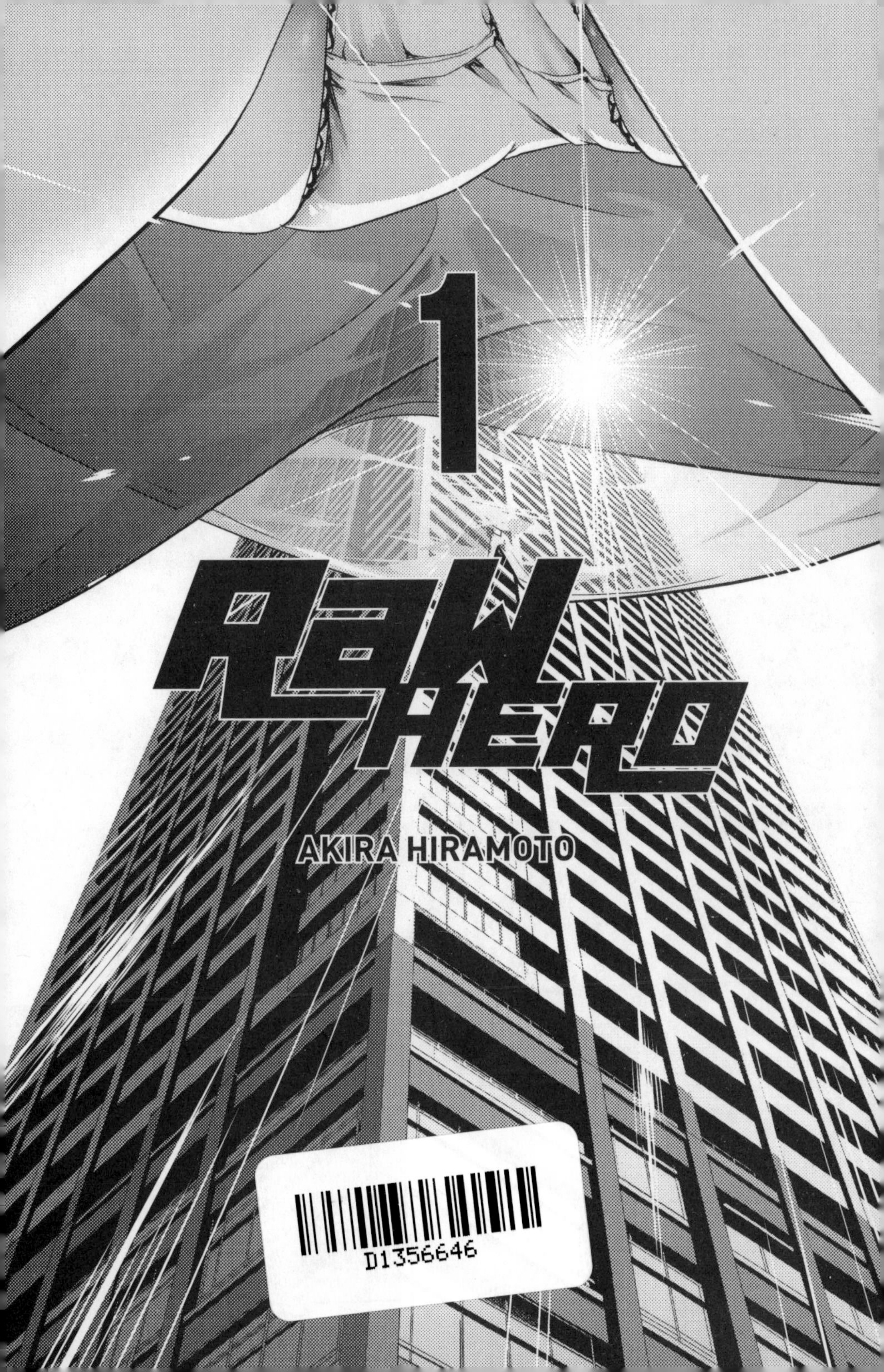
1
AKIRA HIRAMOTO

CONTENTS

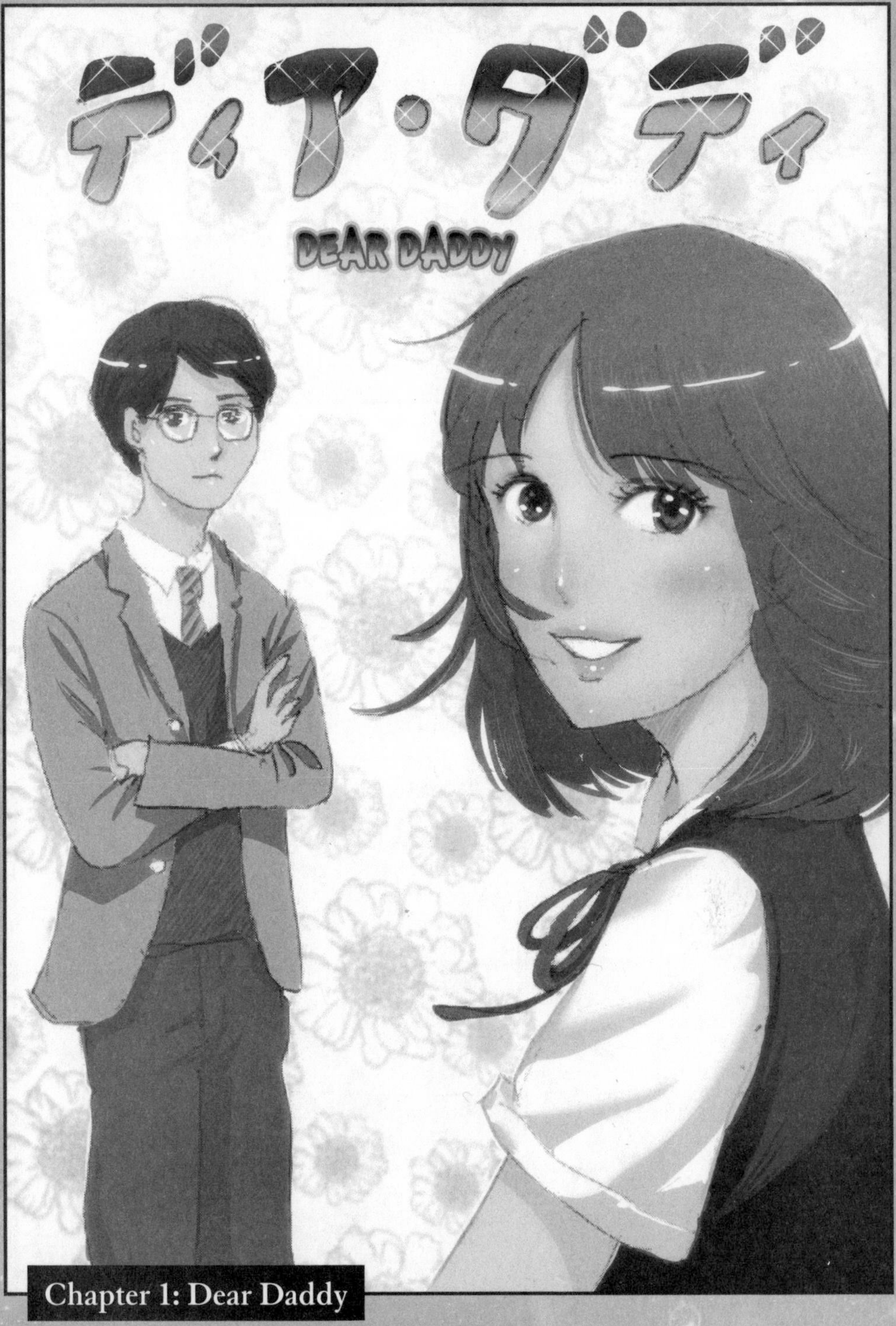
ディア・ダディ
DEAR DADDY

Chapter 1: Dear Daddy

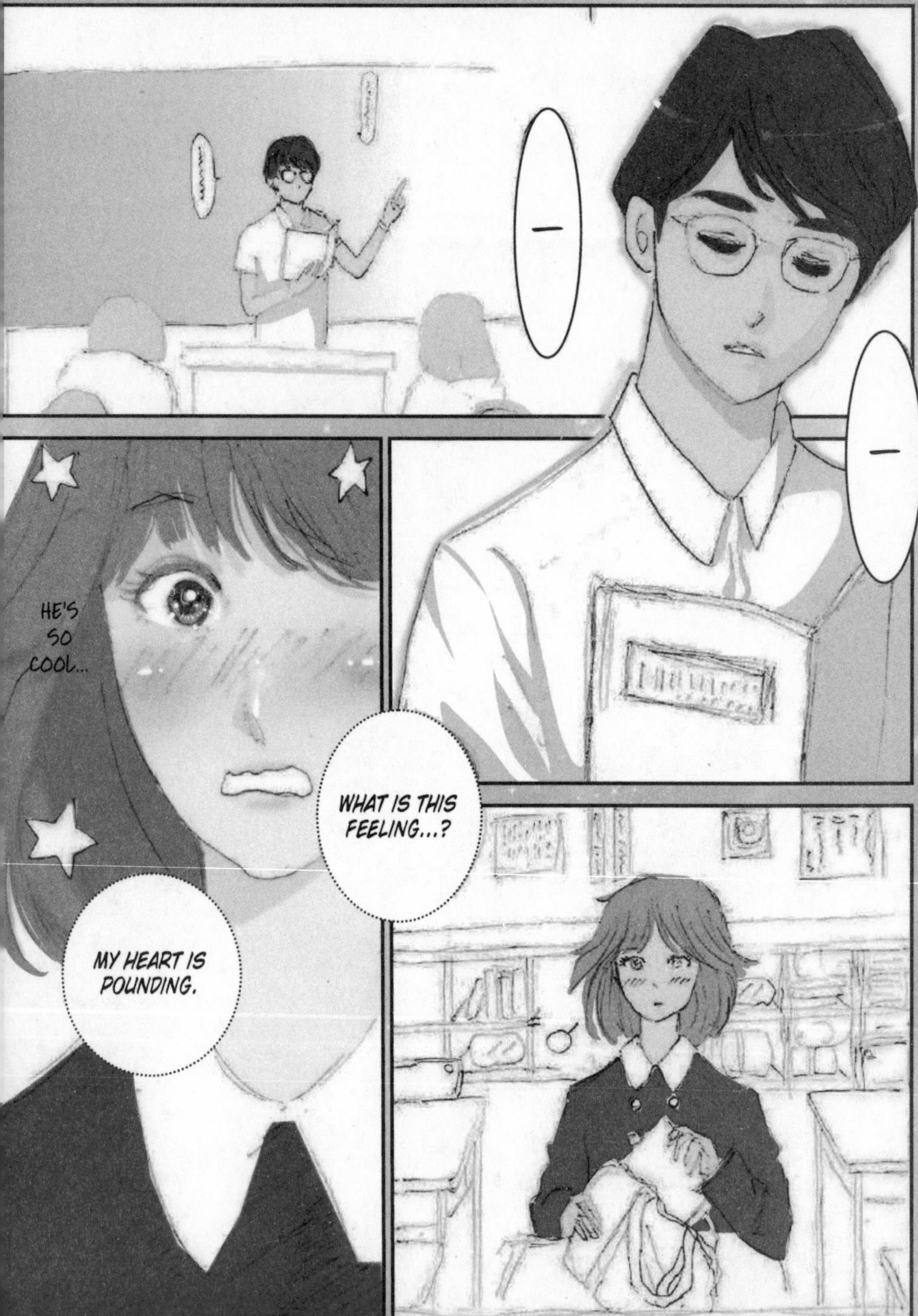

—
—
HE'S SO COOL...
WHAT IS THIS FEELING...?
MY HEART IS POUNDING.

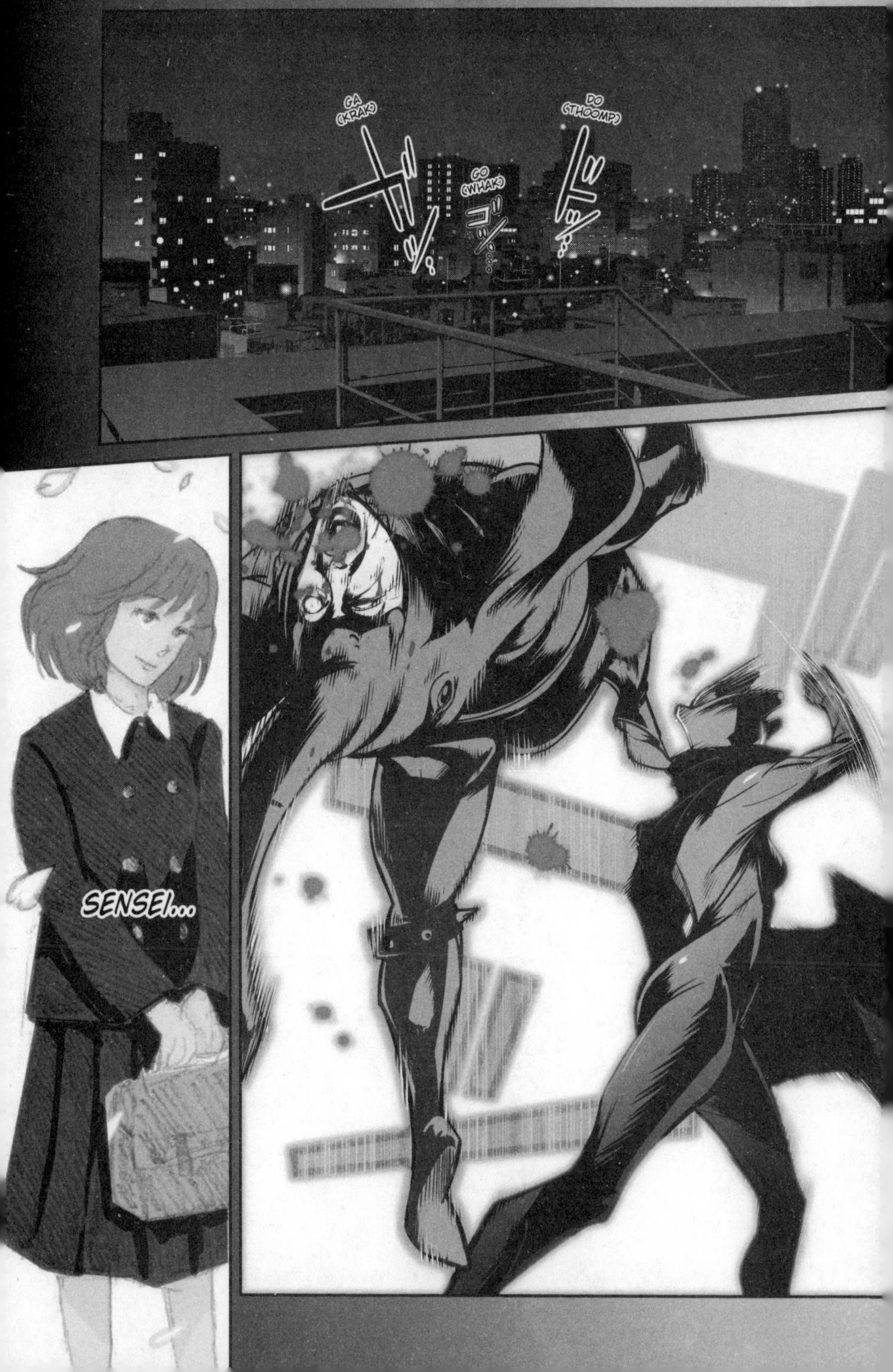
DO (THOOMP)
GO (WHAK)
GA (KRAK)
SENSEI...

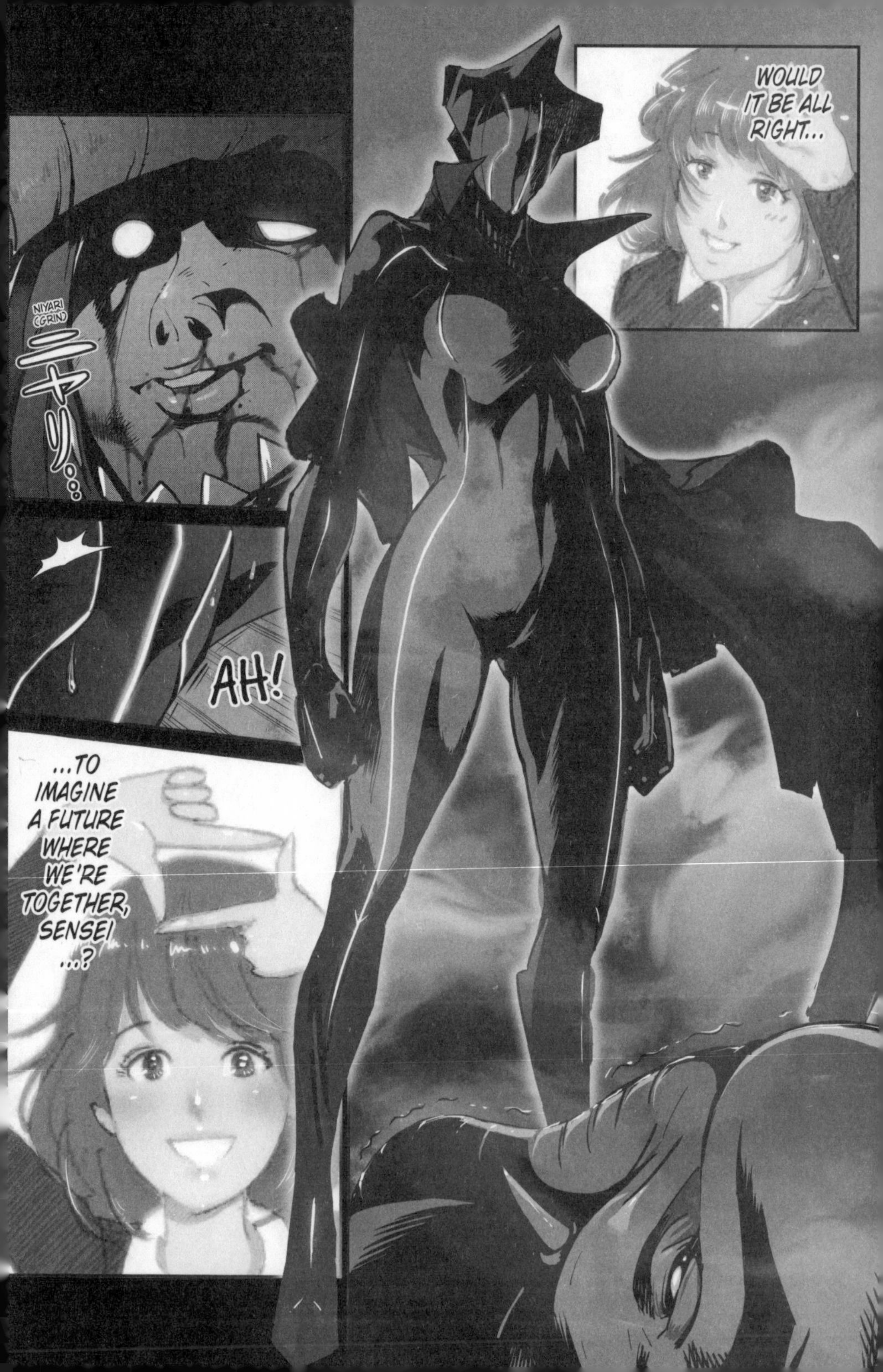
WOULD IT BE ALL RIGHT...
NIYARI (GRIN)
ニヤリ...
AH!
...TO IMAGINE A FUTURE WHERE WE'RE TOGETHER, SENSEI ...?

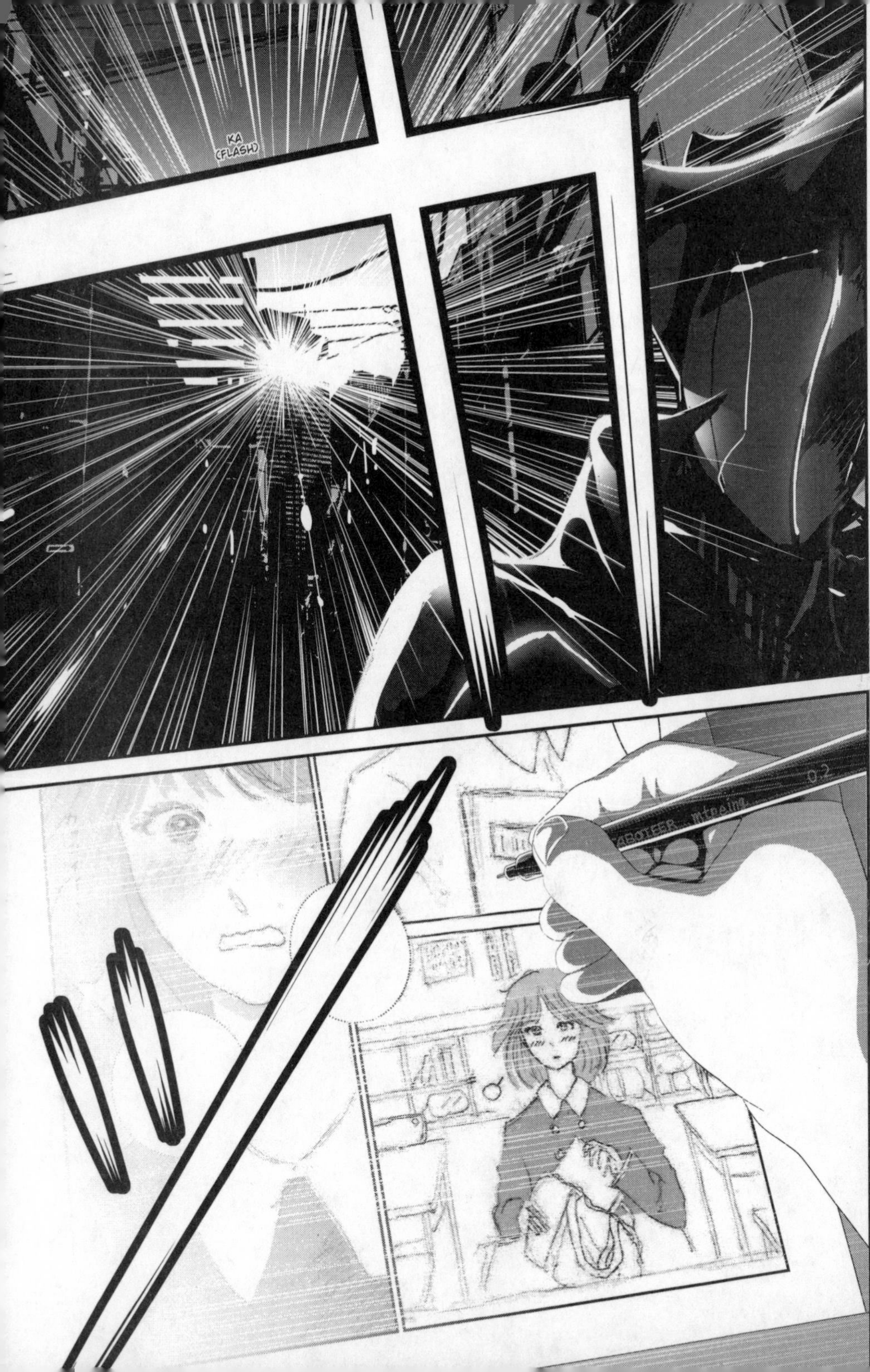
KA
(FLASH)

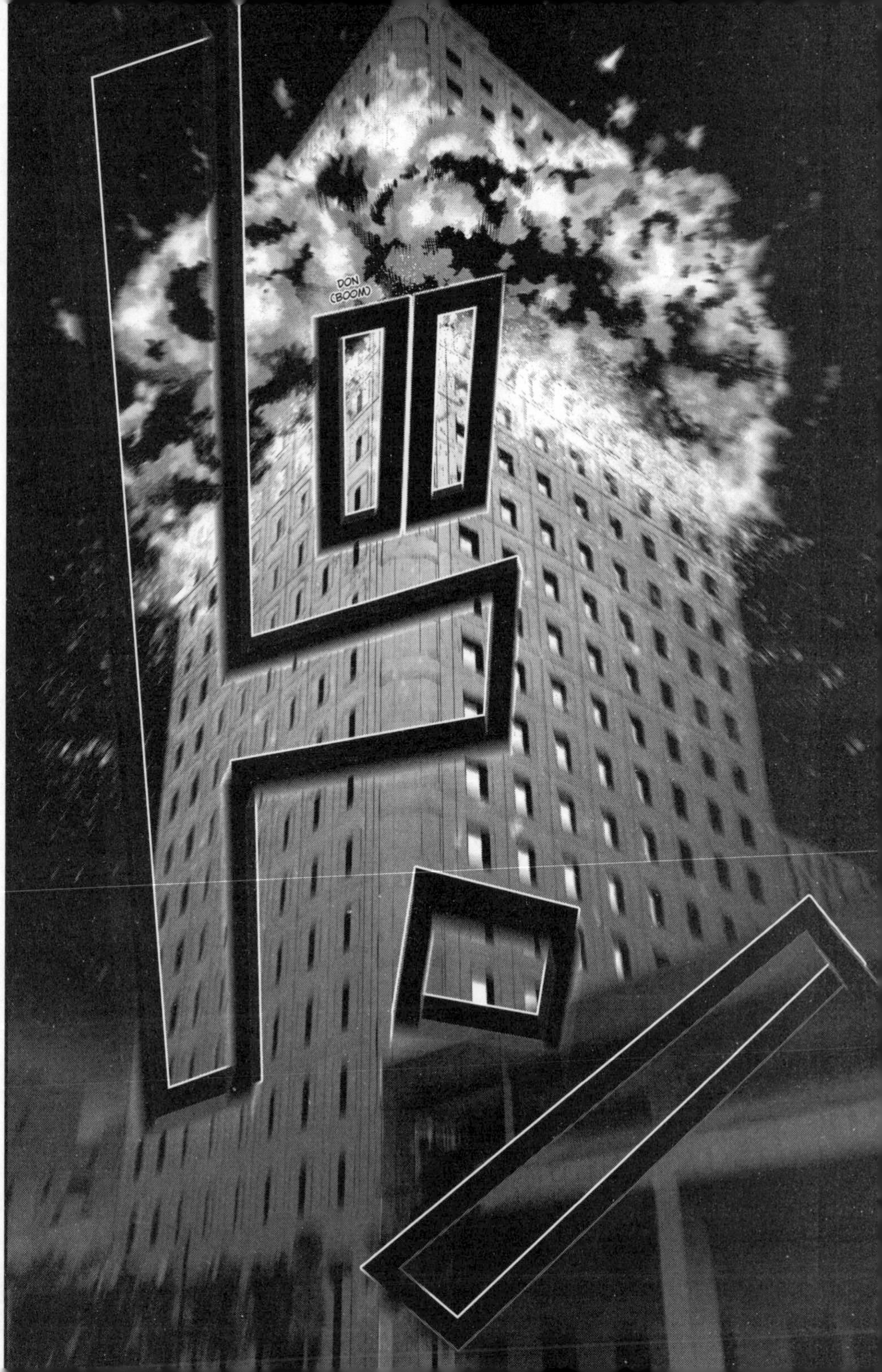
DON
(BOOM)

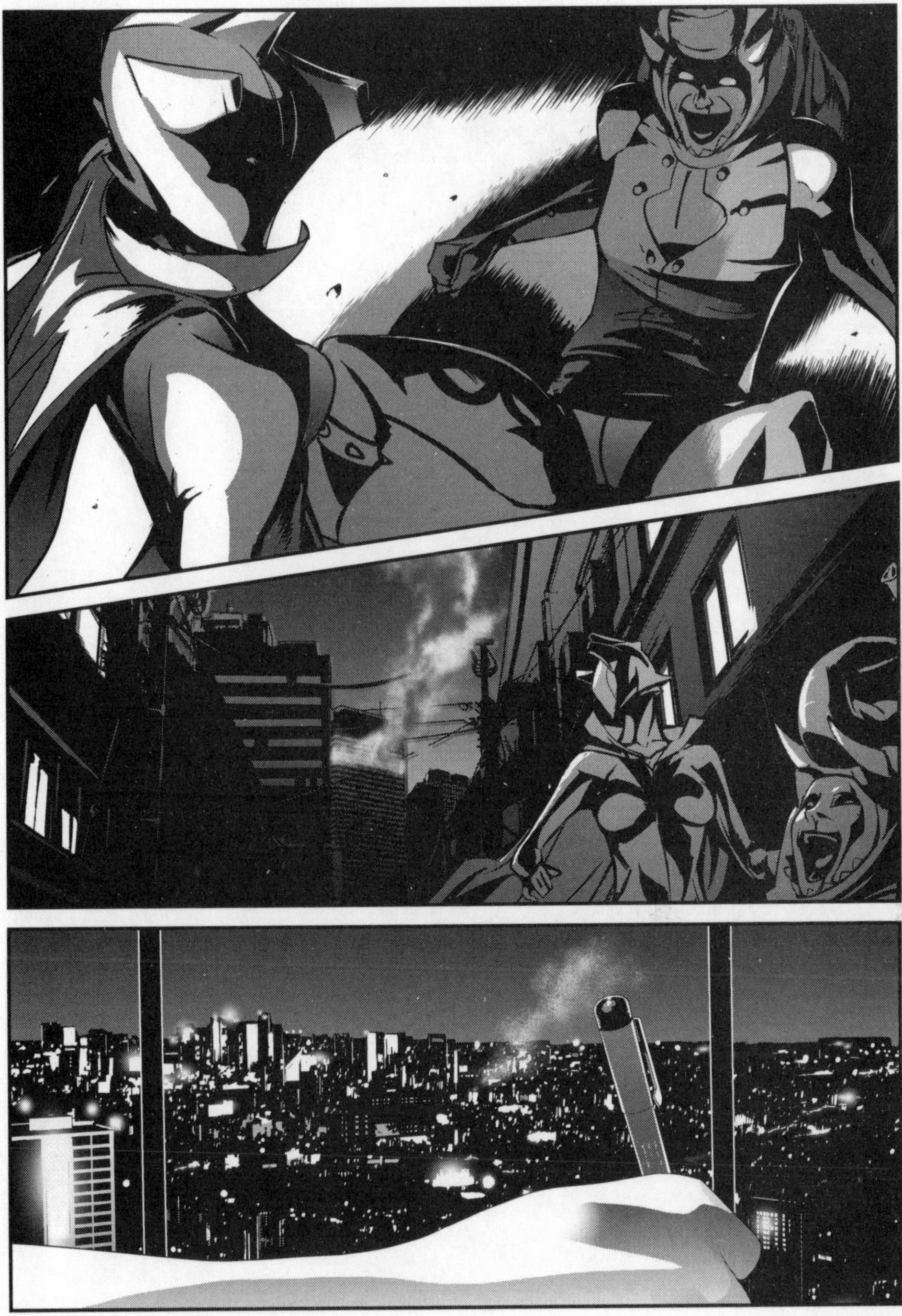

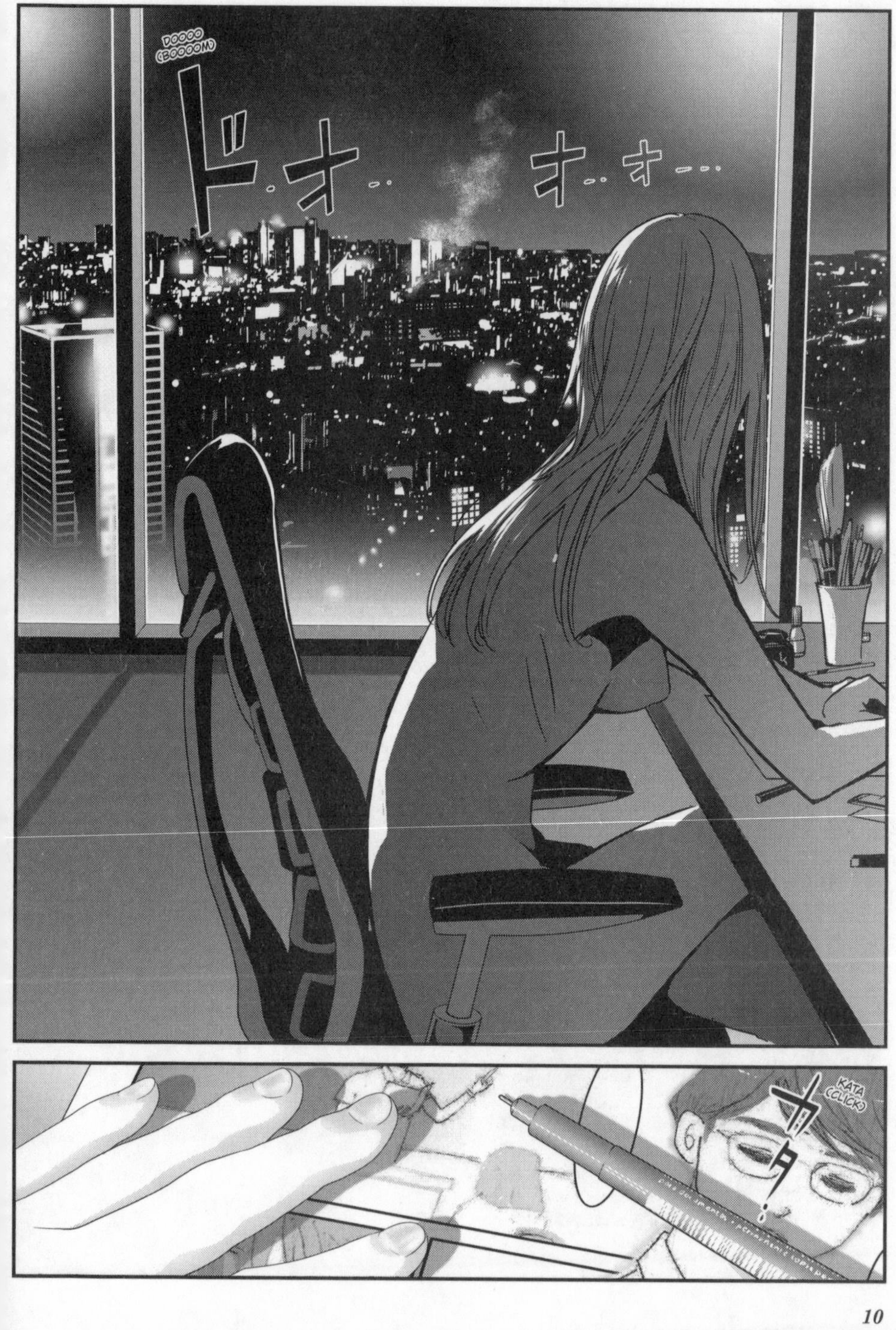
DOOOO (BOOOOM)
ドオ‥オ‥オ…
KATA (CLICK)
カタ!

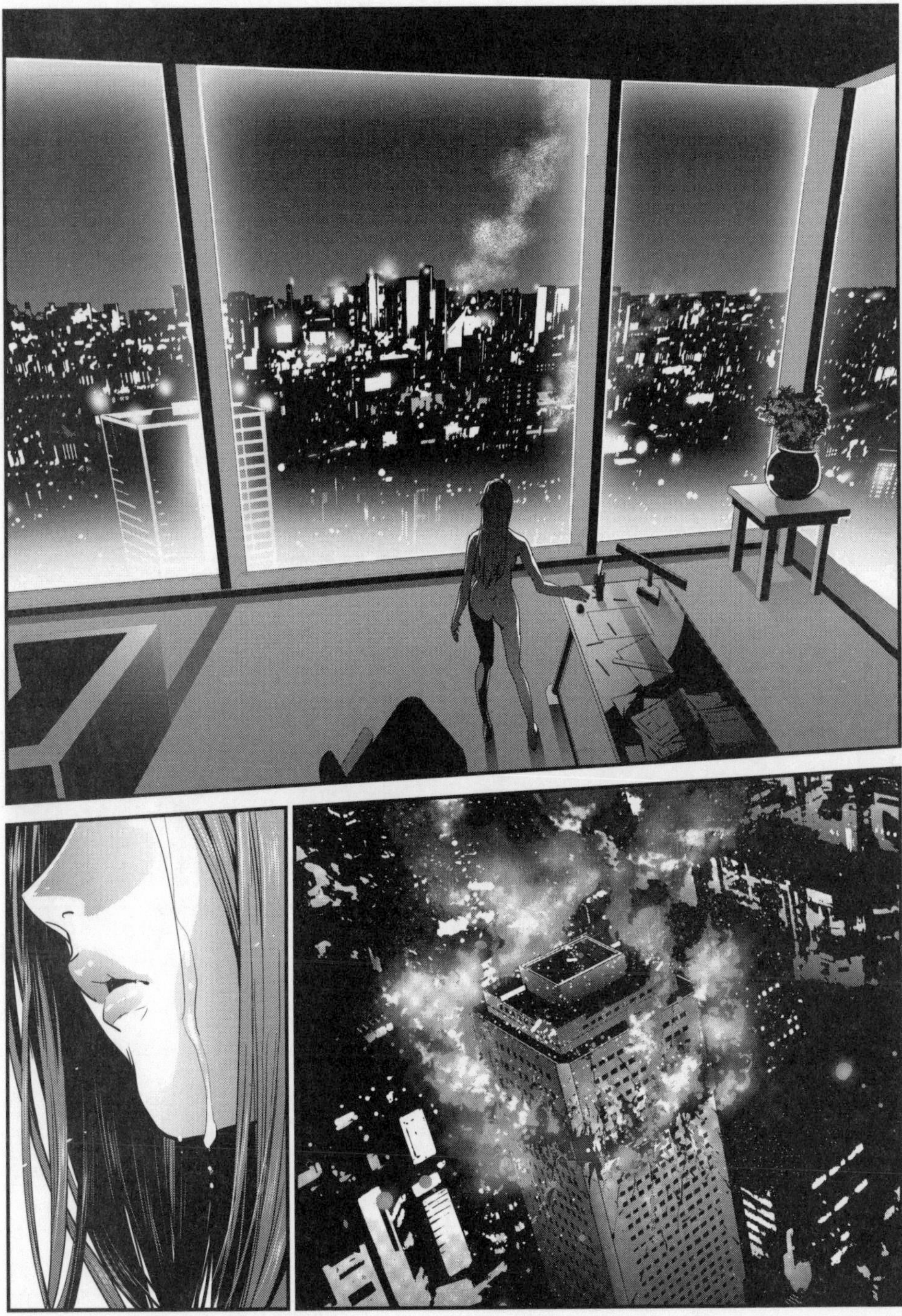

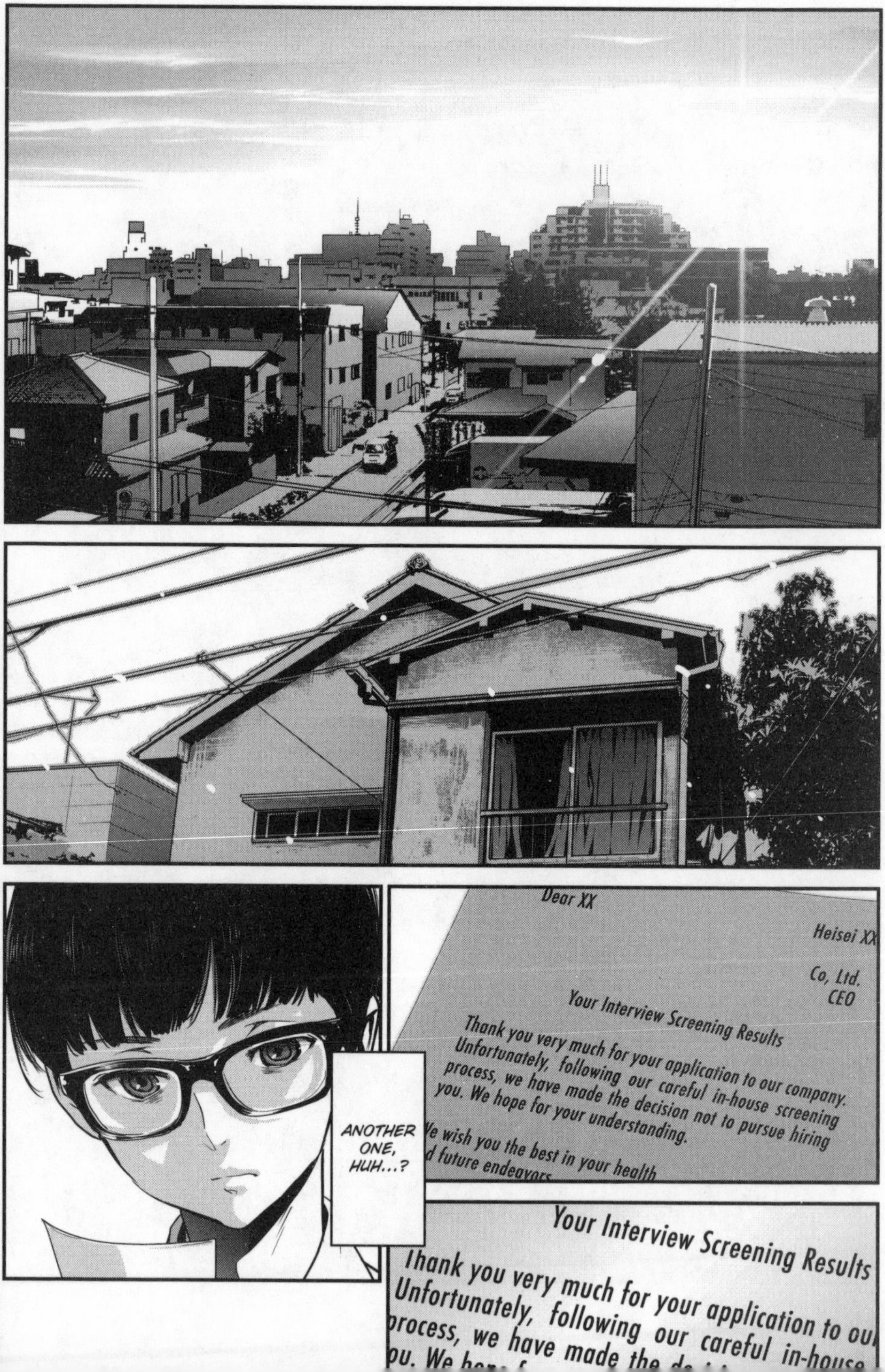
Dear XX
Heisei XX
Co, Ltd.
CEO
Your Interview Screening Results
Thank you very much for your application to our company.
Unfortunately, following our careful in-house screening
process, we have made the decision not to pursue hiring
you. We hope for your understanding.
We wish you the best in your health
d future endeavors
Your Interview Screening Results
Thank you very much for your application to ou
Unfortunately, following our careful in-house
process, we have made the
ANOTHER ONE, HUH...?

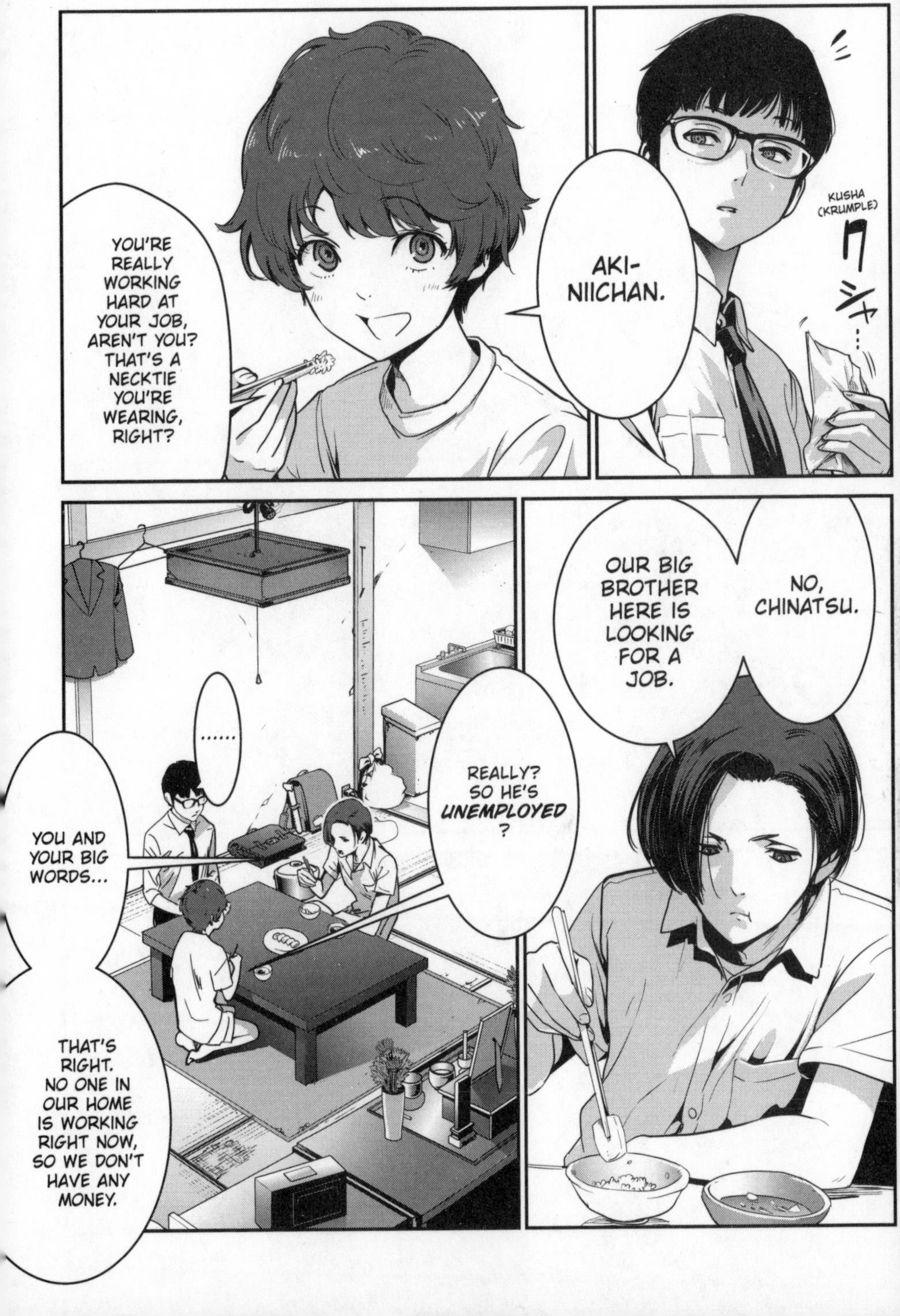
AKI-NIICHAN.
KUSHA (KRUMPLE)
クシャ…
YOU'RE REALLY WORKING HARD AT YOUR JOB, AREN'T YOU? THAT'S A NECKTIE YOU'RE WEARING, RIGHT?
NO, CHINATSU.
OUR BIG BROTHER HERE IS LOOKING FOR A JOB.
REALLY? SO HE'S *UNEMPLOYED*?
......
YOU AND YOUR BIG WORDS...
THAT'S RIGHT. NO ONE IN OUR HOME IS WORKING RIGHT NOW, SO WE DON'T HAVE ANY MONEY.

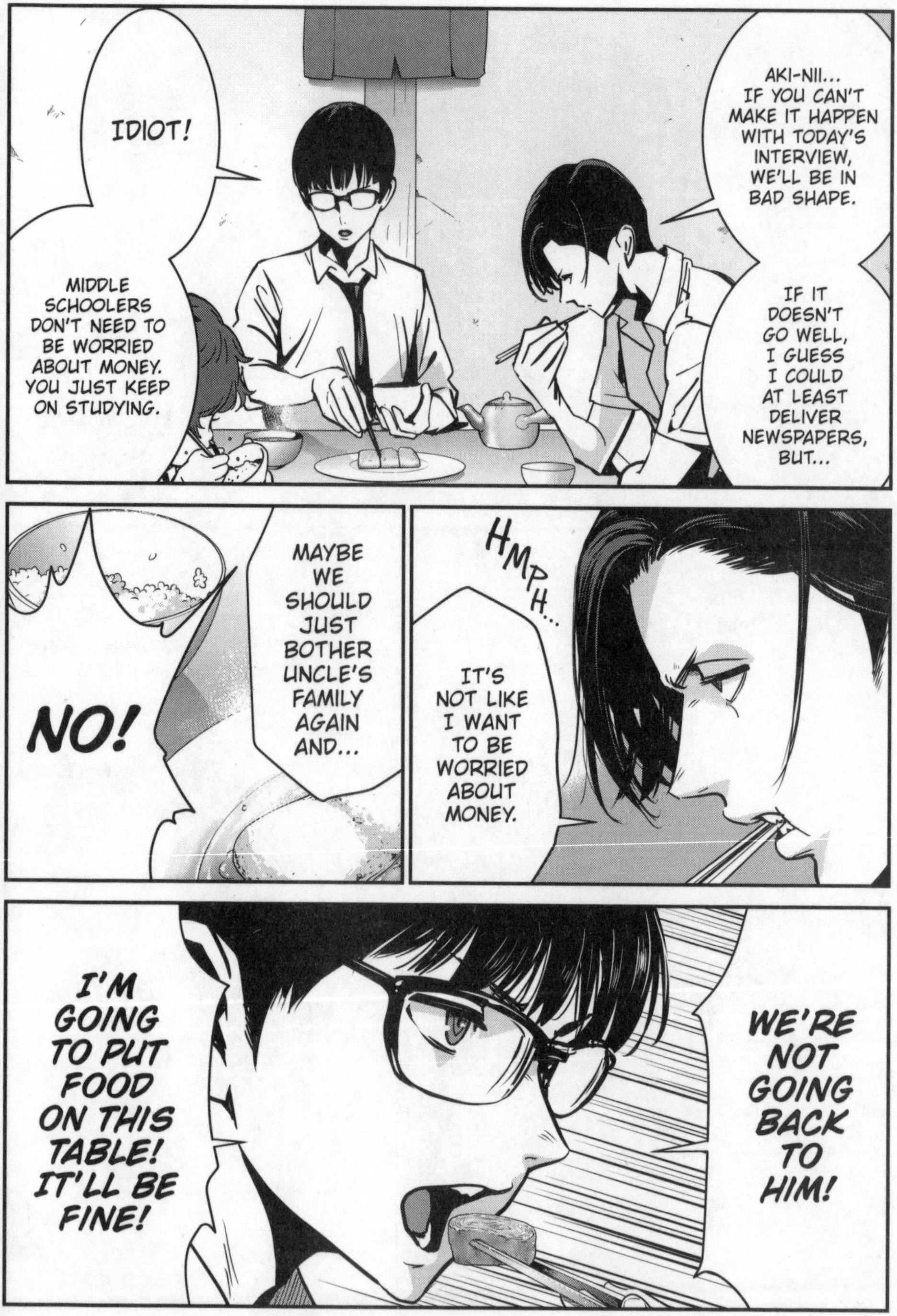
AKI-NII... IF YOU CAN'T MAKE IT HAPPEN WITH TODAY'S INTERVIEW, WE'LL BE IN BAD SHAPE.
IF IT DOESN'T GO WELL, I GUESS I COULD AT LEAST DELIVER NEWSPAPERS, BUT...
IDIOT!
MIDDLE SCHOOLERS DON'T NEED TO BE WORRIED ABOUT MONEY. YOU JUST KEEP ON STUDYING.
HMPH...
IT'S NOT LIKE I WANT TO BE WORRIED ABOUT MONEY.
MAYBE WE SHOULD JUST BOTHER UNCLE'S FAMILY AGAIN AND...
NO!
WE'RE NOT GOING BACK TO HIM!
I'M GOING TO PUT FOOD ON THIS TABLE! IT'LL BE FINE!

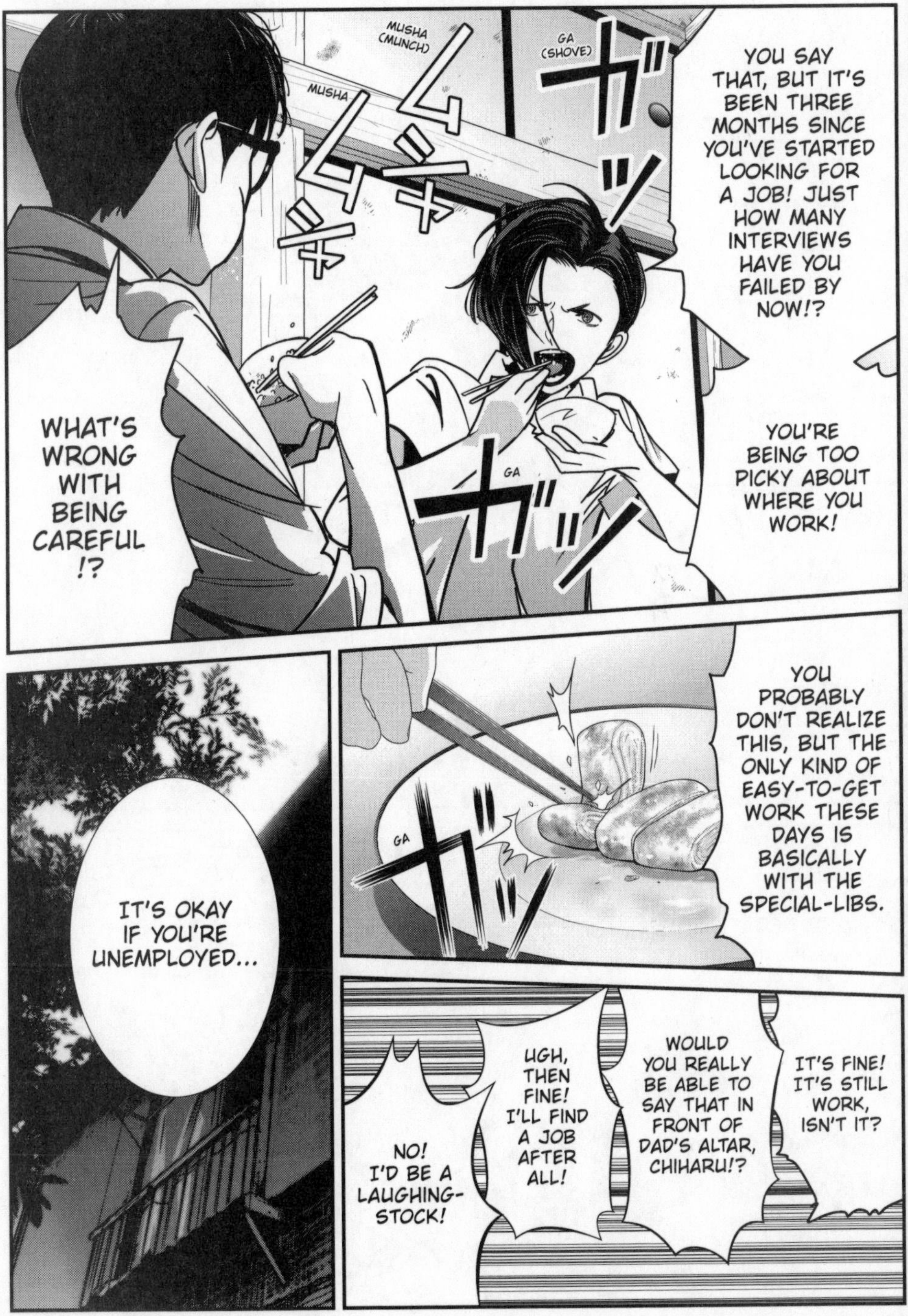
YOU SAY THAT, BUT IT'S BEEN THREE MONTHS SINCE YOU'VE STARTED LOOKING FOR A JOB! JUST HOW MANY INTERVIEWS HAVE YOU FAILED BY NOW!?
GA (SHOVE)
MUSHA (MUNCH)
MUSHA
YOU'RE BEING TOO PICKY ABOUT WHERE YOU WORK!
GA
WHAT'S WRONG WITH BEING CAREFUL!?
YOU PROBABLY DON'T REALIZE THIS, BUT THE ONLY KIND OF EASY-TO-GET WORK THESE DAYS IS BASICALLY WITH THE SPECIAL-LIBS.
GA
IT'S FINE! IT'S STILL WORK, ISN'T IT?
WOULD YOU REALLY BE ABLE TO SAY THAT IN FRONT OF DAD'S ALTAR, CHIHARU!?
UGH, THEN FINE! I'LL FIND A JOB AFTER ALL!
NO! I'D BE A LAUGHING-STOCK!
IT'S OKAY IF YOU'RE UNEMPLOYED...

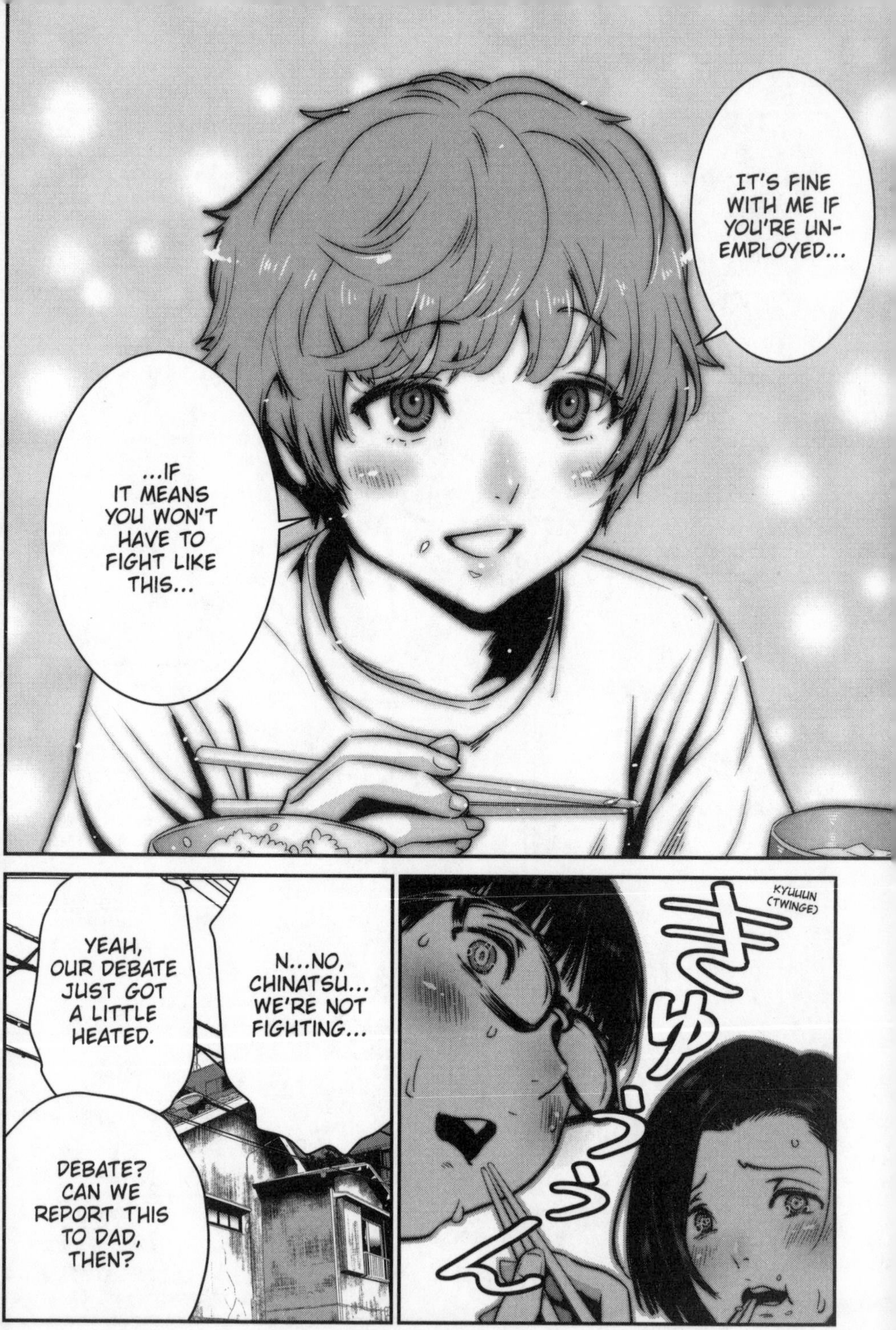
IT'S FINE WITH ME IF YOU'RE UN-EMPLOYED...
...IF IT MEANS YOU WON'T HAVE TO FIGHT LIKE THIS...
KYUUUN (TWINGE)
N...NO, CHINATSU... WE'RE NOT FIGHTING...
YEAH, OUR DEBATE JUST GOT A LITTLE HEATED.
DEBATE? CAN WE REPORT THIS TO DAD, THEN?

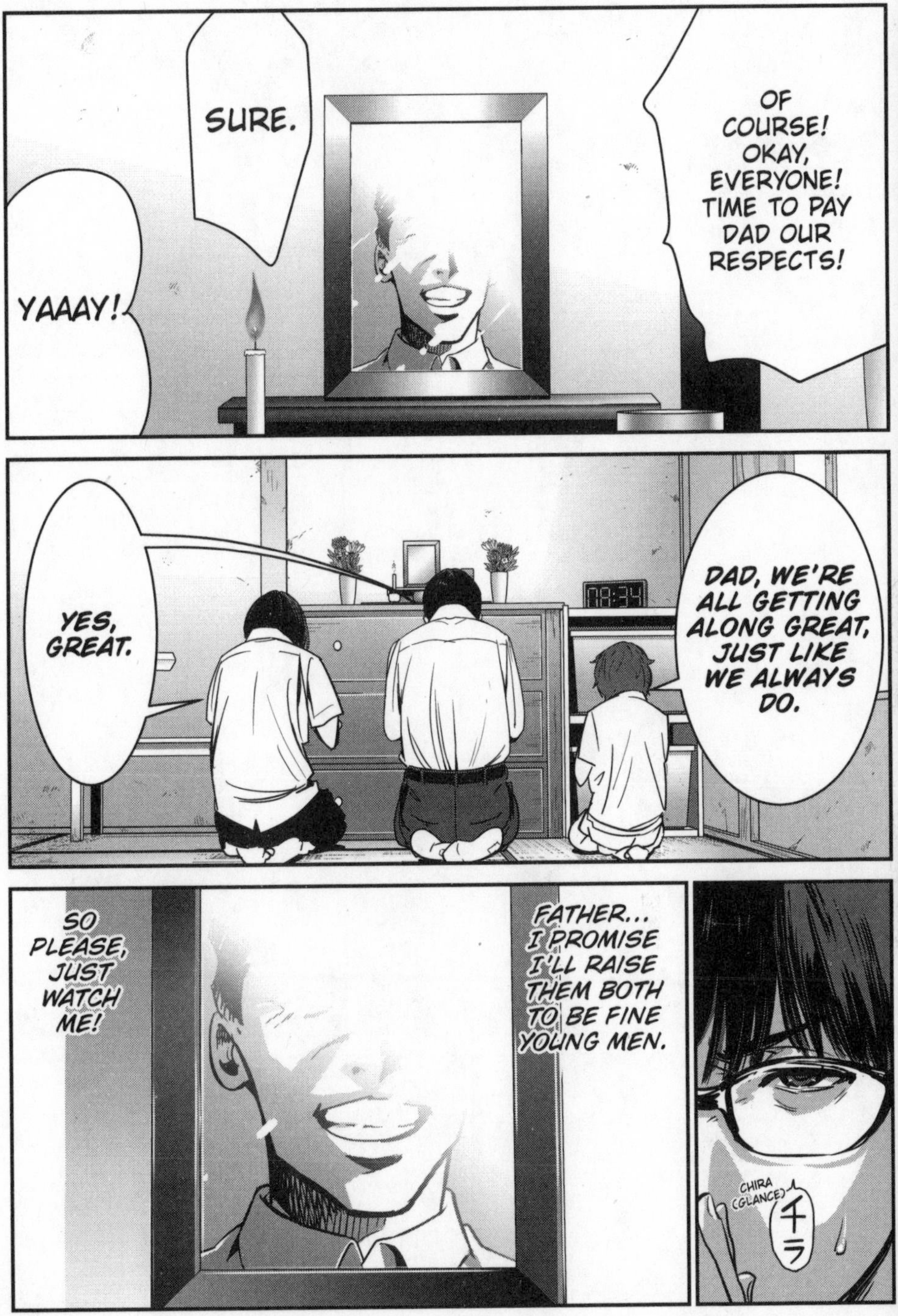
OF COURSE! OKAY, EVERYONE! TIME TO PAY DAD OUR RESPECTS!
SURE.
YAAAY!
DAD, WE'RE ALL GETTING ALONG GREAT, JUST LIKE WE ALWAYS DO.
YES, GREAT.
CHIRA (GLANCE)
チラ
FATHER... I PROMISE I'LL RAISE THEM BOTH TO BE FINE YOUNG MEN.
SO PLEASE, JUST WATCH ME!

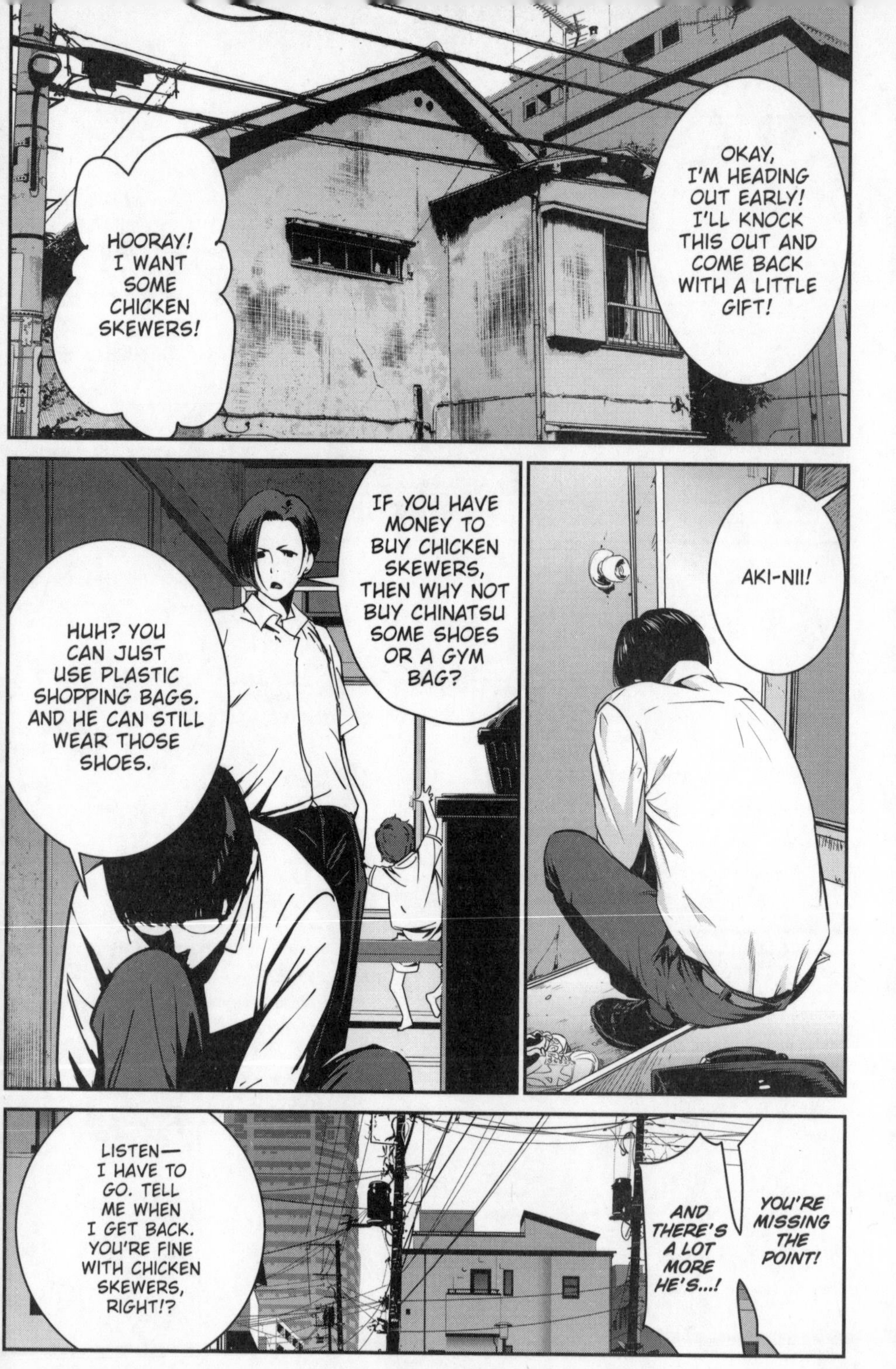
OKAY, I'M HEADING OUT EARLY! I'LL KNOCK THIS OUT AND COME BACK WITH A LITTLE GIFT!
HOORAY! I WANT SOME CHICKEN SKEWERS!
AKI-NII!
IF YOU HAVE MONEY TO BUY CHICKEN SKEWERS, THEN WHY NOT BUY CHINATSU SOME SHOES OR A GYM BAG?
HUH? YOU CAN JUST USE PLASTIC SHOPPING BAGS. AND HE CAN STILL WEAR THOSE SHOES.
YOU'RE MISSING THE POINT!
AND THERE'S A LOT MORE HE'S...!
LISTEN— I HAVE TO GO. TELL ME WHEN I GET BACK. YOU'RE FINE WITH CHICKEN SKEWERS, RIGHT!?

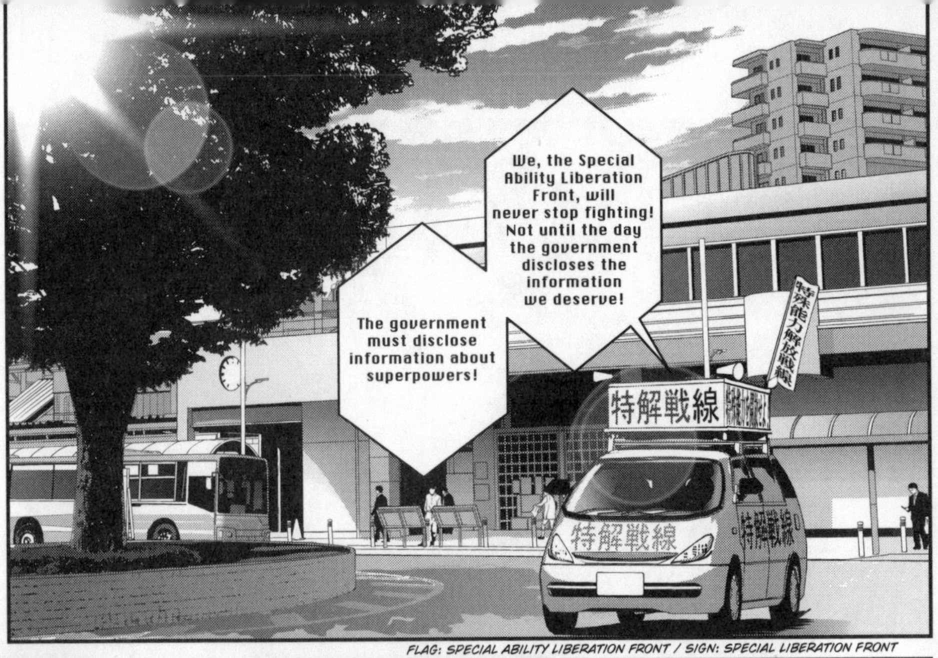
We, the Special Ability Liberation Front, will never stop fighting! Not until the day the government discloses the information we deserve!
The government must disclose information about superpowers!
特殊能力解放戦線
特解戦線
特解戦線
特解戦線

FLAG: SPECIAL ABILITY LIBERATION FRONT / SIGN: SPECIAL LIBERATION FRONT

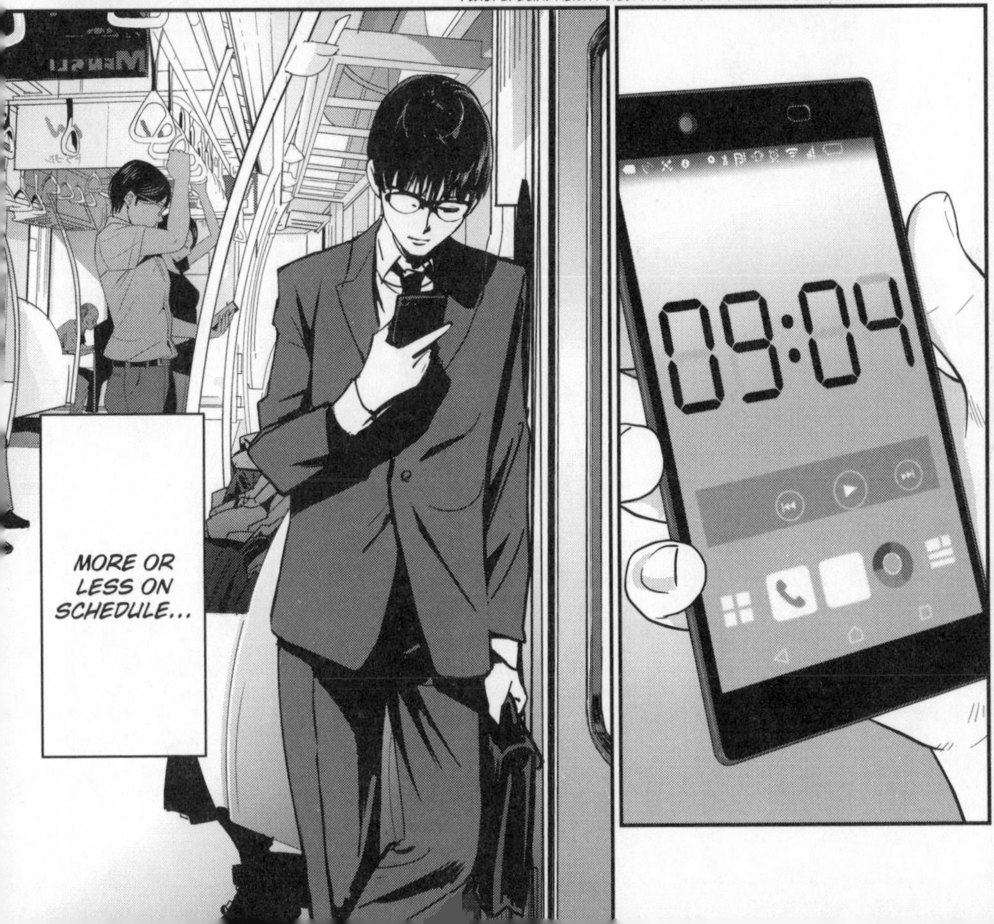
09:04
MORE OR LESS ON SCHEDULE...

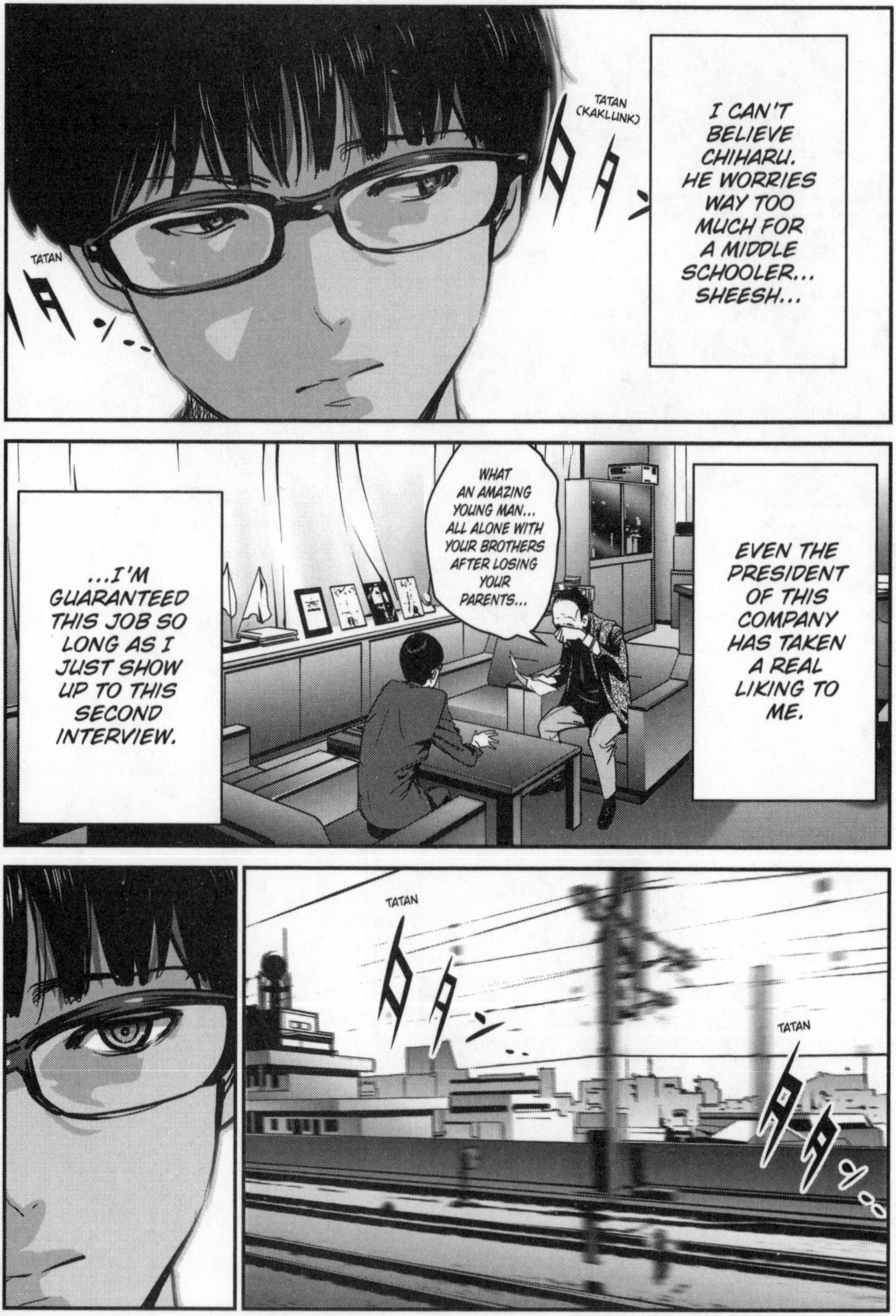
I CAN'T BELIEVE CHIHARU. HE WORRIES WAY TOO MUCH FOR A MIDDLE SCHOOLER... SHEESH...
TATAN (KAKLUNK)
TATAN
EVEN THE PRESIDENT OF THIS COMPANY HAS TAKEN A REAL LIKING TO ME.
WHAT AN AMAZING YOUNG MAN... ALL ALONE WITH YOUR BROTHERS AFTER LOSING YOUR PARENTS...
...I'M GUARANTEED THIS JOB SO LONG AS I JUST SHOW UP TO THIS SECOND INTERVIEW.
TATAN
TATAN

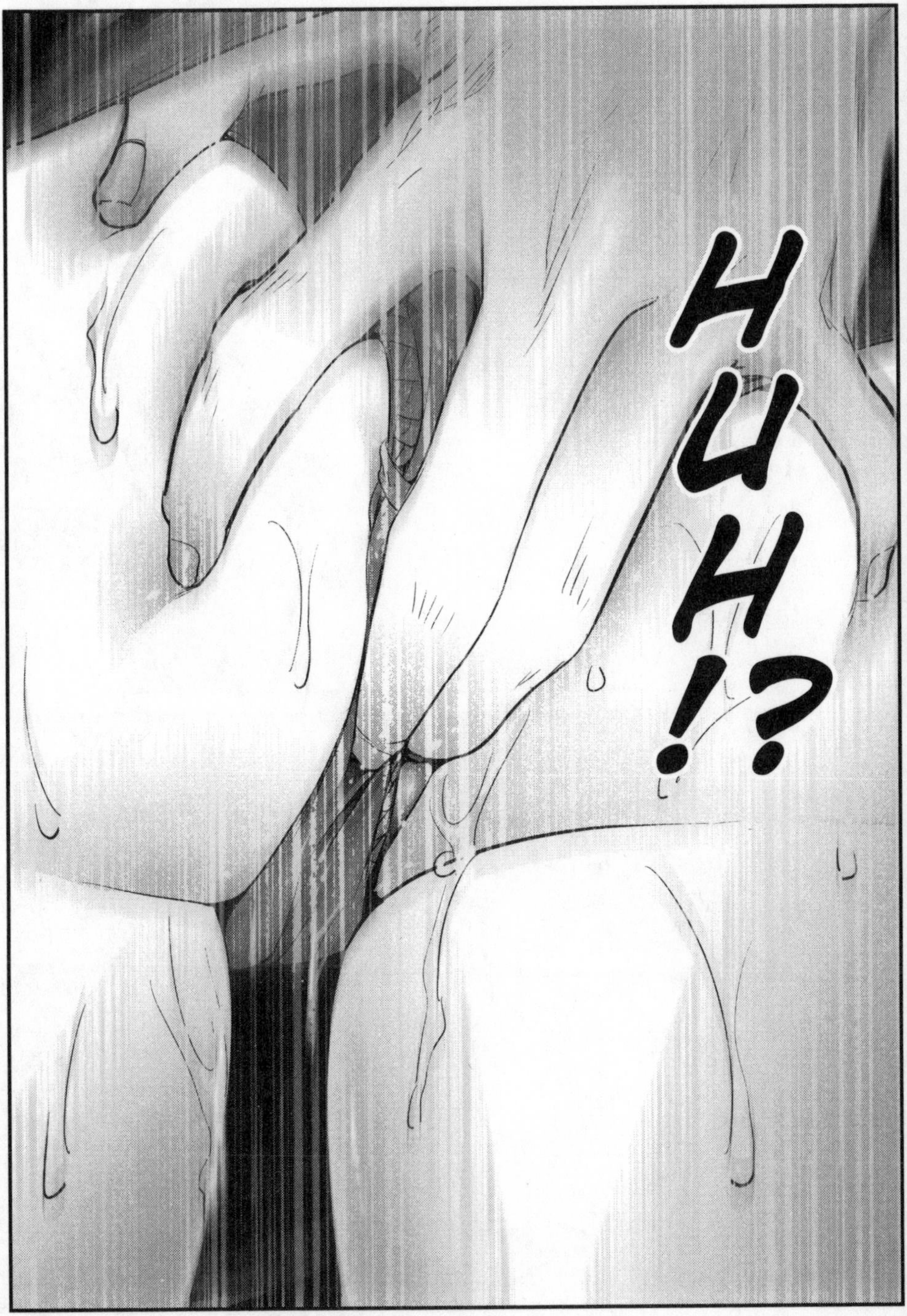
HUH!?

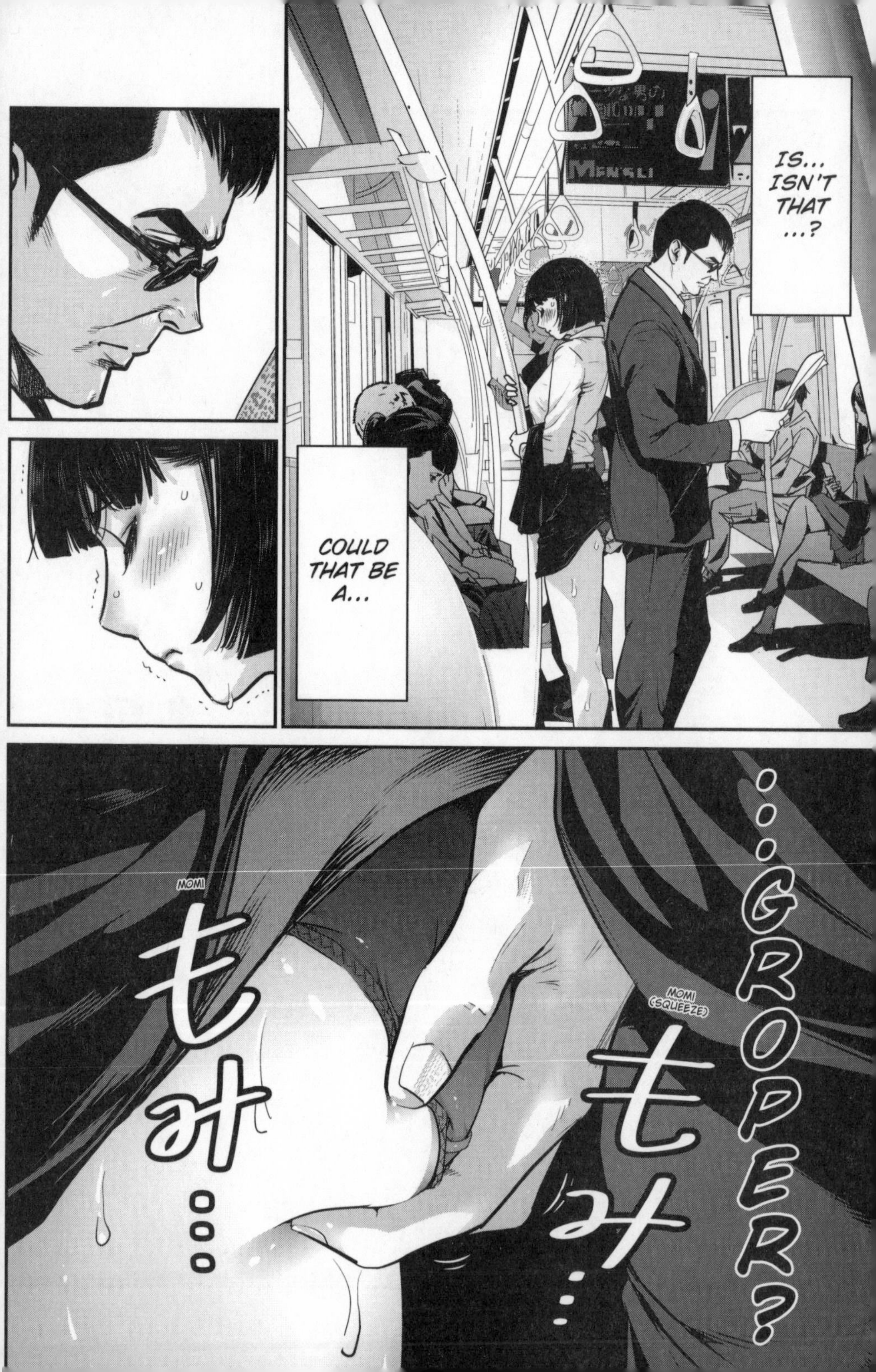

IS... ISN'T THAT...?
COULD THAT BE A...
...GROPER?
MOMI (SQUEEZE)
もみ...
MOMI
もみ...

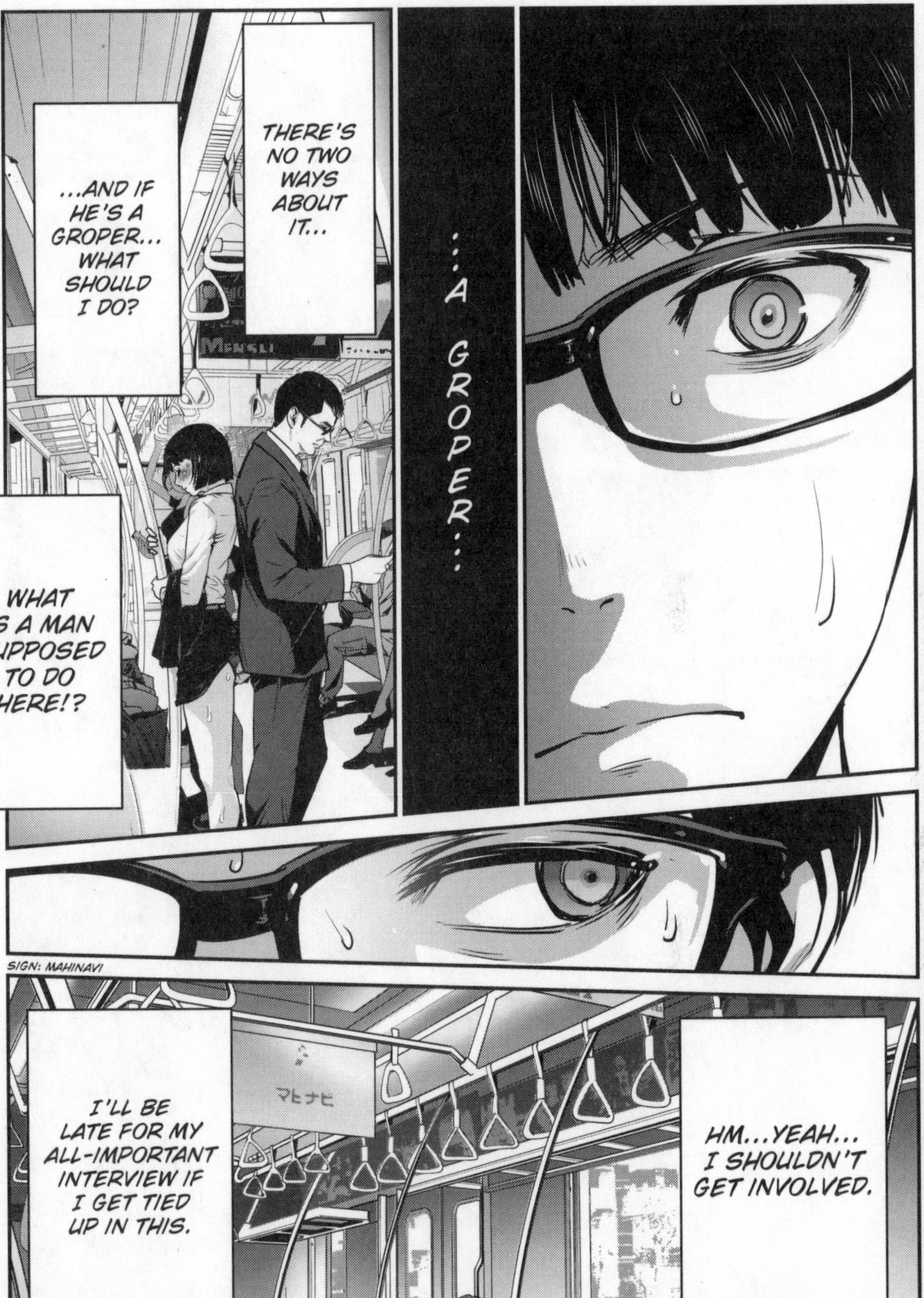
...A GROPER...
THERE'S NO TWO WAYS ABOUT IT...
...AND IF HE'S A GROPER... WHAT SHOULD I DO?
WHAT IS A MAN SUPPOSED TO DO HERE!?
SIGN: MAHINAVI
HM...YEAH... I SHOULDN'T GET INVOLVED.
マヒナビ
I'LL BE LATE FOR MY ALL-IMPORTANT INTERVIEW IF I GET TIED UP IN THIS.

I MAY
BE A MAN,
BUT MORE
IMPORTANTLY,
I'M MY
FAMILY'S
BREAD-
WINNER...

I NEED TO
PUT FOOD ON
THE TABLE
FOR THOSE
BROTHERS
OF MINE...

I'M
SORRY,
MISS...
BUT IF I
DON'T GET
THIS JOB
TODAY,
I WON'T
EVEN BE
ABLE TO
FEED
THEM.

I'M SURE
SOME
KINDHEARTED
HERO WILL
APPEAR
SOON
ENOUGH.

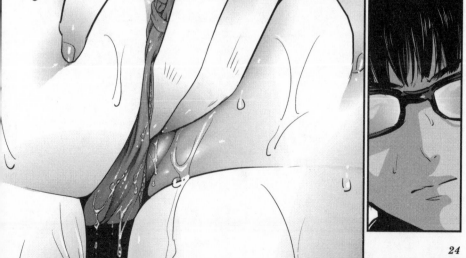

24

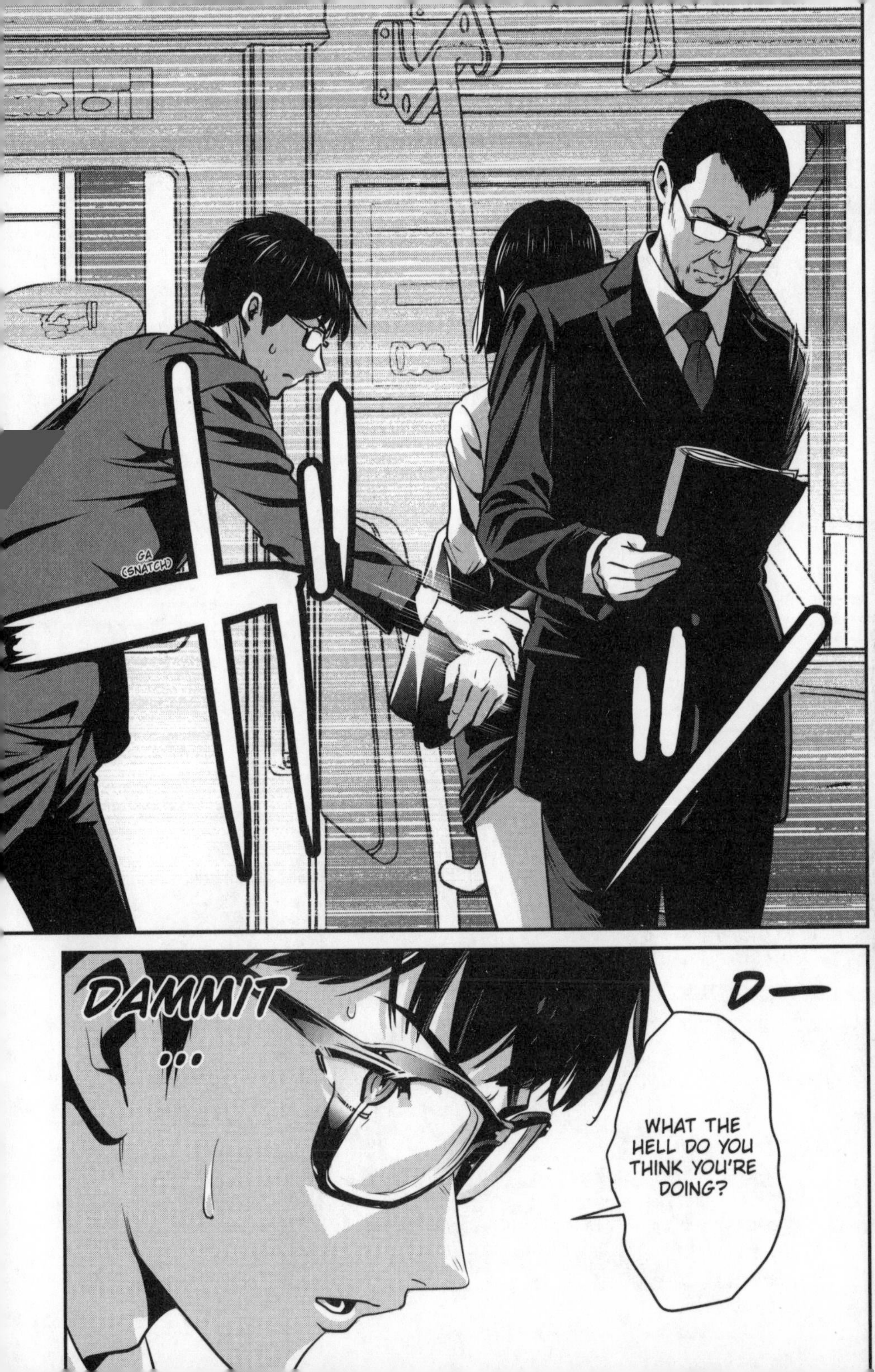
GA (SNATCH)
D—
WHAT THE HELL DO YOU THINK YOU'RE DOING?
DAMMIT ...

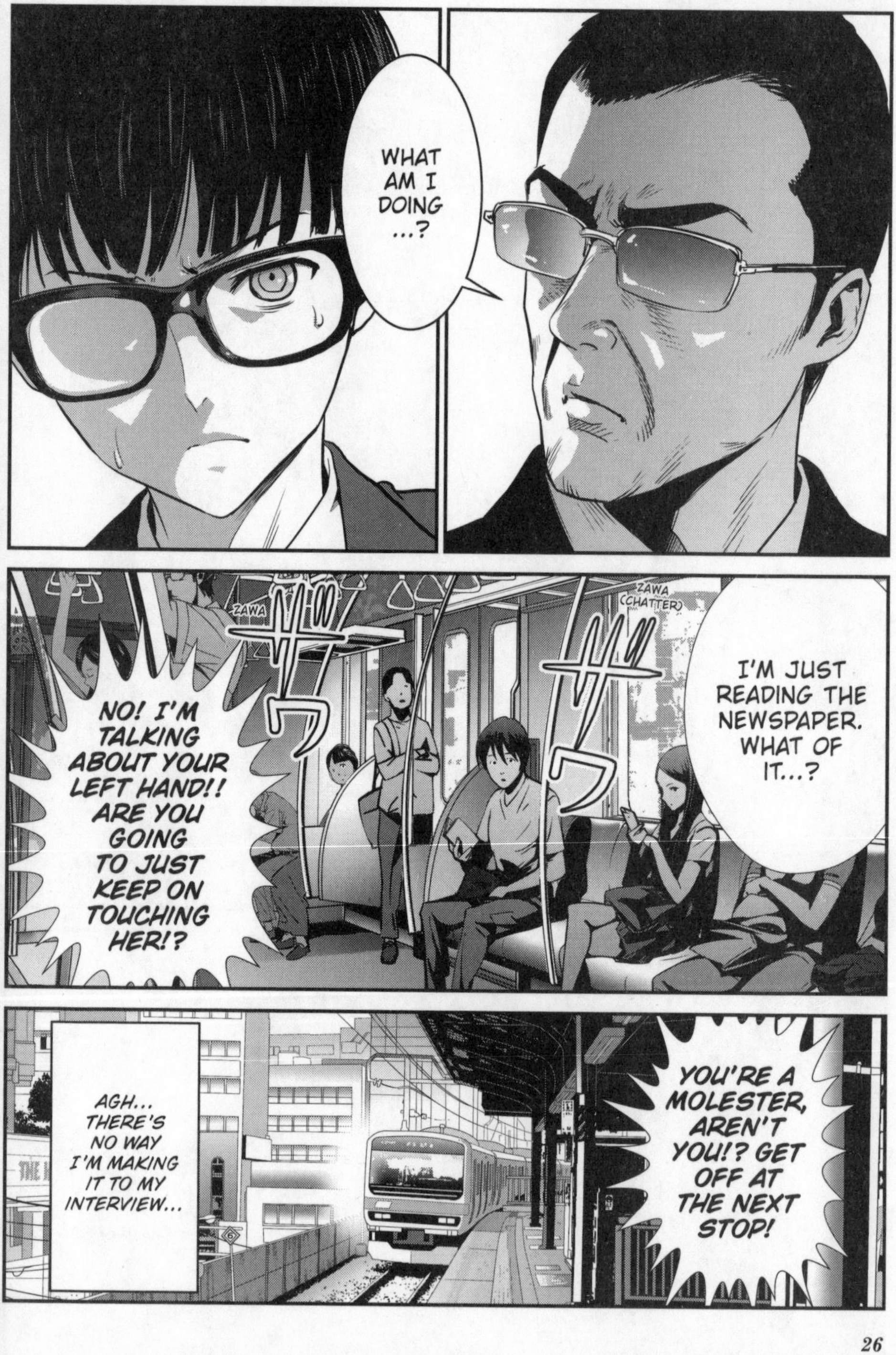
WHAT AM I DOING ...?
I'M JUST READING THE NEWSPAPER. WHAT OF IT...?
ザワ
ZAWA (CHATTER)
ザワ
ZAWA
NO! I'M TALKING ABOUT YOUR LEFT HAND!! ARE YOU GOING TO JUST KEEP ON TOUCHING HER!?
YOU'RE A MOLESTER, AREN'T YOU!? GET OFF AT THE NEXT STOP!
AGH... THERE'S NO WAY I'M MAKING IT TO MY INTERVIEW...

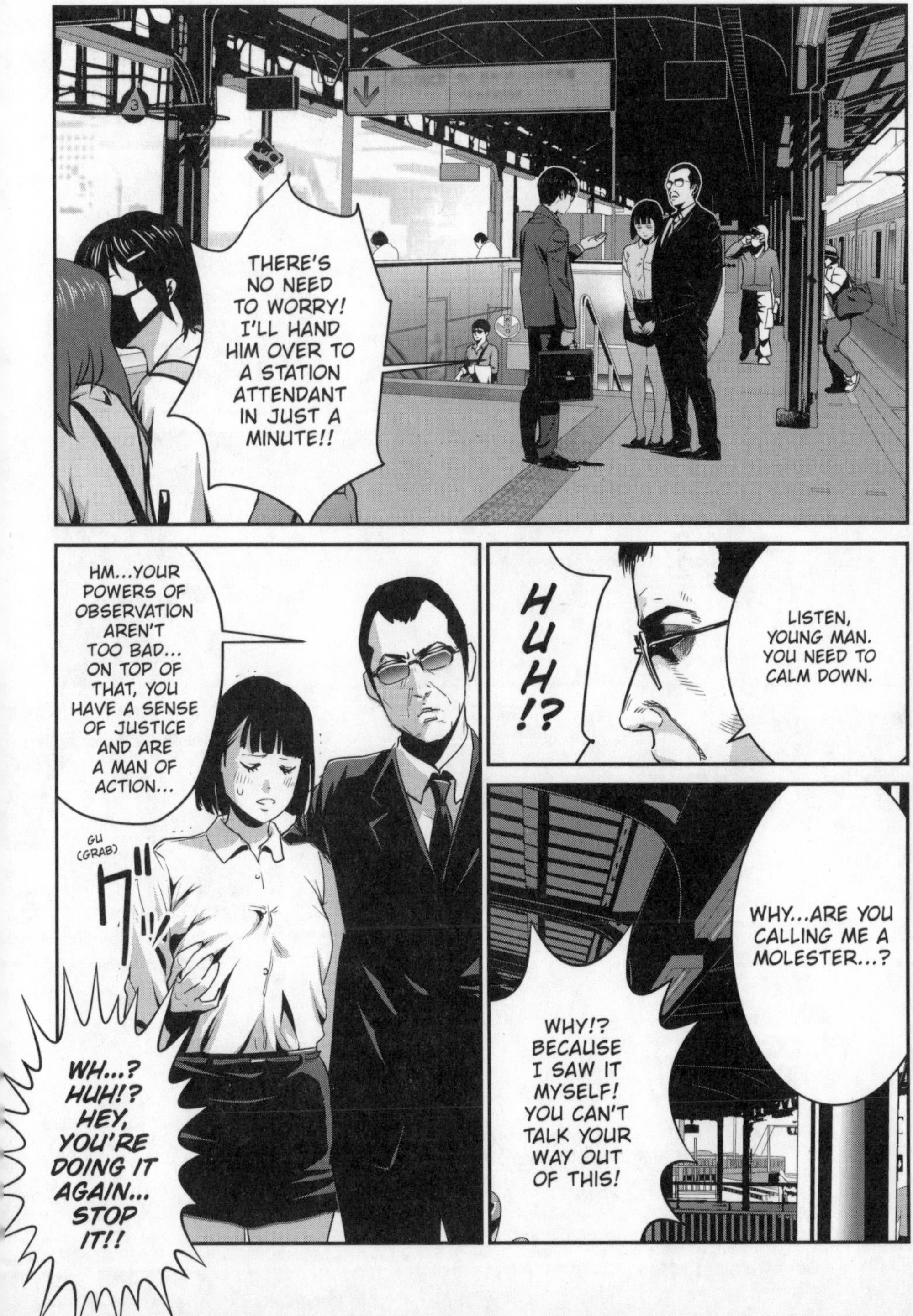
THERE'S NO NEED TO WORRY! I'LL HAND HIM OVER TO A STATION ATTENDANT IN JUST A MINUTE!!
LISTEN, YOUNG MAN. YOU NEED TO CALM DOWN.
HUH!?
WHY...ARE YOU CALLING ME A MOLESTER...?
WHY!? BECAUSE I SAW IT MYSELF! YOU CAN'T TALK YOUR WAY OUT OF THIS!
HM...YOUR POWERS OF OBSERVATION AREN'T TOO BAD... ON TOP OF THAT, YOU HAVE A SENSE OF JUSTICE AND ARE A MAN OF ACTION...
GU (GRAB)
WH...? HUH!? HEY, YOU'RE DOING IT AGAIN... STOP IT!!

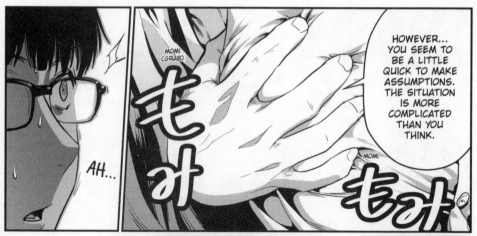

MOMI (GRAB)

も
み

AH...

HOWEVER...
YOU SEEM TO
BE A LITTLE
QUICK TO MAKE
ASSUMPTIONS.
THE SITUATION
IS MORE
COMPLICATED
THAN YOU
THINK.

MOMI

も
み

HFF!
MOMI
HFF!

も
み

HFF!

HFF!

MOMI

も
み

HFF!

I...I'M
SORRY...

HFF!

HFF!

THAT'S
RIGHT.

WE'RE
JUST
ROLE-
PLAYING
A TRAIN
GROPER
SCENE.

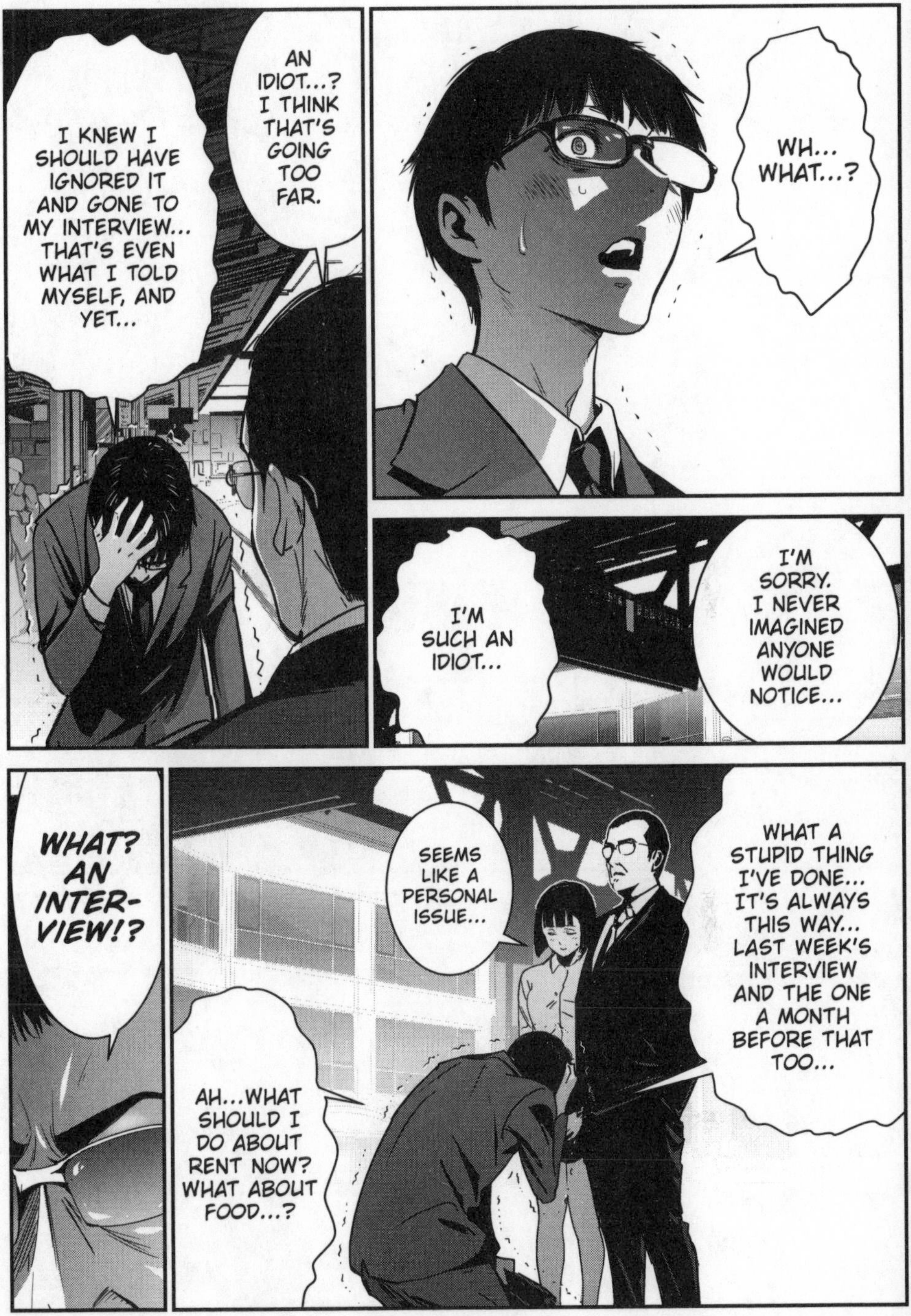
WH... WHAT...?
I'M SORRY. I NEVER IMAGINED ANYONE WOULD NOTICE...
I'M SUCH AN IDIOT...
AN IDIOT...? I THINK THAT'S GOING TOO FAR.
I KNEW I SHOULD HAVE IGNORED IT AND GONE TO MY INTERVIEW... THAT'S EVEN WHAT I TOLD MYSELF, AND YET...
WHAT A STUPID THING I'VE DONE... IT'S ALWAYS THIS WAY... LAST WEEK'S INTERVIEW AND THE ONE A MONTH BEFORE THAT TOO...
SEEMS LIKE A PERSONAL ISSUE...
AH...WHAT SHOULD I DO ABOUT RENT NOW? WHAT ABOUT FOOD...?
WHAT? AN INTER-VIEW!?

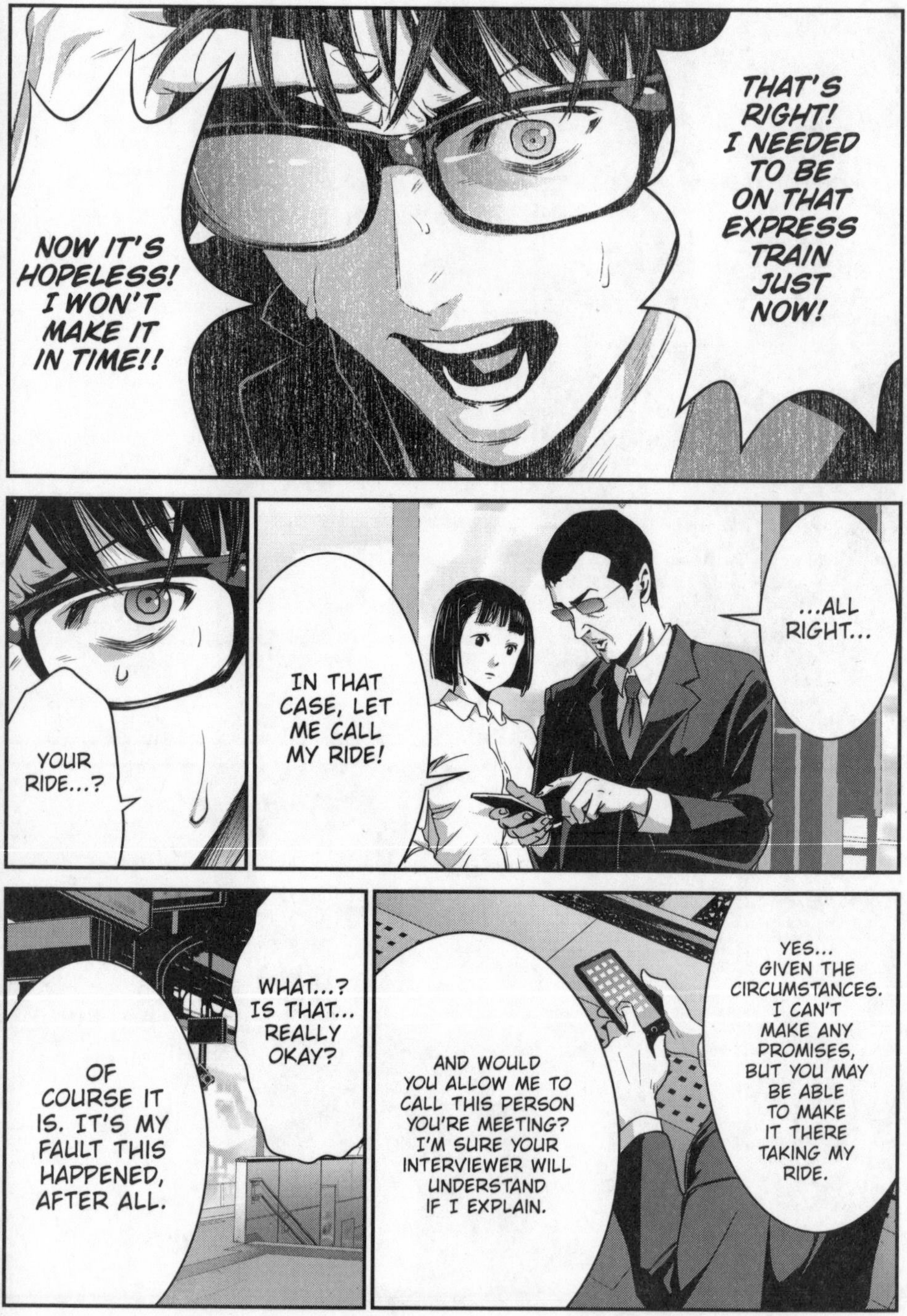
THAT'S RIGHT! I NEEDED TO BE ON THAT EXPRESS TRAIN JUST NOW!
NOW IT'S HOPELESS! I WON'T MAKE IT IN TIME!!
...ALL RIGHT...
IN THAT CASE, LET ME CALL MY RIDE!
YOUR RIDE...?
YES... GIVEN THE CIRCUMSTANCES. I CAN'T MAKE ANY PROMISES, BUT YOU MAY BE ABLE TO MAKE IT THERE TAKING MY RIDE.
AND WOULD YOU ALLOW ME TO CALL THIS PERSON YOU'RE MEETING? I'M SURE YOUR INTERVIEWER WILL UNDERSTAND IF I EXPLAIN.
WHAT...? IS THAT... REALLY OKAY?
OF COURSE IT IS. IT'S MY FAULT THIS HAPPENED, AFTER ALL.

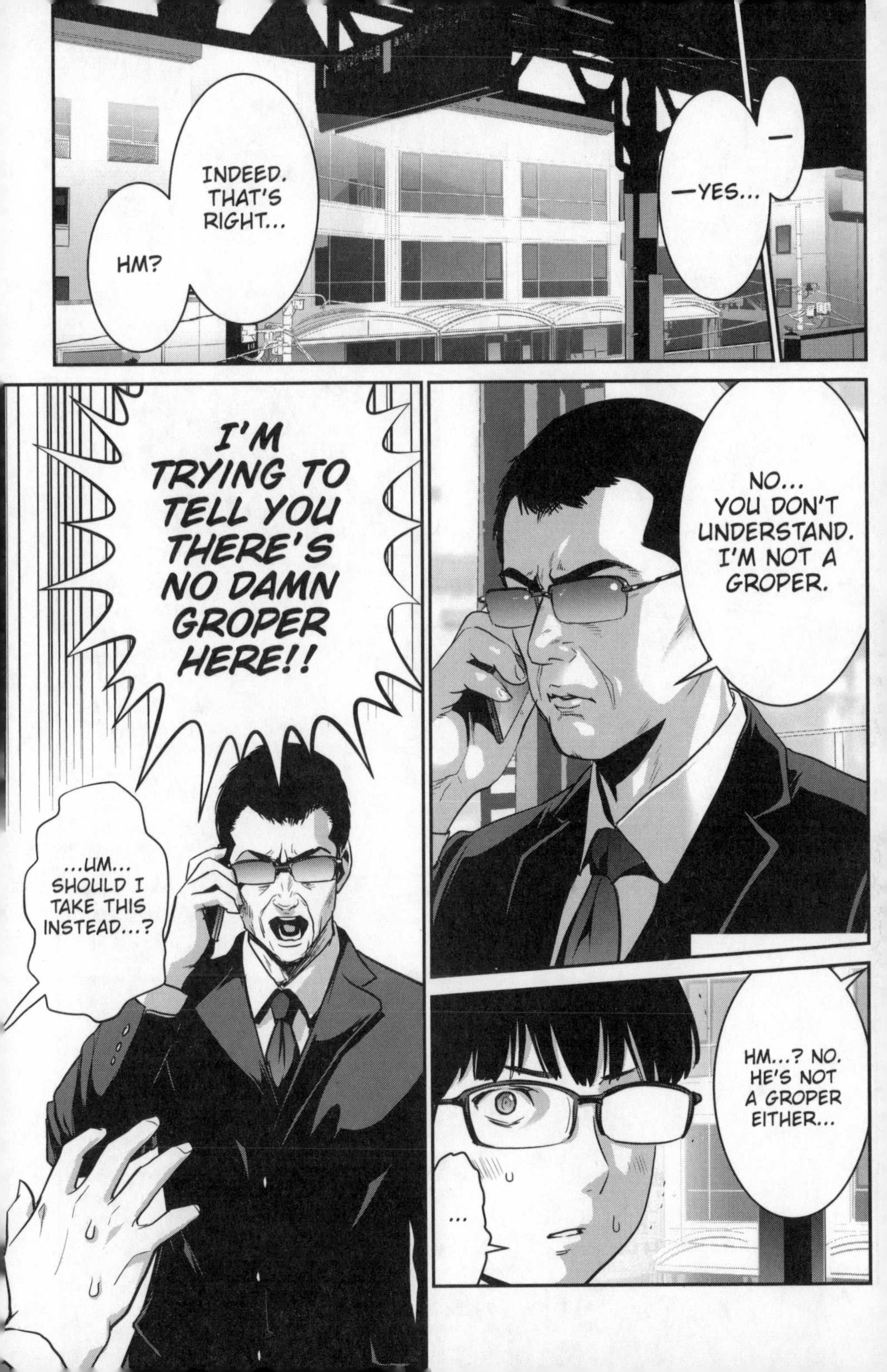
—
—YES...
INDEED. THAT'S RIGHT...
HM?
NO... YOU DON'T UNDERSTAND. I'M NOT A GROPER.
HM...? NO. HE'S NOT A GROPER EITHER...
...
I'M TRYING TO TELL YOU THERE'S NO DAMN GROPER HERE!!
...UM... SHOULD I TAKE THIS INSTEAD...?

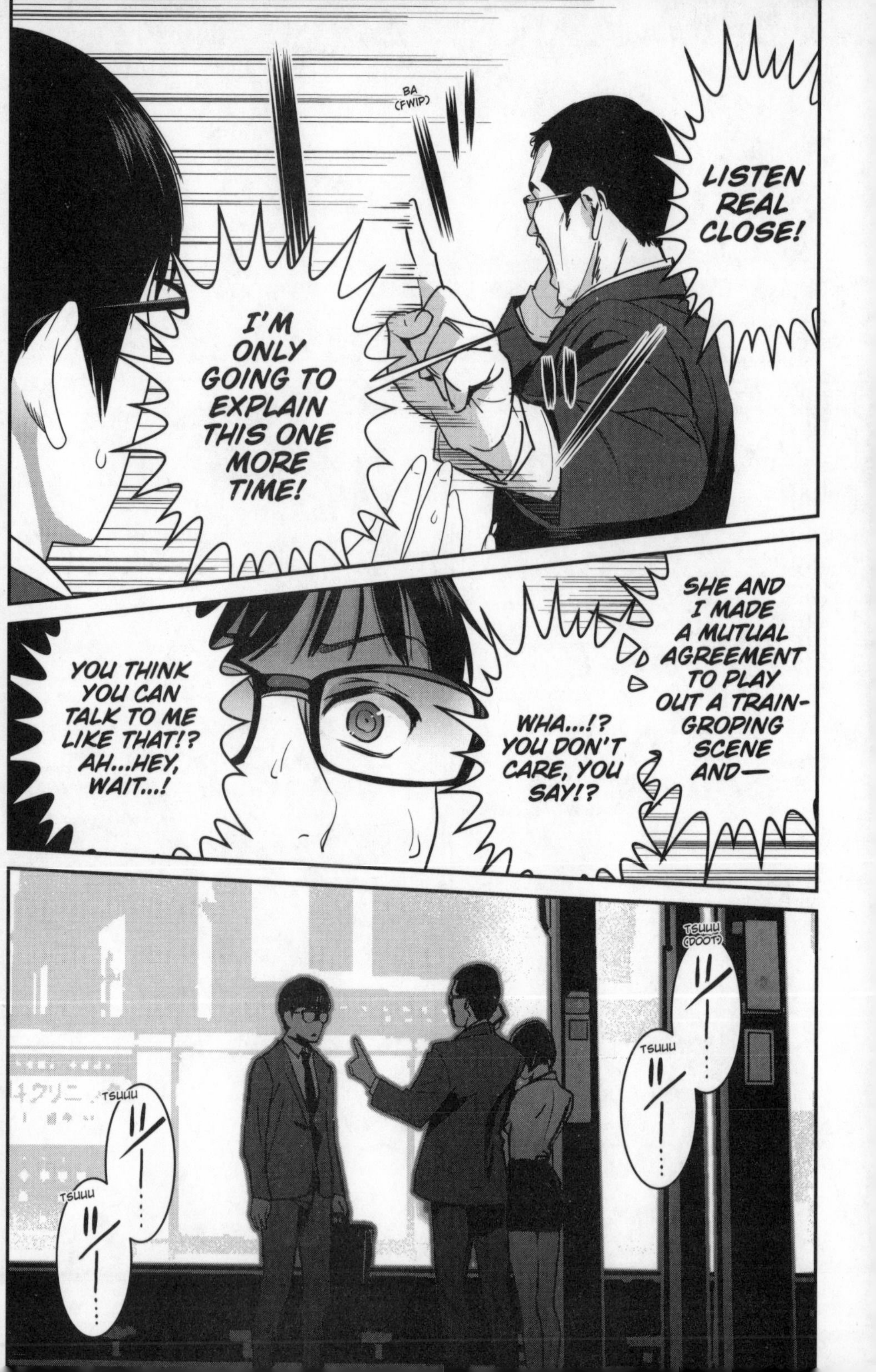
BA (FWIP)
LISTEN REAL CLOSE!
I'M ONLY GOING TO EXPLAIN THIS ONE MORE TIME!
SHE AND I MADE A MUTUAL AGREEMENT TO PLAY OUT A TRAIN-GROPING SCENE AND—
WHA...!? YOU DON'T CARE, YOU SAY!?
YOU THINK YOU CAN TALK TO ME LIKE THAT!? AH...HEY, WAIT...!
TSUUU (DOOT)
TSUUU
TSUUU
TSUUU

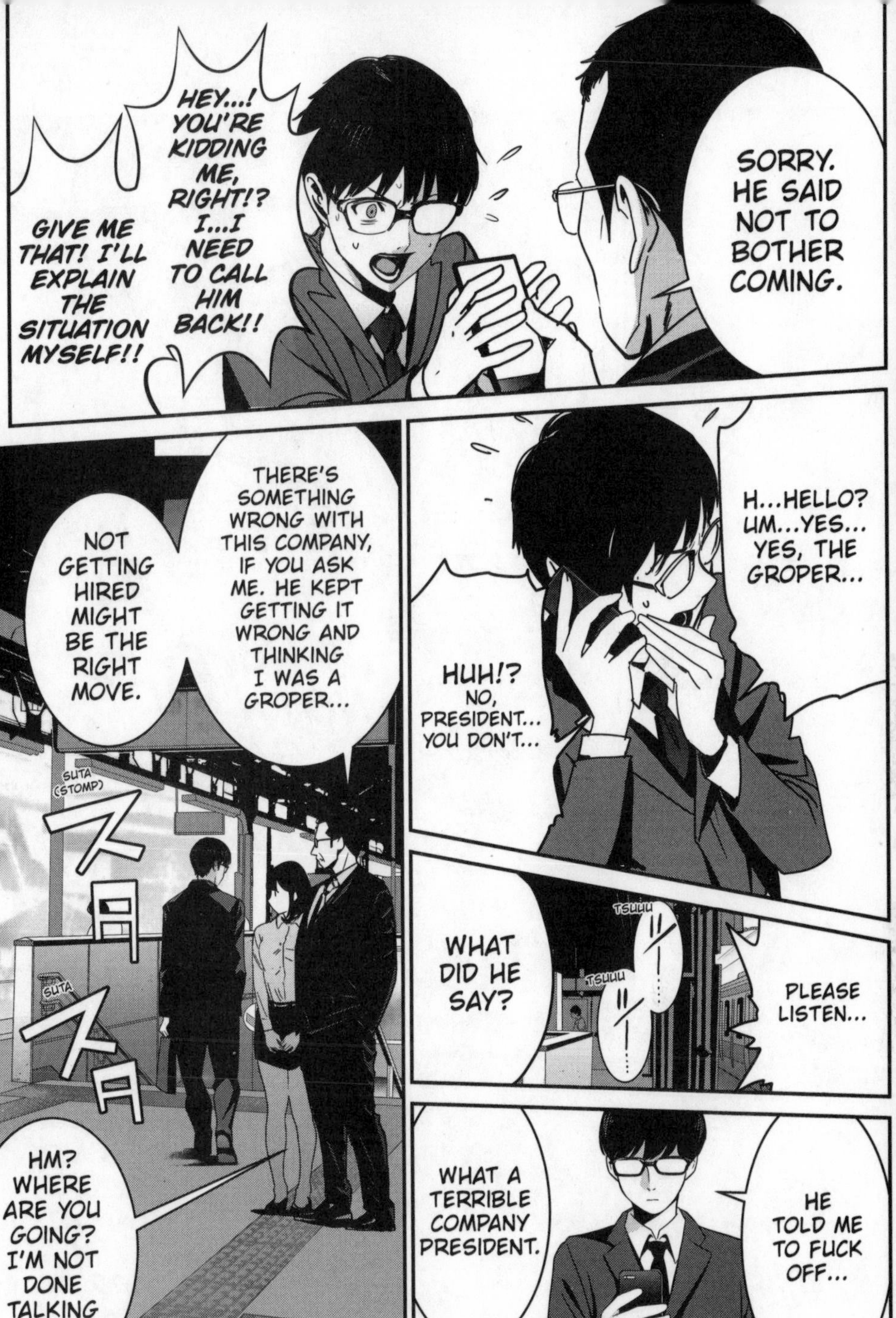
SORRY. HE SAID NOT TO BOTHER COMING.
HEY...! YOU'RE KIDDING ME, RIGHT!? I...I NEED TO CALL HIM BACK!!
GIVE ME THAT! I'LL EXPLAIN THE SITUATION MYSELF!!
H...HELLO? UM...YES... YES, THE GROPER...
HUH!? NO, PRESIDENT... YOU DON'T...
PLEASE LISTEN...
TSUUU
TSUUU
WHAT DID HE SAY?
HE TOLD ME TO FUCK OFF...
WHAT A TERRIBLE COMPANY PRESIDENT.
THERE'S SOMETHING WRONG WITH THIS COMPANY, IF YOU ASK ME. HE KEPT GETTING IT WRONG AND THINKING I WAS A GROPER...
NOT GETTING HIRED MIGHT BE THE RIGHT MOVE.
SUTA (STOMP)
SUTA
HM? WHERE ARE YOU GOING? I'M NOT DONE TALKING TO—

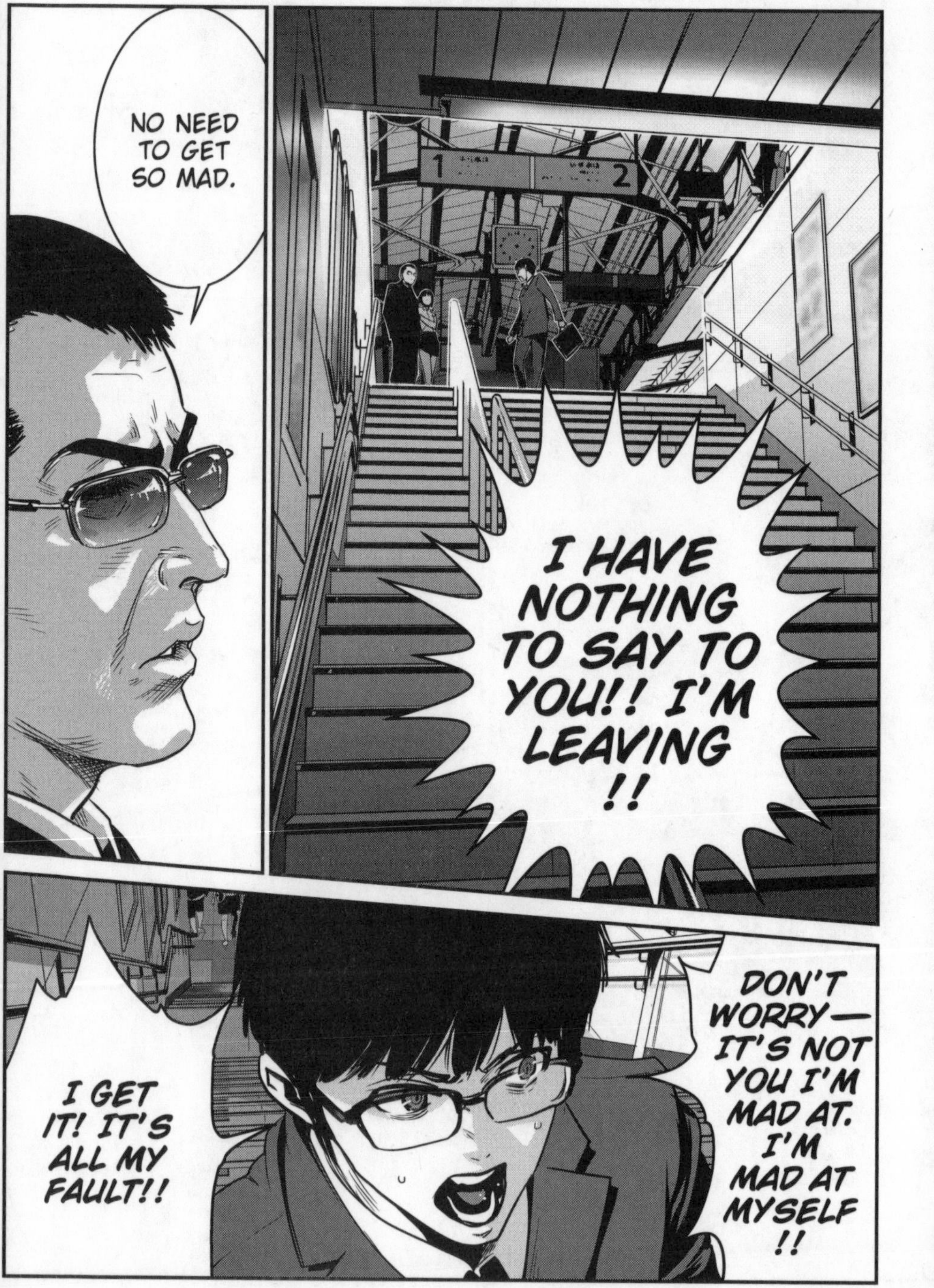
I HAVE NOTHING TO SAY TO YOU!! I'M LEAVING !!
NO NEED TO GET SO MAD.
DON'T WORRY— IT'S NOT YOU I'M MAD AT. I'M MAD AT MYSELF !!
I GET IT! IT'S ALL MY FAULT!!

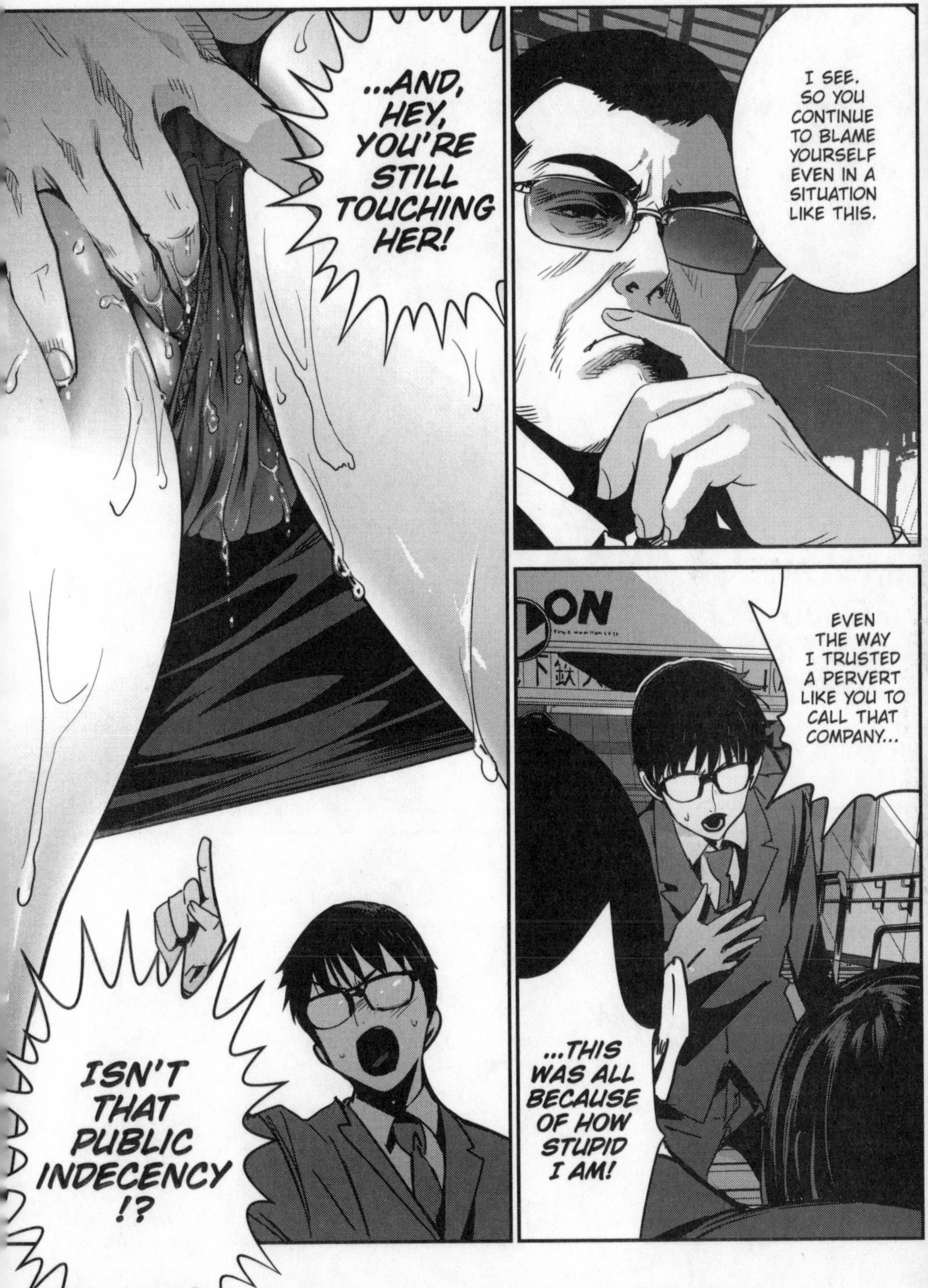
I SEE. SO YOU CONTINUE TO BLAME YOURSELF EVEN IN A SITUATION LIKE THIS.
EVEN THE WAY I TRUSTED A PERVERT LIKE YOU TO CALL THAT COMPANY...
...THIS WAS ALL BECAUSE OF HOW STUPID I AM!
...AND, HEY, YOU'RE STILL TOUCHING HER!
ISN'T THAT PUBLIC INDECENCY!?

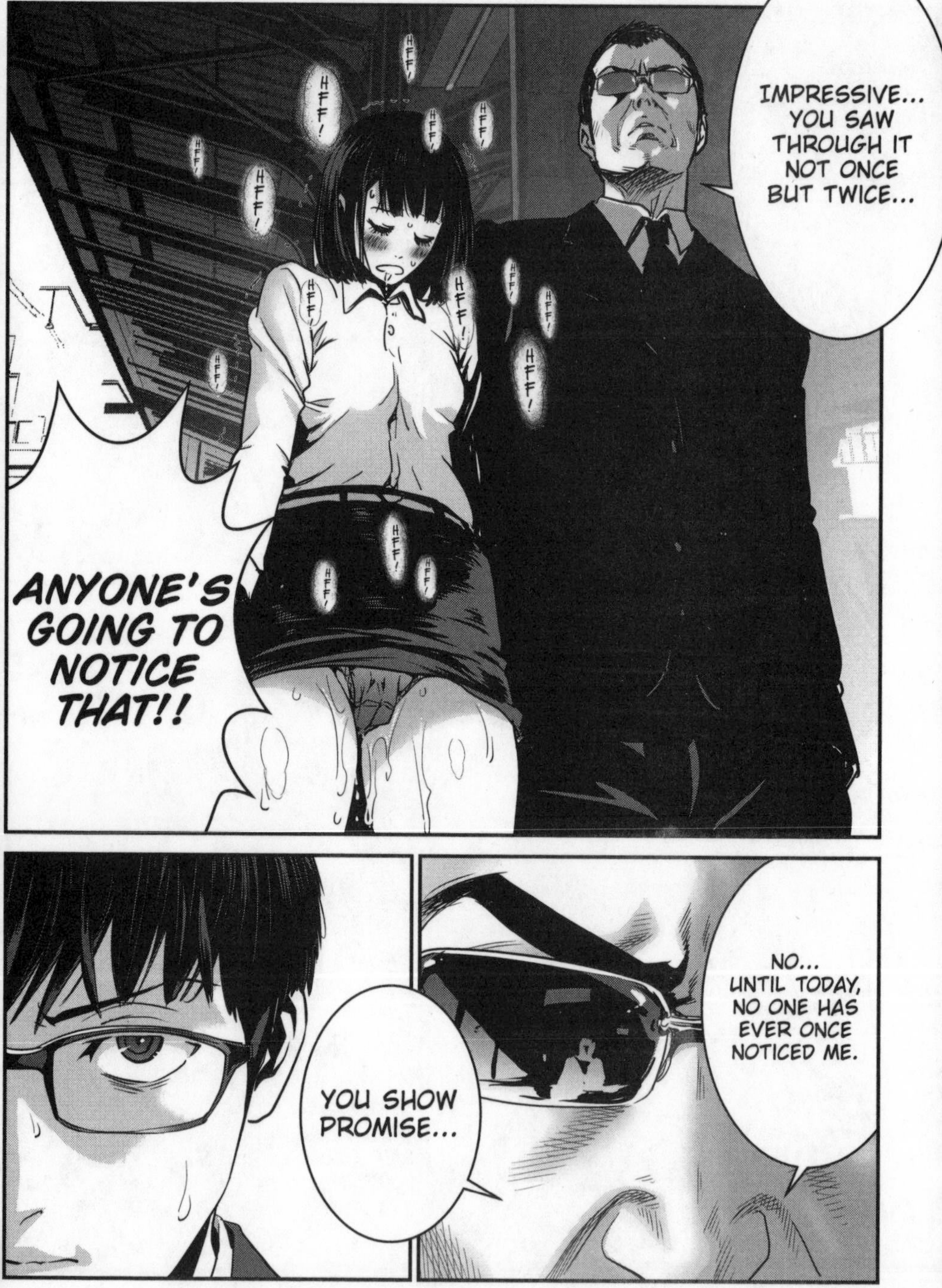
IMPRESSIVE... YOU SAW THROUGH IT NOT ONCE BUT TWICE...
HFF!
HFF!
HFF!
HFF!
HFF!
HFF!
HFF!
HFF!
HFF!
HFF!
HFF!
HFF!
HFF!
HFF!
HFF!
ANYONE'S GOING TO NOTICE THAT!!
NO... UNTIL TODAY, NO ONE HAS EVER ONCE NOTICED ME.
YOU SHOW PROMISE...

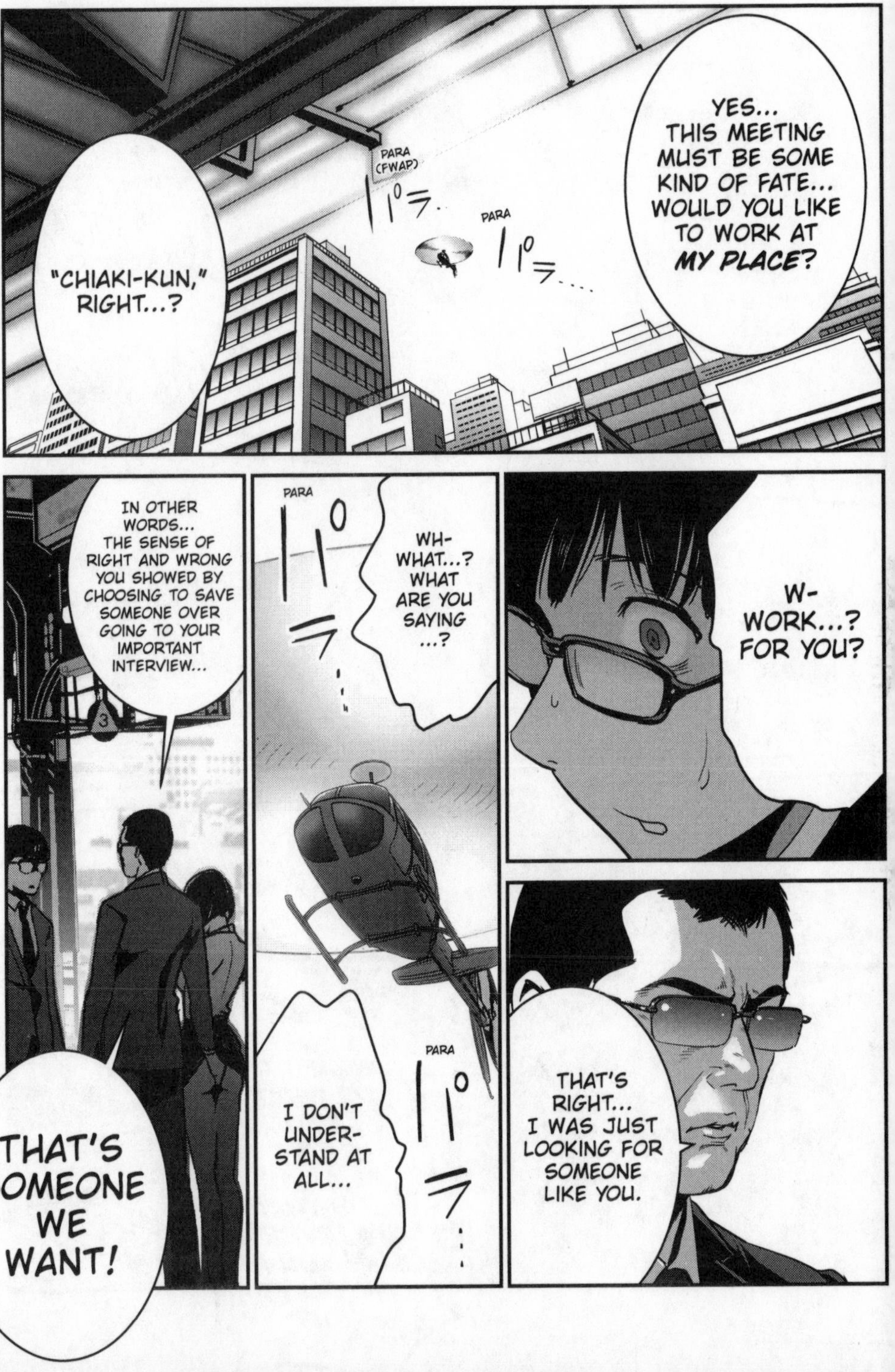
YES... THIS MEETING MUST BE SOME KIND OF FATE... WOULD YOU LIKE TO WORK AT *MY PLACE*?
PARA (FWAP)
PARA
"CHIAKI-KUN," RIGHT...?
W-WORK...? FOR YOU?
THAT'S RIGHT... I WAS JUST LOOKING FOR SOMEONE LIKE YOU.
PARA
WH-WHAT...? WHAT ARE YOU SAYING ...?
PARA
I DON'T UNDER-STAND AT ALL...
IN OTHER WORDS... THE SENSE OF RIGHT AND WRONG YOU SHOWED BY CHOOSING TO SAVE SOMEONE OVER GOING TO YOUR IMPORTANT INTERVIEW...
THAT'S SOMEONE WE WANT!

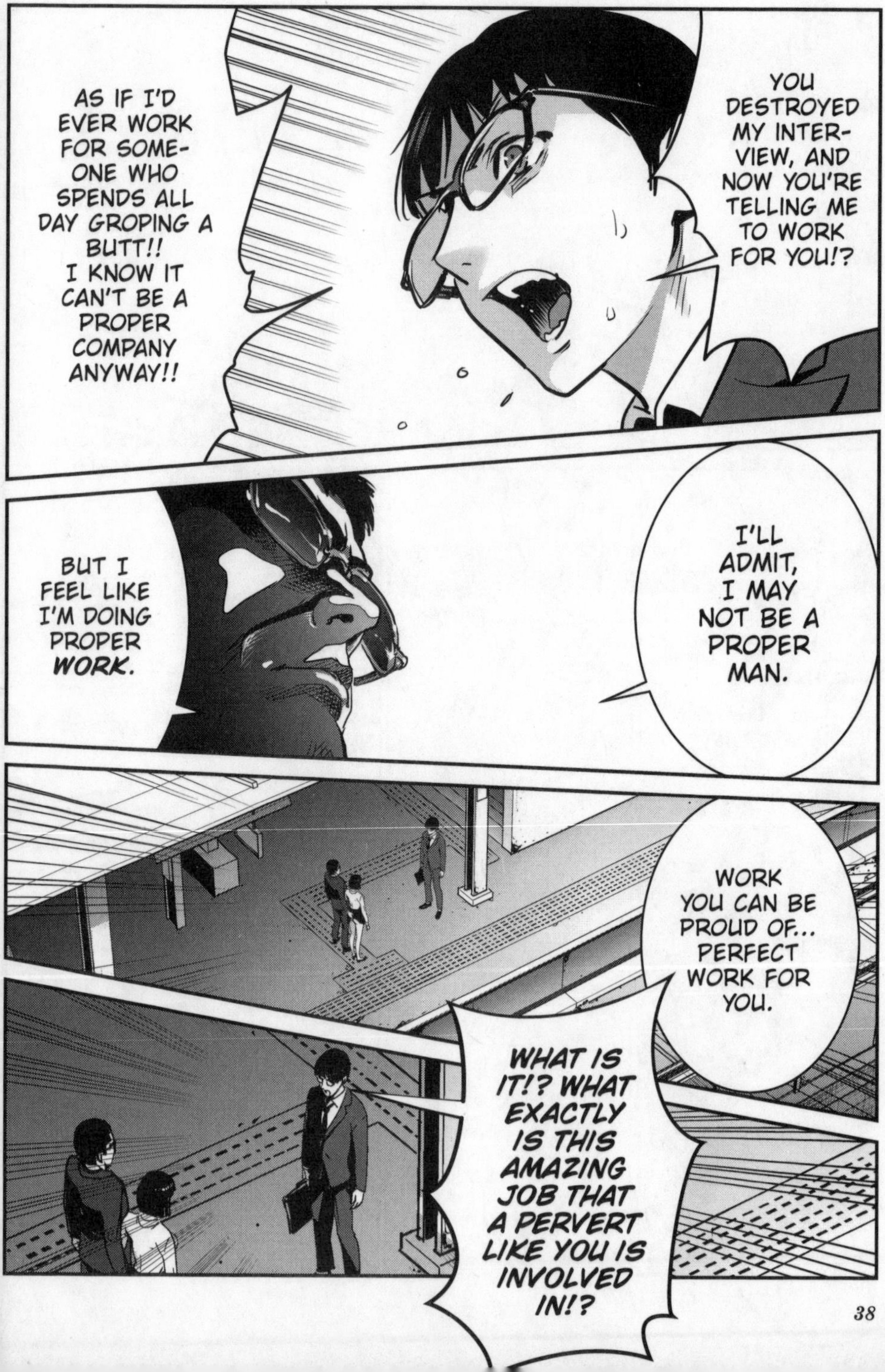
YOU DESTROYED MY INTER-VIEW, AND NOW YOU'RE TELLING ME TO WORK FOR YOU!?
AS IF I'D EVER WORK FOR SOME-ONE WHO SPENDS ALL DAY GROPING A BUTT!! I KNOW IT CAN'T BE A PROPER COMPANY ANYWAY!!
I'LL ADMIT, I MAY NOT BE A PROPER MAN.
BUT I FEEL LIKE I'M DOING PROPER *WORK*.
WORK YOU CAN BE PROUD OF... PERFECT WORK FOR YOU.
WHAT IS IT!? WHAT EXACTLY IS THIS AMAZING JOB THAT A PERVERT LIKE YOU IS INVOLVED IN!?

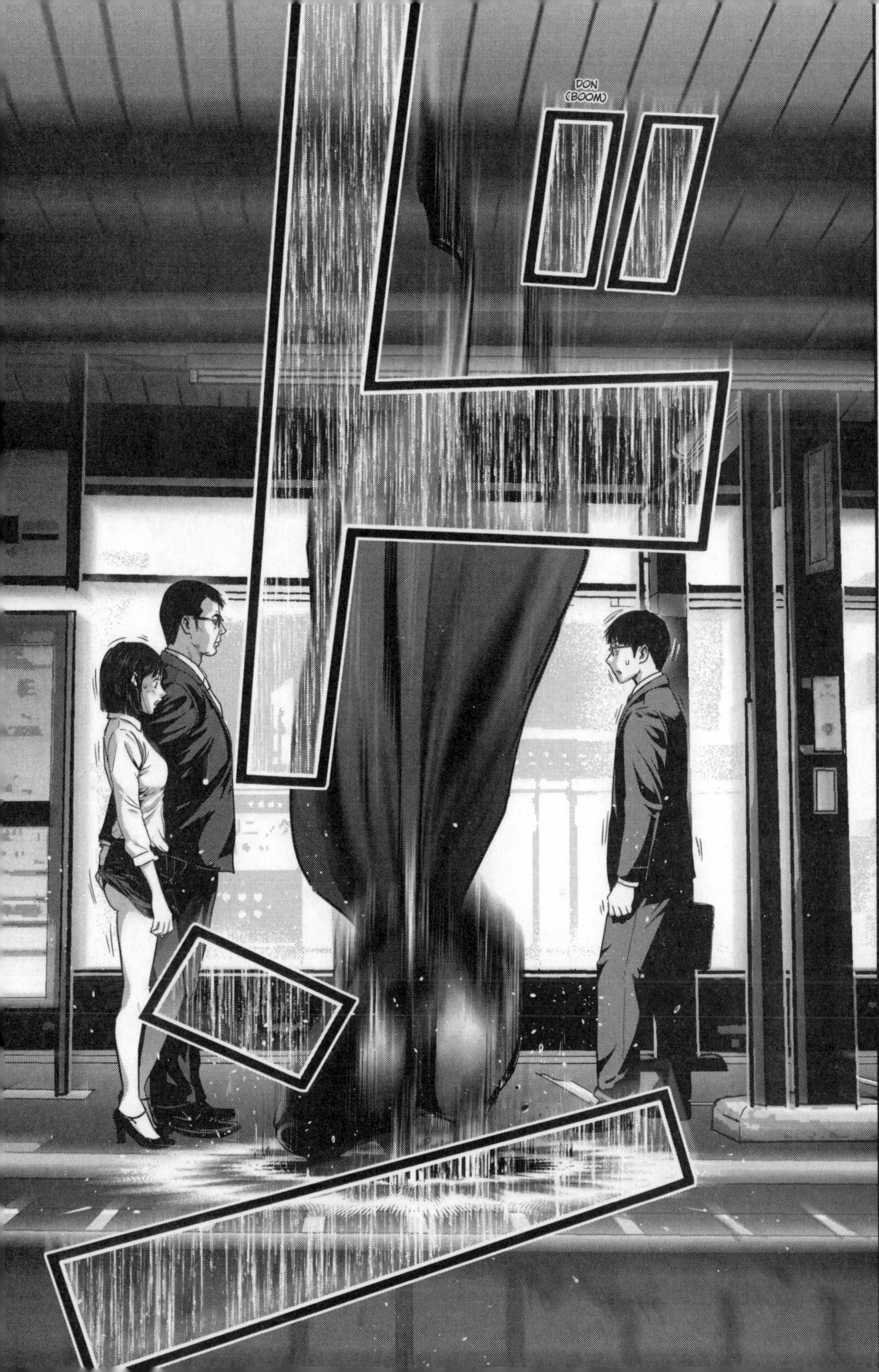
DON
(BOOM)

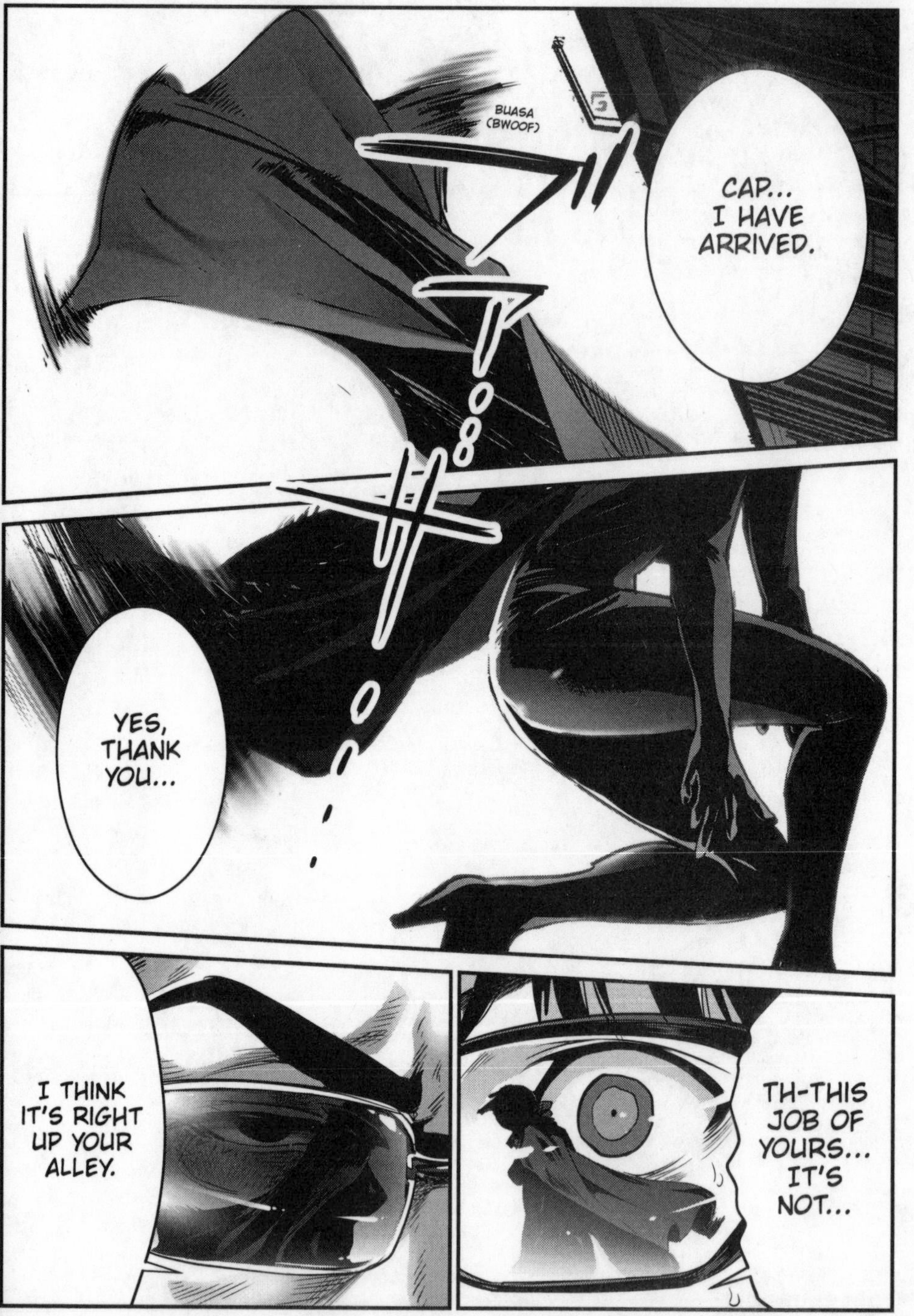
CAP... I HAVE ARRIVED.
BUASA (BWOOF)
YES, THANK YOU...
TH-THIS JOB OF YOURS... IT'S NOT...
I THINK IT'S RIGHT UP YOUR ALLEY.

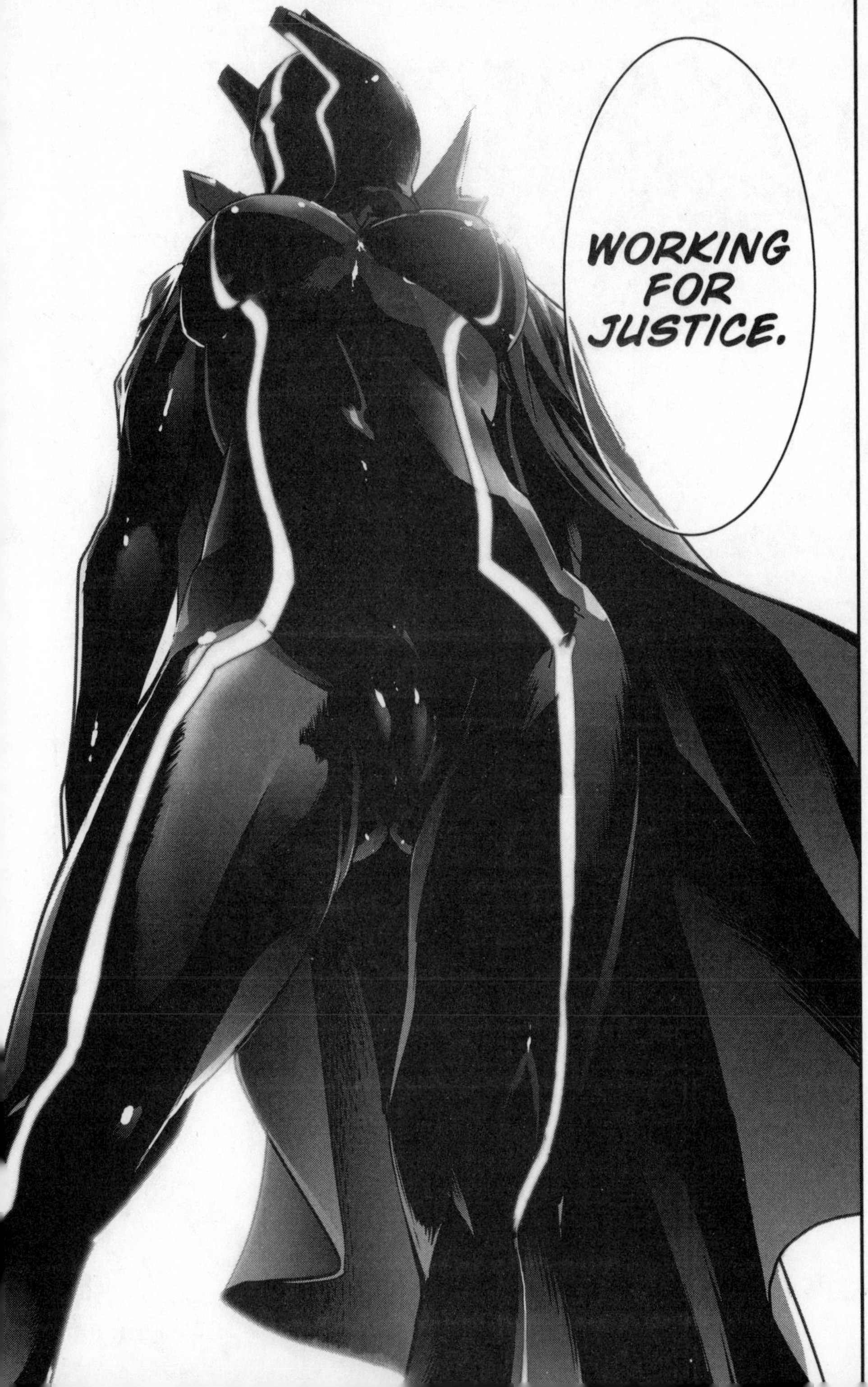
WORKING FOR JUSTICE.

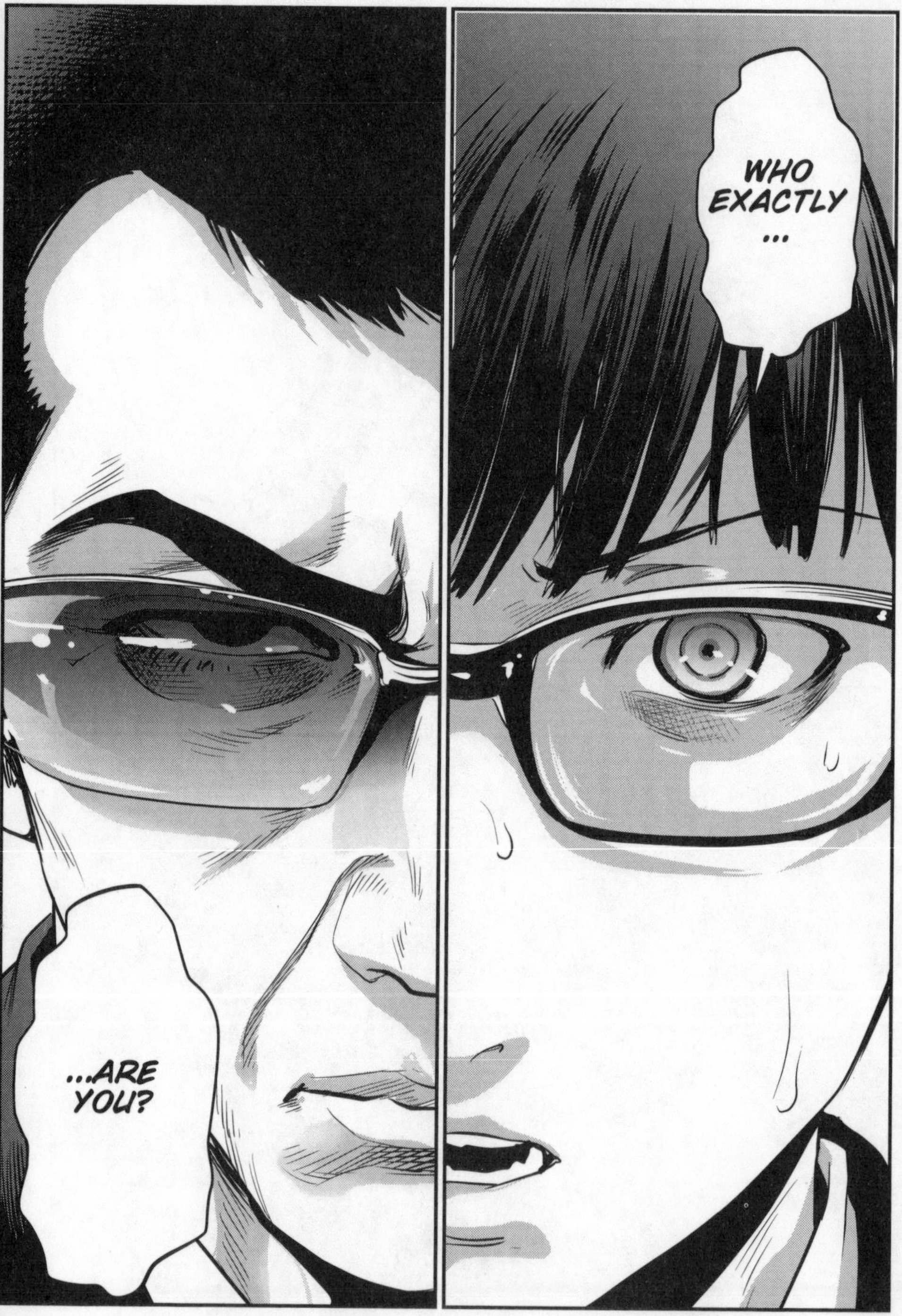
WHO EXACTLY ...
...ARE YOU?

Chapter 1: End

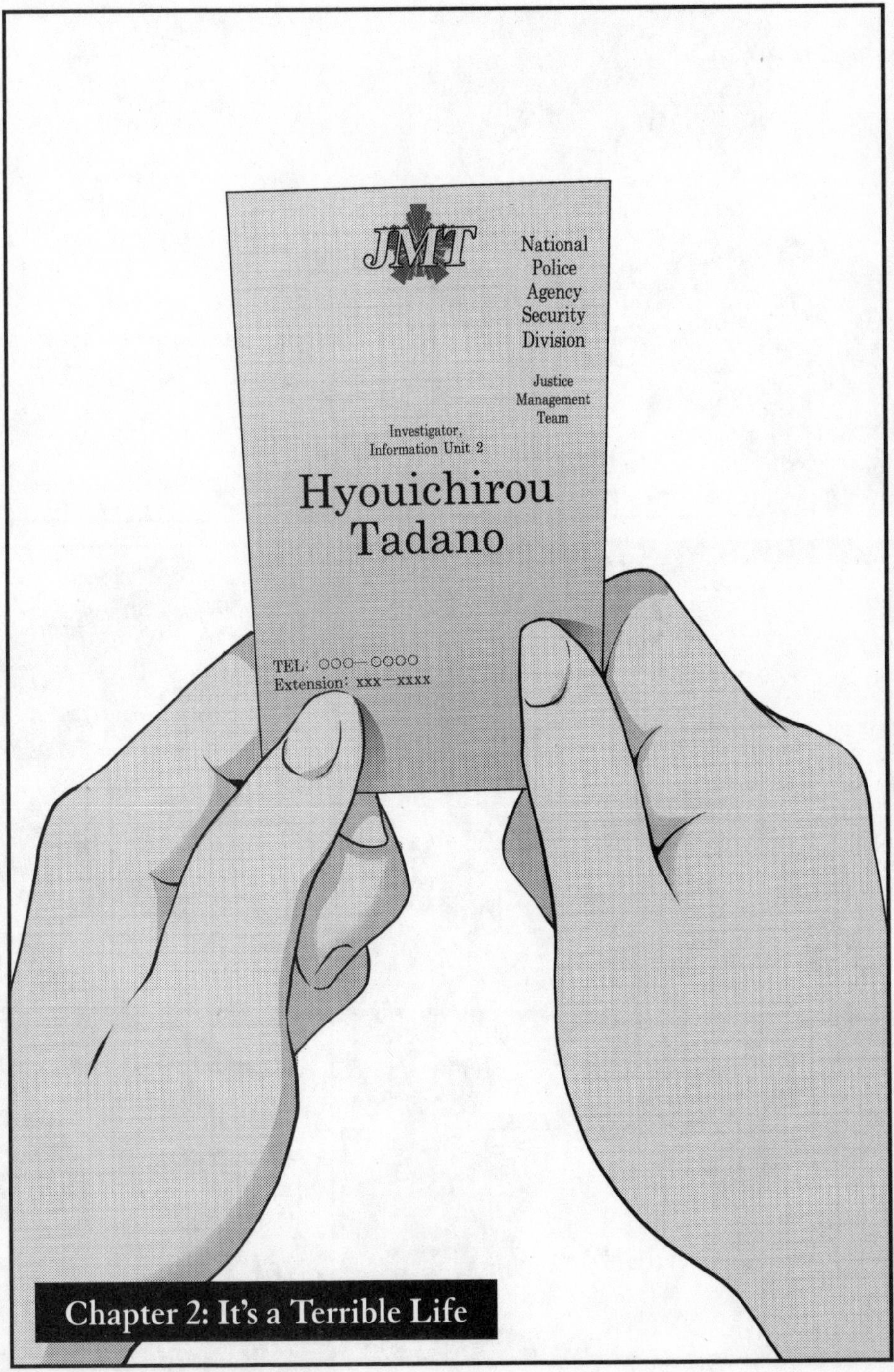
JMT
National
Police
Agency
Security
Division
Justice
Management
Team
Investigator,
Information Unit 2
Hyouichirou
Tadano
TEL: ○○○—○○○○
Extension: xxx—xxxx
Chapter 2: It's a Terrible Life

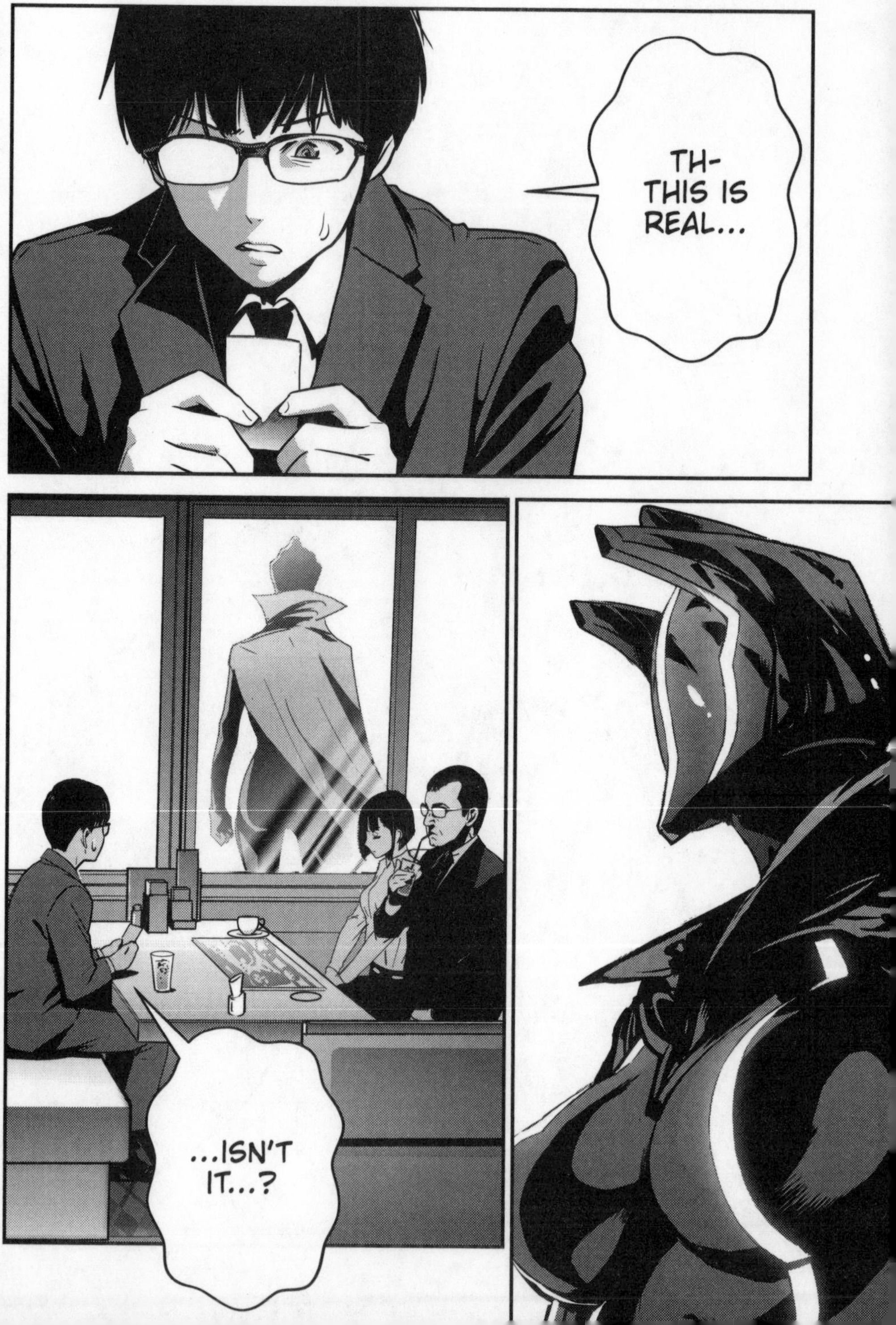
TH- THIS IS REAL...
...ISN'T IT...?

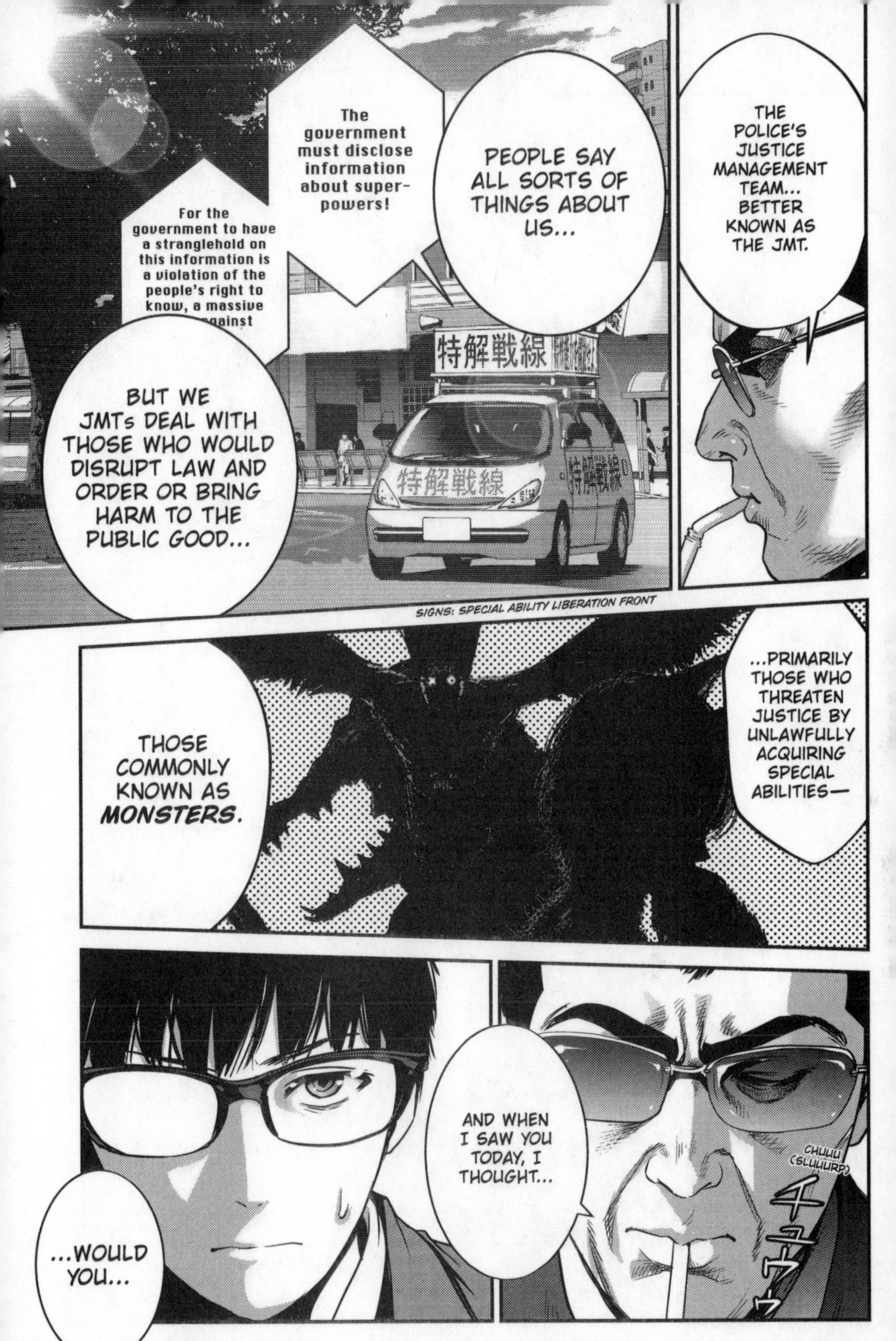
THE POLICE'S JUSTICE MANAGEMENT TEAM... BETTER KNOWN AS THE JMT.
PEOPLE SAY ALL SORTS OF THINGS ABOUT US...
The government must disclose information about super-powers!
For the government to have a stranglehold on this information is a violation of the people's right to know, a massive
against
特解戦線
BUT WE JMTs DEAL WITH THOSE WHO WOULD DISRUPT LAW AND ORDER OR BRING HARM TO THE PUBLIC GOOD...
SIGNS: SPECIAL ABILITY LIBERATION FRONT
...PRIMARILY THOSE WHO THREATEN JUSTICE BY UNLAWFULLY ACQUIRING SPECIAL ABILITIES—
THOSE COMMONLY KNOWN AS *MONSTERS*.
AND WHEN I SAW YOU TODAY, I THOUGHT...
CHUUU (SLUUURP)
...WOULD YOU...

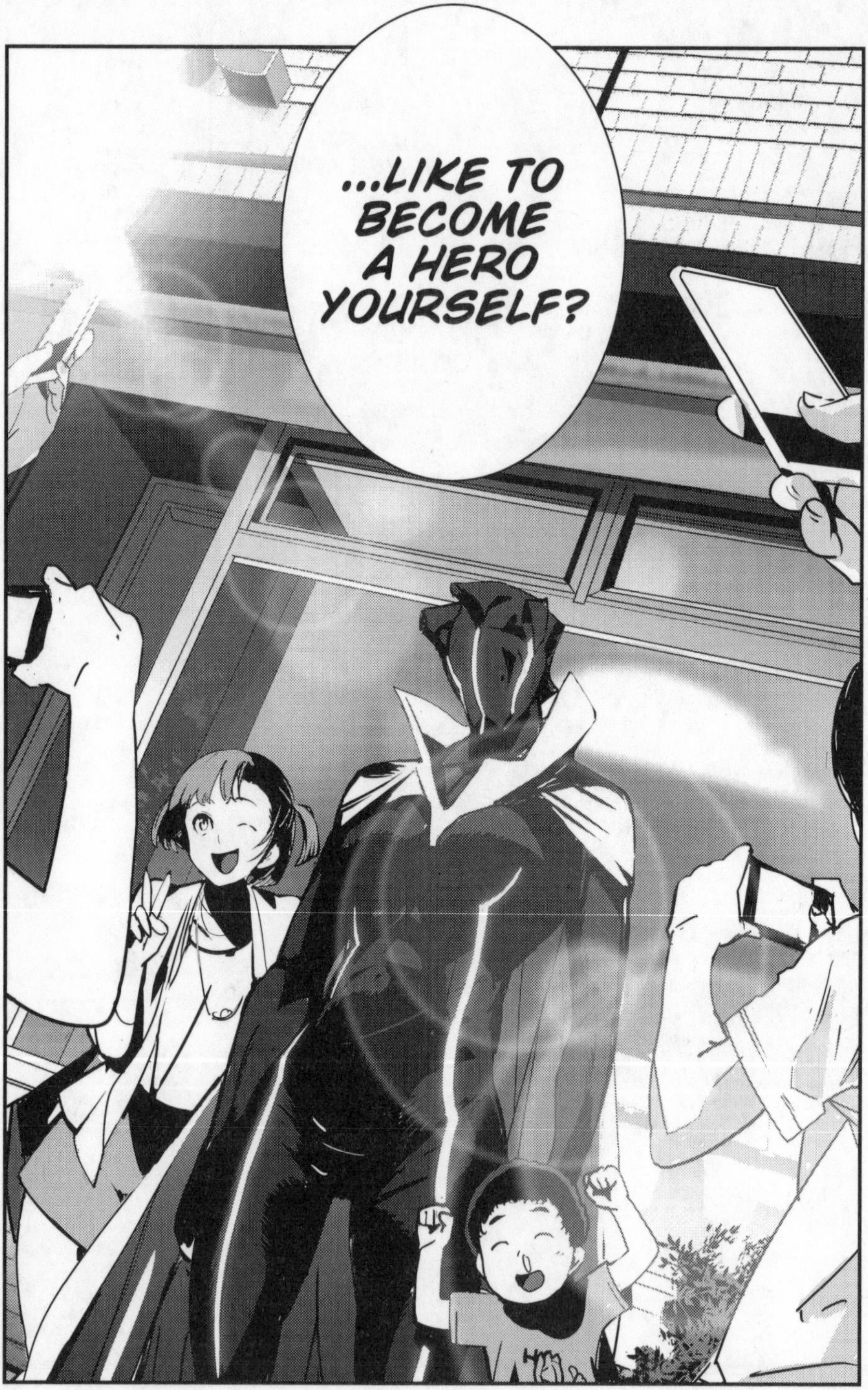
...LIKE TO BECOME A HERO YOURSELF?

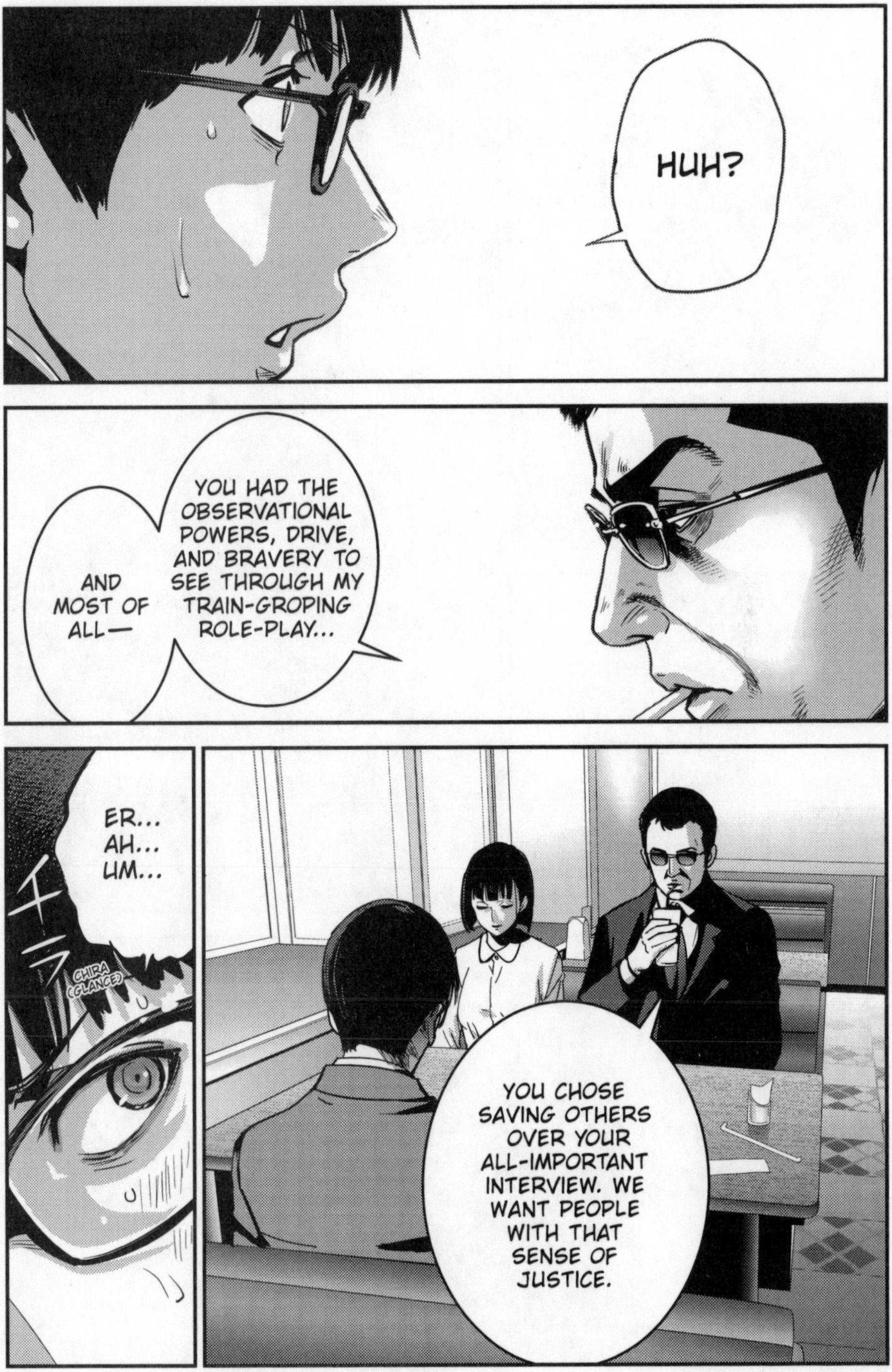
HUH?
YOU HAD THE OBSERVATIONAL POWERS, DRIVE, AND BRAVERY TO SEE THROUGH MY TRAIN-GROPING ROLE-PLAY...
AND MOST OF ALL—
YOU CHOSE SAVING OTHERS OVER YOUR ALL-IMPORTANT INTERVIEW. WE WANT PEOPLE WITH THAT SENSE OF JUSTICE.
ER... AH... UM...
CHIRA (GLANCE)

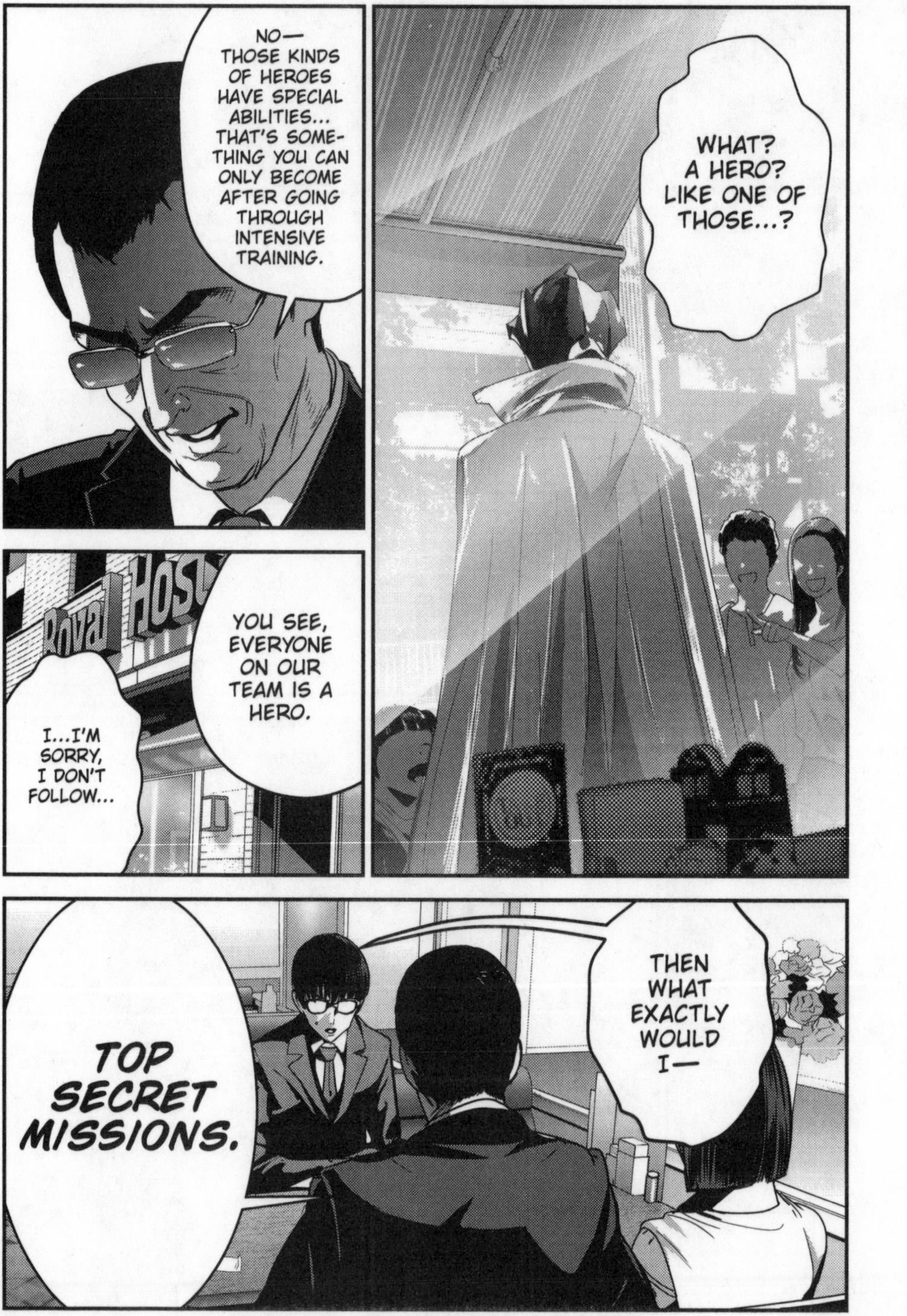
WHAT? A HERO? LIKE ONE OF THOSE...?
NO— THOSE KINDS OF HEROES HAVE SPECIAL ABILITIES... THAT'S SOMETHING YOU CAN ONLY BECOME AFTER GOING THROUGH INTENSIVE TRAINING.
YOU SEE, EVERYONE ON OUR TEAM IS A HERO.
I...I'M SORRY, I DON'T FOLLOW...
THEN WHAT EXACTLY WOULD I—
TOP SECRET MISSIONS.

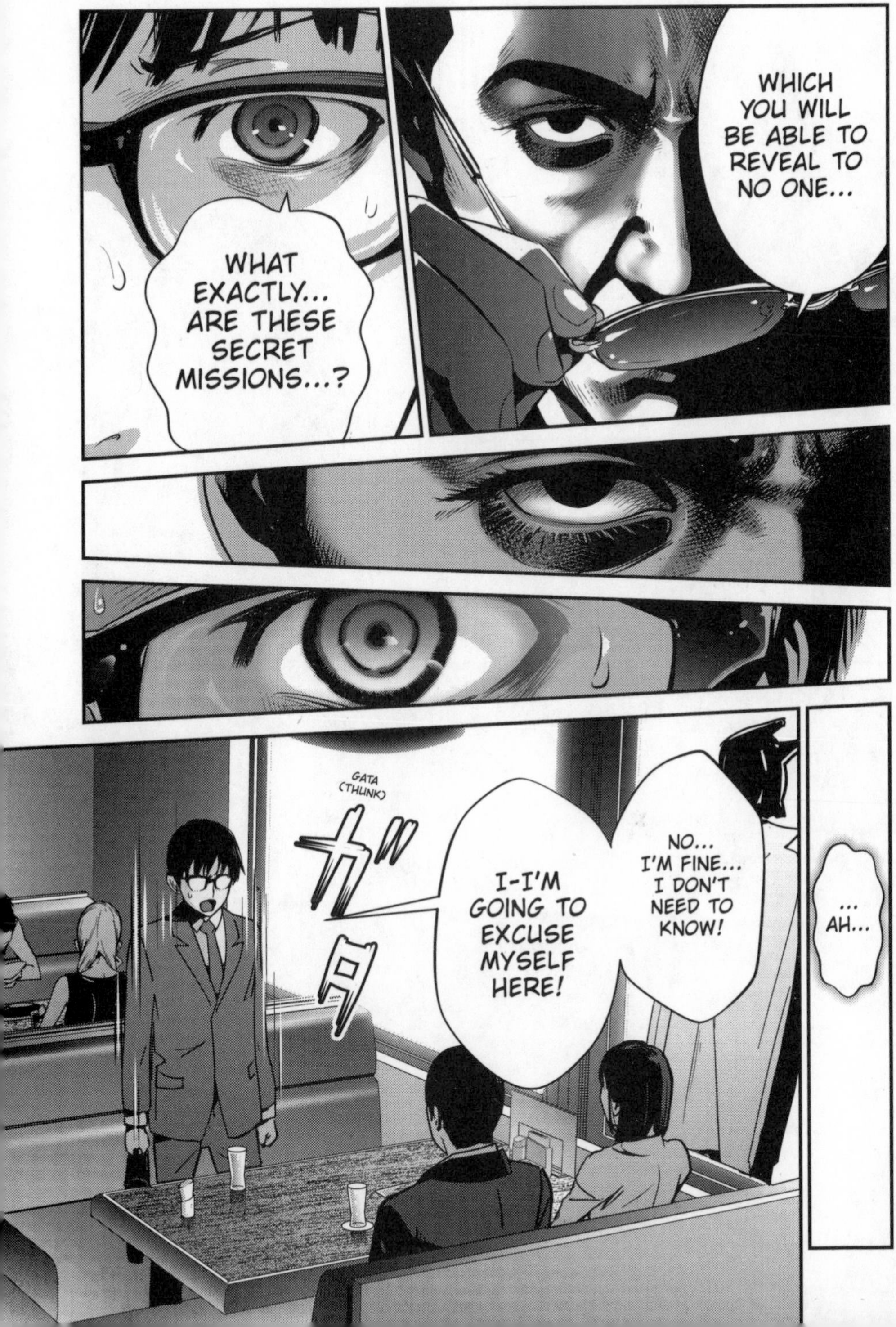
WHICH YOU WILL BE ABLE TO REVEAL TO NO ONE...
WHAT EXACTLY... ARE THESE SECRET MISSIONS...?
... AH...
NO... I'M FINE... I DON'T NEED TO KNOW!
I-I'M GOING TO EXCUSE MYSELF HERE!
GATA (THUNK)

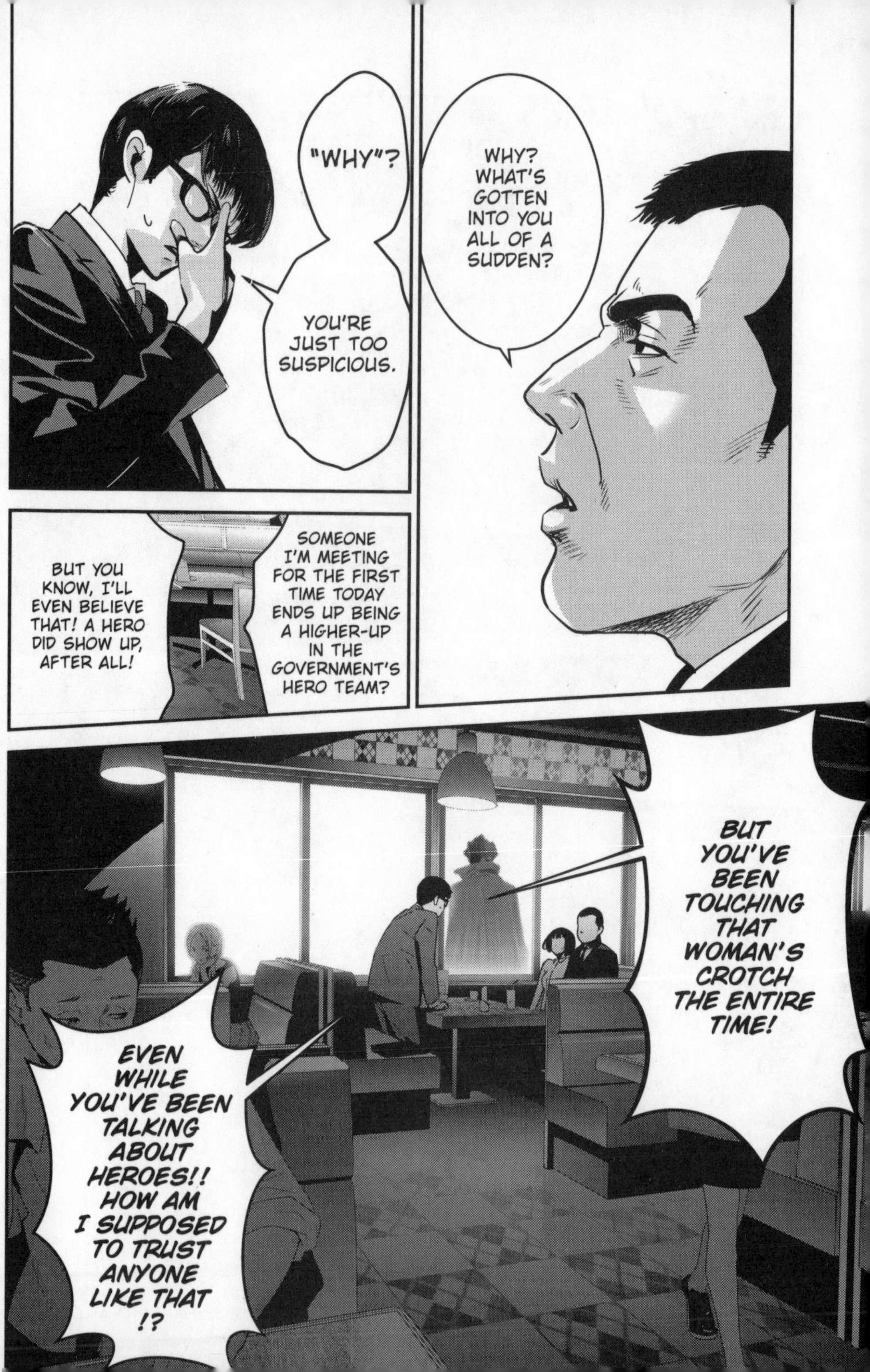
WHY? WHAT'S GOTTEN INTO YOU ALL OF A SUDDEN?
"WHY"?
YOU'RE JUST TOO SUSPICIOUS.
SOMEONE I'M MEETING FOR THE FIRST TIME TODAY ENDS UP BEING A HIGHER-UP IN THE GOVERNMENT'S HERO TEAM?
BUT YOU KNOW, I'LL EVEN BELIEVE THAT! A HERO DID SHOW UP, AFTER ALL!
BUT YOU'VE BEEN TOUCHING THAT WOMAN'S CROTCH THE ENTIRE TIME!
EVEN WHILE YOU'VE BEEN TALKING ABOUT HEROES!! HOW AM I SUPPOSED TO TRUST ANYONE LIKE THAT !?

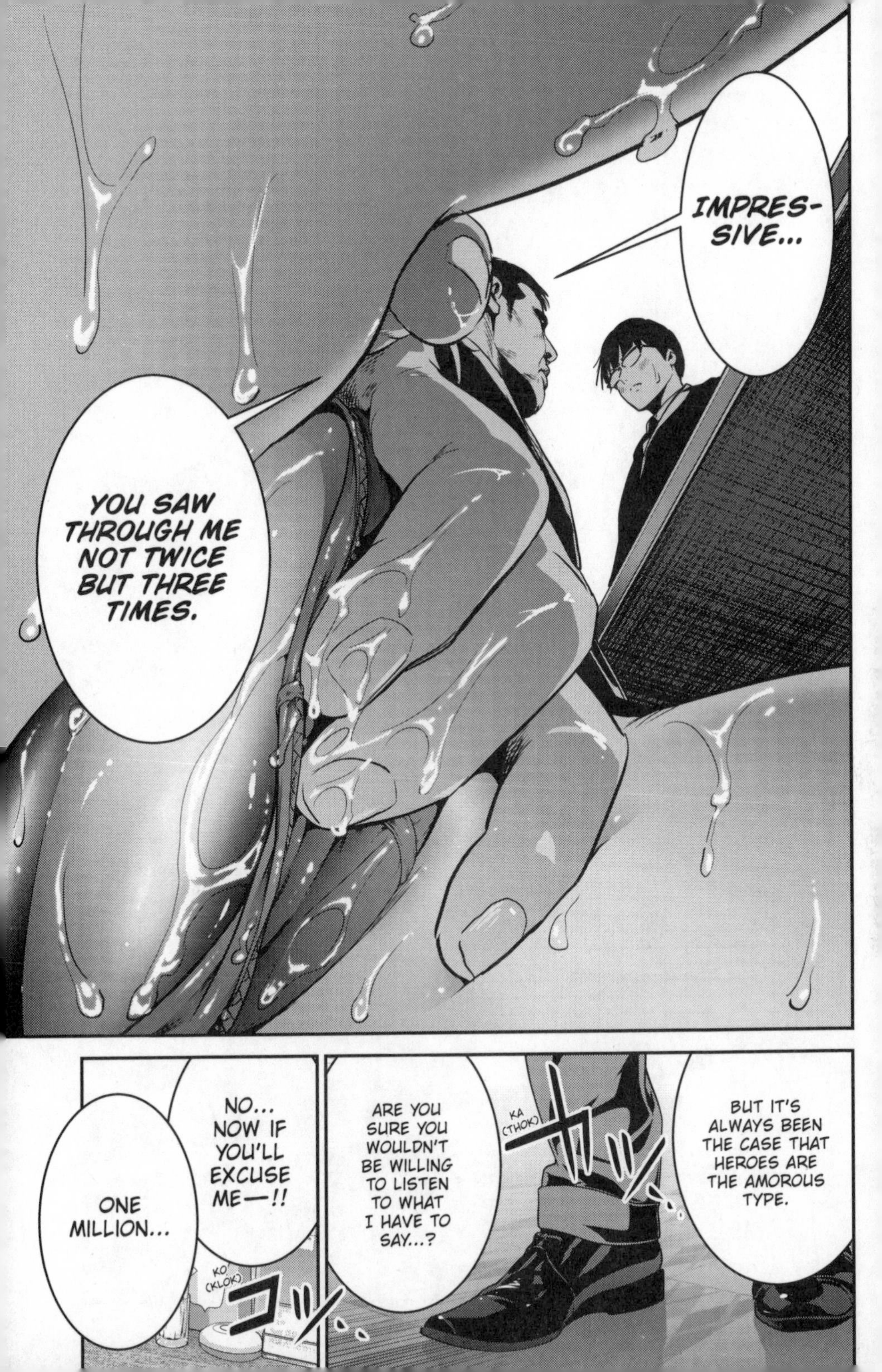
IMPRES-SIVE...
YOU SAW THROUGH ME NOT TWICE BUT THREE TIMES.
BUT IT'S ALWAYS BEEN THE CASE THAT HEROES ARE THE AMOROUS TYPE.
KA (THOK)
ARE YOU SURE YOU WOULDN'T BE WILLING TO LISTEN TO WHAT I HAVE TO SAY...?
NO... NOW IF YOU'LL EXCUSE ME—!!
KO (KLOK)
ONE MILLION...

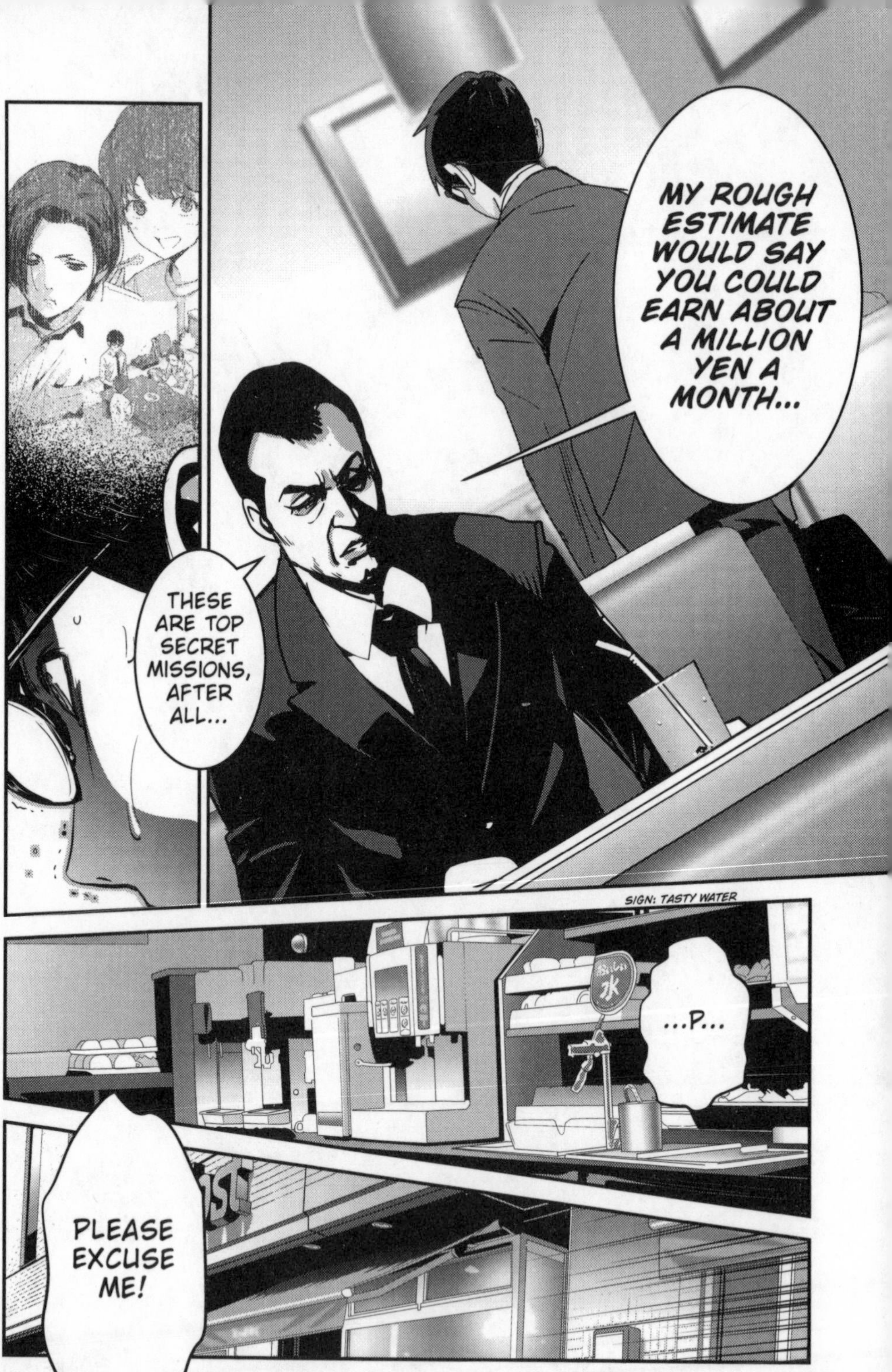
MY ROUGH ESTIMATE WOULD SAY YOU COULD EARN ABOUT A MILLION YEN A MONTH...
THESE ARE TOP SECRET MISSIONS, AFTER ALL...
SIGN: TASTY WATER
...P...
PLEASE EXCUSE ME!

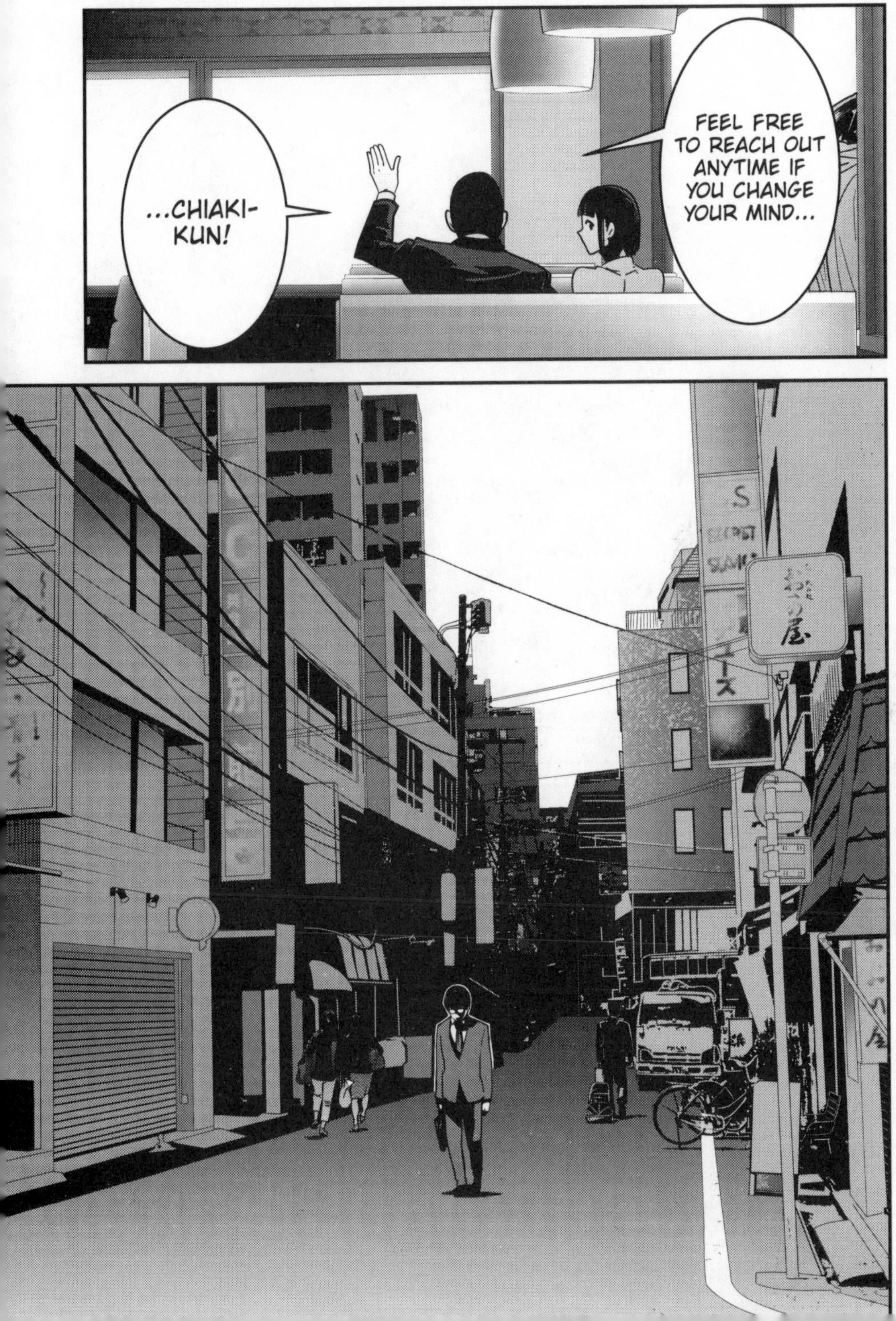
FEEL FREE TO REACH OUT ANYTIME IF YOU CHANGE YOUR MIND...
...CHIAKI-KUN!

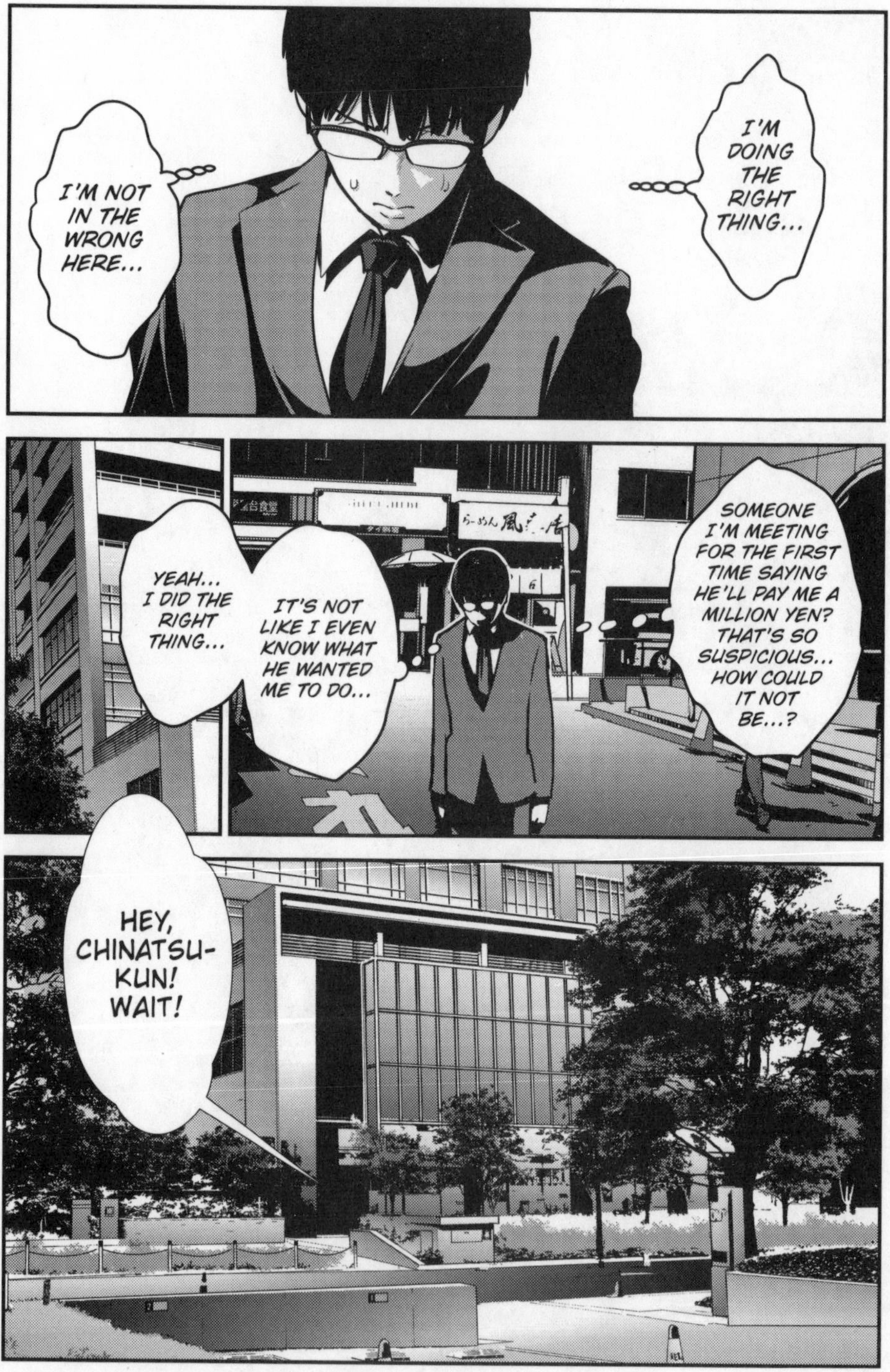
I'M DOING THE RIGHT THING...
I'M NOT IN THE WRONG HERE...
SOMEONE I'M MEETING FOR THE FIRST TIME SAYING HE'LL PAY ME A MILLION YEN? THAT'S SO SUSPICIOUS... HOW COULD IT NOT BE...?
IT'S NOT LIKE I EVEN KNOW WHAT HE WANTED ME TO DO...
YEAH... I DID THE RIGHT THING...
HEY, CHINATSU-KUN! WAIT!

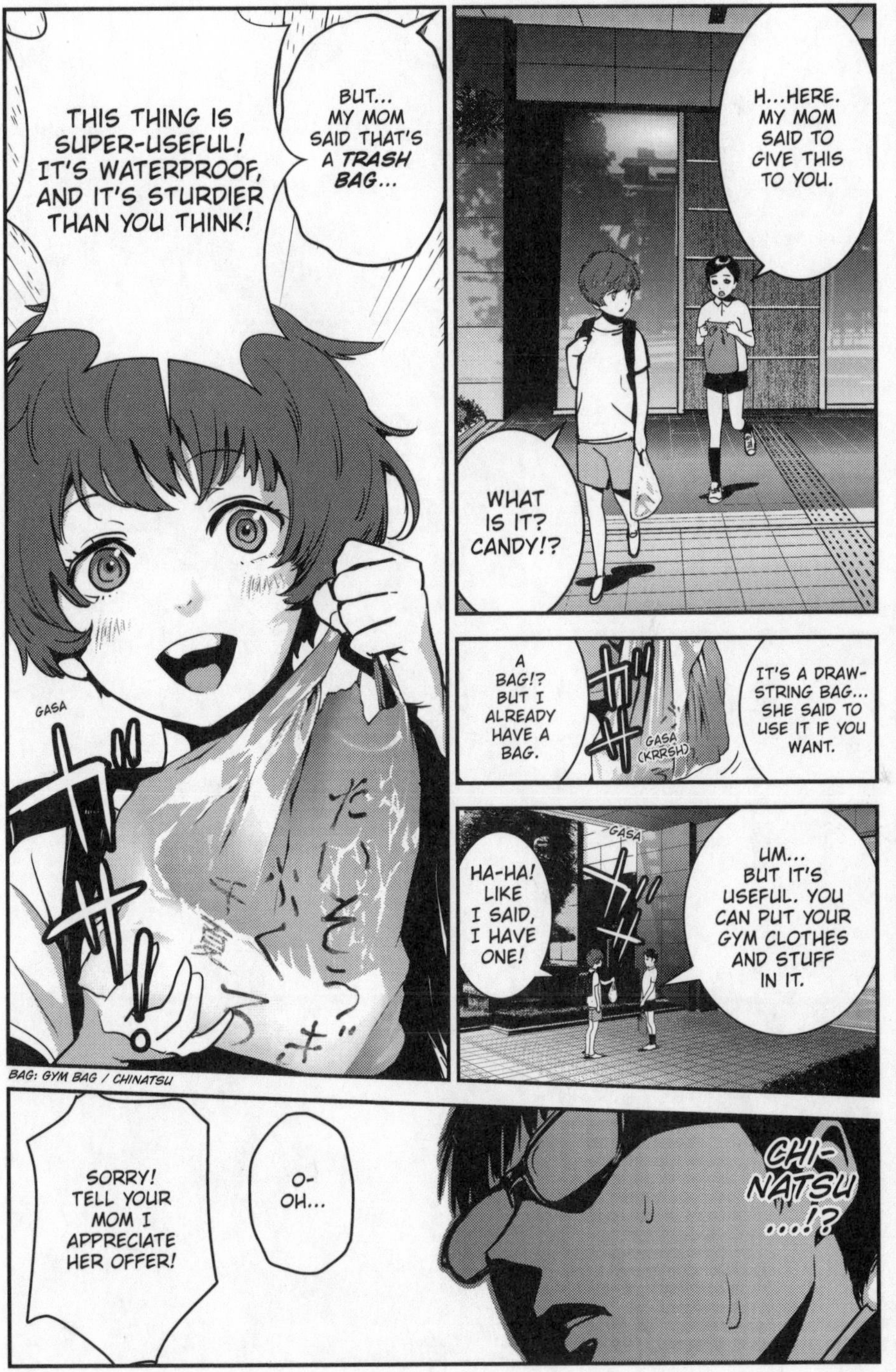
H...HERE. MY MOM SAID TO GIVE THIS TO YOU.
WHAT IS IT? CANDY!?
IT'S A DRAW-STRING BAG... SHE SAID TO USE IT IF YOU WANT.
GASA (KRRSH)
A BAG!? BUT I ALREADY HAVE A BAG.
GASA
UM... BUT IT'S USEFUL. YOU CAN PUT YOUR GYM CLOTHES AND STUFF IN IT.
HA-HA! LIKE I SAID, I HAVE ONE!
BUT... MY MOM SAID THAT'S A *TRASH BAG*...
THIS THING IS SUPER-USEFUL! IT'S WATERPROOF, AND IT'S STURDIER THAN YOU THINK!
GASA
BAG: GYM BAG / CHINATSU
CHI-NATSU...!?
O-OH...
SORRY! TELL YOUR MOM I APPRECIATE HER OFFER!

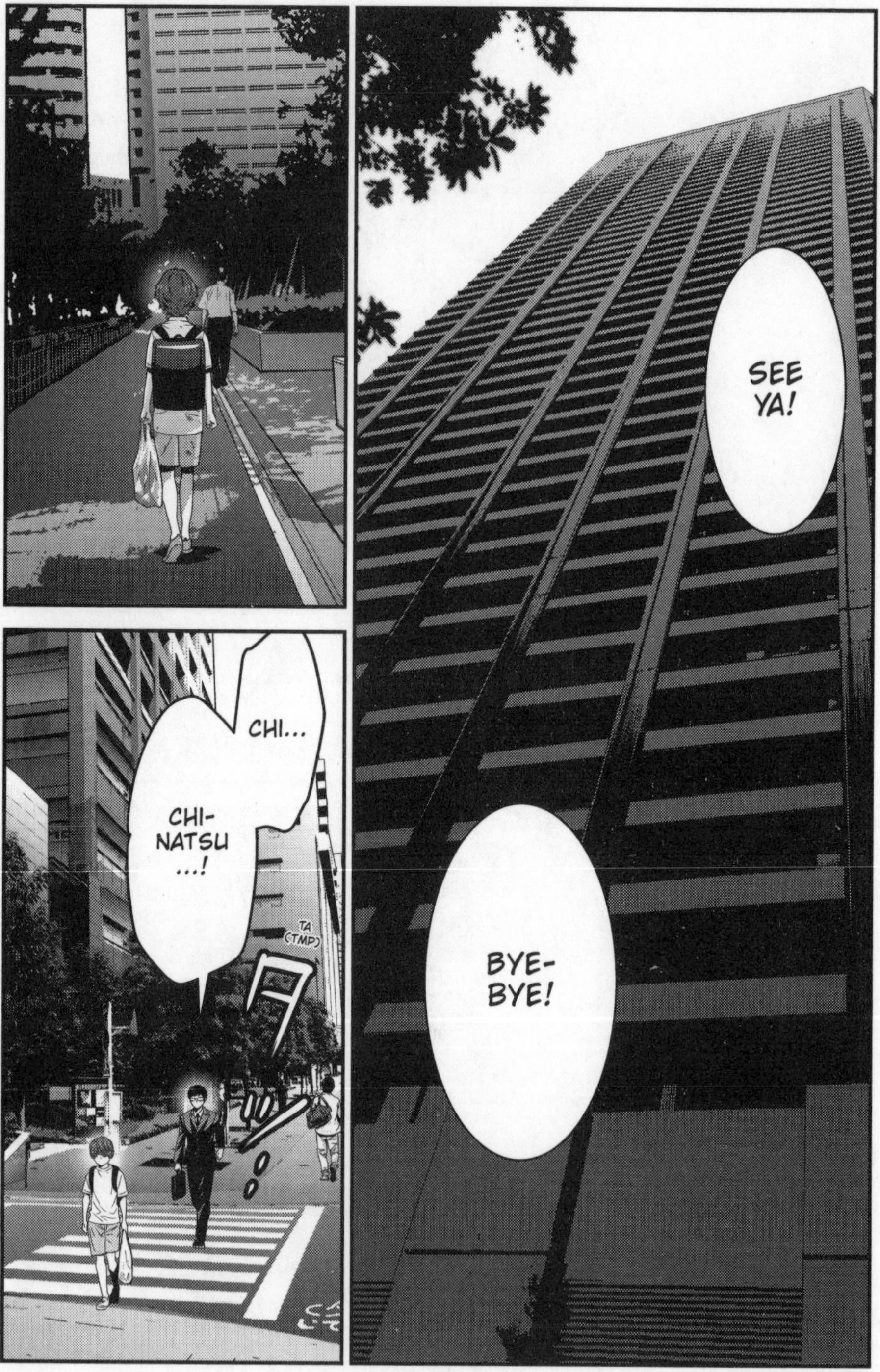
SEE YA!
BYE-BYE!
CHI...
CHI-NATSU ...!
TA (TMP)

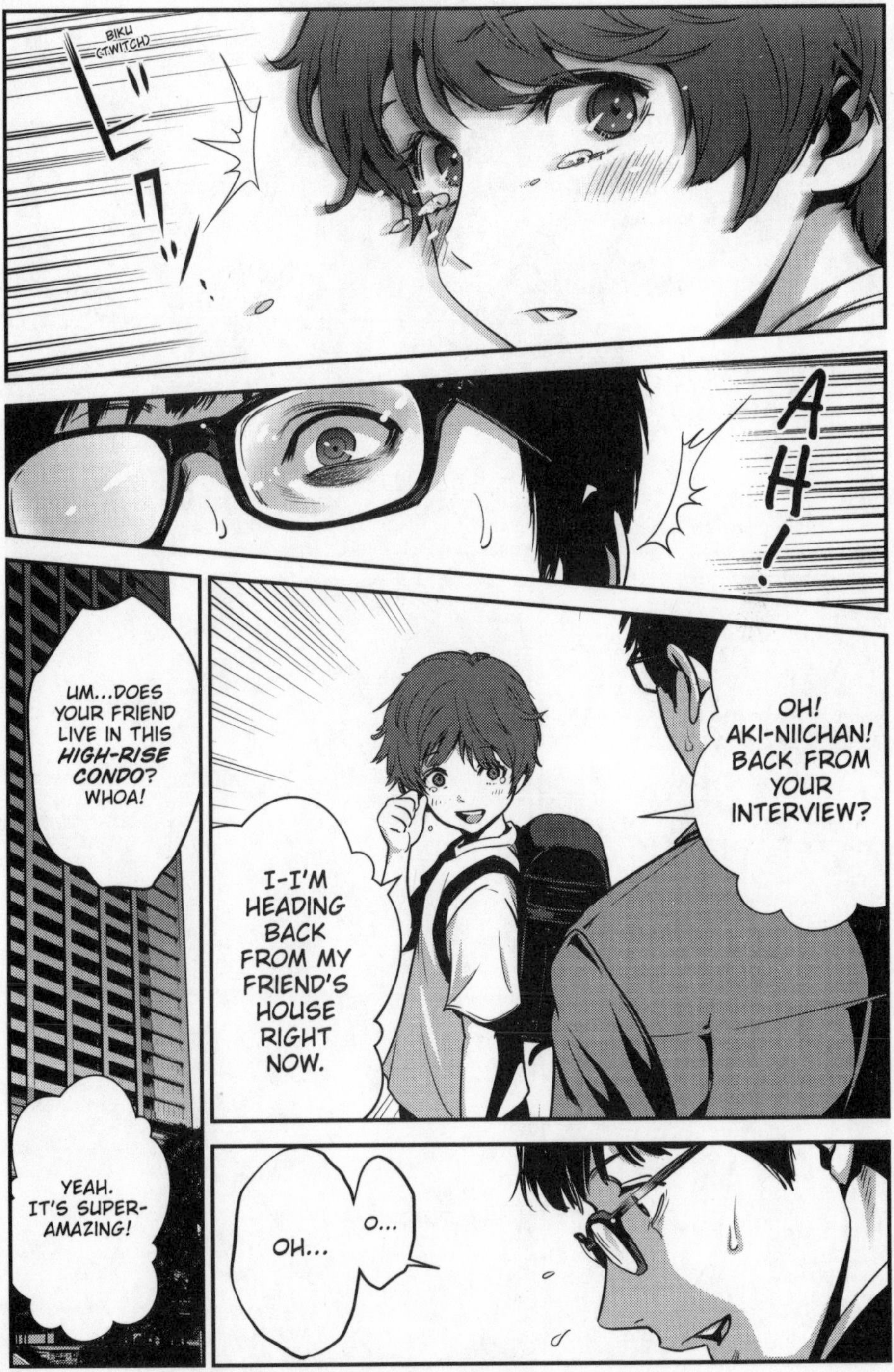
BIKU (TWITCH)
AH!
OH! AKI-NIICHAN! BACK FROM YOUR INTERVIEW?
I-I'M HEADING BACK FROM MY FRIEND'S HOUSE RIGHT NOW.
O... OH...
UM...DOES YOUR FRIEND LIVE IN THIS *HIGH-RISE CONDO*? WHOA!
YEAH. IT'S SUPER-AMAZING!

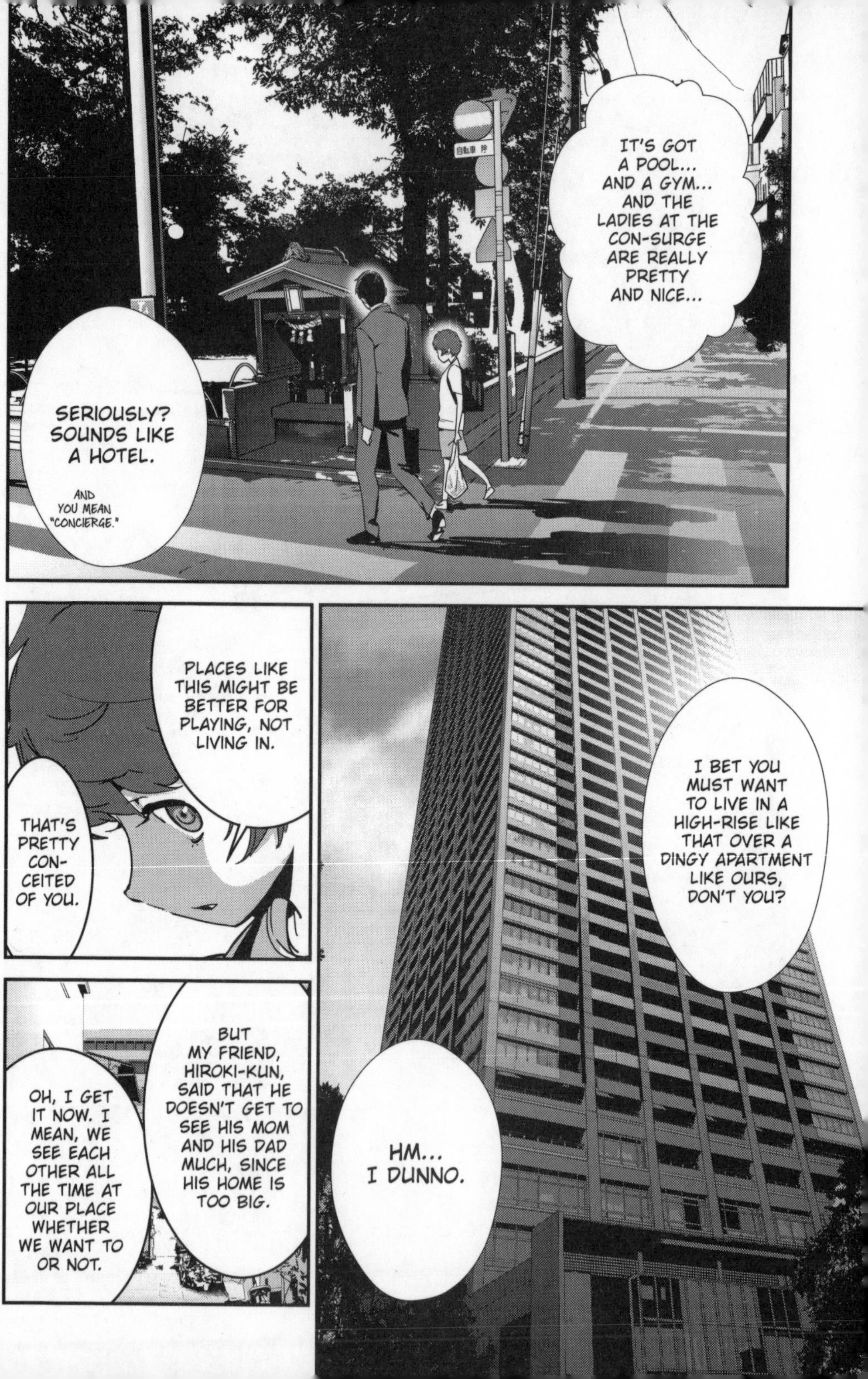
IT'S GOT A POOL... AND A GYM... AND THE LADIES AT THE CON-SURGE ARE REALLY PRETTY AND NICE...
SERIOUSLY? SOUNDS LIKE A HOTEL.
AND YOU MEAN "CONCIERGE."
I BET YOU MUST WANT TO LIVE IN A HIGH-RISE LIKE THAT OVER A DINGY APARTMENT LIKE OURS, DON'T YOU?
HM... I DUNNO.
PLACES LIKE THIS MIGHT BE BETTER FOR PLAYING, NOT LIVING IN.
THAT'S PRETTY CON-CEITED OF YOU.
BUT MY FRIEND, HIROKI-KUN, SAID THAT HE DOESN'T GET TO SEE HIS MOM AND HIS DAD MUCH, SINCE HIS HOME IS TOO BIG.
OH, I GET IT NOW. I MEAN, WE SEE EACH OTHER ALL THE TIME AT OUR PLACE WHETHER WE WANT TO OR NOT.

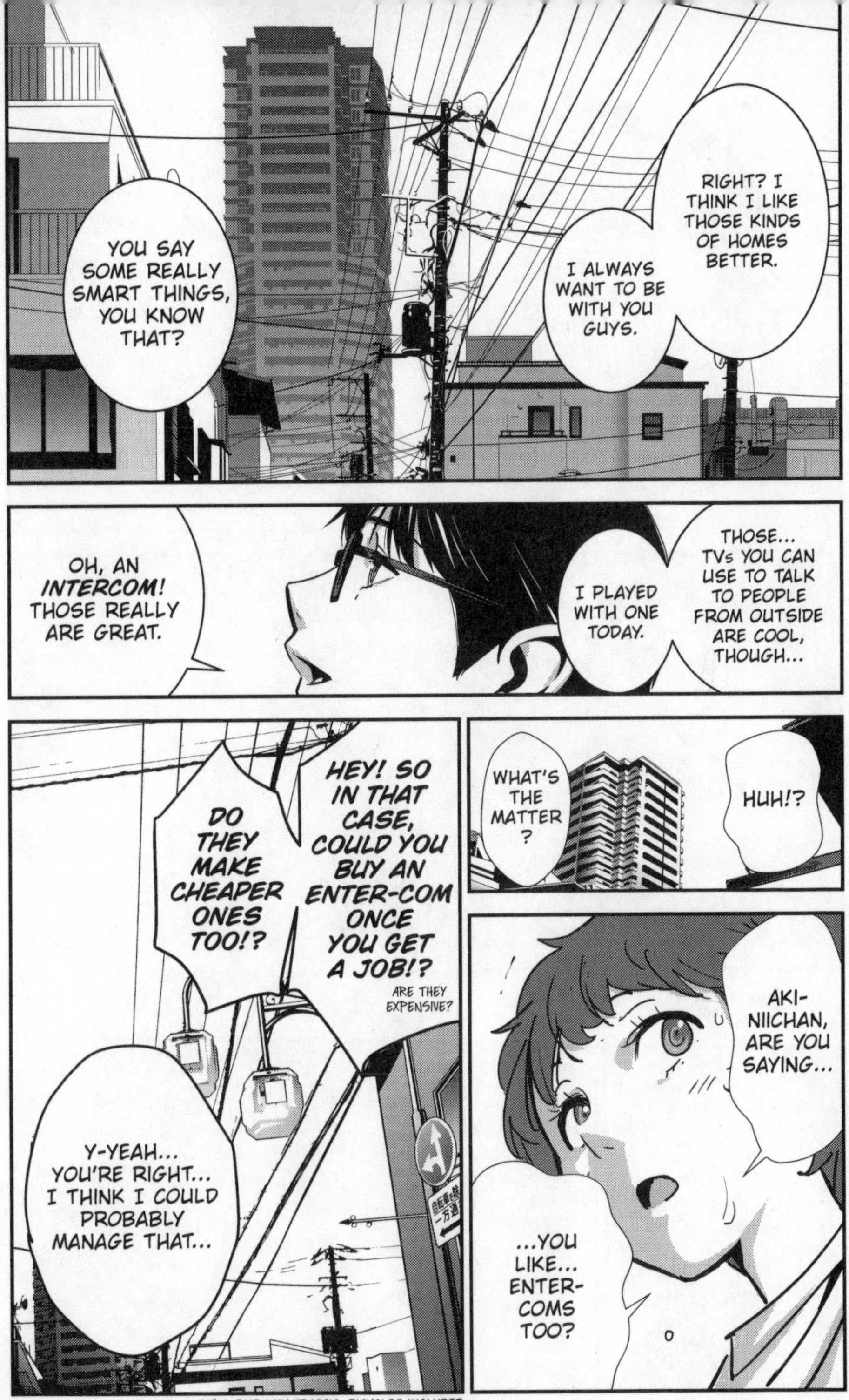
RIGHT? I THINK I LIKE THOSE KINDS OF HOMES BETTER.
I ALWAYS WANT TO BE WITH YOU GUYS.
YOU SAY SOME REALLY SMART THINGS, YOU KNOW THAT?
THOSE... TVs YOU CAN USE TO TALK TO PEOPLE FROM OUTSIDE ARE COOL, THOUGH...
I PLAYED WITH ONE TODAY.
OH, AN *INTERCOM!* THOSE REALLY ARE GREAT.
HUH!?
WHAT'S THE MATTER?
AKI-NIICHAN, ARE YOU SAYING...
...YOU LIKE... ENTER-COMS TOO?
HEY! SO IN THAT CASE, COULD YOU BUY AN ENTER-COM ONCE YOU GET A JOB!?
ARE THEY EXPENSIVE?
DO THEY MAKE CHEAPER ONES TOO!?
Y-YEAH... YOU'RE RIGHT... I THINK I COULD PROBABLY MANAGE THAT...
SIGN: ONE-WAY TRAFFIC, BICYCLES INCLUDED

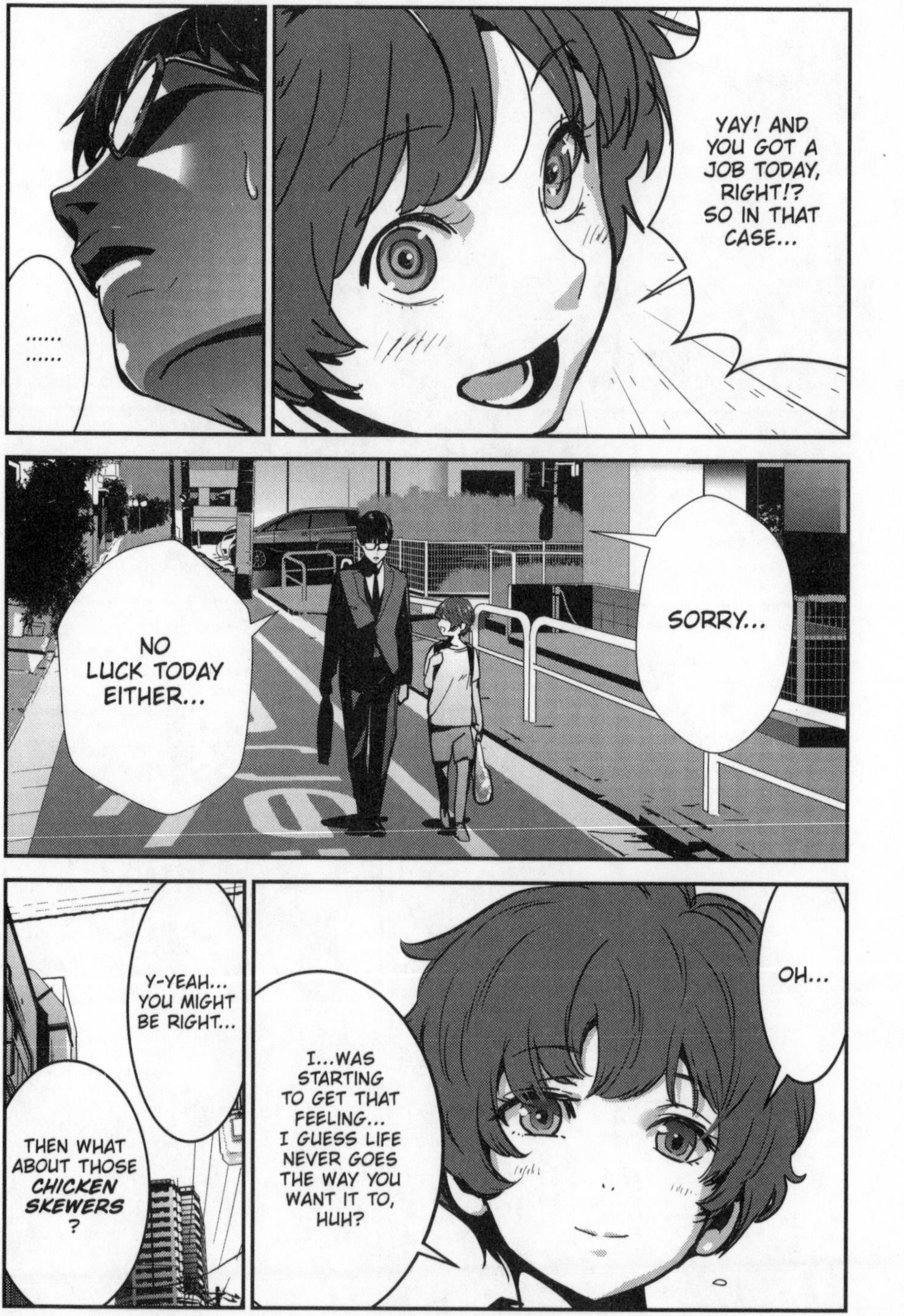
YAY! AND YOU GOT A JOB TODAY, RIGHT!? SO IN THAT CASE...
....
SORRY...
NO LUCK TODAY EITHER...
OH...
I...WAS STARTING TO GET THAT FEELING... I GUESS LIFE NEVER GOES THE WAY YOU WANT IT TO, HUH?
Y-YEAH... YOU MIGHT BE RIGHT...
THEN WHAT ABOUT THOSE *CHICKEN SKEWERS* ?

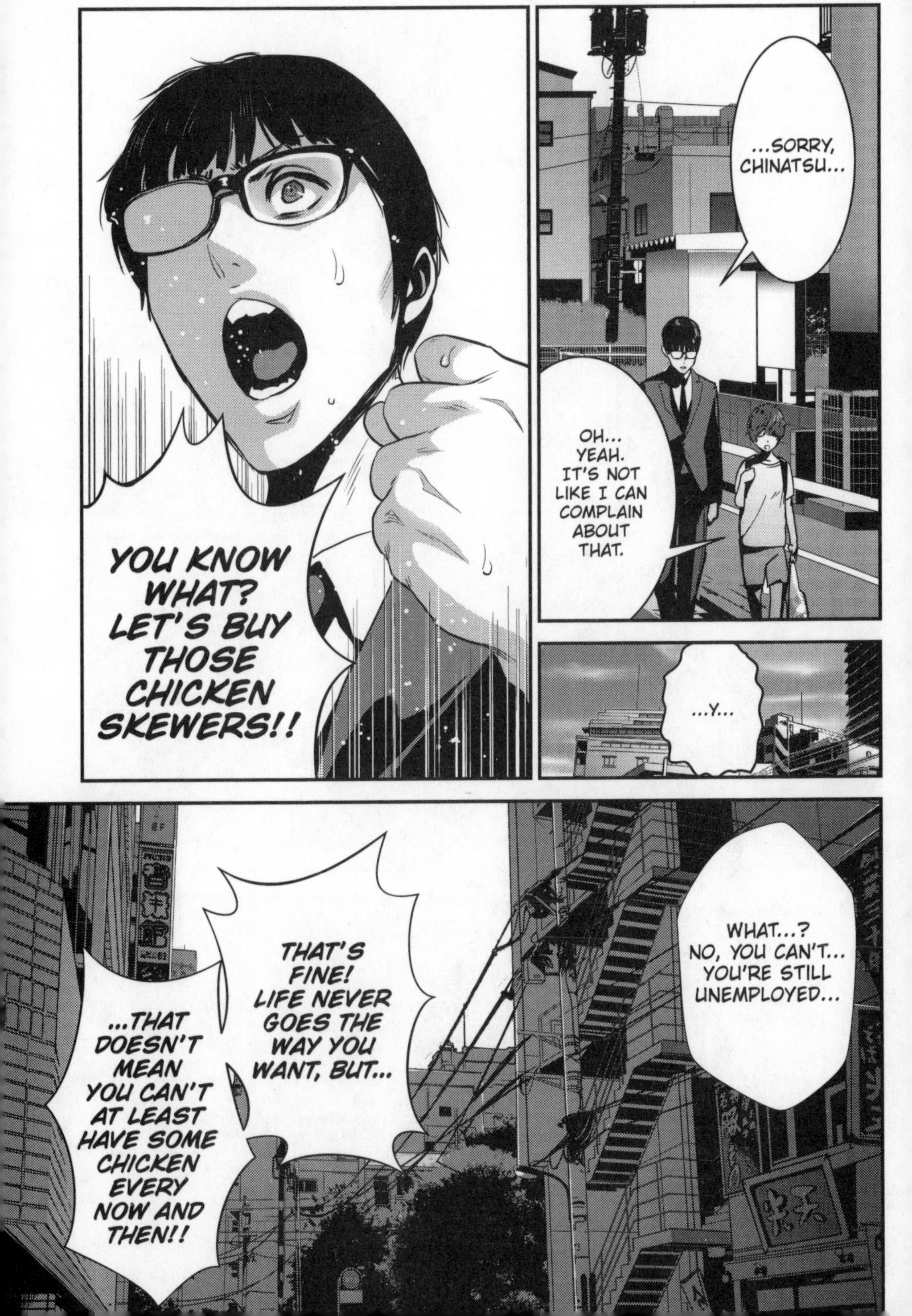
...SORRY, CHINATSU...
OH... YEAH. IT'S NOT LIKE I CAN COMPLAIN ABOUT THAT.
...Y...
YOU KNOW WHAT? LET'S BUY THOSE CHICKEN SKEWERS!!
WHAT...? NO, YOU CAN'T... YOU'RE STILL UNEMPLOYED...
THAT'S FINE! LIFE NEVER GOES THE WAY YOU WANT, BUT...
...THAT DOESN'T MEAN YOU CAN'T AT LEAST HAVE SOME CHICKEN EVERY NOW AND THEN!!

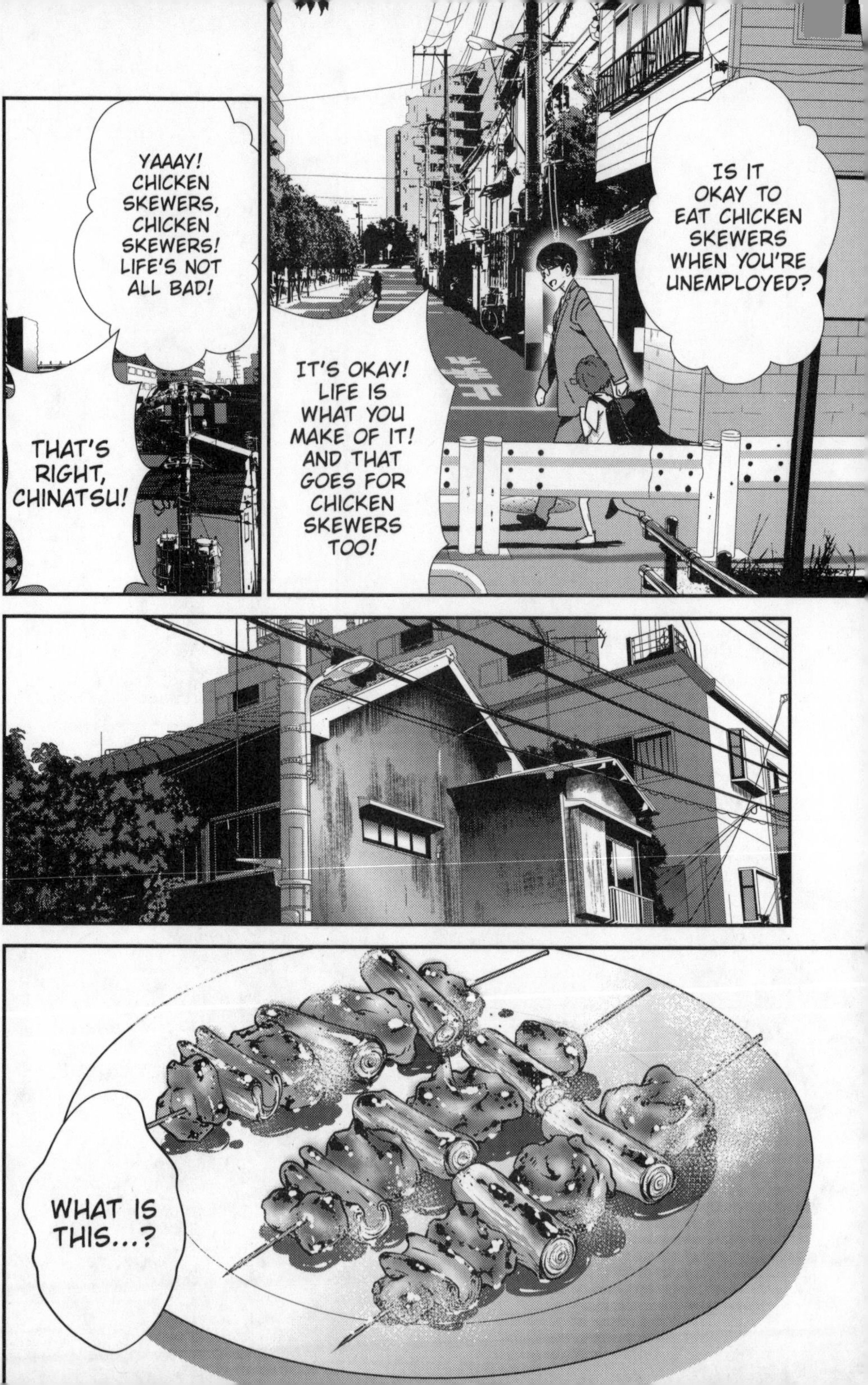
IS IT OKAY TO EAT CHICKEN SKEWERS WHEN YOU'RE UNEMPLOYED?
IT'S OKAY! LIFE IS WHAT YOU MAKE OF IT! AND THAT GOES FOR CHICKEN SKEWERS TOO!
YAAAY! CHICKEN SKEWERS, CHICKEN SKEWERS! LIFE'S NOT ALL BAD!
THAT'S RIGHT, CHINATSU!
WHAT IS THIS...?

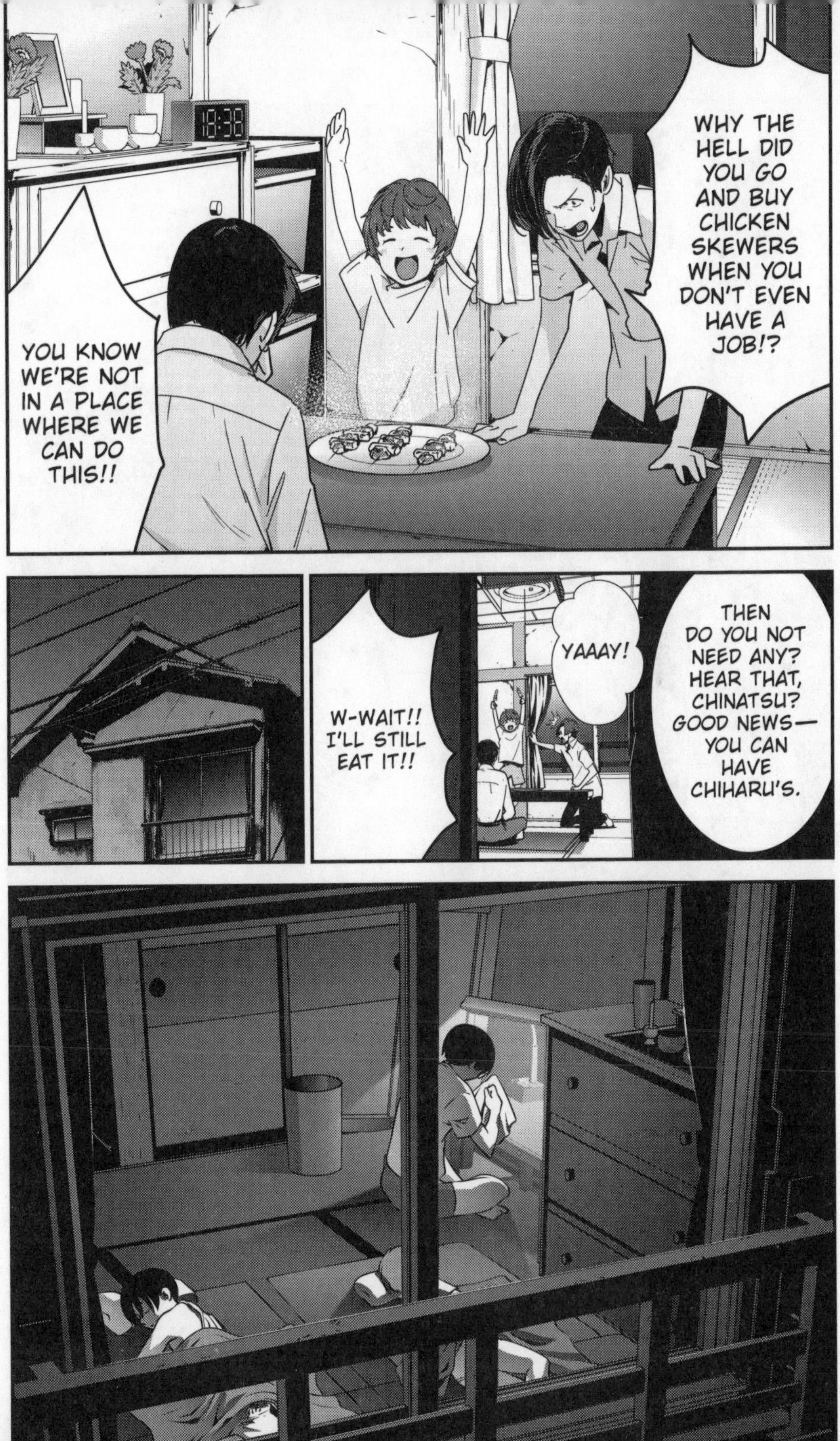
WHY THE HELL DID YOU GO AND BUY CHICKEN SKEWERS WHEN YOU DON'T EVEN HAVE A JOB!?
YOU KNOW WE'RE NOT IN A PLACE WHERE WE CAN DO THIS!!
THEN DO YOU NOT NEED ANY? HEAR THAT, CHINATSU? GOOD NEWS—YOU CAN HAVE CHIHARU'S.
YAAAY!
W-WAIT!! I'LL STILL EAT IT!!

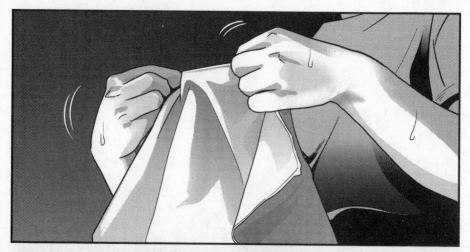

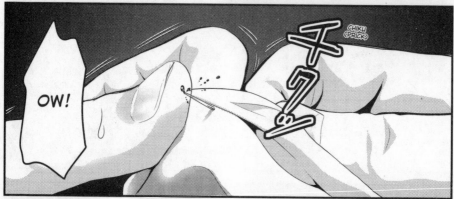

OW!

CHIKU
(PRICK)

MRRGH...

DAMMIT...

MOMS OUT THERE ARE AMAZING... GYM BAGS ARE SUPER-HARD TO MAKE...

WANNA...
LIVE...
HIGH...
RISE...

WHAT
AM I
DOING
...?

KUSHA
(KRRSH)

WHAT
...

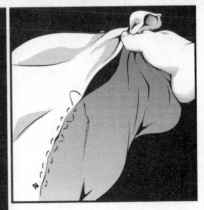

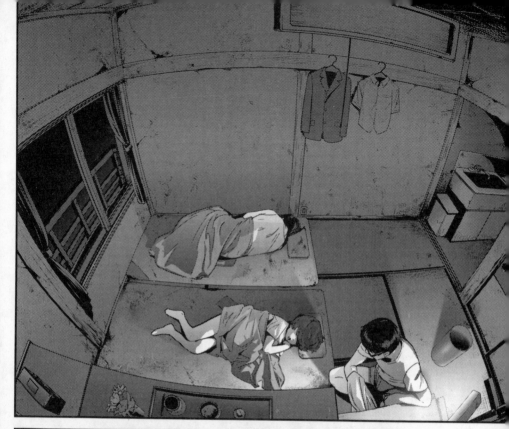

IF I
ONLY HAD
MONEY...

GYU
(SQUEEZE)

POTA
(DRIP)

MONEY...

...RISE...
CONDO...

HIGH...

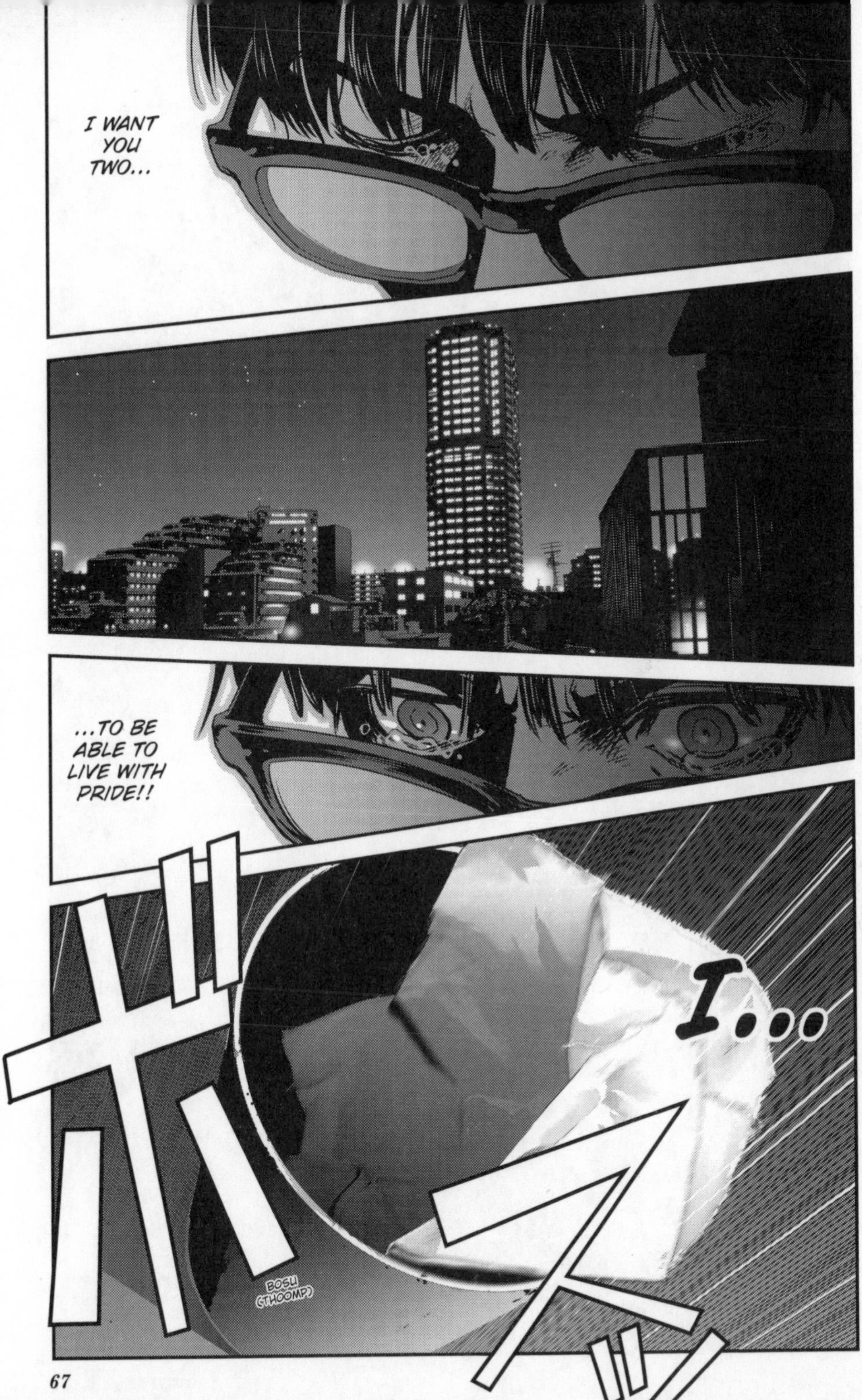
I WANT YOU TWO...
...TO BE ABLE TO LIVE WITH PRIDE!!
I...
BOSU (THOOMP)

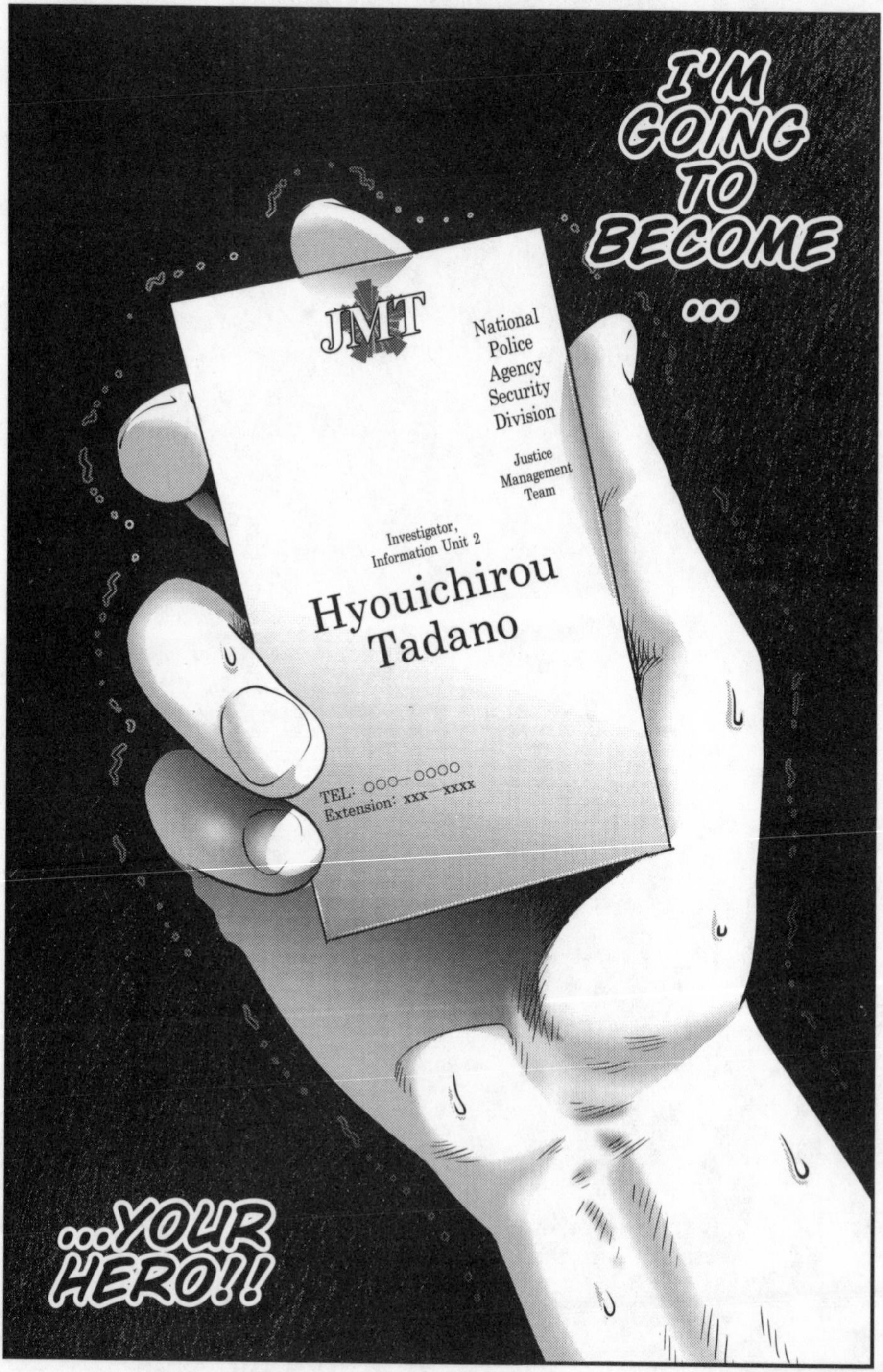
I'M GOING TO BECOME ...
JMT
National Police Agency Security Division
Justice Management Team
Investigator, Information Unit 2
Hyouichirou Tadano
TEL: ○○○-○○○○
Extension: xxx-xxxx
...YOUR HERO!!

Chapter 2: End

Chapter 3: For My Brothers

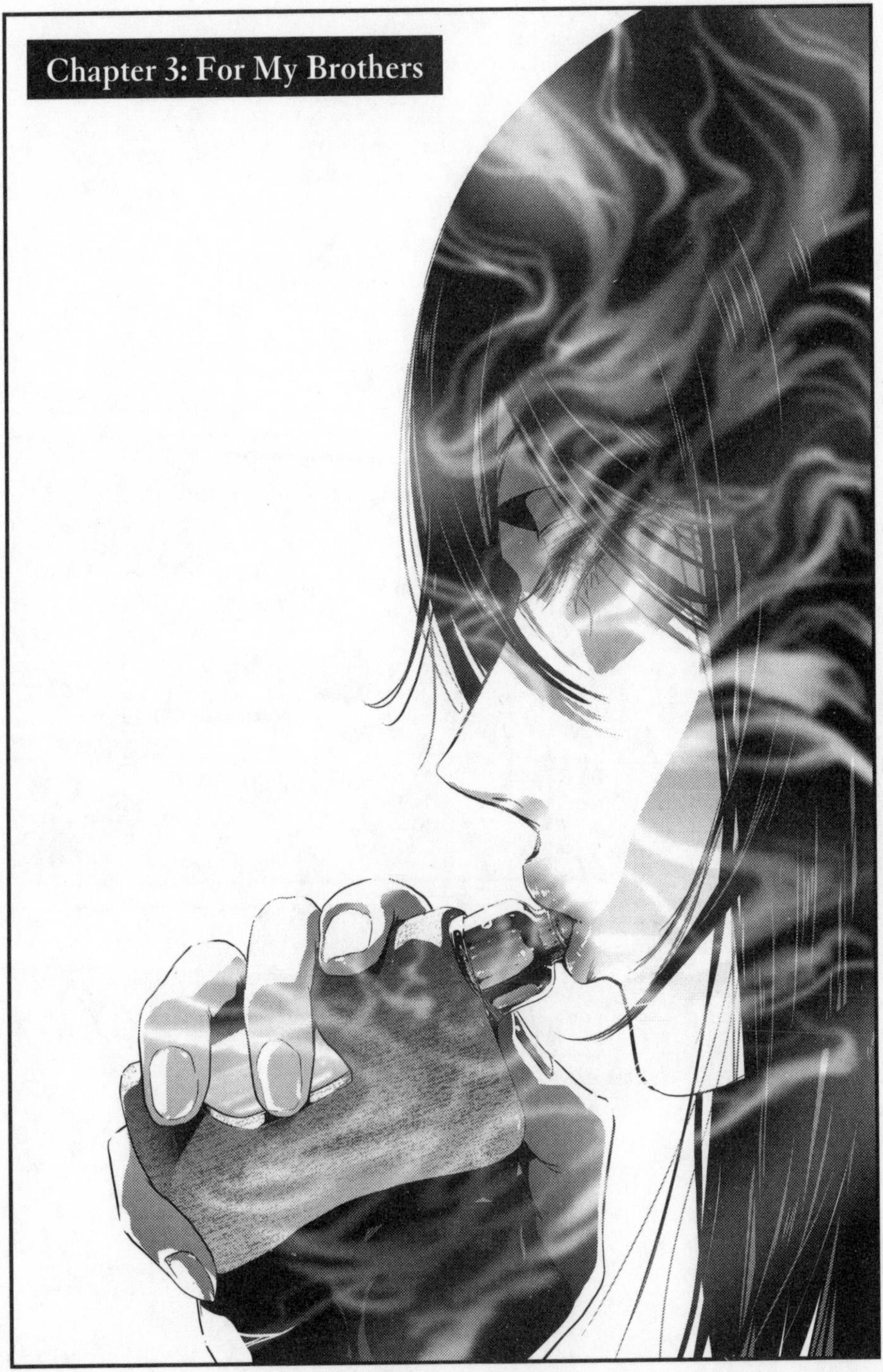

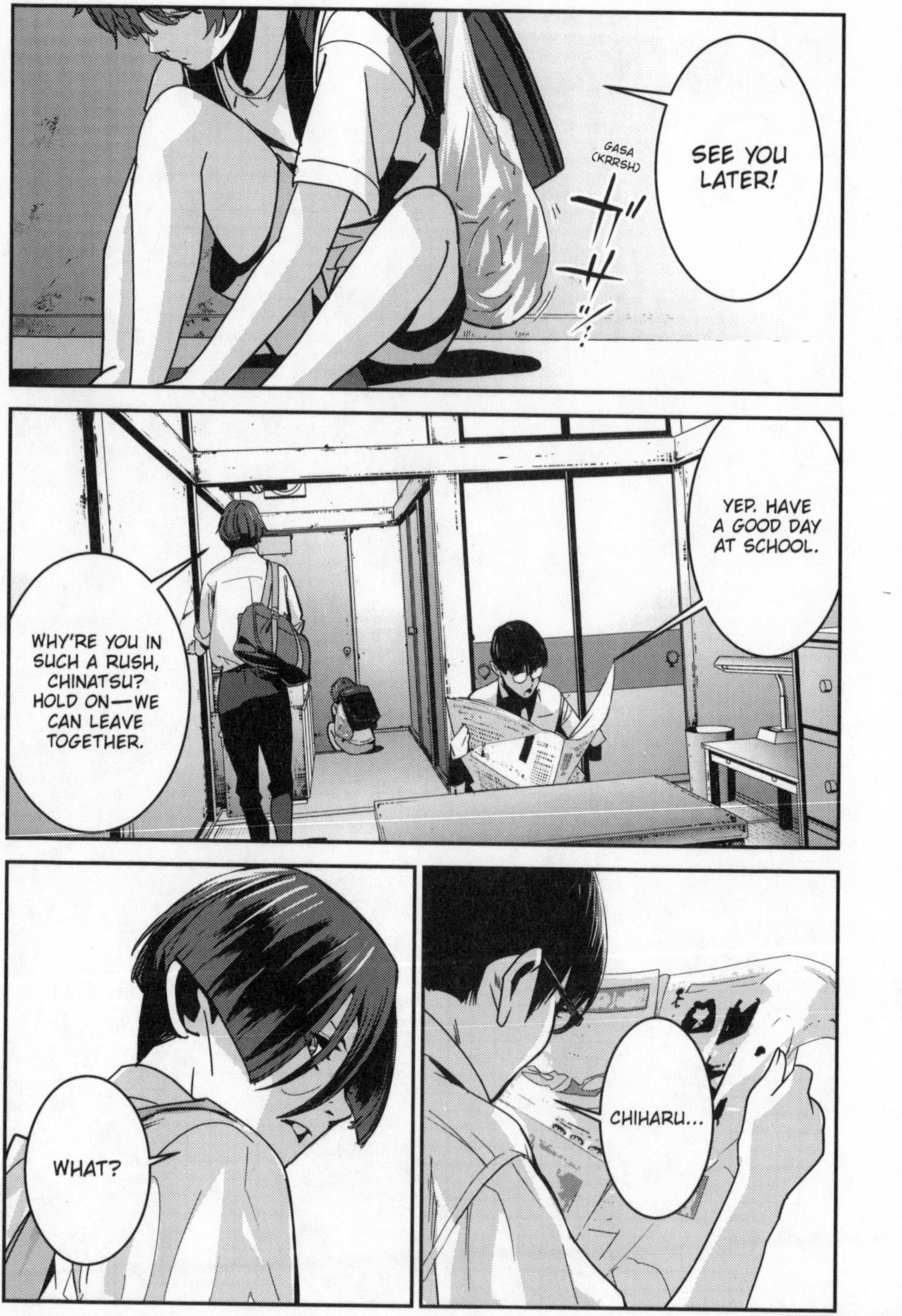
SEE YOU LATER!
GASA (KRRSH)
YEP. HAVE A GOOD DAY AT SCHOOL.
WHY'RE YOU IN SUCH A RUSH, CHINATSU? HOLD ON—WE CAN LEAVE TOGETHER.
CHIHARU...
WHAT?

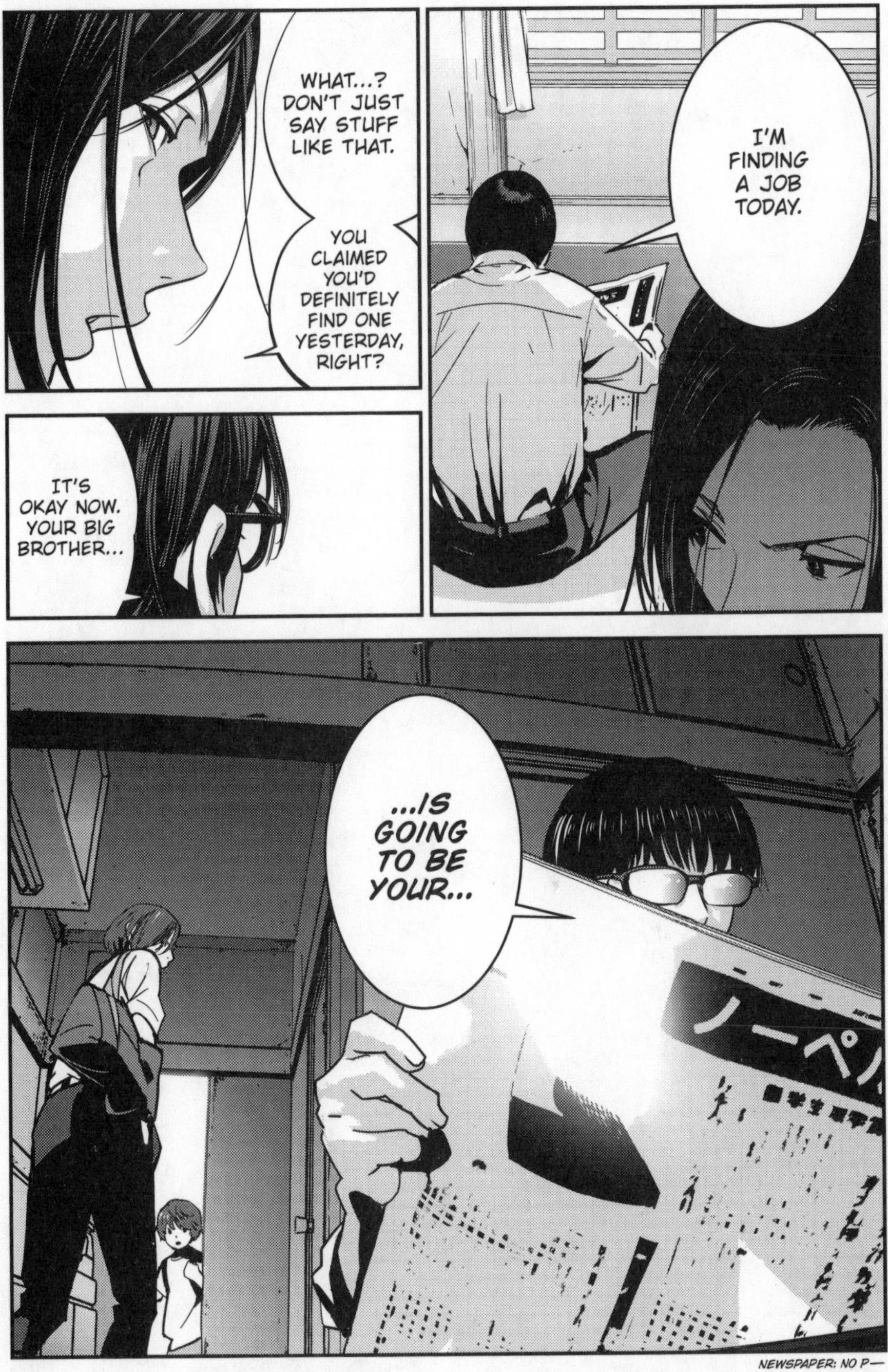
I'M FINDING A JOB TODAY.
WHAT...? DON'T JUST SAY STUFF LIKE THAT.
YOU CLAIMED YOU'D DEFINITELY FIND ONE YESTERDAY, RIGHT?
IT'S OKAY NOW. YOUR BIG BROTHER...
...IS GOING TO BE YOUR...
ノーペ

NEWSPAPER: NO P—

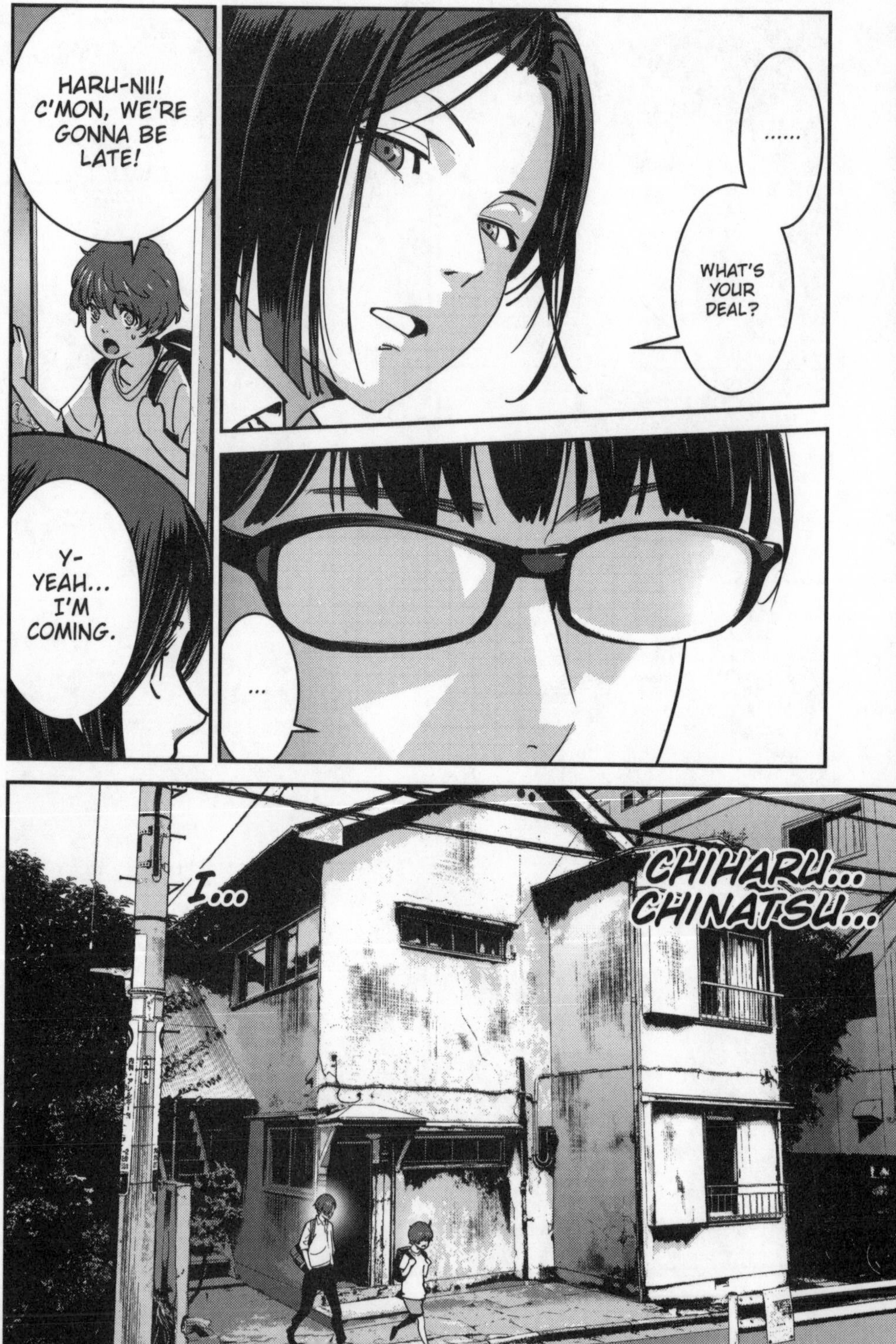
......
WHAT'S YOUR DEAL?
HARU-NII! C'MON, WE'RE GONNA BE LATE!
...
Y- YEAH... I'M COMING.
CHIHARU... CHINATSU...
I...

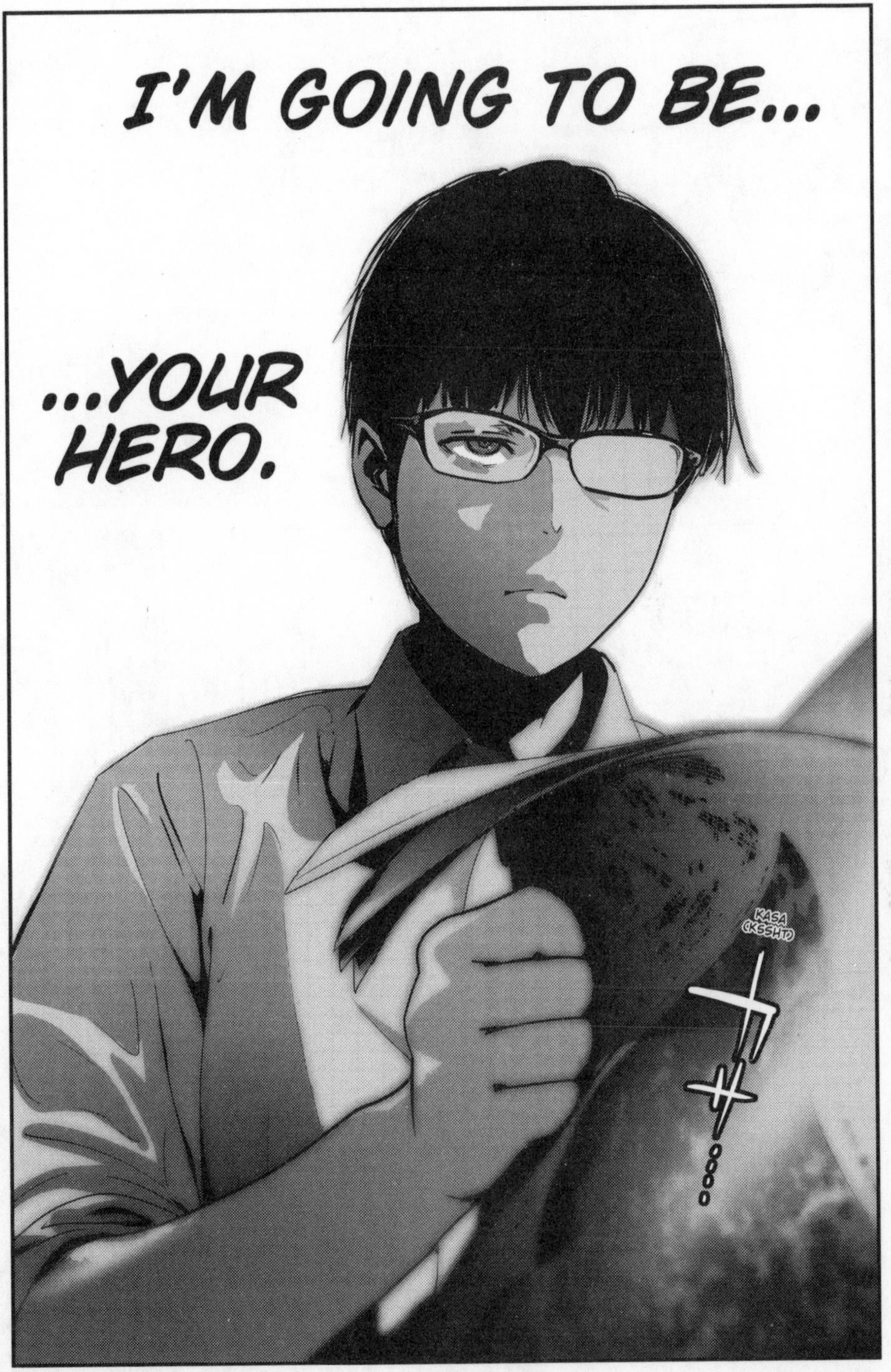
I'M GOING TO BE...
...YOUR HERO.
KASA (KSSHT)

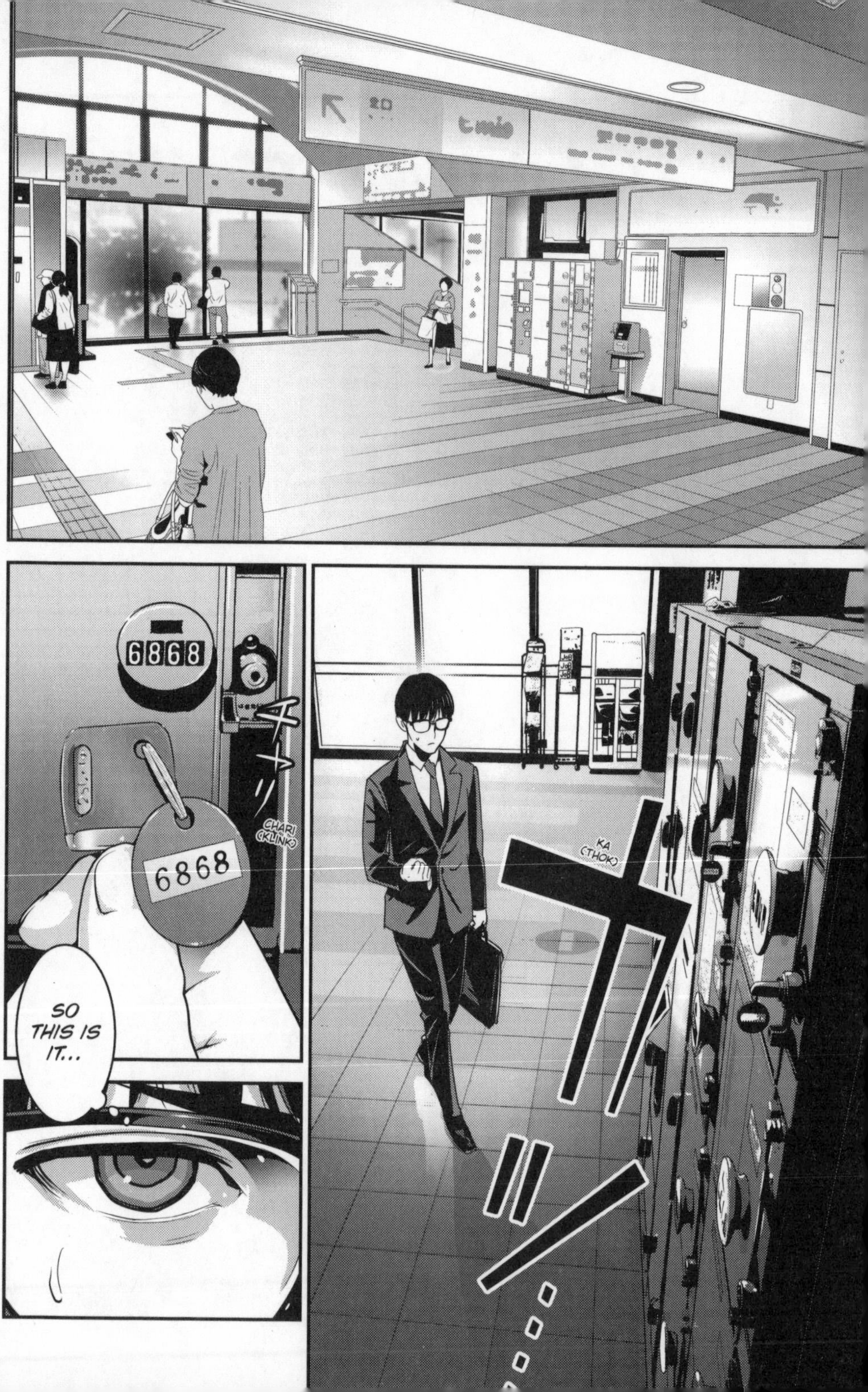
KA
(THOK)
6868
6868
CHARI
(KLINK)
SO THIS IS IT...

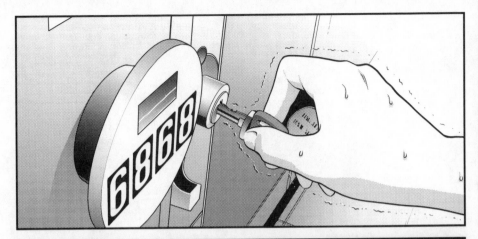

......

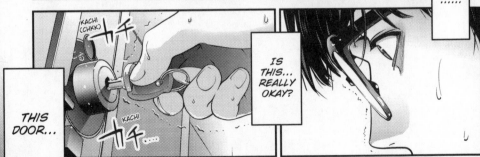

THIS
DOOR...

KACHI
CCHKKO

KACHI

IS
THIS...
REALLY
OKAY?

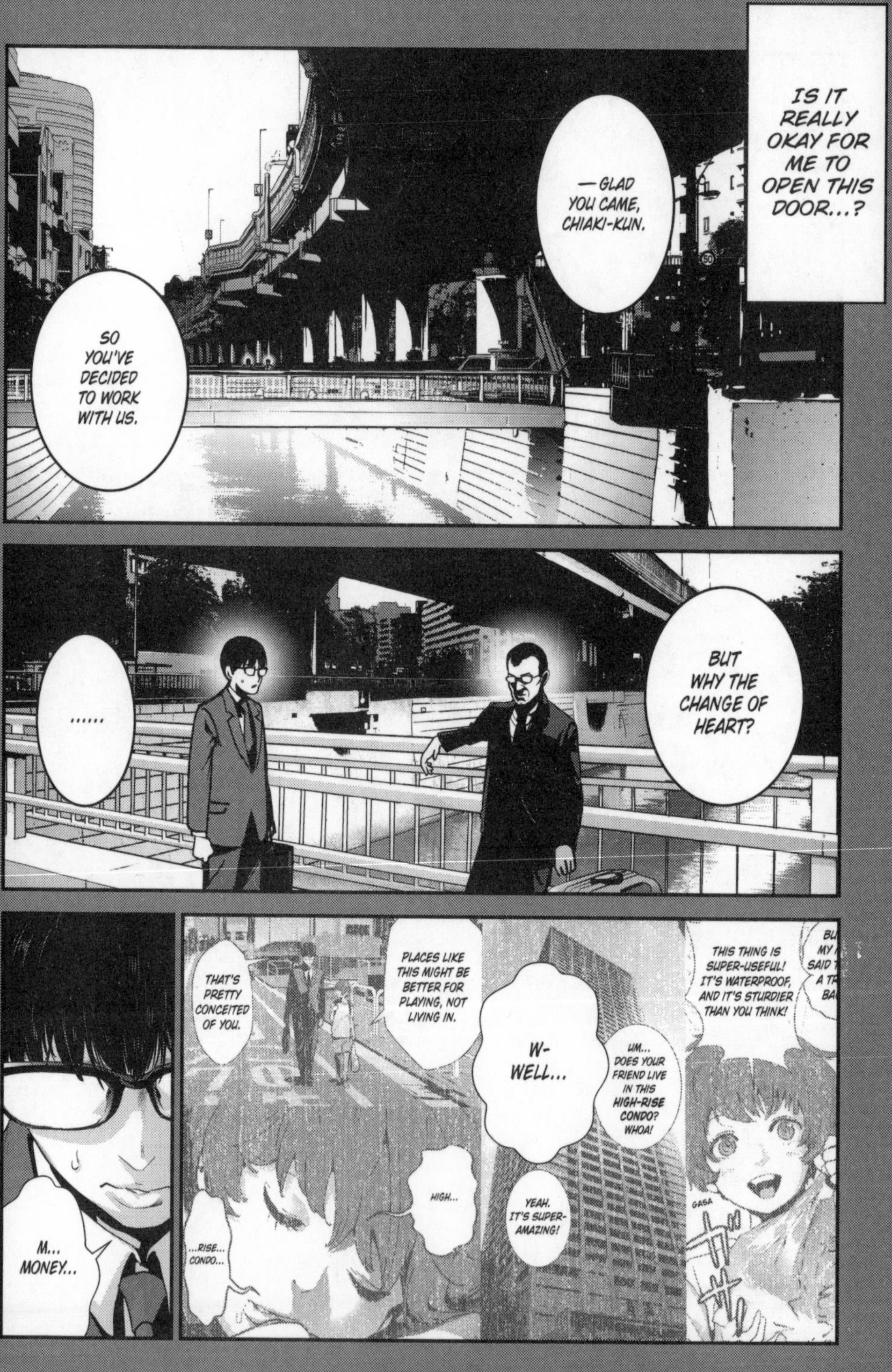
IS IT REALLY OKAY FOR ME TO OPEN THIS DOOR...?
—GLAD YOU CAME, CHIAKI-KUN.
SO YOU'VE DECIDED TO WORK WITH US.
BUT WHY THE CHANGE OF HEART?
......
THIS THING IS SUPER-USEFUL! IT'S WATERPROOF, AND IT'S STURDIER THAN YOU THINK!
GASA
UM... DOES YOUR FRIEND LIVE IN THIS HIGH-RISE CONDO? WHOA!
W-WELL...
YEAH. IT'S SUPER-AMAZING!
PLACES LIKE THIS MIGHT BE BETTER FOR PLAYING, NOT LIVING IN.
THAT'S PRETTY CONCEITED OF YOU.
HIGH...
...RISE... CONDO...
M... MONEY...

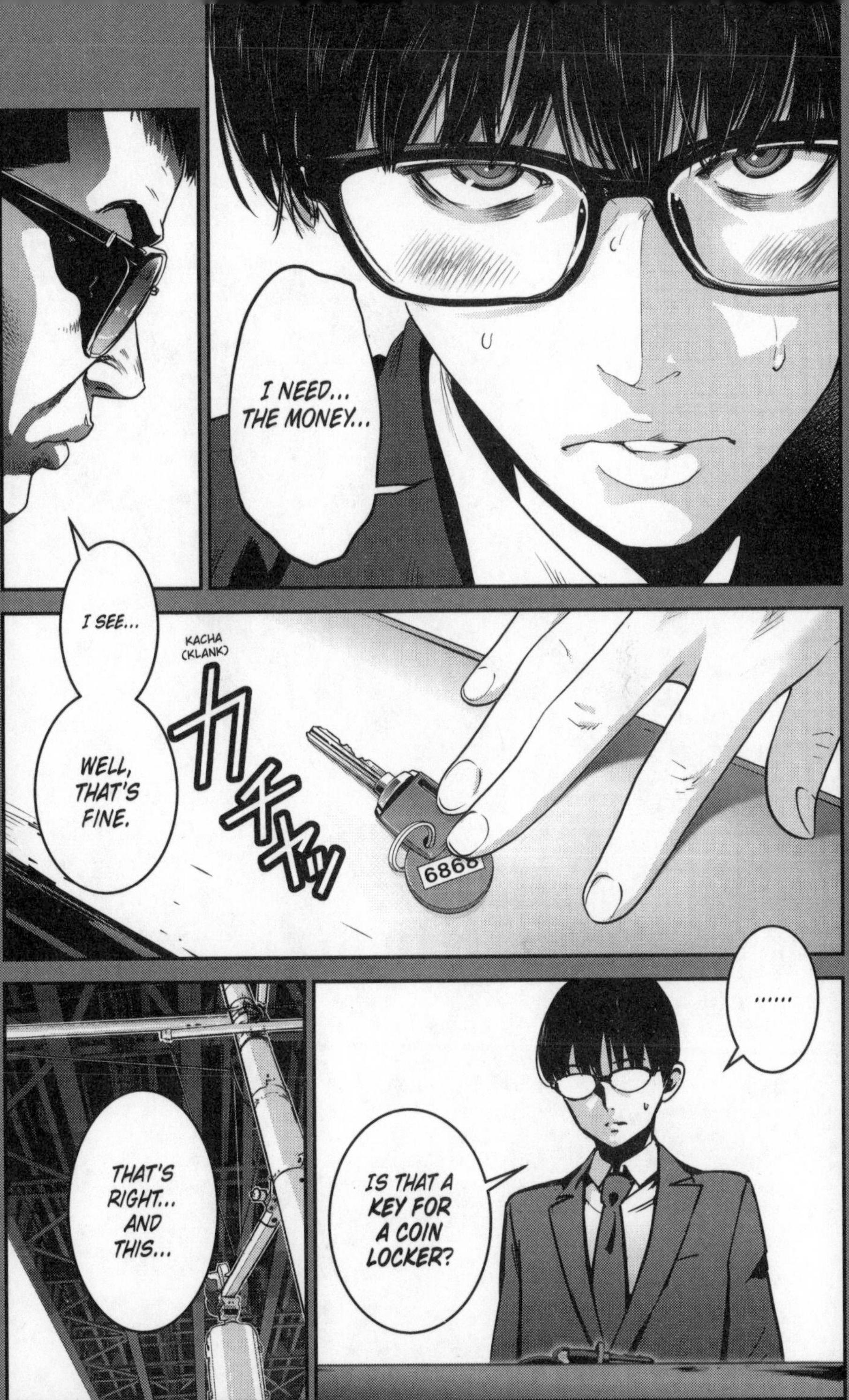
I NEED... THE MONEY...
I SEE...
WELL, THAT'S FINE.
KACHA (KLANK)
6868
......
IS THAT A KEY FOR A COIN LOCKER?
THAT'S RIGHT... AND THIS...

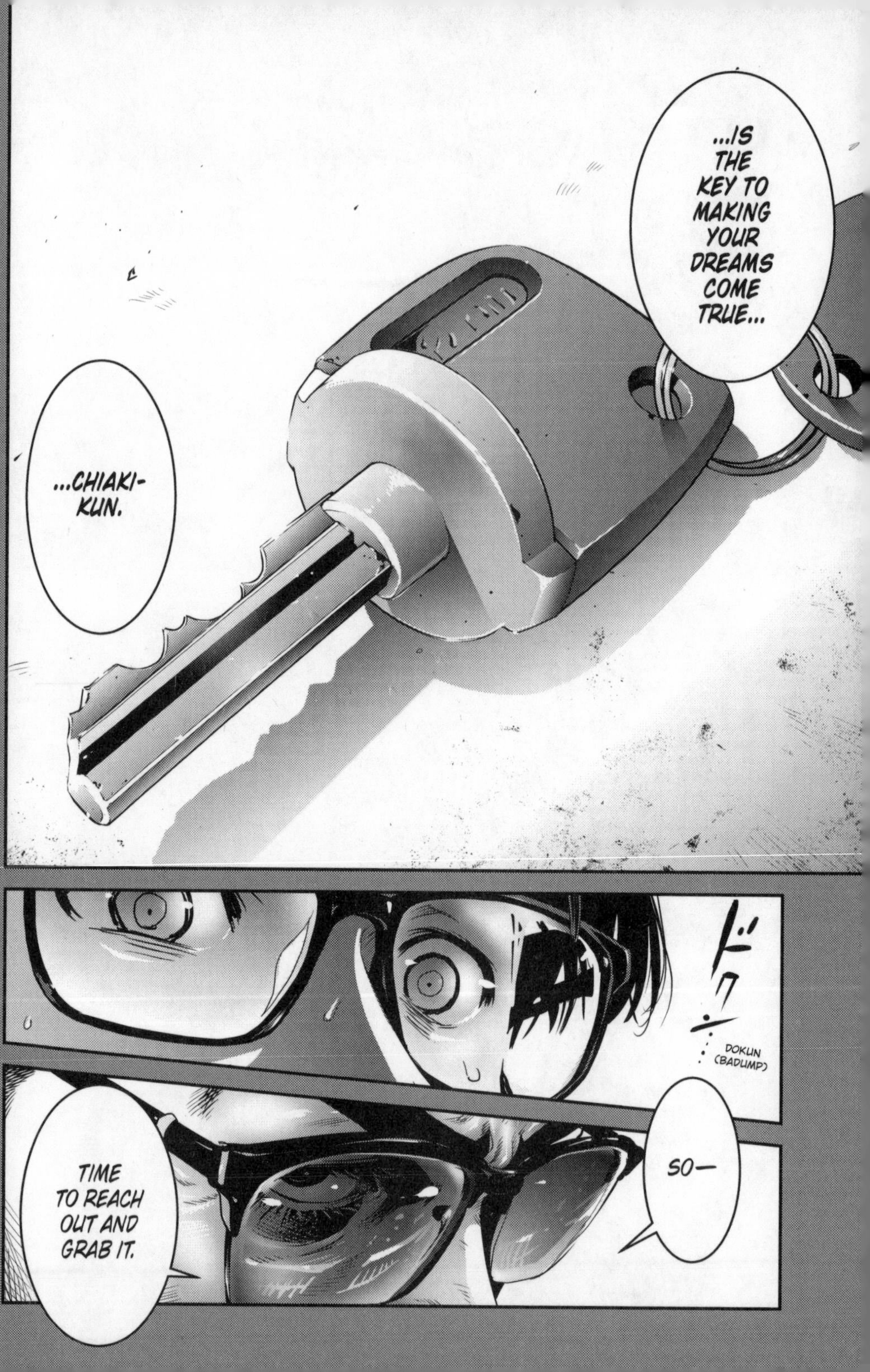
...IS THE KEY TO MAKING YOUR DREAMS COME TRUE...
...CHIAKI-KUN.
DOKUN (BADUMP)
SO—
TIME TO REACH OUT AND GRAB IT.

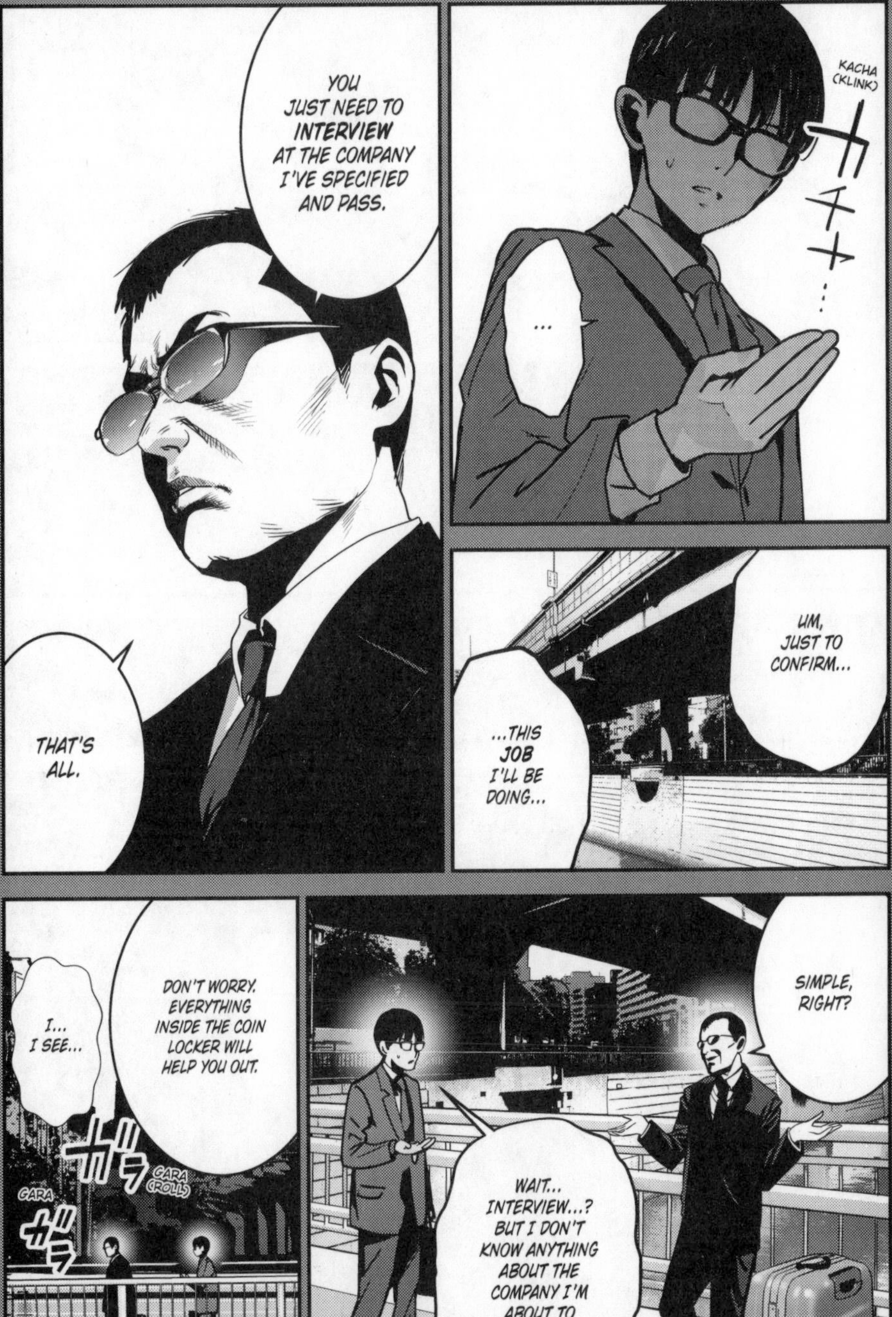
KACHA (KLINK)
...
UM, JUST TO CONFIRM...
...THIS JOB I'LL BE DOING...
YOU JUST NEED TO INTERVIEW AT THE COMPANY I'VE SPECIFIED AND PASS.
THAT'S ALL.
SIMPLE, RIGHT?
WAIT... INTERVIEW...? BUT I DON'T KNOW ANYTHING ABOUT THE COMPANY I'M ABOUT TO VISIT.
DON'T WORRY. EVERYTHING INSIDE THE COIN LOCKER WILL HELP YOU OUT.
I... I SEE...
GARA (ROLL)
GARA

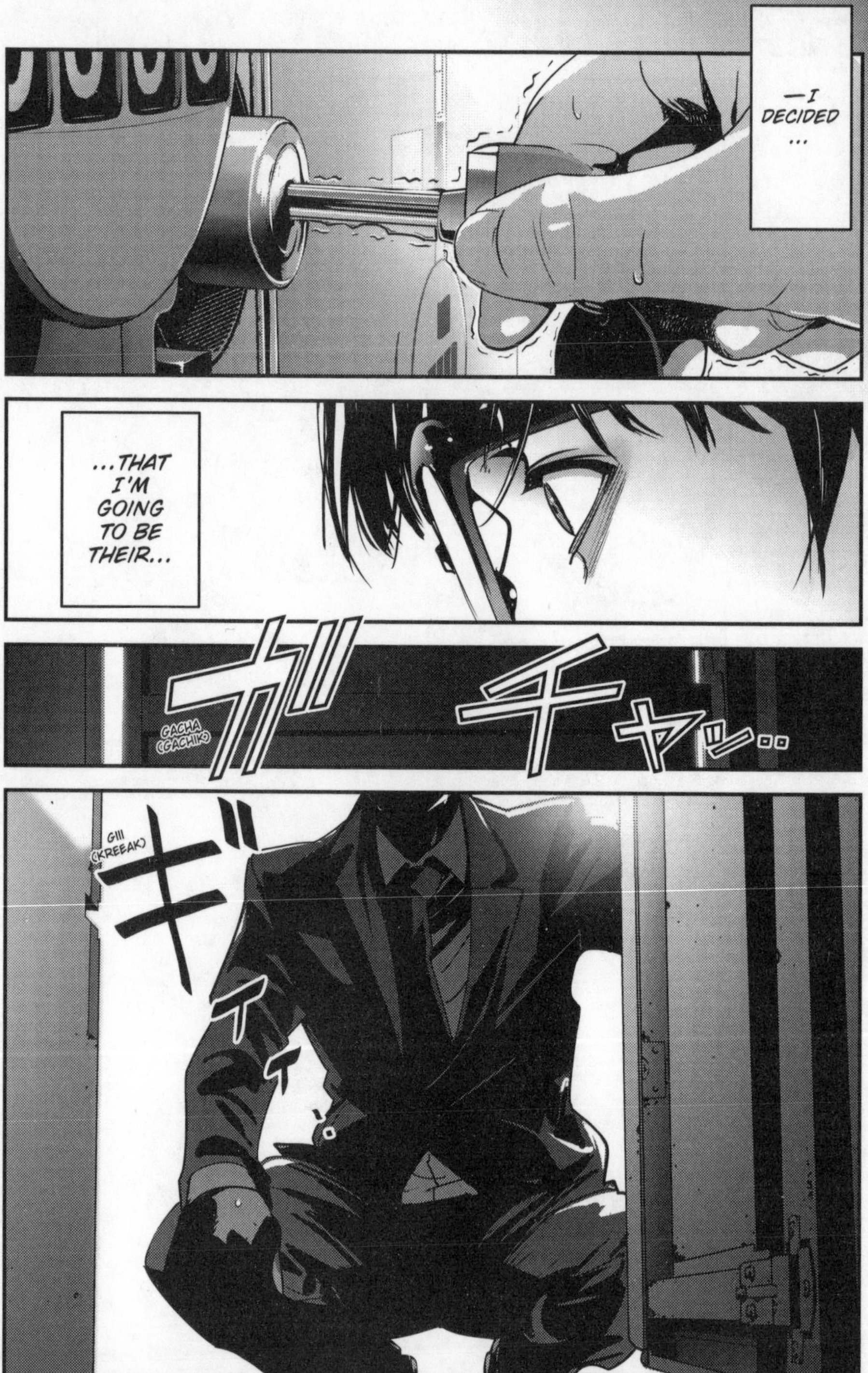
—I DECIDED ...
...THAT I'M GOING TO BE THEIR...
GACHA (GACHIK)
GIII (KREEAK)

GOTO
CTHUNK

ゴトッ

A SUIT-CASE...? SO ARE THERE THINGS FOR MY INTERVIEW INSIDE...?

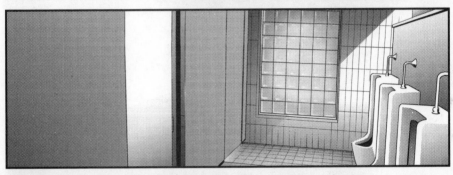

WHA—

....

81

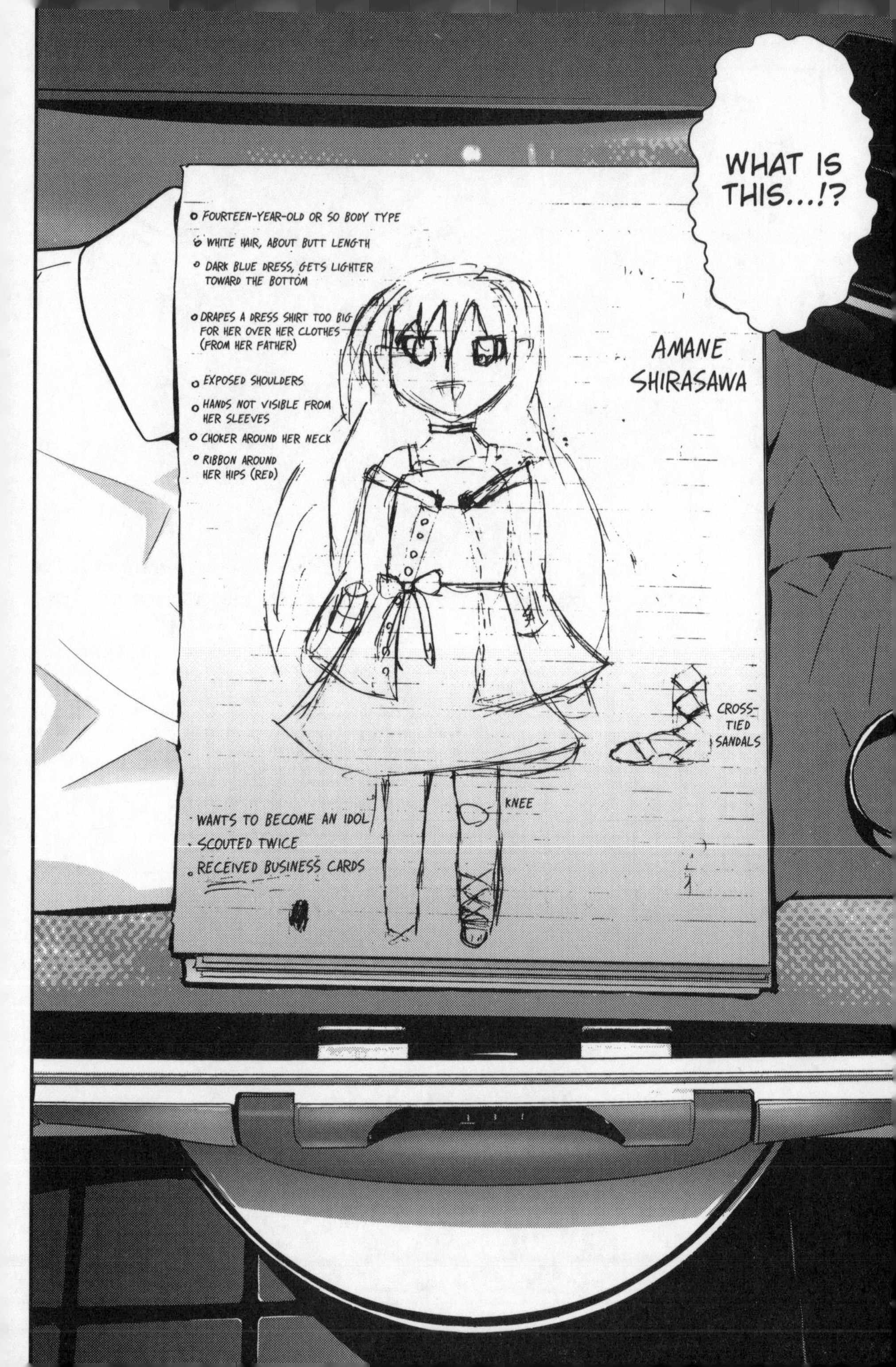
WHAT IS THIS...!?
FOURTEEN-YEAR-OLD OR SO BODY TYPE
WHITE HAIR, ABOUT BUTT LENGTH
DARK BLUE DRESS, GETS LIGHTER TOWARD THE BOTTOM
DRAPES A DRESS SHIRT TOO BIG FOR HER OVER HER CLOTHES (FROM HER FATHER)
EXPOSED SHOULDERS
HANDS NOT VISIBLE FROM HER SLEEVES
CHOKER AROUND HER NECK
RIBBON AROUND HER HIPS (RED)
AMANE SHIRASAWA
CROSS-TIED SANDALS
KNEE
WANTS TO BECOME AN IDOL
SCOUTED TWICE
RECEIVED BUSINESS CARDS

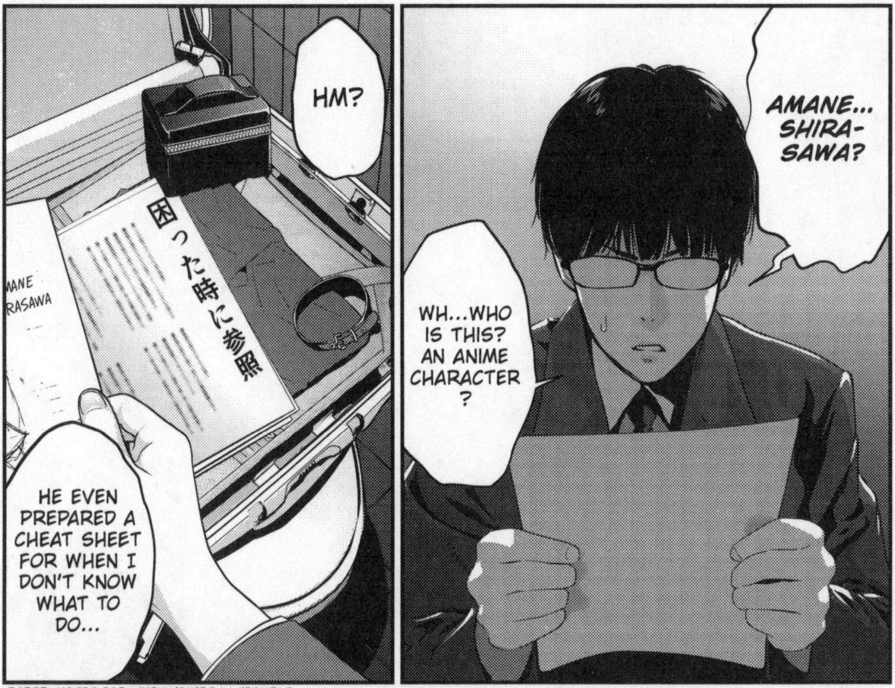
AMANE... SHIRA-SAWA?
WH...WHO IS THIS? AN ANIME CHARACTER?
HM?
困った時に参照
AMANE SHIRASAWA
HE EVEN PREPARED A CHEAT SHEET FOR WHEN I DON'T KNOW WHAT TO DO...

PAPER: NOTES FOR WHEN YOU'RE IN TROUBLE

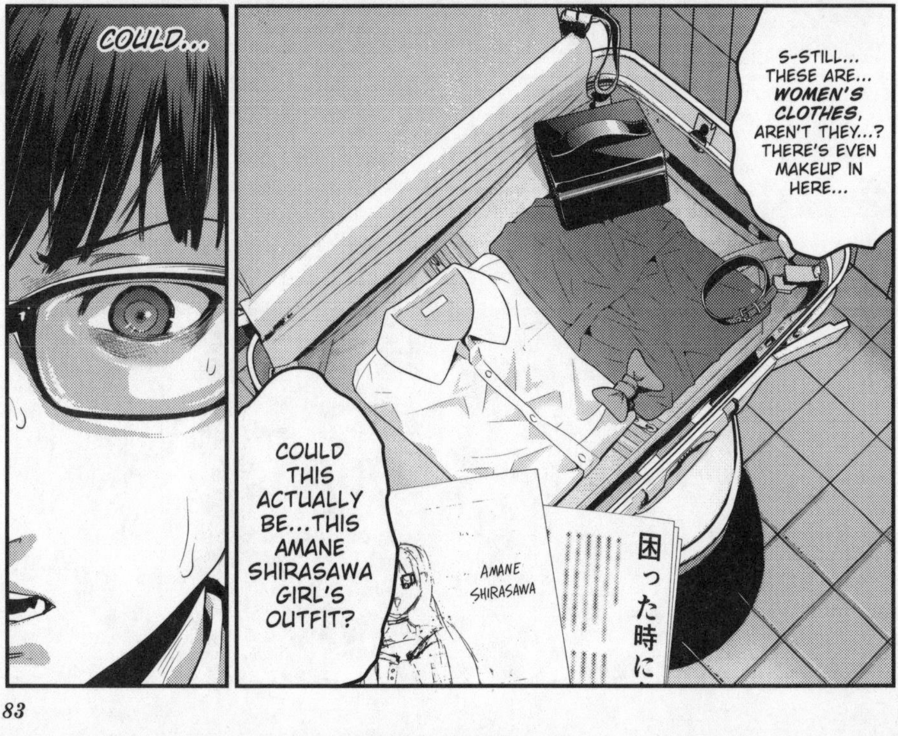
S-STILL... THESE ARE... WOMEN'S CLOTHES, AREN'T THEY...? THERE'S EVEN MAKEUP IN HERE...
COULD THIS ACTUALLY BE...THIS AMANE SHIRASAWA GIRL'S OUTFIT?
困った時に
AMANE SHIRASAWA
COULD...

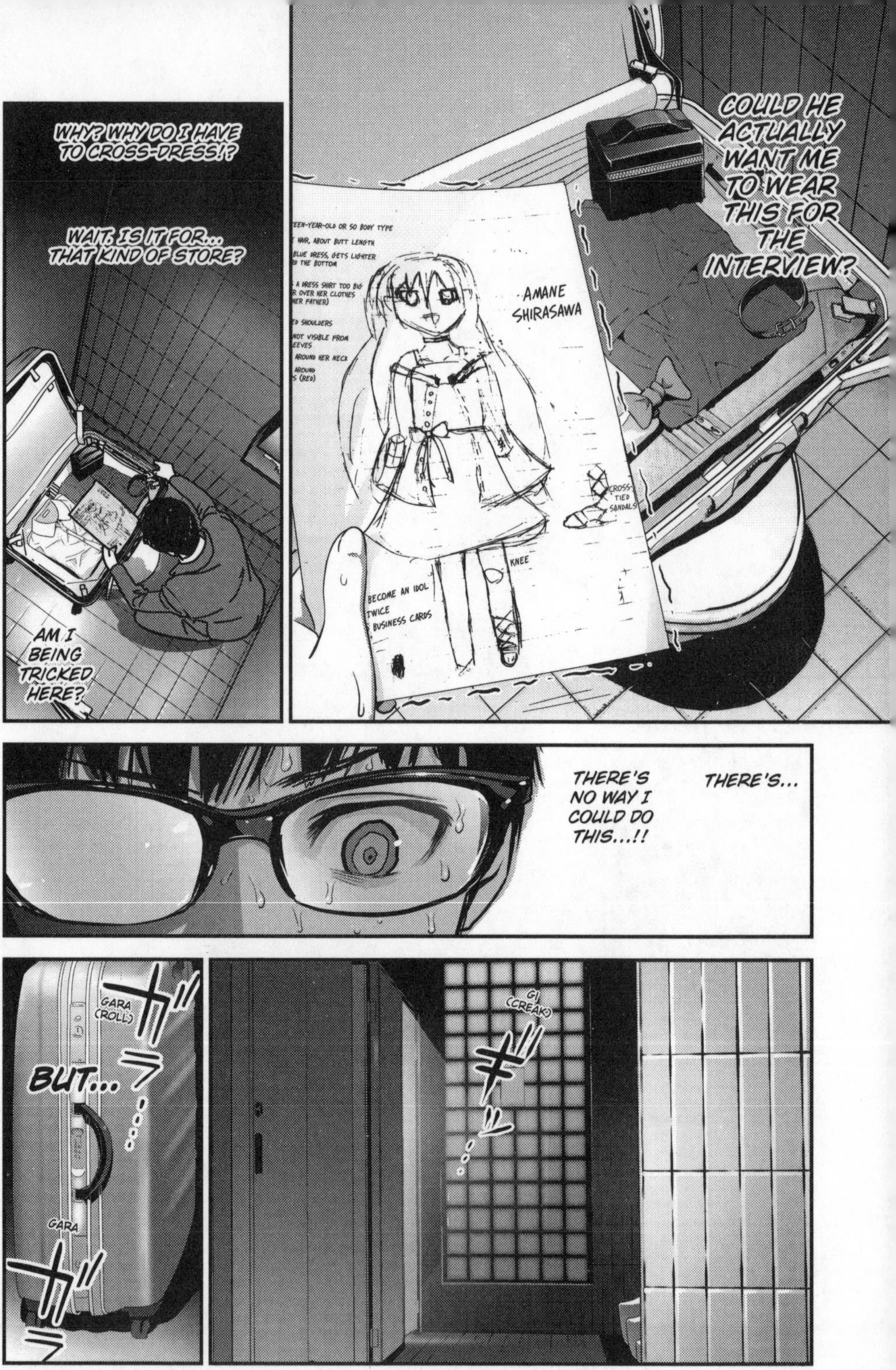
COULD HE ACTUALLY WANT ME TO WEAR THIS FOR THE INTERVIEW?
EEN-YEAR-OLD OR SO BODY TYPE
HAIR, ABOUT BUTT LENGTH
BLUE DRESS, GETS LIGHTER
D THE BOTTOM
A DRESS SHIRT TOO BIG
R OVER HER CLOTHES
HER FATHER)
ED SHOULDERS
NOT VISIBLE FROM
EEVES
AROUND HER NECK
AROUND
S (RED)
AMANE SHIRASAWA
CROSS-TIED SANDALS
KNEE
BECOME AN IDOL
TWICE
BUSINESS CARDS
WHY? WHY DO I HAVE TO CROSS-DRESS!?
WAIT. IS IT FOR... THAT KIND OF STORE?
AM I BEING TRICKED HERE?
THERE'S...
THERE'S NO WAY I COULD DO THIS...!!
GI (CREAK)
GARA (ROLL)
BUT...
GARA

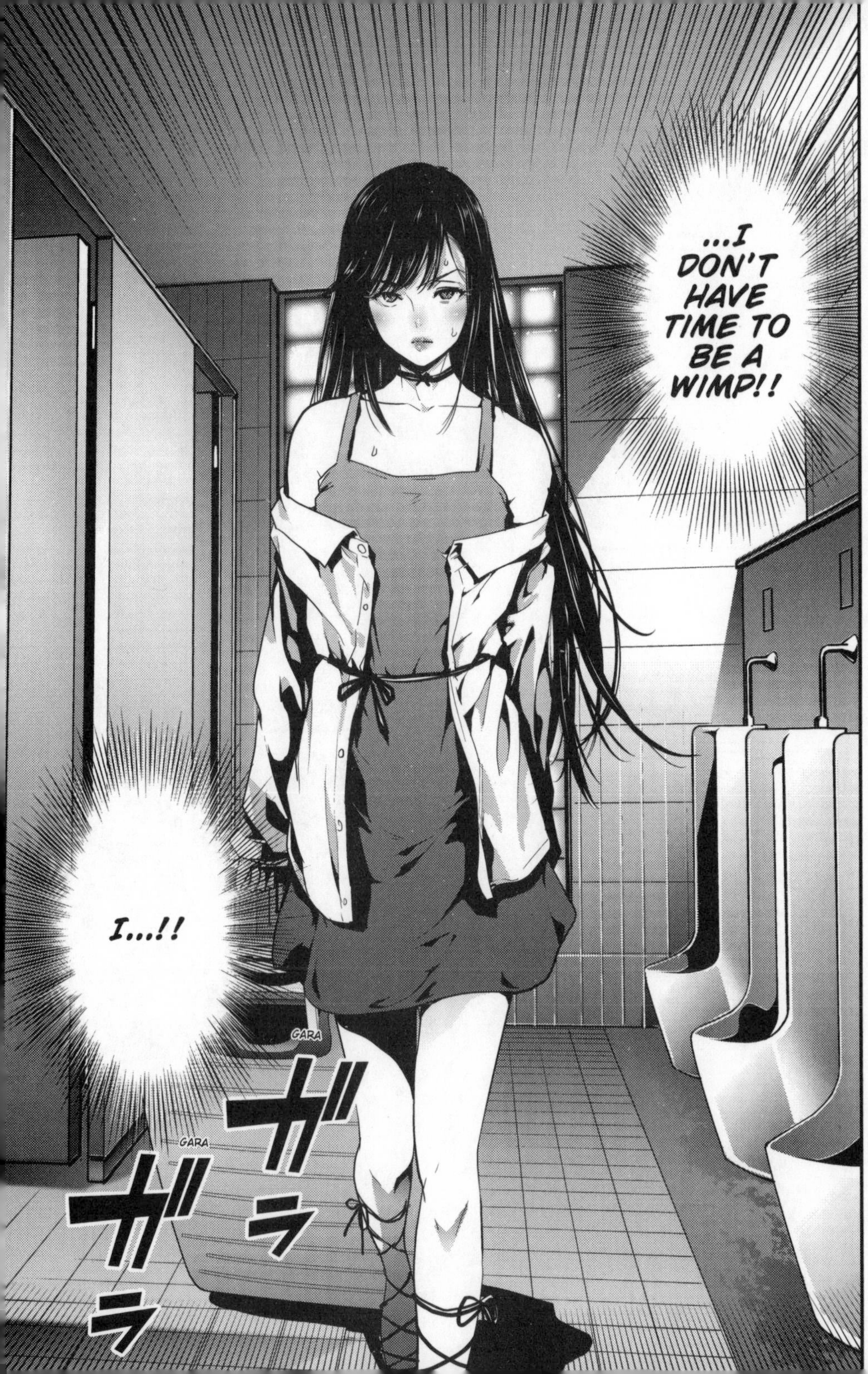
...I DON'T HAVE TIME TO BE A WIMP!!
I...!!
ガラ
GARA
ガラ
GARA

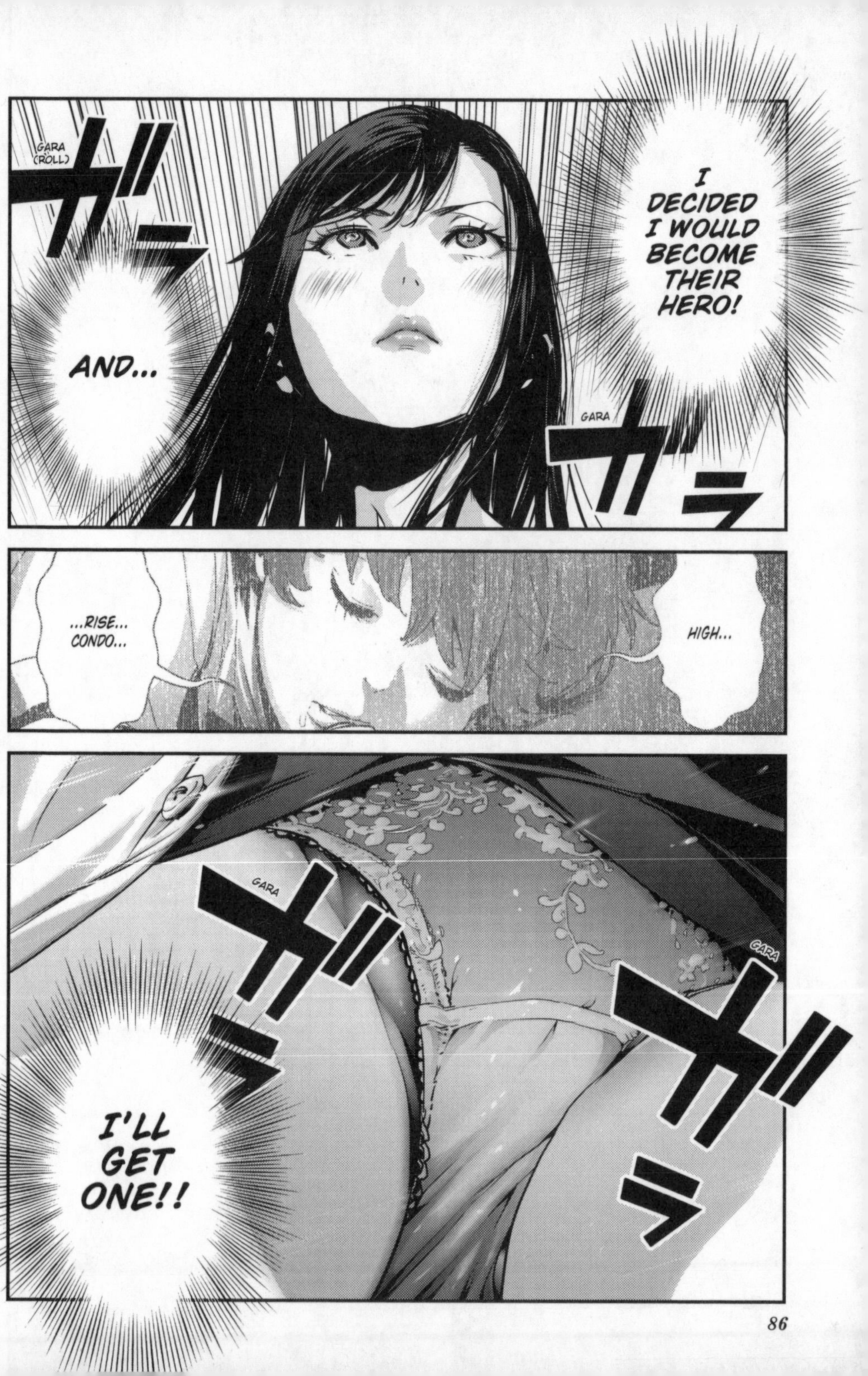
I DECIDED I WOULD BECOME THEIR HERO!
GARA
AND...
GARA (ROLL)
HIGH...
...RISE... CONDO...
GARA
GARA
I'LL GET ONE!!

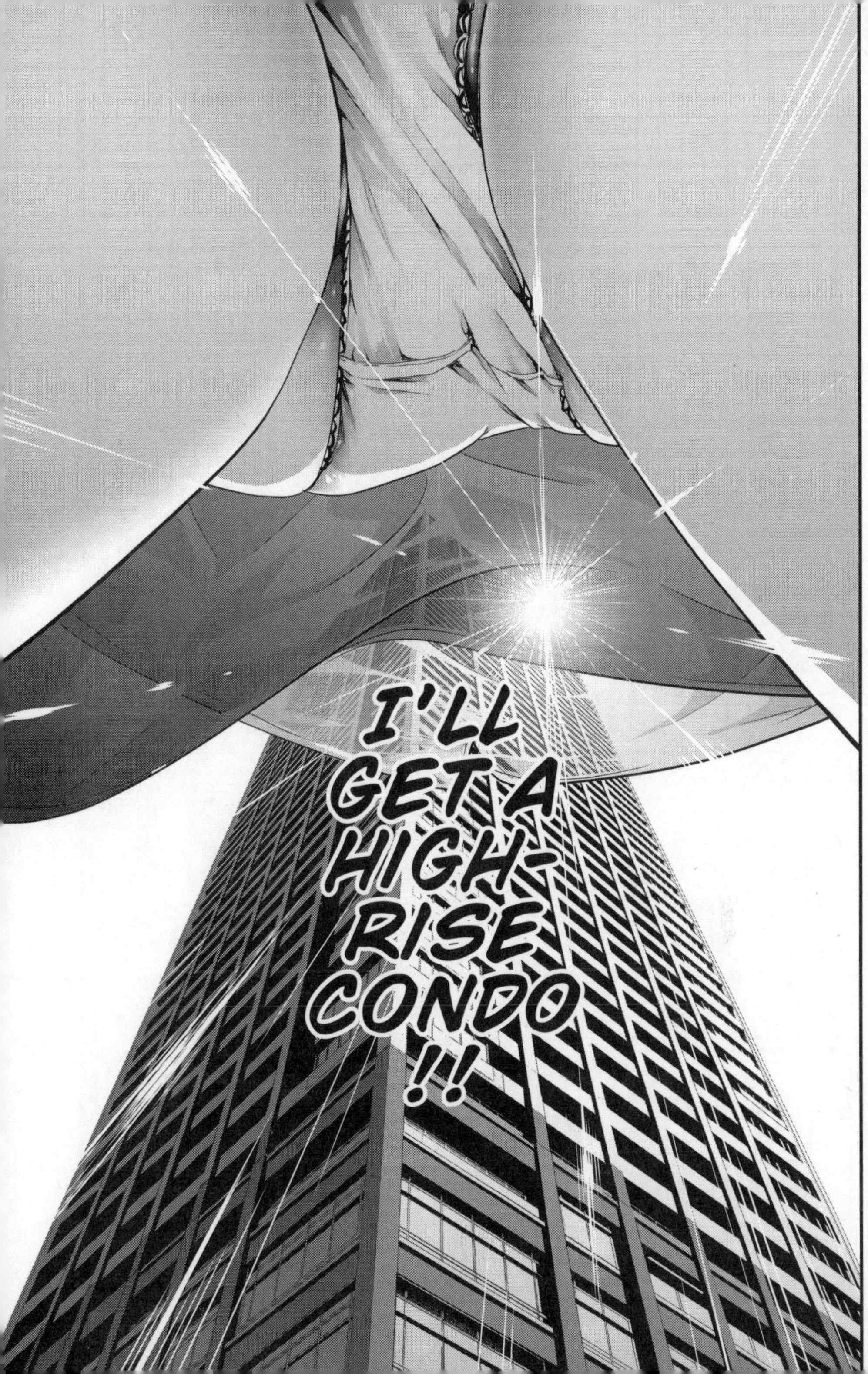
I'LL GET A HIGH-RISE CONDO!!

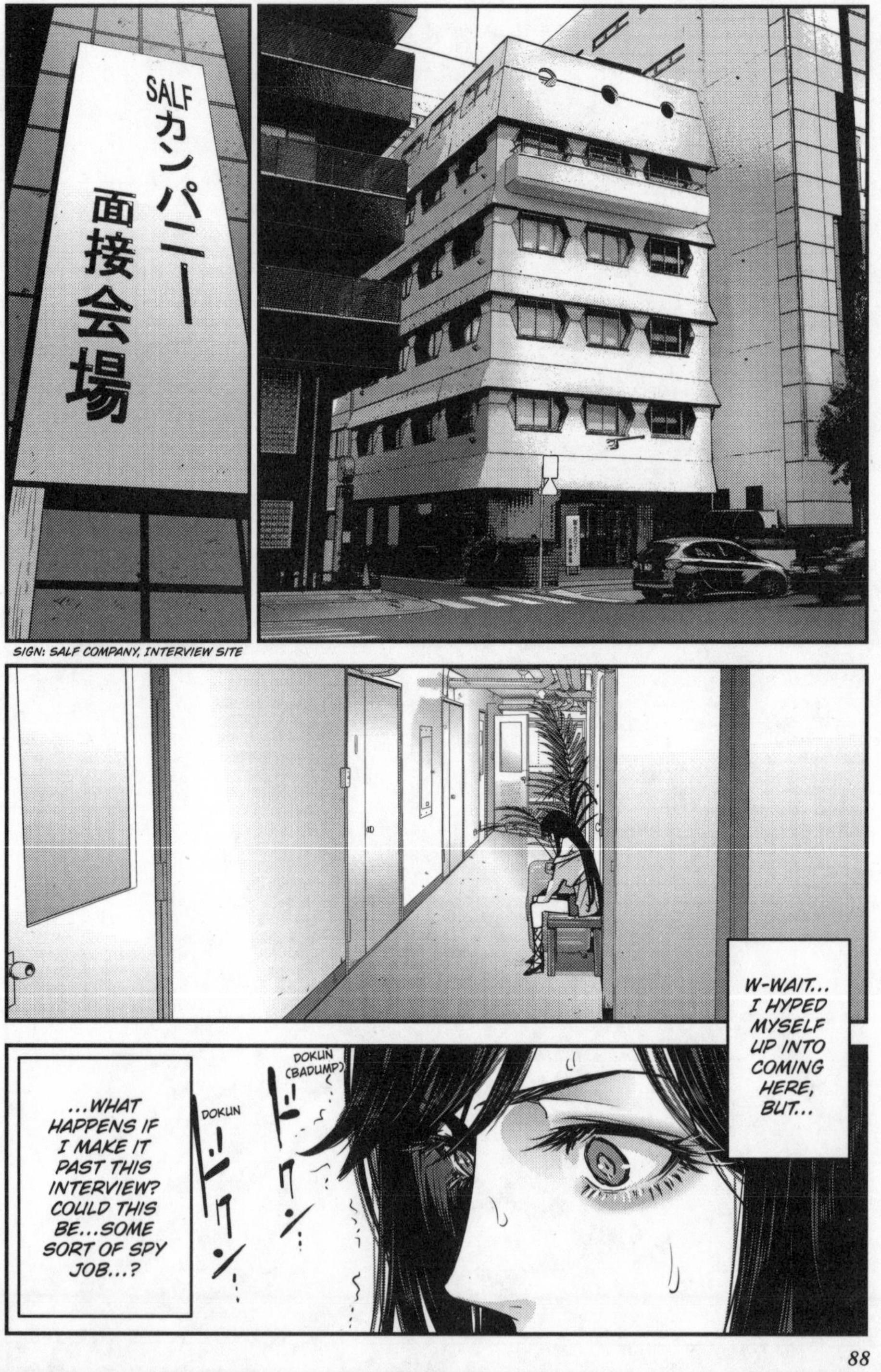
SALF カンパニー 面接会場
SIGN: SALF COMPANY, INTERVIEW SITE
W-WAIT... I HYPED MYSELF UP INTO COMING HERE, BUT...
DOKUN (BADUMP)
ドクン
DOKUN
ドクン
...WHAT HAPPENS IF I MAKE IT PAST THIS INTERVIEW? COULD THIS BE...SOME SORT OF SPY JOB...?

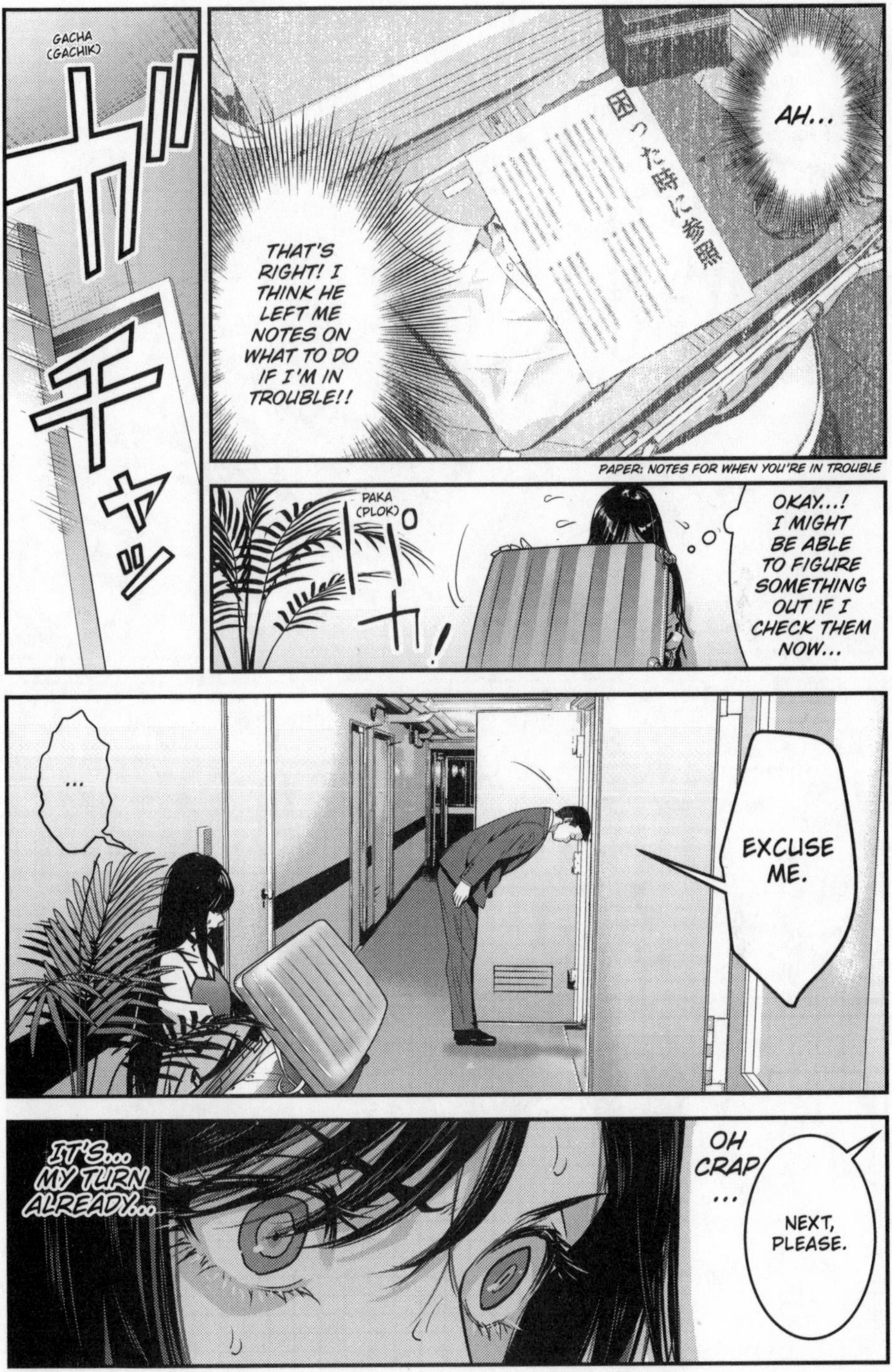
AH...
THAT'S RIGHT! I THINK HE LEFT ME NOTES ON WHAT TO DO IF I'M IN TROUBLE!!
困った時に参照
PAPER: NOTES FOR WHEN YOU'RE IN TROUBLE
OKAY...! I MIGHT BE ABLE TO FIGURE SOMETHING OUT IF I CHECK THEM NOW...
PAKA (PLOK)
GACHA (GACHIK)
EXCUSE ME.
...
NEXT, PLEASE.
OH CRAP...
IT'S... MY TURN ALREADY...

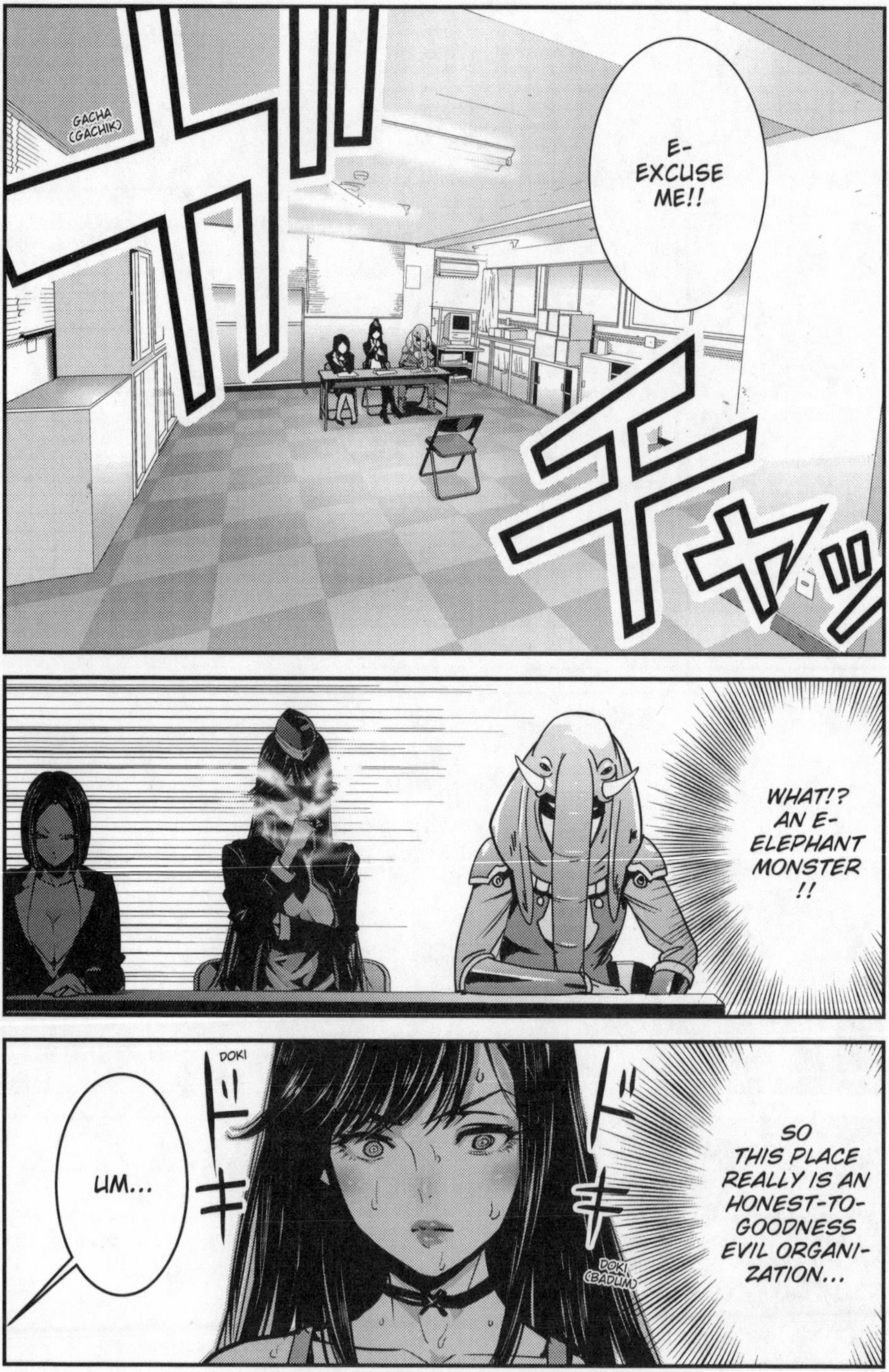
E-EXCUSE ME!!
GACHA (GACHIK)
WHAT!? AN E-ELEPHANT MONSTER !!
SO THIS PLACE REALLY IS AN HONEST-TO-GOODNESS EVIL ORGANI-ZATION...
DOKI (BADUM)
DOKI
UM...

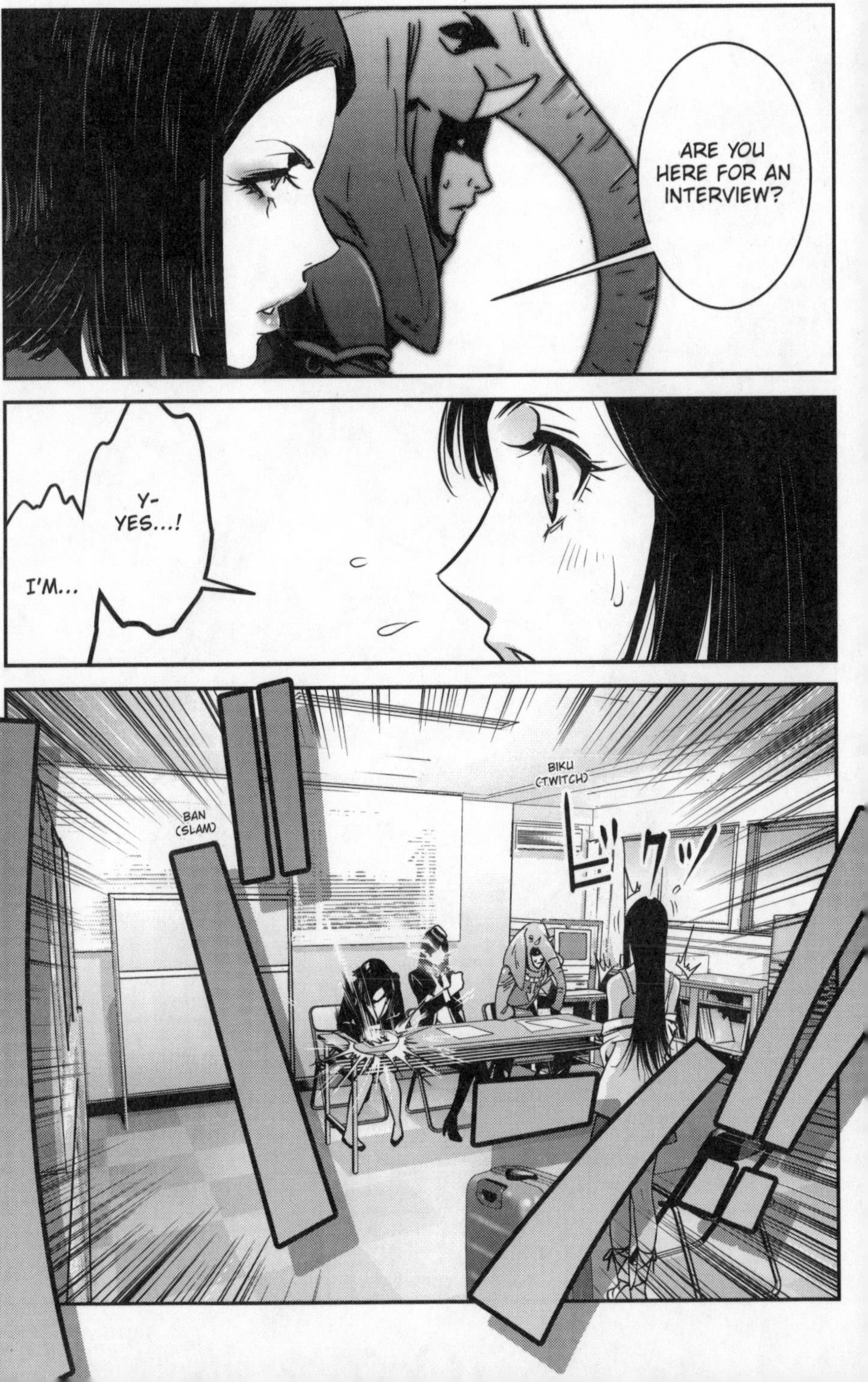
ARE YOU HERE FOR AN INTERVIEW?
Y- YES...!
I'M...
BIKU (TWITCH)
BAN (SLAM)

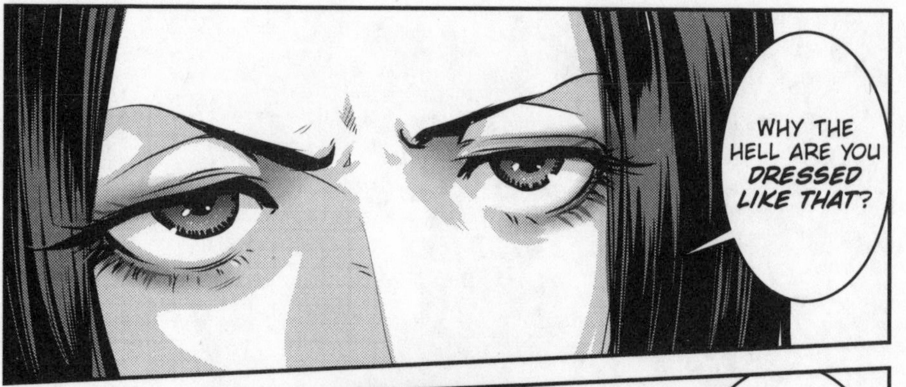
WHY THE HELL ARE YOU DRESSED LIKE THAT?

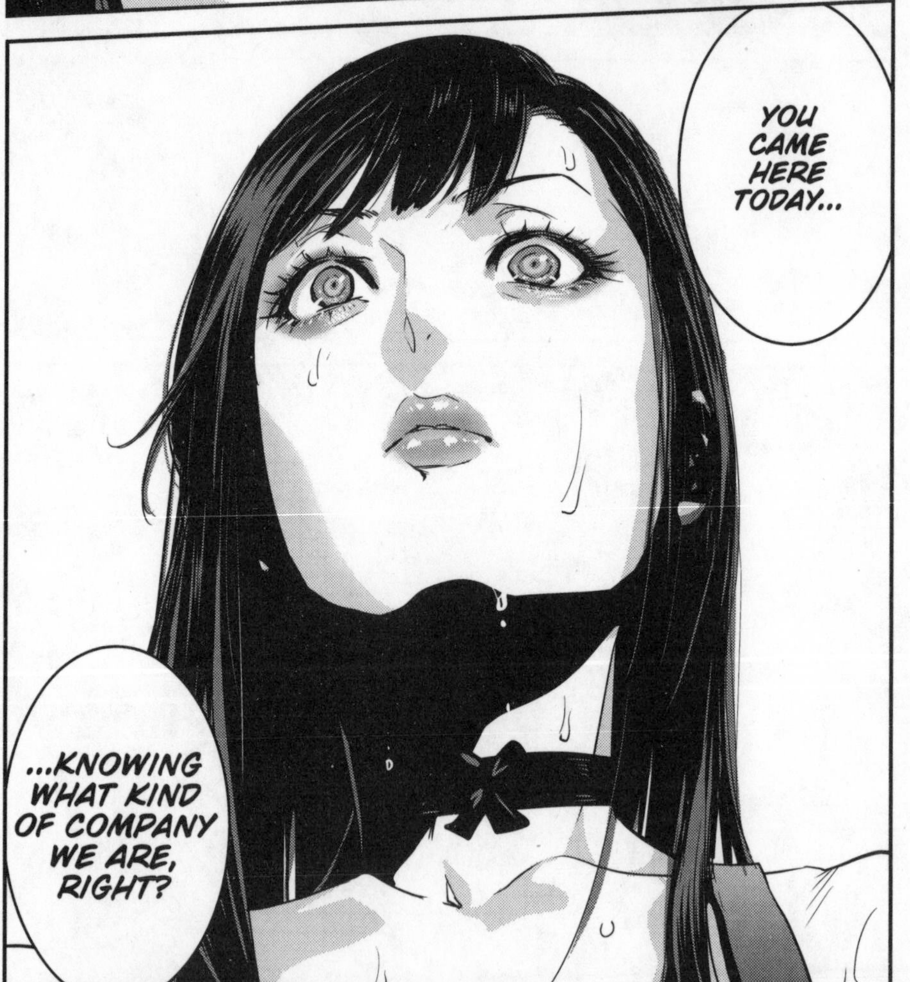
YOU CAME HERE TODAY...
...KNOWING WHAT KIND OF COMPANY WE ARE, RIGHT?

Chapter 3: End

Chapter 4: Exam

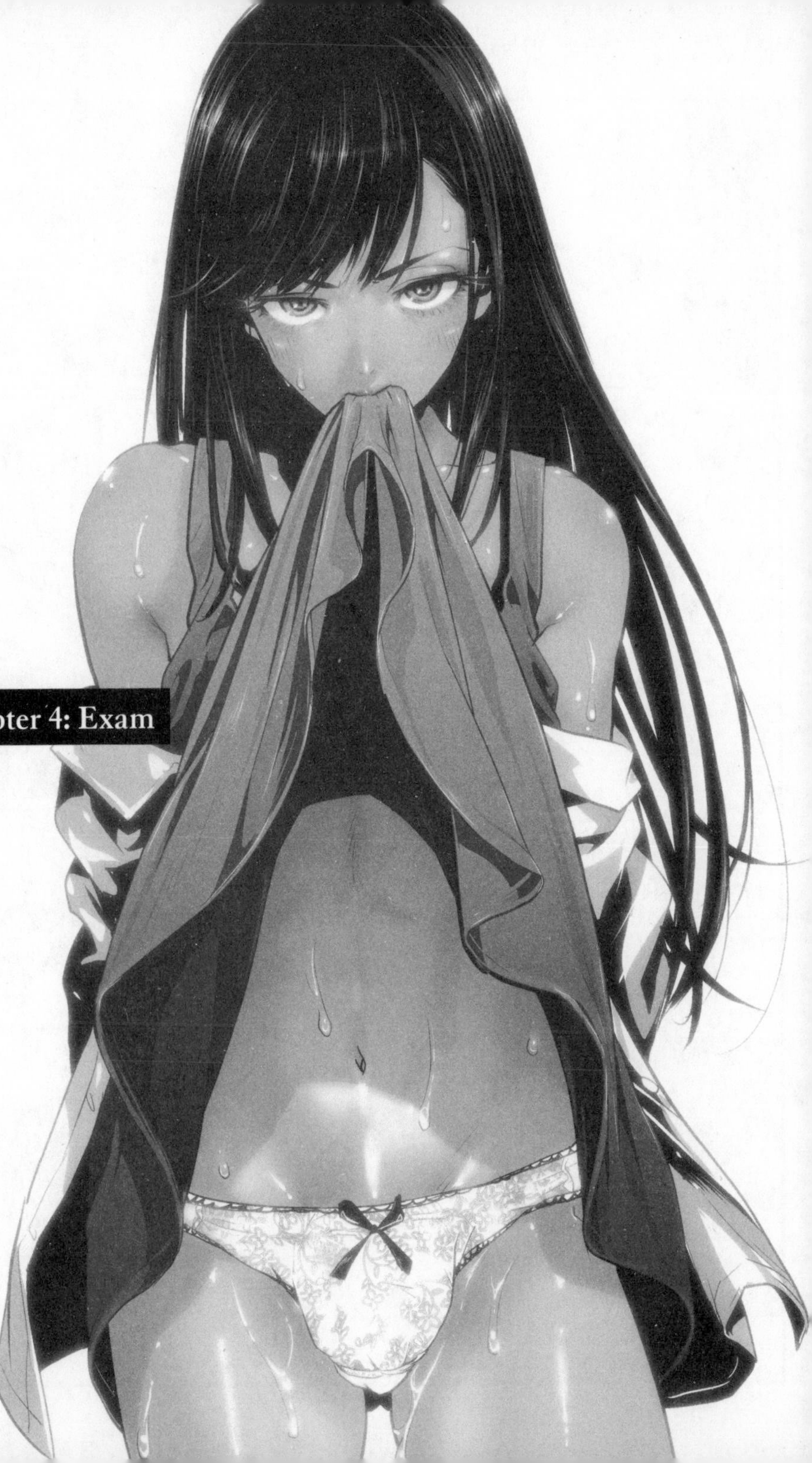

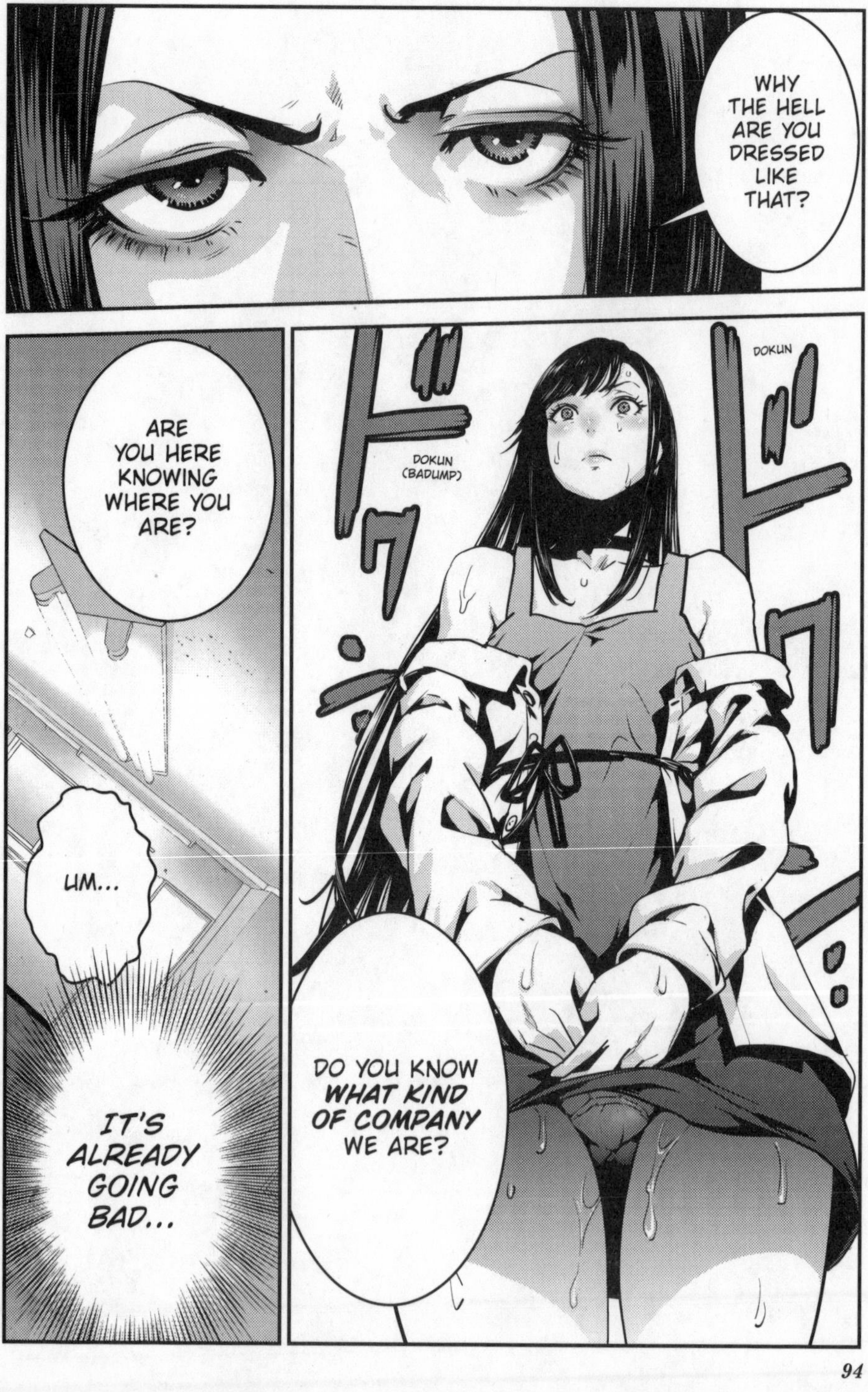
WHY THE HELL ARE YOU DRESSED LIKE THAT?
DOKUN
DOKUN (BADUMP)
DO YOU KNOW *WHAT KIND* OF COMPANY WE ARE?
ARE YOU HERE KNOWING WHERE YOU ARE?
UM...
IT'S ALREADY GOING BAD...

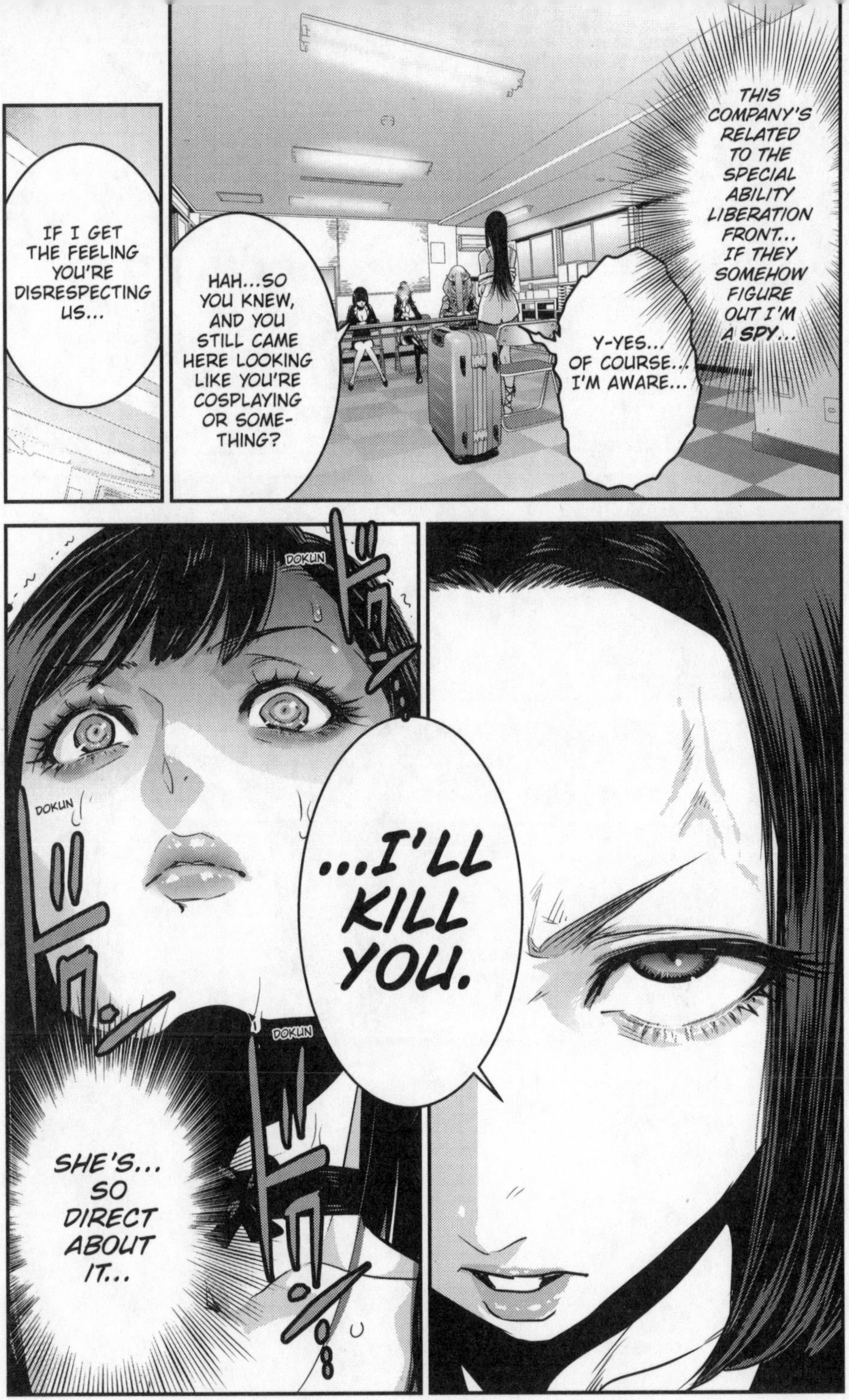
THIS COMPANY'S RELATED TO THE SPECIAL ABILITY LIBERATION FRONT... IF THEY SOMEHOW FIGURE OUT I'M A SPY...
Y-YES... OF COURSE... I'M AWARE...
HAH...SO YOU KNEW, AND YOU STILL CAME HERE LOOKING LIKE YOU'RE COSPLAYING OR SOME-THING?
IF I GET THE FEELING YOU'RE DISRESPECTING US...
...I'LL KILL YOU.
DOKUN
DOKUN
DOKUN
SHE'S... SO DIRECT ABOUT IT...

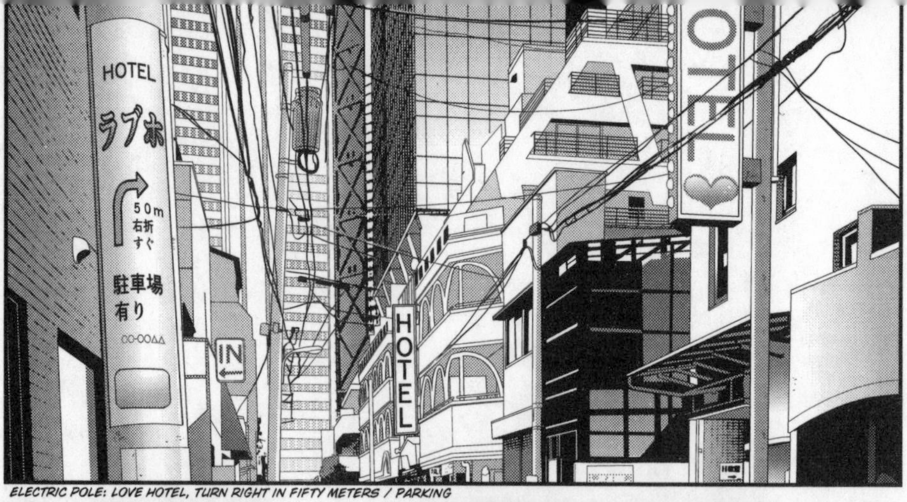
HOTEL
ラブホ
50m
右折
すぐ
駐車場
有り
IN
HOTEL
HOTEL
ELECTRIC POLE: LOVE HOTEL, TURN RIGHT IN FIFTY METERS / PARKING

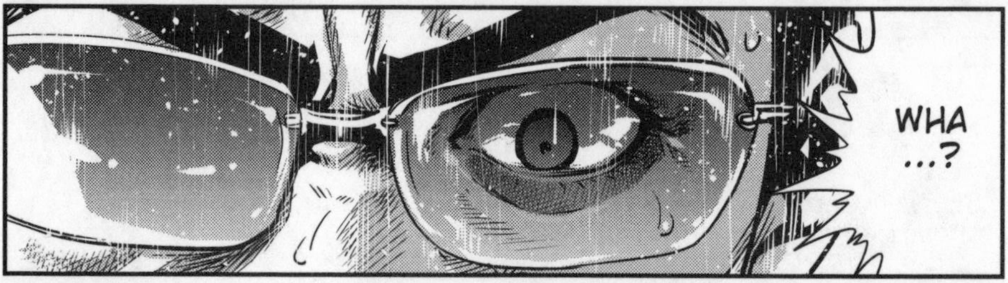
WHA
...?

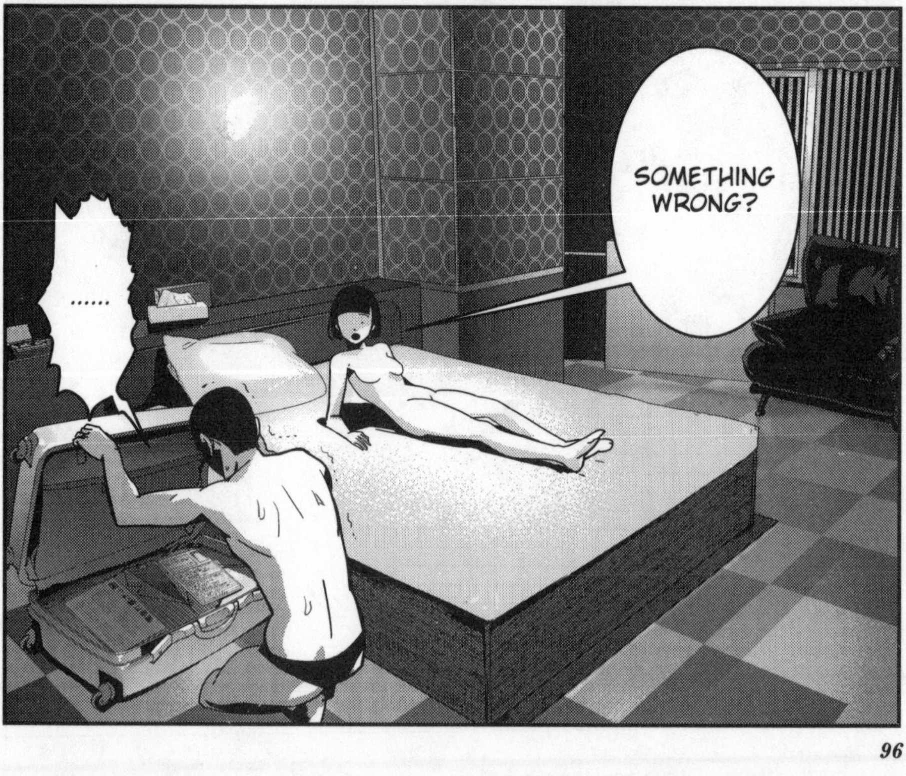
SOMETHING WRONG?
......

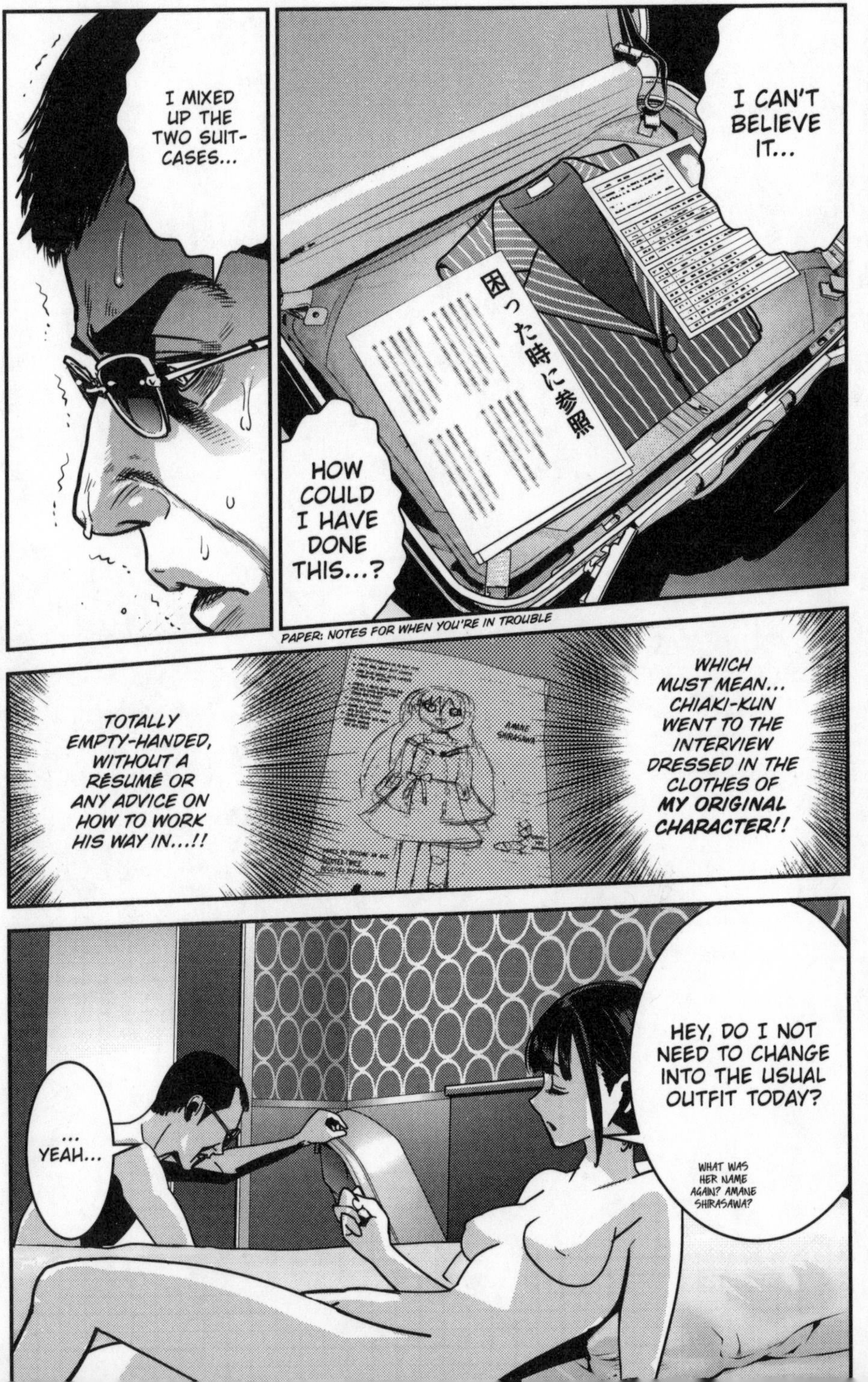
I CAN'T BELIEVE IT...
困った時に参照
HOW COULD I HAVE DONE THIS...?
I MIXED UP THE TWO SUIT-CASES...
PAPER: NOTES FOR WHEN YOU'RE IN TROUBLE
WHICH MUST MEAN... CHIAKI-KUN WENT TO THE INTERVIEW DRESSED IN THE CLOTHES OF MY ORIGINAL CHARACTER!!
AMANE SHIRASAWA
TOTALLY EMPTY-HANDED, WITHOUT A RÉSUMÉ OR ANY ADVICE ON HOW TO WORK HIS WAY IN...!!
HEY, DO I NOT NEED TO CHANGE INTO THE USUAL OUTFIT TODAY?
WHAT WAS HER NAME AGAIN? AMANE SHIRASAWA?
... YEAH...

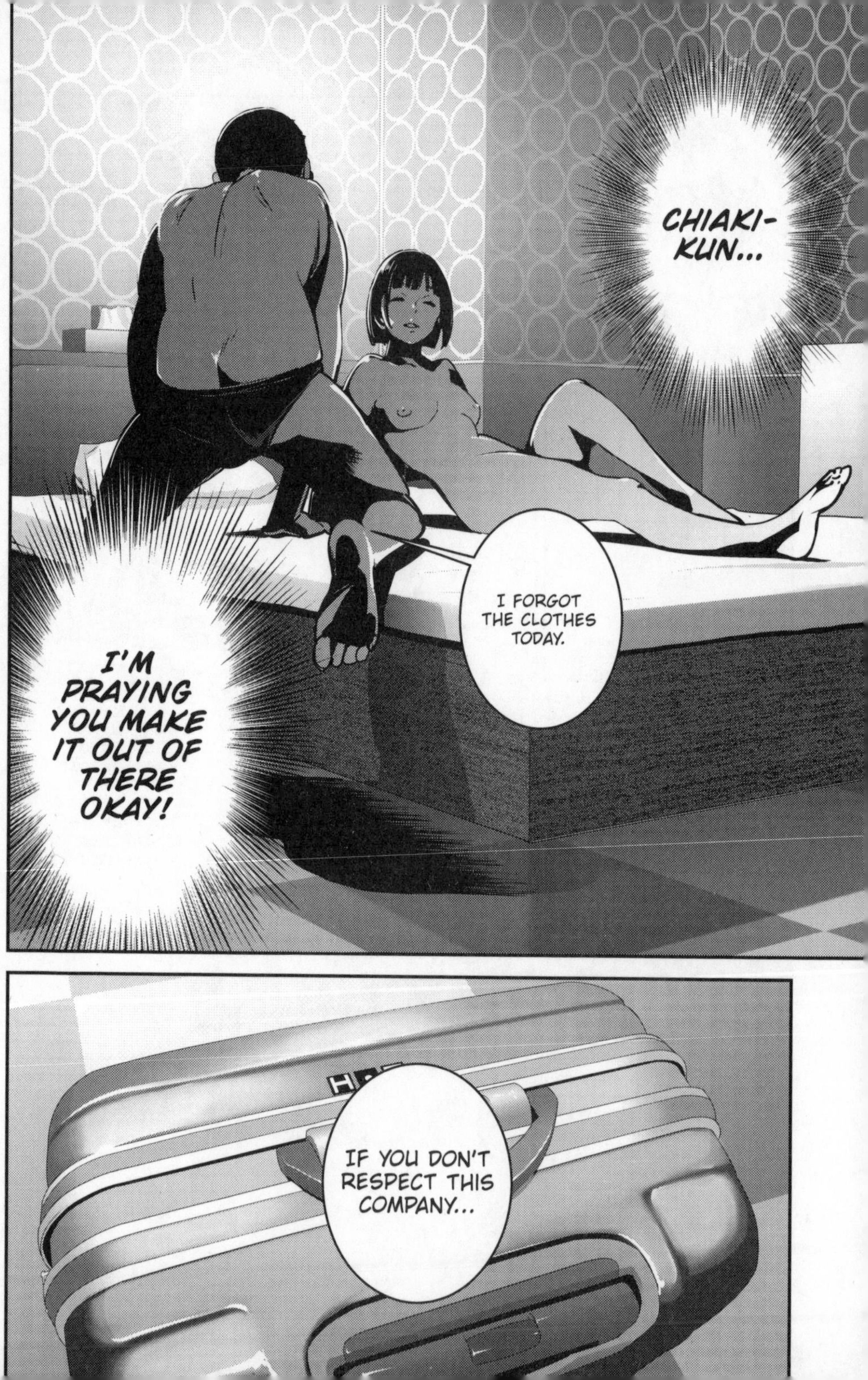
CHIAKI-KUN...
I FORGOT THE CLOTHES TODAY.
I'M PRAYING YOU MAKE IT OUT OF THERE OKAY!
IF YOU DON'T RESPECT THIS COMPANY...

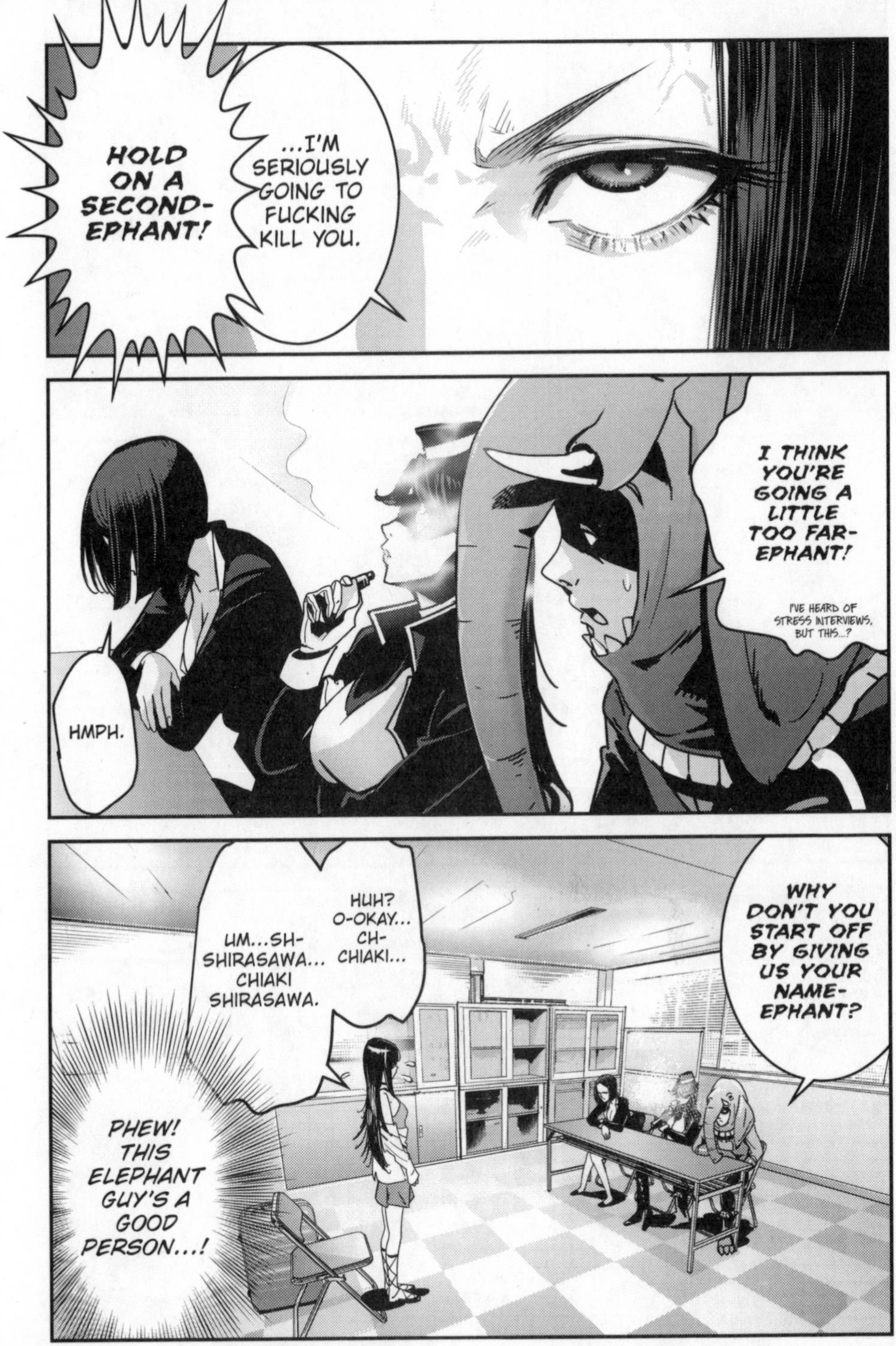
...I'M SERIOUSLY GOING TO FUCKING KILL YOU.
HOLD ON A SECOND-EPHANT!
I THINK YOU'RE GOING A LITTLE TOO FAR-EPHANT!
I'VE HEARD OF STRESS INTERVIEWS, BUT THIS...?
HMPH.
WHY DON'T YOU START OFF BY GIVING US YOUR NAME-EPHANT?
HUH? O-OKAY... CH-CHIAKI...
UM...SH-SHIRASAWA... CHIAKI SHIRASAWA.
PHEW! THIS ELEPHANT GUY'S A GOOD PERSON...!

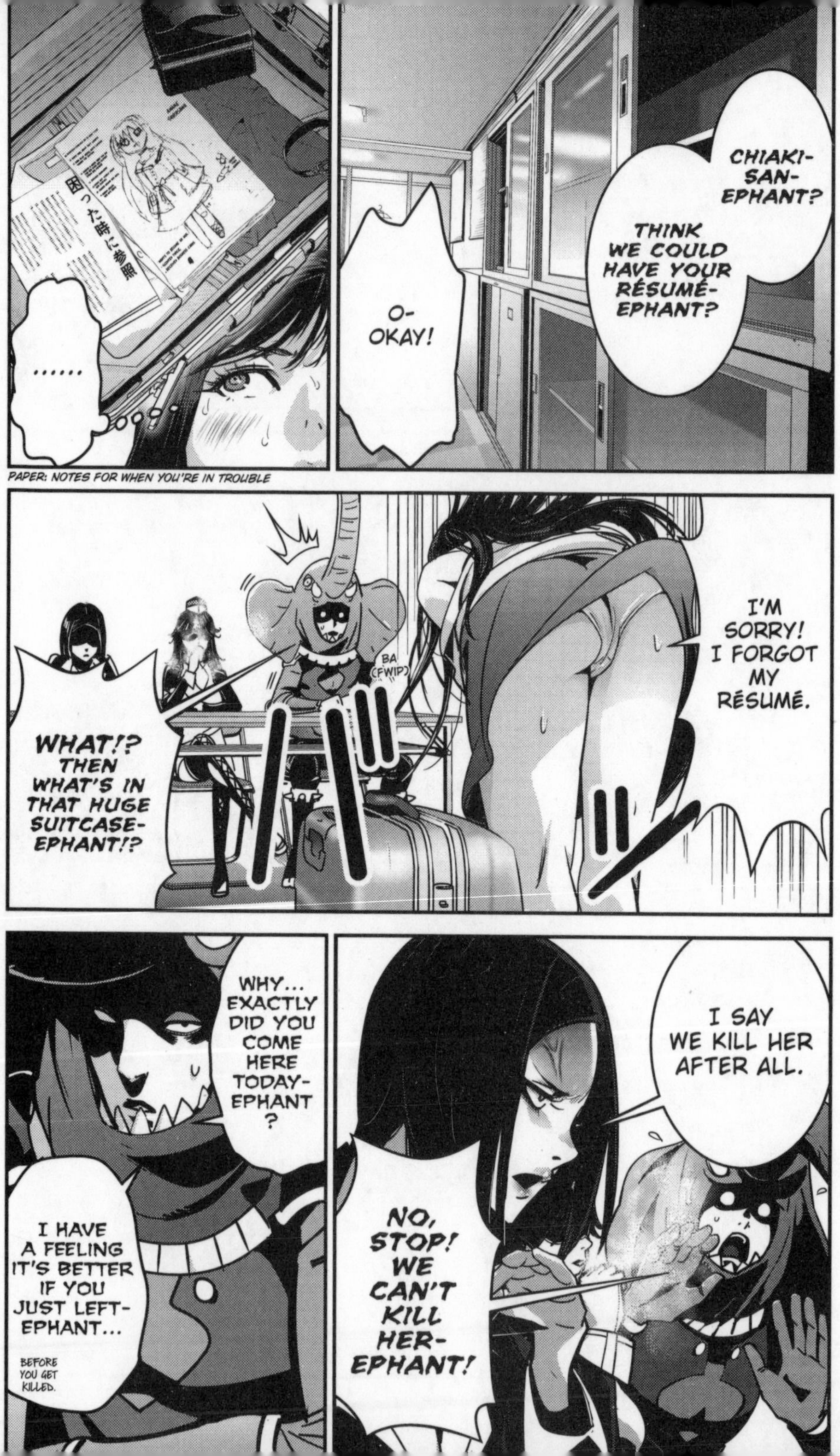
CHIAKI-SAN-EPHANT?
THINK WE COULD HAVE YOUR RÉSUMÉ-EPHANT?
O-OKAY!
困った時に参照
......
PAPER: NOTES FOR WHEN YOU'RE IN TROUBLE
I'M SORRY! I FORGOT MY RÉSUMÉ.
BA (FWIP)
WHAT!? THEN WHAT'S IN THAT HUGE SUITCASE-EPHANT!?
I SAY WE KILL HER AFTER ALL.
NO, STOP! WE CAN'T KILL HER-EPHANT!
WHY... EXACTLY DID YOU COME HERE TODAY-EPHANT?
I HAVE A FEELING IT'S BETTER IF YOU JUST LEFT-EPHANT...
BEFORE YOU GET KILLED.

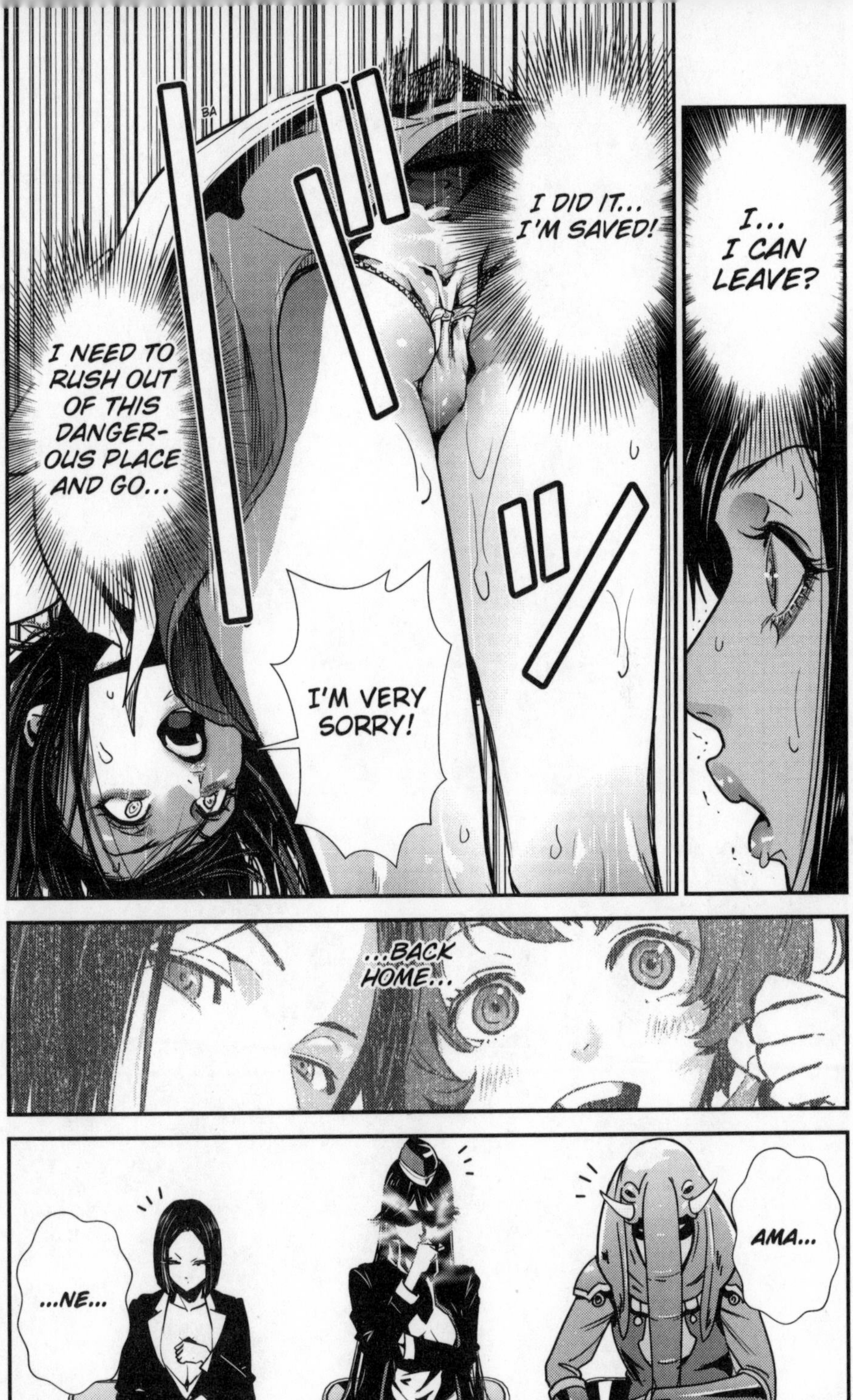
I...
I CAN LEAVE?
I DID IT... I'M SAVED!
BA
I NEED TO RUSH OUT OF THIS DANGER-OUS PLACE AND GO...
I'M VERY SORRY!
...BACK HOME...
AMA...
...NE...

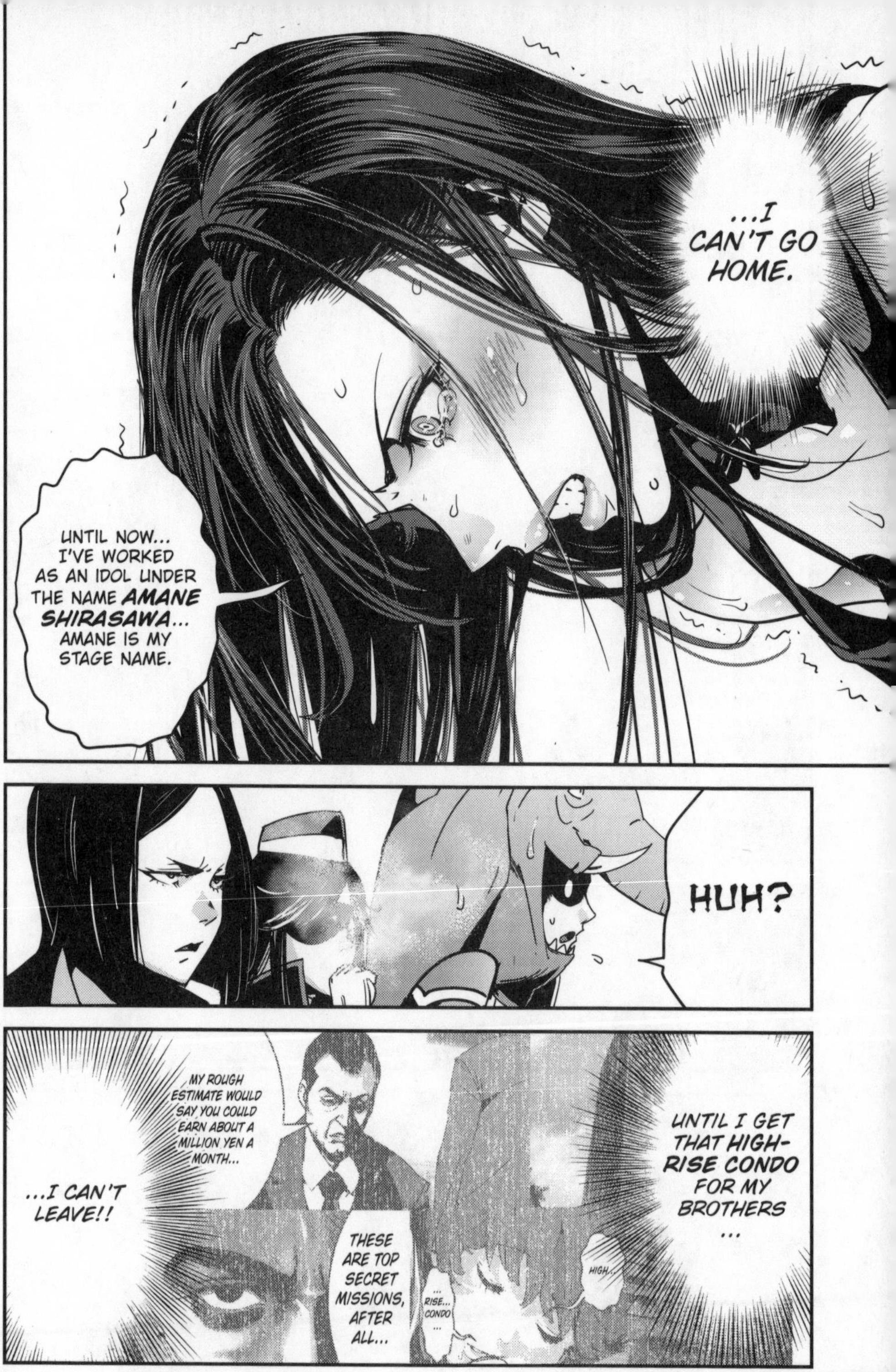
...I CAN'T GO HOME.
UNTIL NOW... I'VE WORKED AS AN IDOL UNDER THE NAME **AMANE SHIRASAWA**... AMANE IS MY STAGE NAME.
HUH?
UNTIL I GET THAT HIGH-RISE CONDO FOR MY BROTHERS ...
MY ROUGH ESTIMATE WOULD SAY YOU COULD EARN ABOUT A MILLION YEN A MONTH...
HIGH...
... RISE... CONDO ...
THESE ARE TOP SECRET MISSIONS, AFTER ALL...
...I CAN'T LEAVE!!

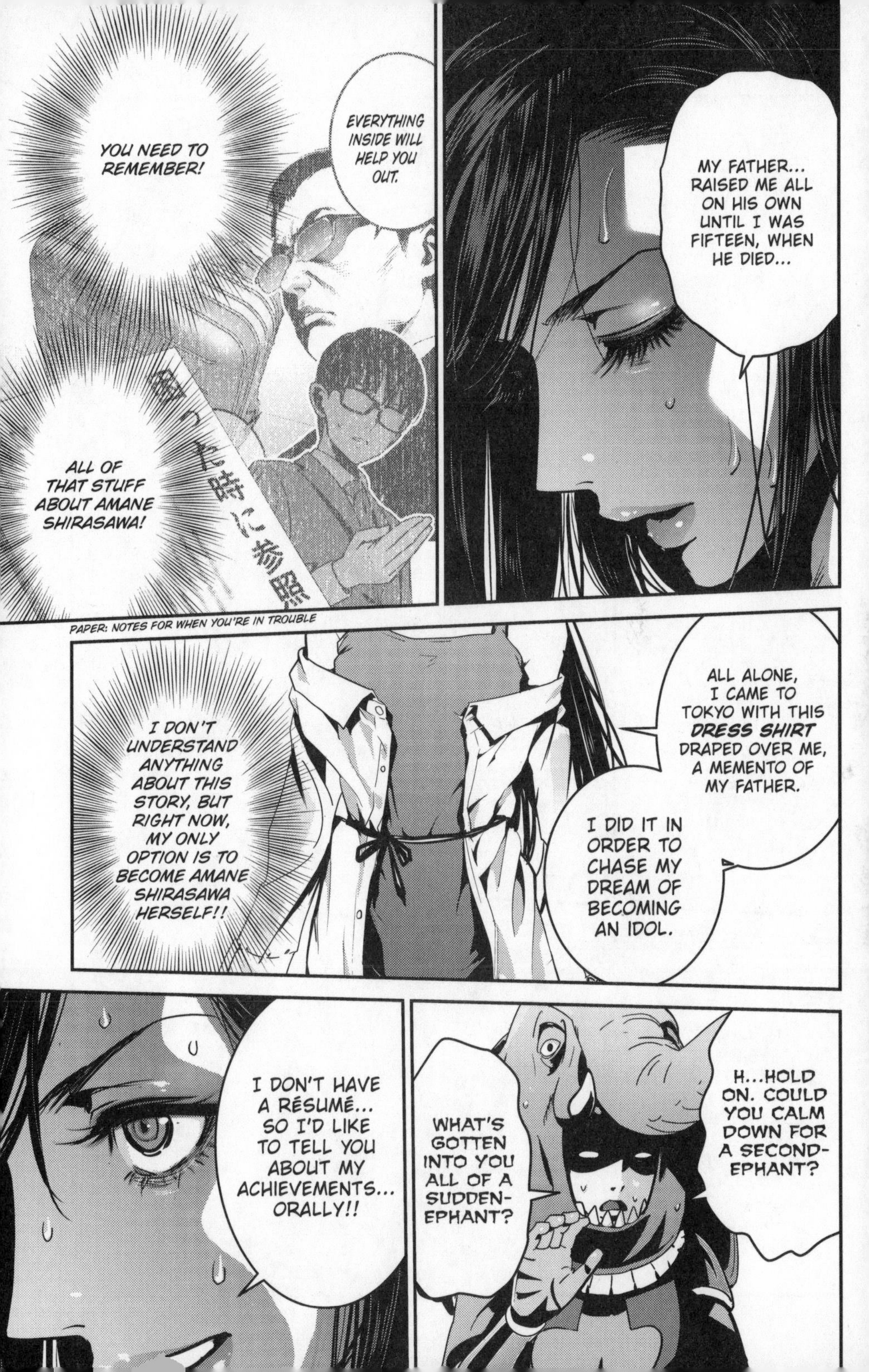
MY FATHER... RAISED ME ALL ON HIS OWN UNTIL I WAS FIFTEEN, WHEN HE DIED...
EVERYTHING INSIDE WILL HELP YOU OUT.
YOU NEED TO REMEMBER!
ALL OF THAT STUFF ABOUT AMANE SHIRASAWA!
った時に参照
PAPER: NOTES FOR WHEN YOU'RE IN TROUBLE
ALL ALONE, I CAME TO TOKYO WITH THIS ***DRESS SHIRT*** DRAPED OVER ME, A MEMENTO OF MY FATHER.
I DID IT IN ORDER TO CHASE MY DREAM OF BECOMING AN IDOL.
I DON'T UNDERSTAND ANYTHING ABOUT THIS STORY, BUT RIGHT NOW, MY ONLY OPTION IS TO BECOME AMANE SHIRASAWA HERSELF!!
H...HOLD ON. COULD YOU CALM DOWN FOR A SECOND-EPHANT?
WHAT'S GOTTEN INTO YOU ALL OF A SUDDEN-EPHANT?
I DON'T HAVE A RÉSUMÉ... SO I'D LIKE TO TELL YOU ABOUT MY ACHIEVEMENTS... ORALLY!!

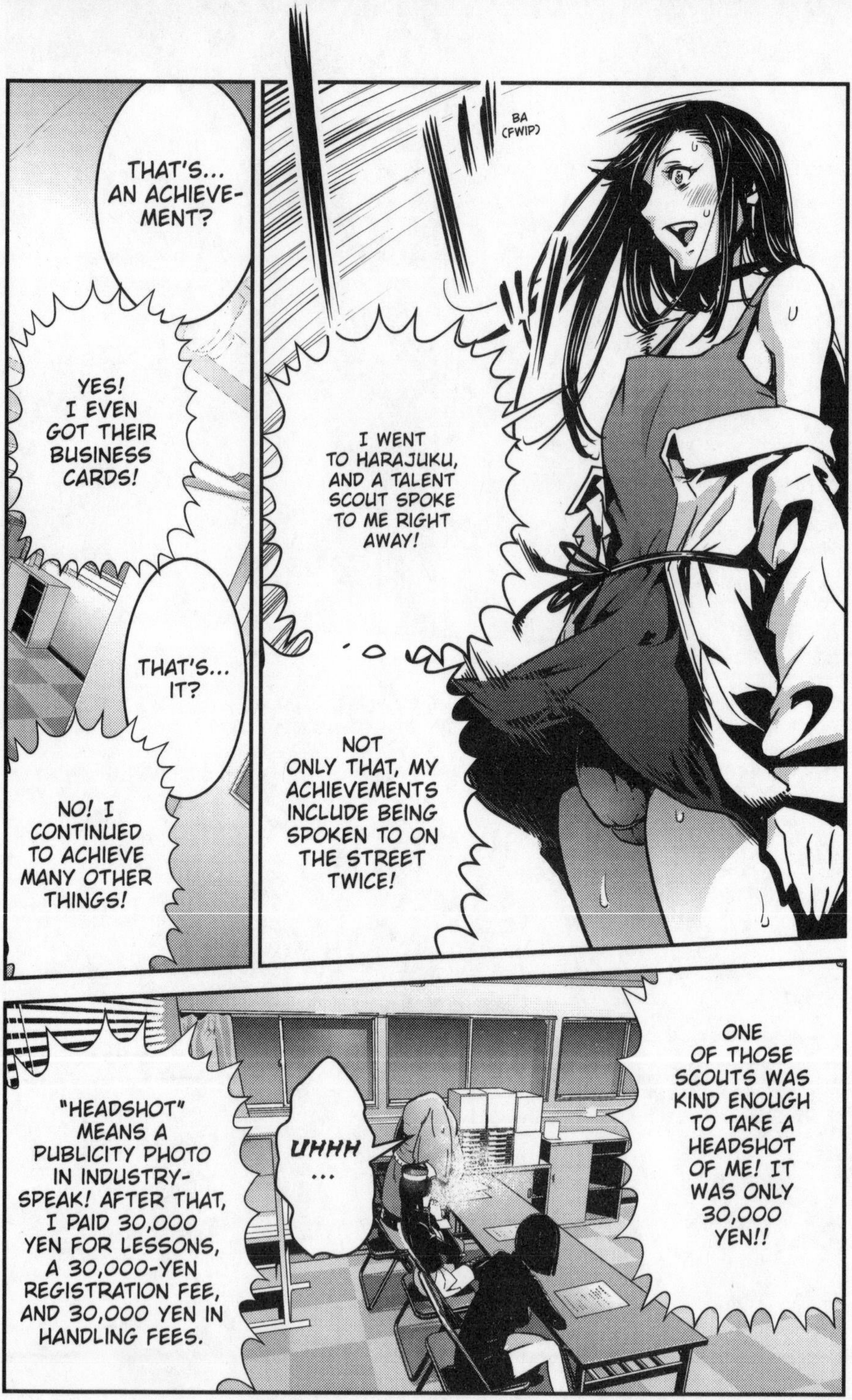
BA (FWIP)
I WENT TO HARAJUKU, AND A TALENT SCOUT SPOKE TO ME RIGHT AWAY!
NOT ONLY THAT, MY ACHIEVEMENTS INCLUDE BEING SPOKEN TO ON THE STREET TWICE!
THAT'S... AN ACHIEVE-MENT?
YES! I EVEN GOT THEIR BUSINESS CARDS!
THAT'S... IT?
NO! I CONTINUED TO ACHIEVE MANY OTHER THINGS!
ONE OF THOSE SCOUTS WAS KIND ENOUGH TO TAKE A HEADSHOT OF ME! IT WAS ONLY 30,000 YEN!!
UHHH ...
"HEADSHOT" MEANS A PUBLICITY PHOTO IN INDUSTRY-SPEAK! AFTER THAT, I PAID 30,000 YEN FOR LESSONS, A 30,000-YEN REGISTRATION FEE, AND 30,000 YEN IN HANDLING FEES.

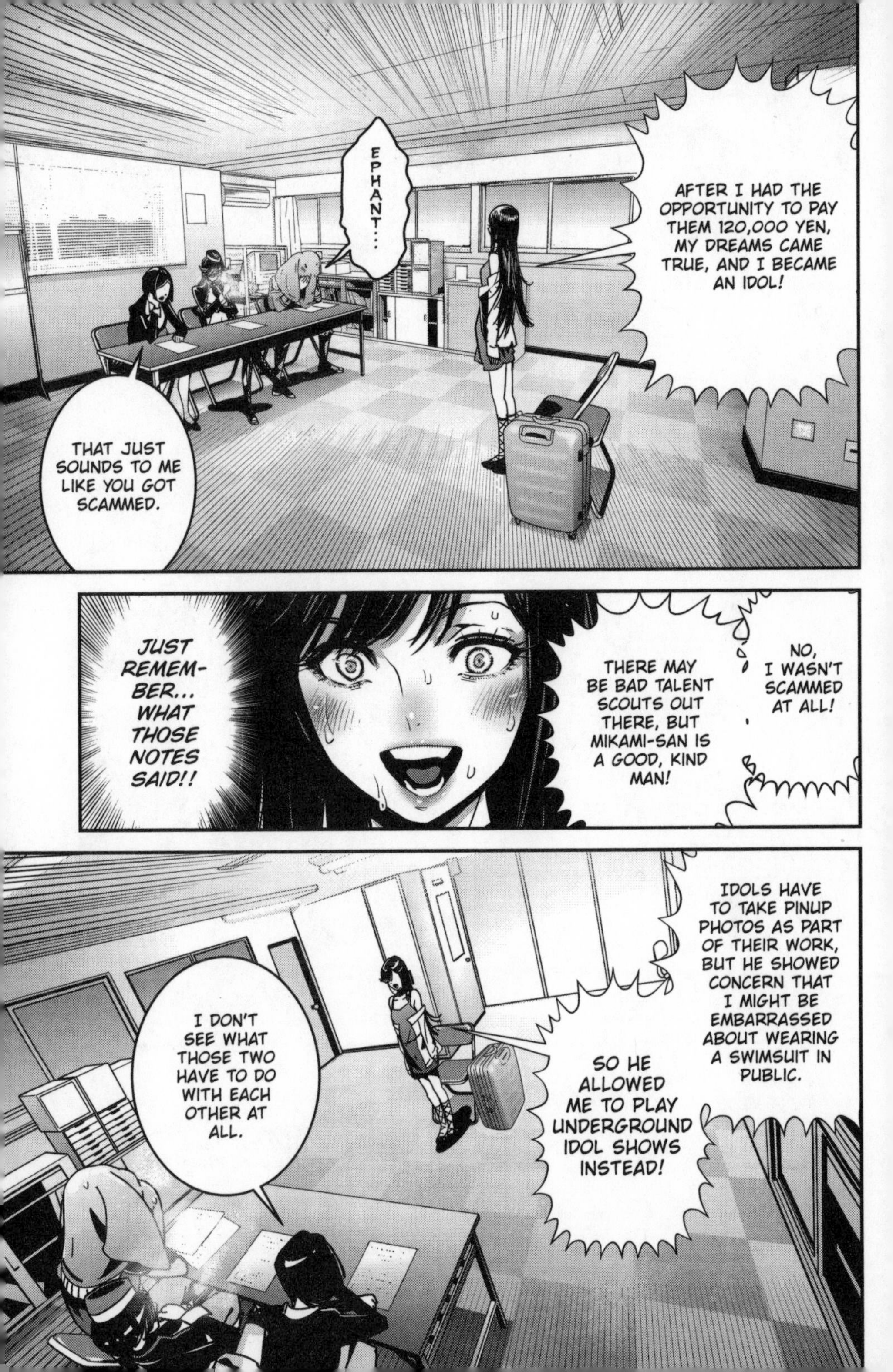
AFTER I HAD THE OPPORTUNITY TO PAY THEM 120,000 YEN, MY DREAMS CAME TRUE, AND I BECAME AN IDOL!
EPHANT...
THAT JUST SOUNDS TO ME LIKE YOU GOT SCAMMED.
NO, I WASN'T SCAMMED AT ALL!
THERE MAY BE BAD TALENT SCOUTS OUT THERE, BUT MIKAMI-SAN IS A GOOD, KIND MAN!
JUST REMEMBER... WHAT THOSE NOTES SAID!!
IDOLS HAVE TO TAKE PINUP PHOTOS AS PART OF THEIR WORK, BUT HE SHOWED CONCERN THAT I MIGHT BE EMBARRASSED ABOUT WEARING A SWIMSUIT IN PUBLIC.
SO HE ALLOWED ME TO PLAY UNDERGROUND IDOL SHOWS INSTEAD!
I DON'T SEE WHAT THOSE TWO HAVE TO DO WITH EACH OTHER AT ALL.

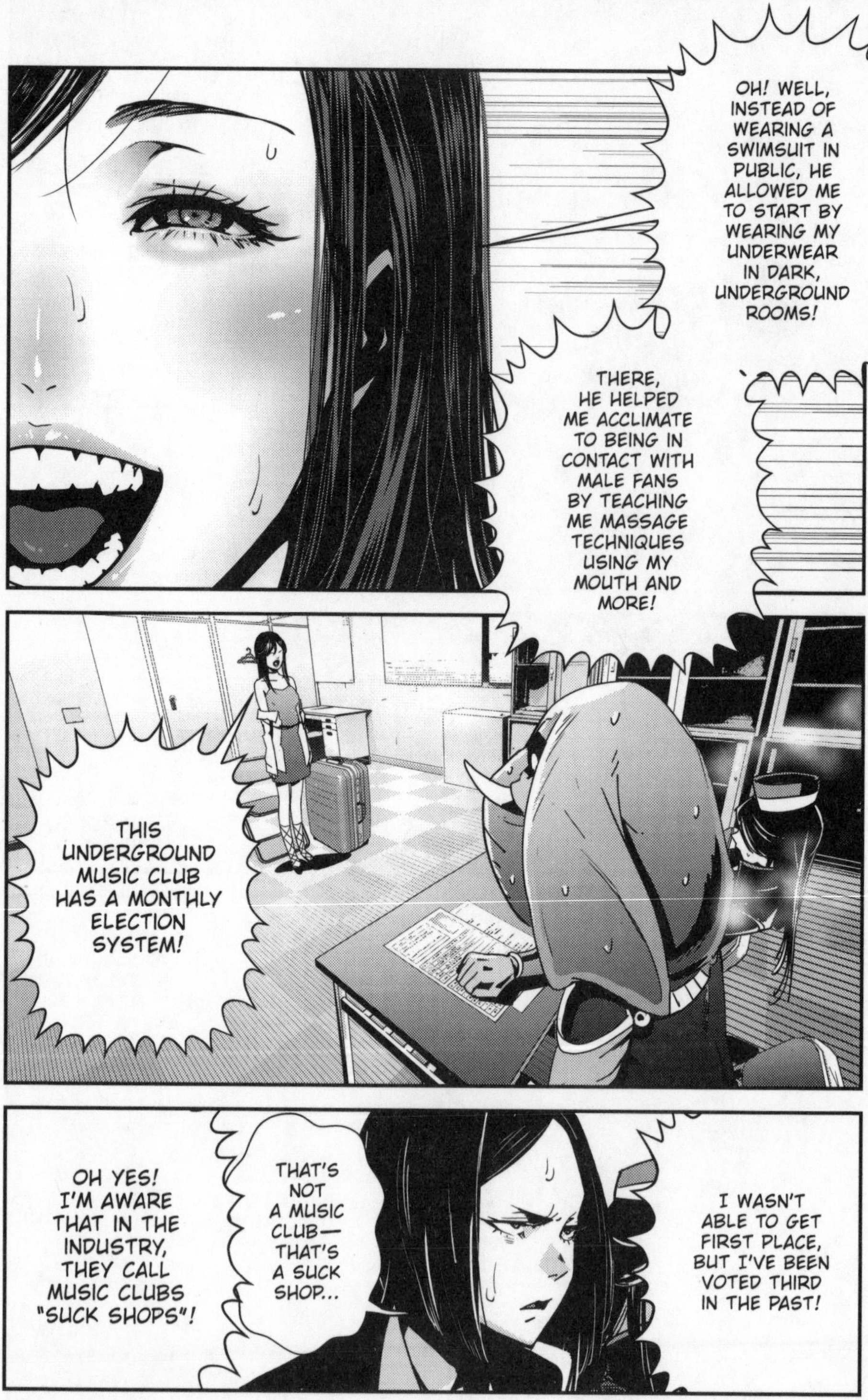
OH! WELL, INSTEAD OF WEARING A SWIMSUIT IN PUBLIC, HE ALLOWED ME TO START BY WEARING MY UNDERWEAR IN DARK, UNDERGROUND ROOMS!
THERE, HE HELPED ME ACCLIMATE TO BEING IN CONTACT WITH MALE FANS BY TEACHING ME MASSAGE TECHNIQUES USING MY MOUTH AND MORE!
THIS UNDERGROUND MUSIC CLUB HAS A MONTHLY ELECTION SYSTEM!
I WASN'T ABLE TO GET FIRST PLACE, BUT I'VE BEEN VOTED THIRD IN THE PAST!
THAT'S NOT A MUSIC CLUB—THAT'S A SUCK SHOP...
OH YES! I'M AWARE THAT IN THE INDUSTRY, THEY CALL MUSIC CLUBS "SUCK SHOPS"!

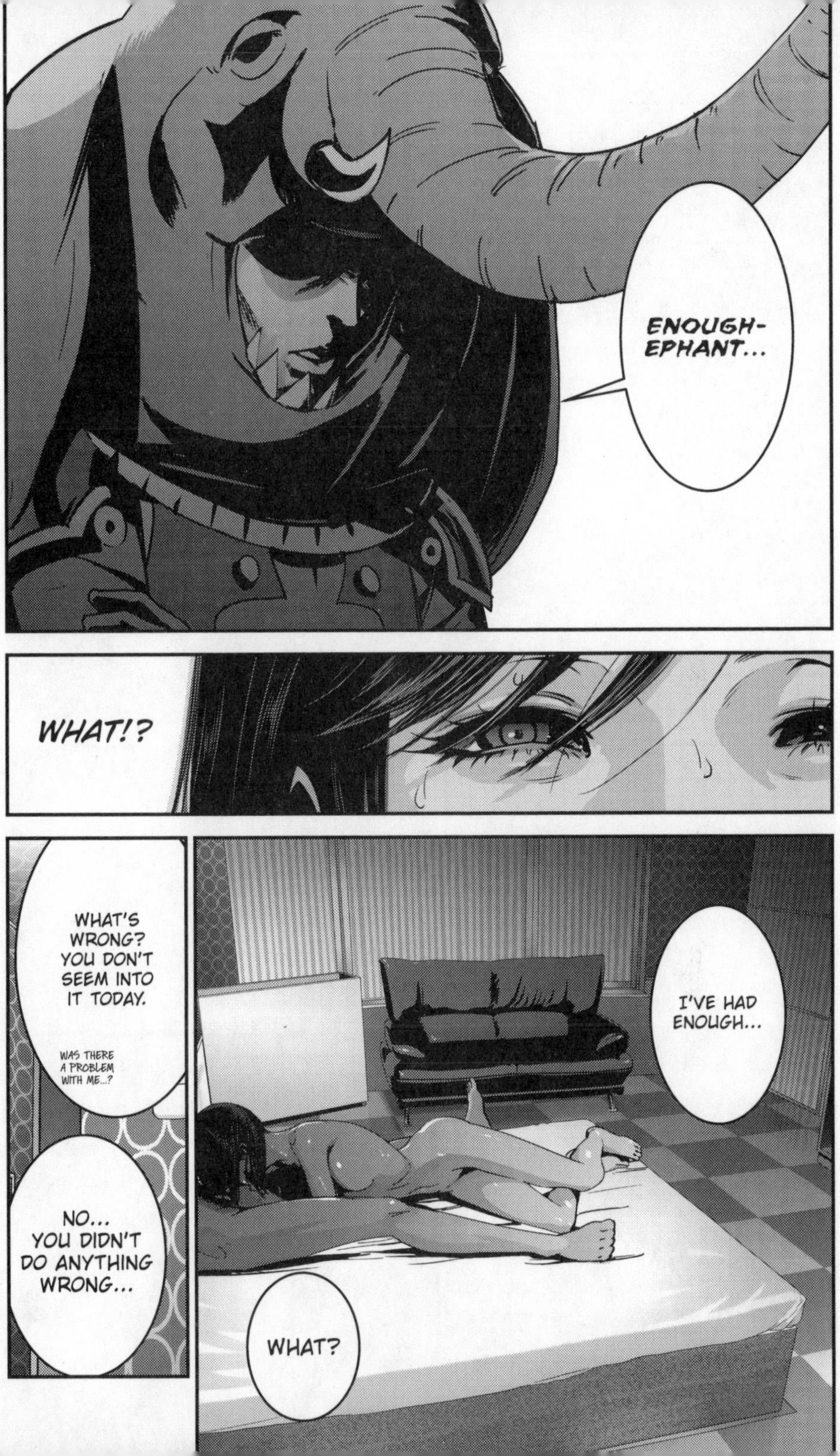
ENOUGH-EPHANT...
WHAT!?
I'VE HAD ENOUGH...
WHAT?
WHAT'S WRONG? YOU DON'T SEEM INTO IT TODAY.
WAS THERE A PROBLEM WITH ME...?
NO... YOU DIDN'T DO ANYTHING WRONG...

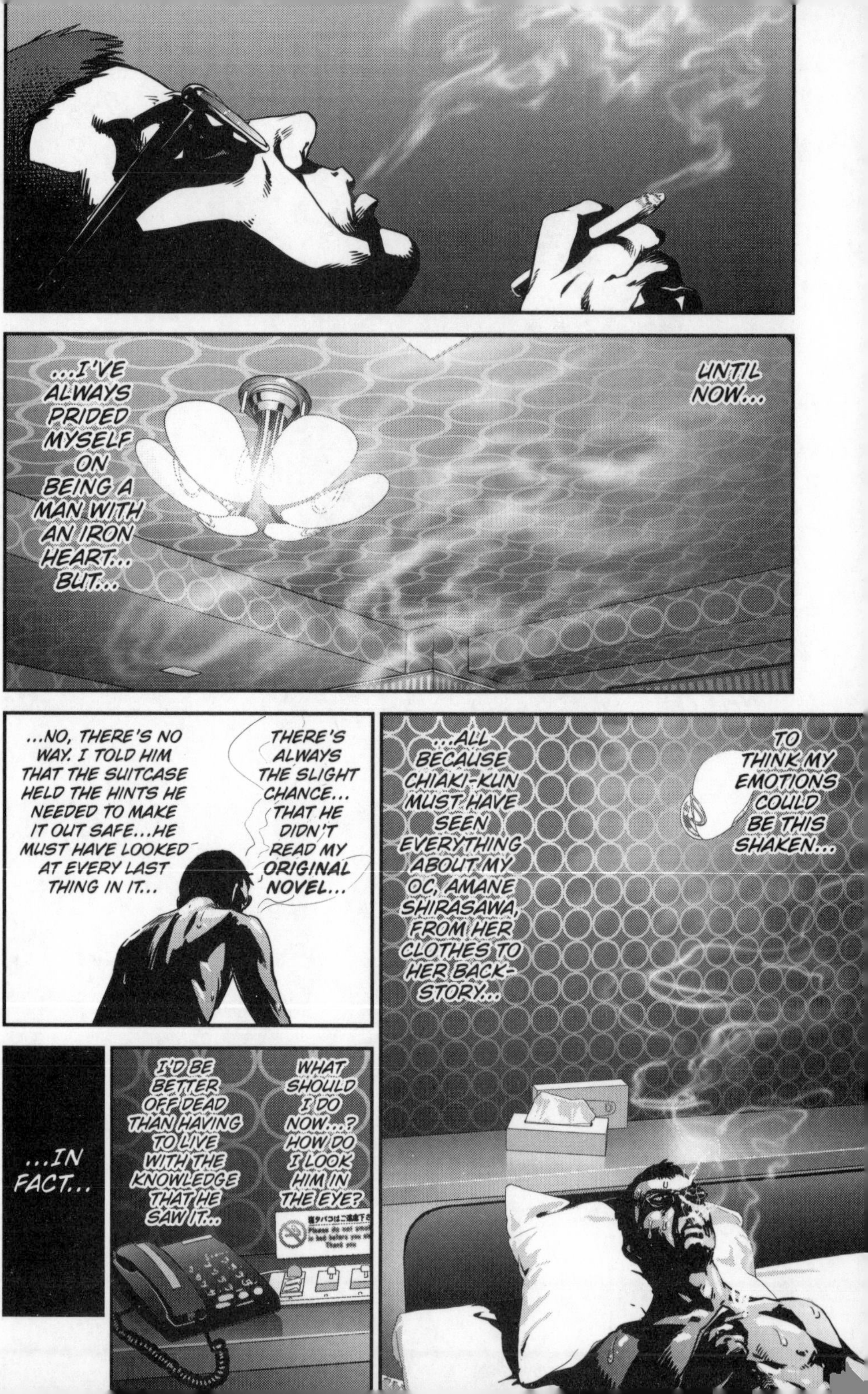
UNTIL NOW...
...I'VE ALWAYS PRIDED MYSELF ON BEING A MAN WITH AN IRON HEART... BUT...
TO THINK MY EMOTIONS COULD BE THIS SHAKEN...
...ALL BECAUSE CHIAKI-KUN MUST HAVE SEEN EVERYTHING ABOUT MY OC, AMANE SHIRASAWA, FROM HER CLOTHES TO HER BACK-STORY...
THERE'S ALWAYS THE SLIGHT CHANCE... THAT HE DIDN'T READ MY ORIGINAL NOVEL...
...NO, THERE'S NO WAY. I TOLD HIM THAT THE SUITCASE HELD THE HINTS HE NEEDED TO MAKE IT OUT SAFE...HE MUST HAVE LOOKED AT EVERY LAST THING IN IT...
WHAT SHOULD I DO NOW...? HOW DO I LOOK HIM IN THE EYE?
I'D BE BETTER OFF DEAD THAN HAVING TO LIVE WITH THE KNOWLEDGE THAT HE SAW IT...
...IN FACT...

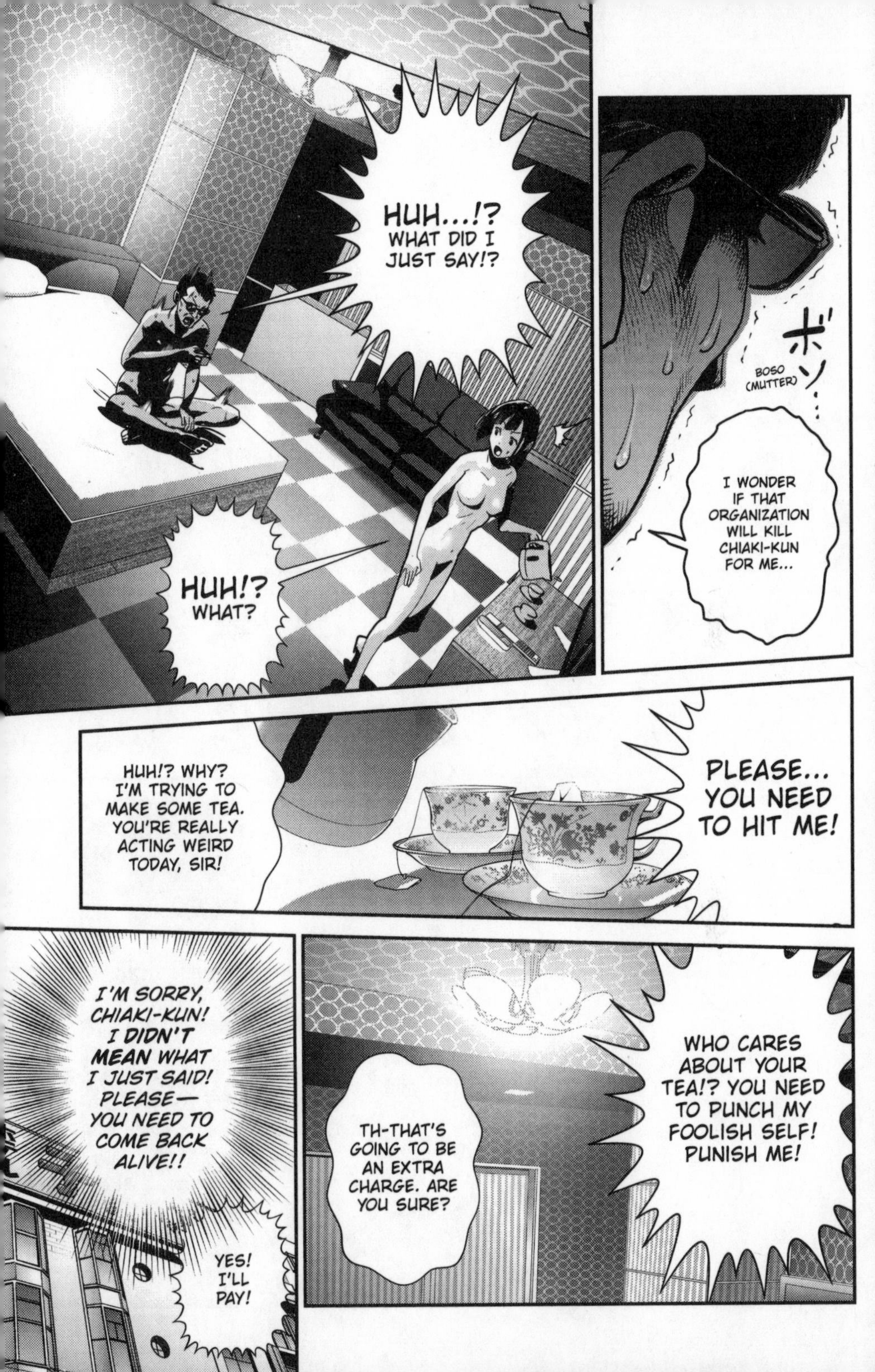
ボソ
BOSO (MUTTER)
I WONDER IF THAT ORGANIZATION WILL KILL CHIAKI-KUN FOR ME...
HUH...!? WHAT DID I JUST SAY!?
HUH!? WHAT?
PLEASE... YOU NEED TO HIT ME!
HUH!? WHY? I'M TRYING TO MAKE SOME TEA. YOU'RE REALLY ACTING WEIRD TODAY, SIR!
WHO CARES ABOUT YOUR TEA!? YOU NEED TO PUNCH MY FOOLISH SELF! PUNISH ME!
TH-THAT'S GOING TO BE AN EXTRA CHARGE. ARE YOU SURE?
I'M SORRY, CHIAKI-KUN! I DIDN'T MEAN WHAT I JUST SAID! PLEASE—YOU NEED TO COME BACK ALIVE!!
YES! I'LL PAY!

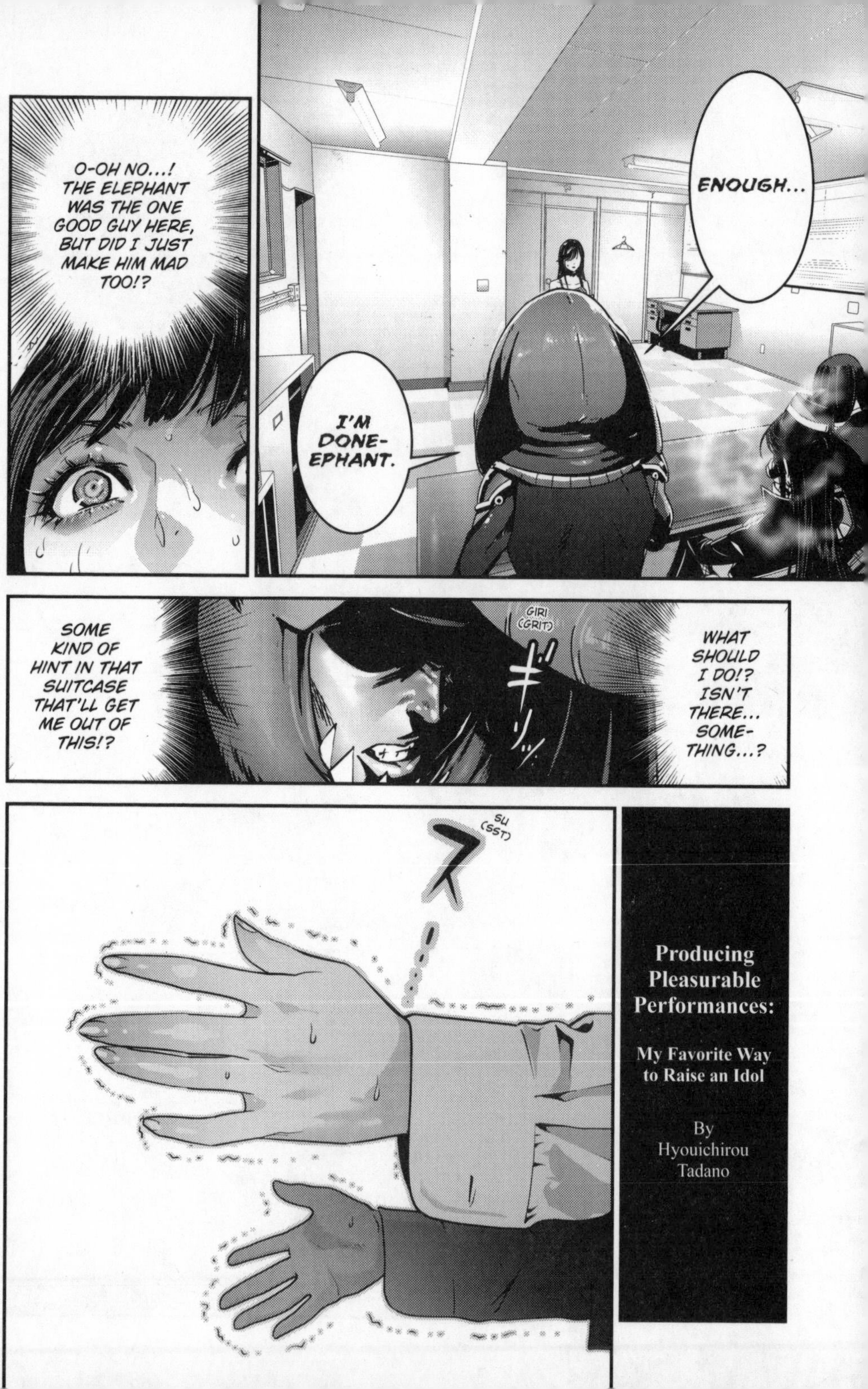
ENOUGH...
I'M DONE-EPHANT.
O-OH NO...! THE ELEPHANT WAS THE ONE GOOD GUY HERE, BUT DID I JUST MAKE HIM MAD TOO!?
GIRI (GRIT)
WHAT SHOULD I DO!? ISN'T THERE... SOME-THING...?
SOME KIND OF HINT IN THAT SUITCASE THAT'LL GET ME OUT OF THIS!?
Producing Pleasurable Performances:
My Favorite Way to Raise an Idol
By Hyouichirou Tadano
SU (SST)

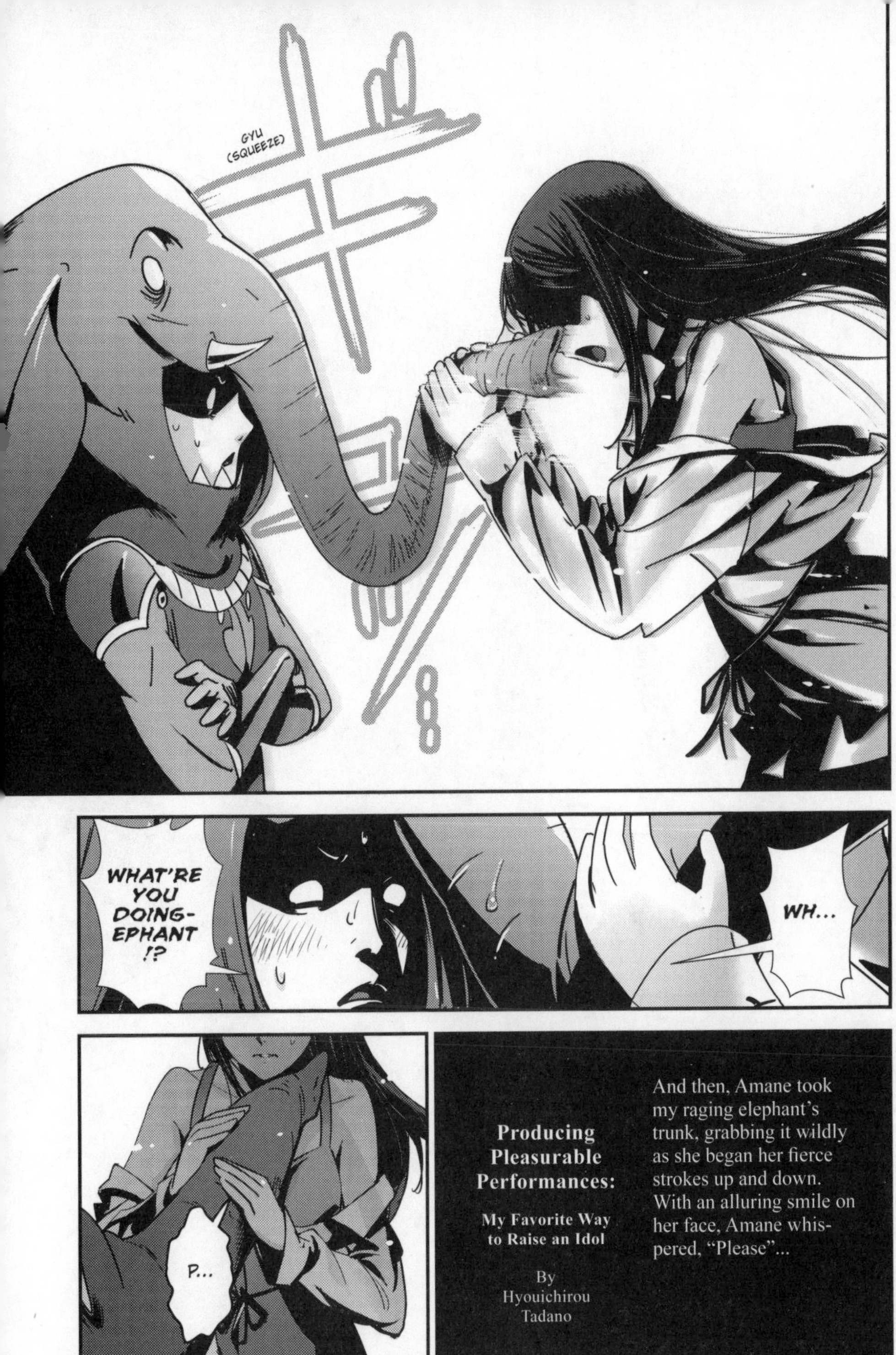
GYU (SQUEEZE)
WH...
WHAT'RE YOU DOING-EPHANT !?
Producing Pleasurable Performances:
My Favorite Way to Raise an Idol
By Hyouichirou Tadano
And then, Amane took my raging elephant's trunk, grabbing it wildly as she began her fierce strokes up and down. With an alluring smile on her face, Amane whispered, "Please"...
P...

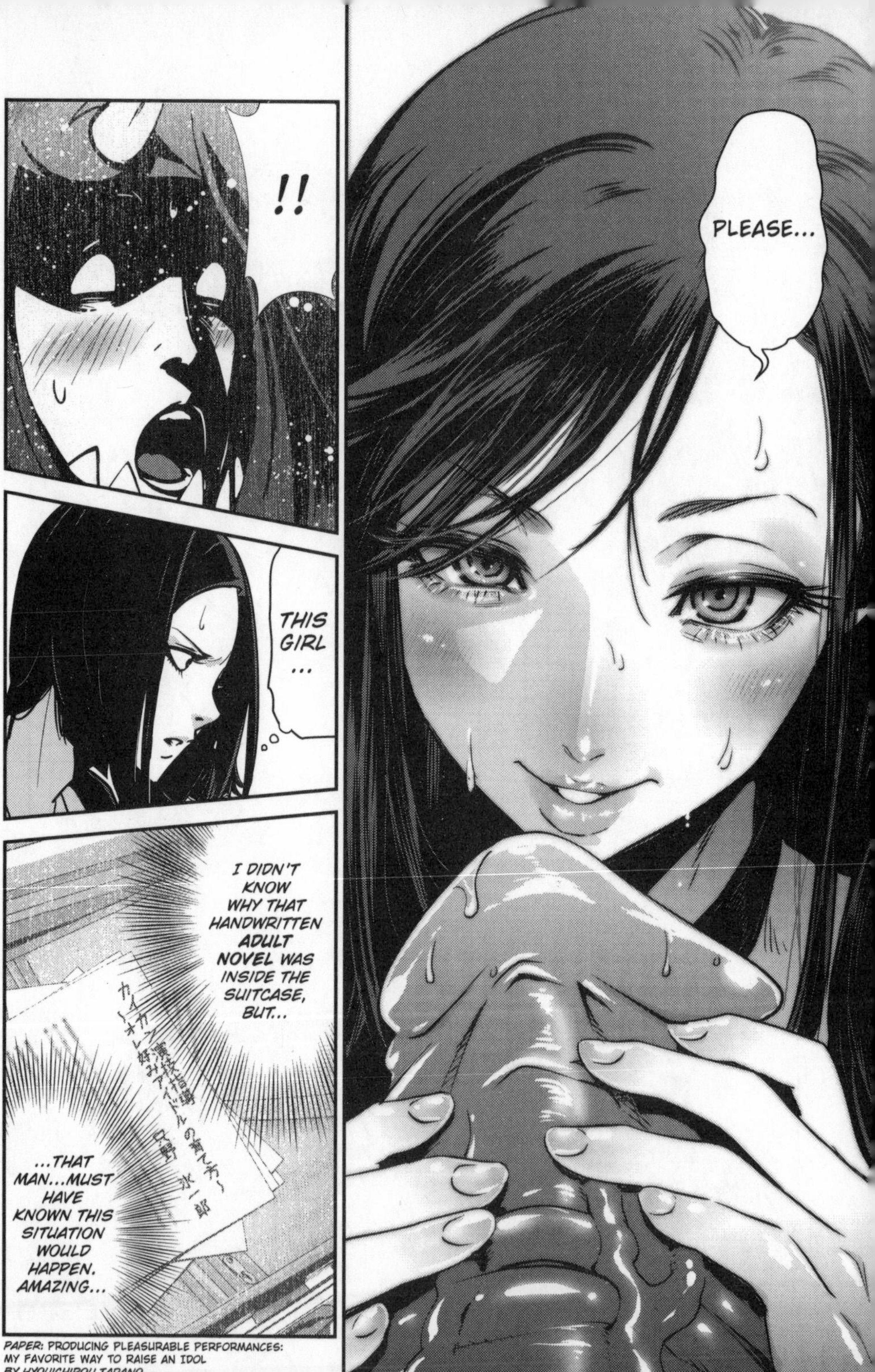
PLEASE...
!!
THIS GIRL ...
I DIDN'T KNOW WHY THAT HANDWRITTEN ADULT NOVEL WAS INSIDE THE SUITCASE, BUT...
カイカン演技指導
〜オレ好みアイドルの育て方〜
只野 氷一郎
...THAT MAN...MUST HAVE KNOWN THIS SITUATION WOULD HAPPEN. AMAZING...

PAPER: PRODUCING PLEASURABLE PERFORMANCES: MY FAVORITE WAY TO RAISE AN IDOL BY HYOUICHIROU TADANO

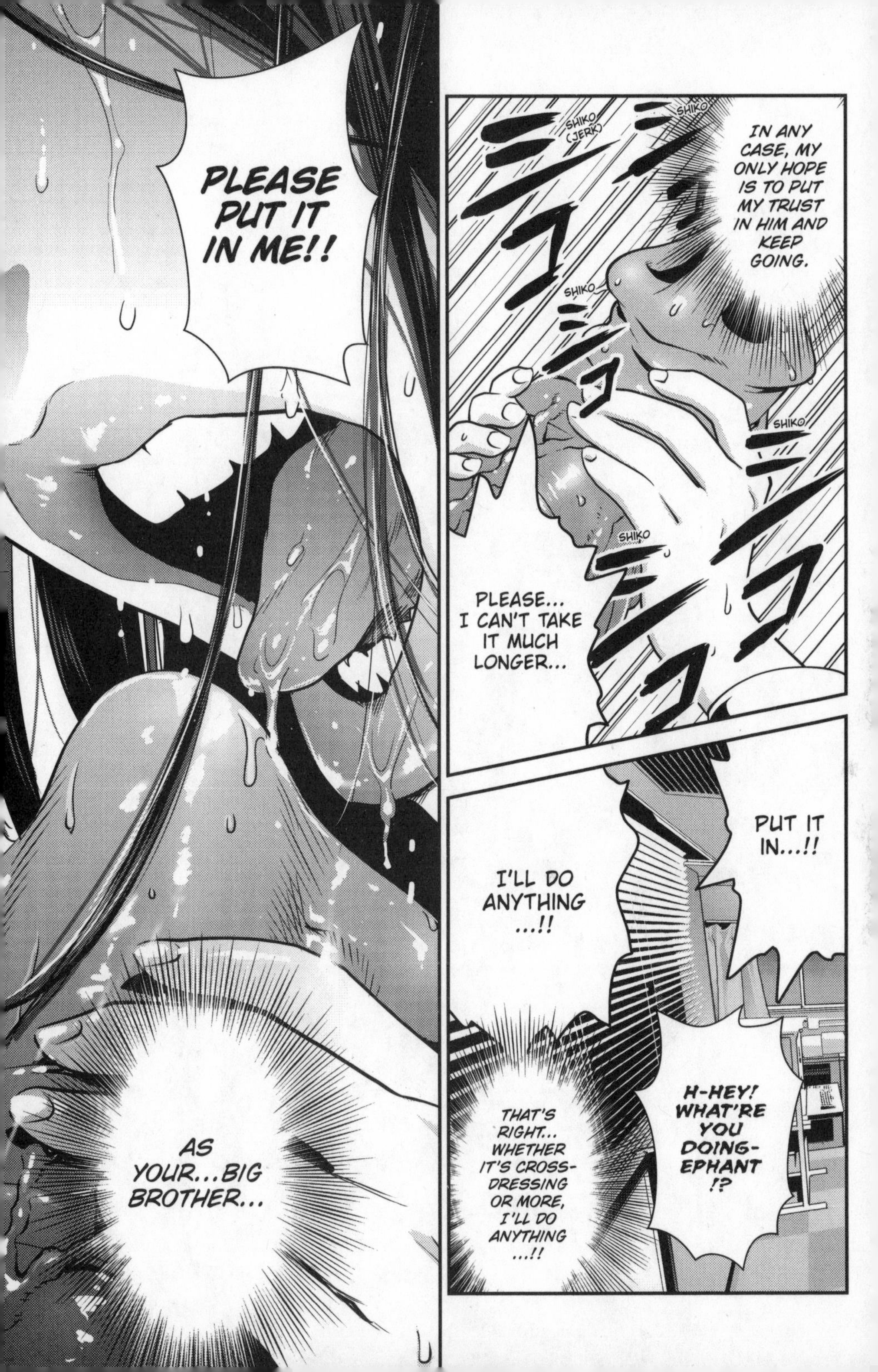
SHIKO
SHIKO (JERK)
IN ANY CASE, MY ONLY HOPE IS TO PUT MY TRUST IN HIM AND KEEP GOING.
SHIKO
SHIKO
SHIKO
PLEASE... I CAN'T TAKE IT MUCH LONGER...
PUT IT IN...!!
I'LL DO ANYTHING ...!!
H-HEY! WHAT'RE YOU DOING-EPHANT !?
THAT'S RIGHT... WHETHER IT'S CROSS-DRESSING OR MORE, I'LL DO ANYTHING ...!!
PLEASE PUT IT IN ME!!
AS YOUR...BIG BROTHER...

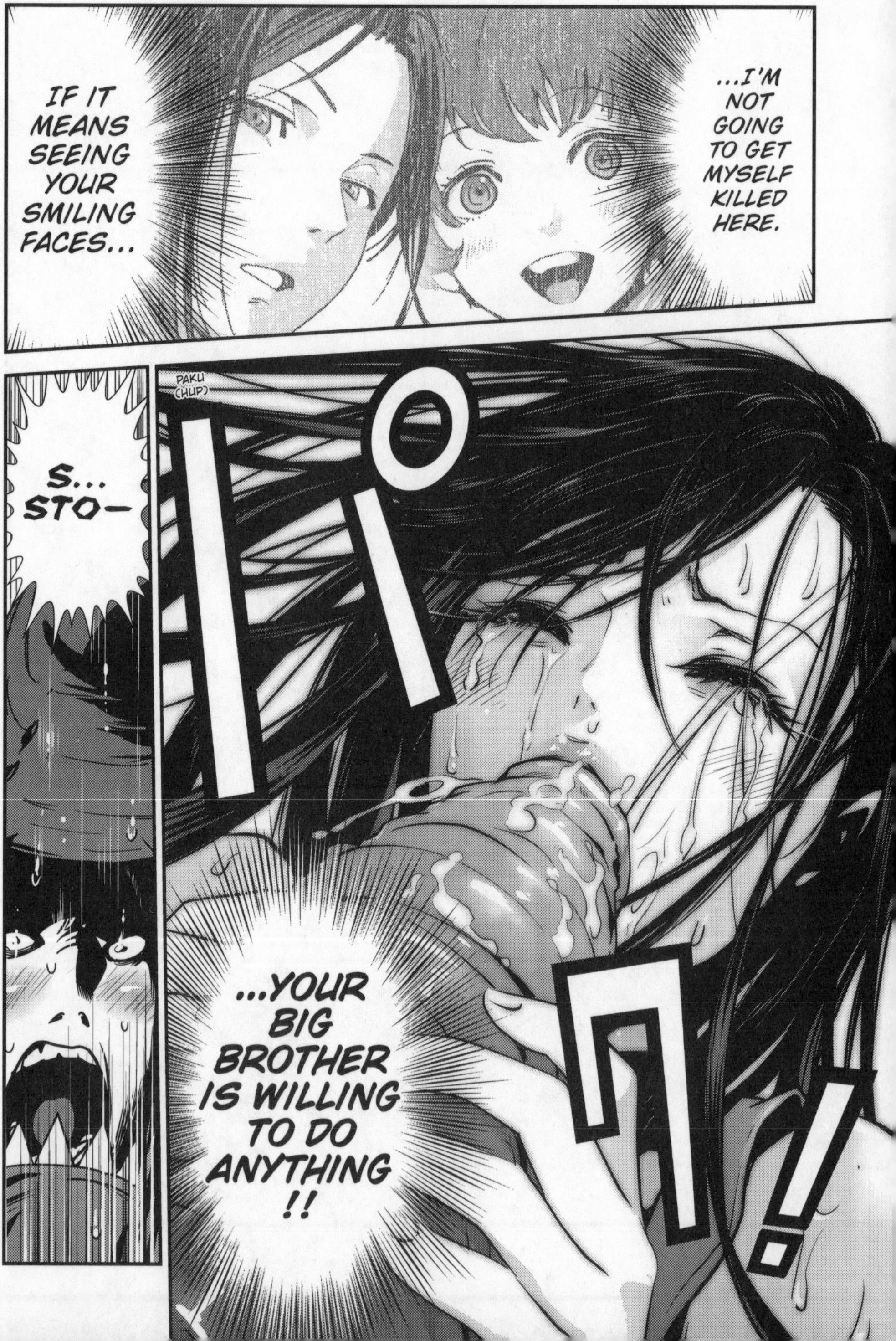
...I'M NOT GOING TO GET MYSELF KILLED HERE.
IF IT MEANS SEEING YOUR SMILING FACES...
PAKU (HUP)
...YOUR BIG BROTHER IS WILLING TO DO ANYTHING!!
S... STO—

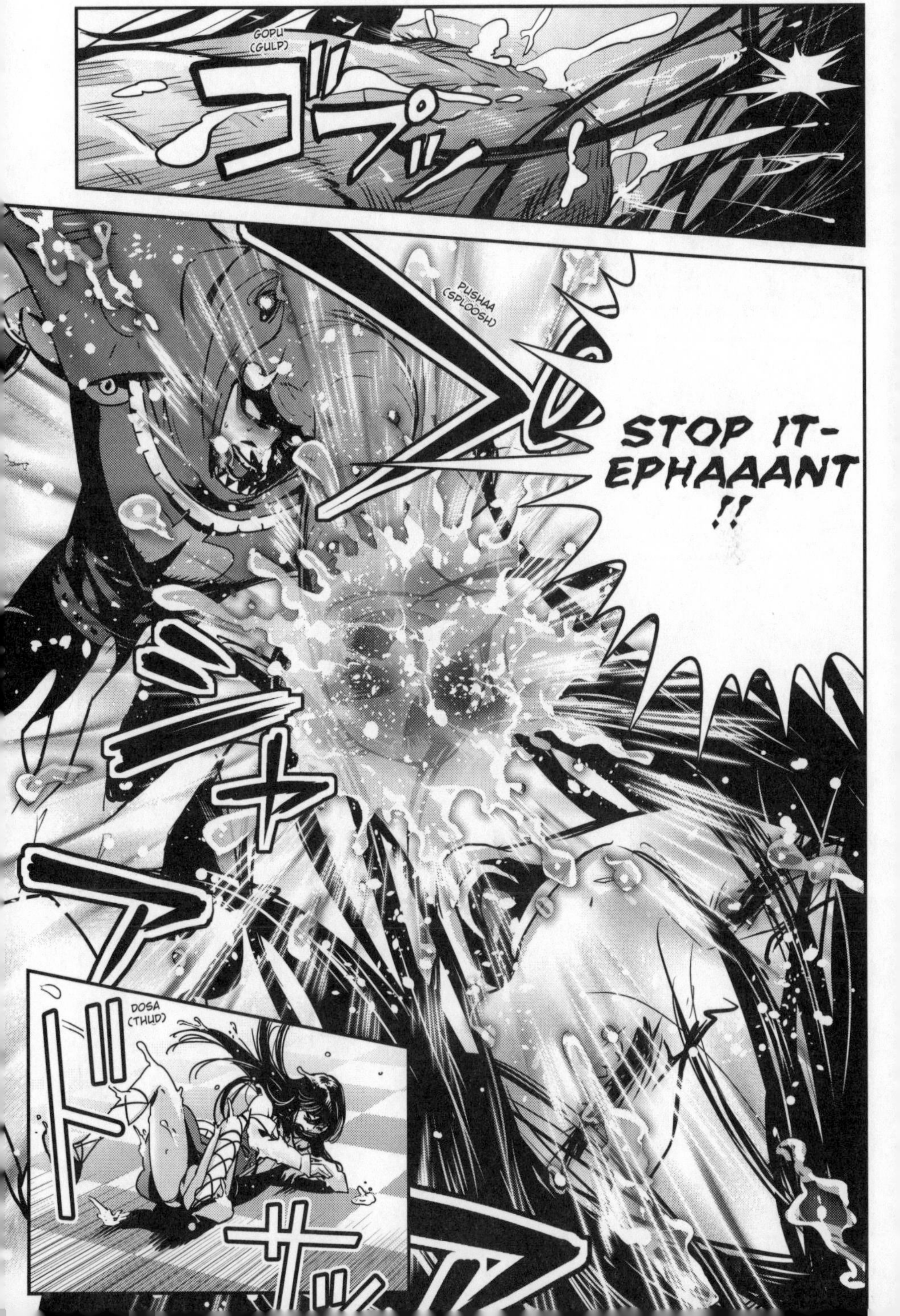
GOPU
(GULP)
PUSHAA
(SPLOOSH)
STOP IT-
EPHAAANT
!!
DOSA
(THUD)

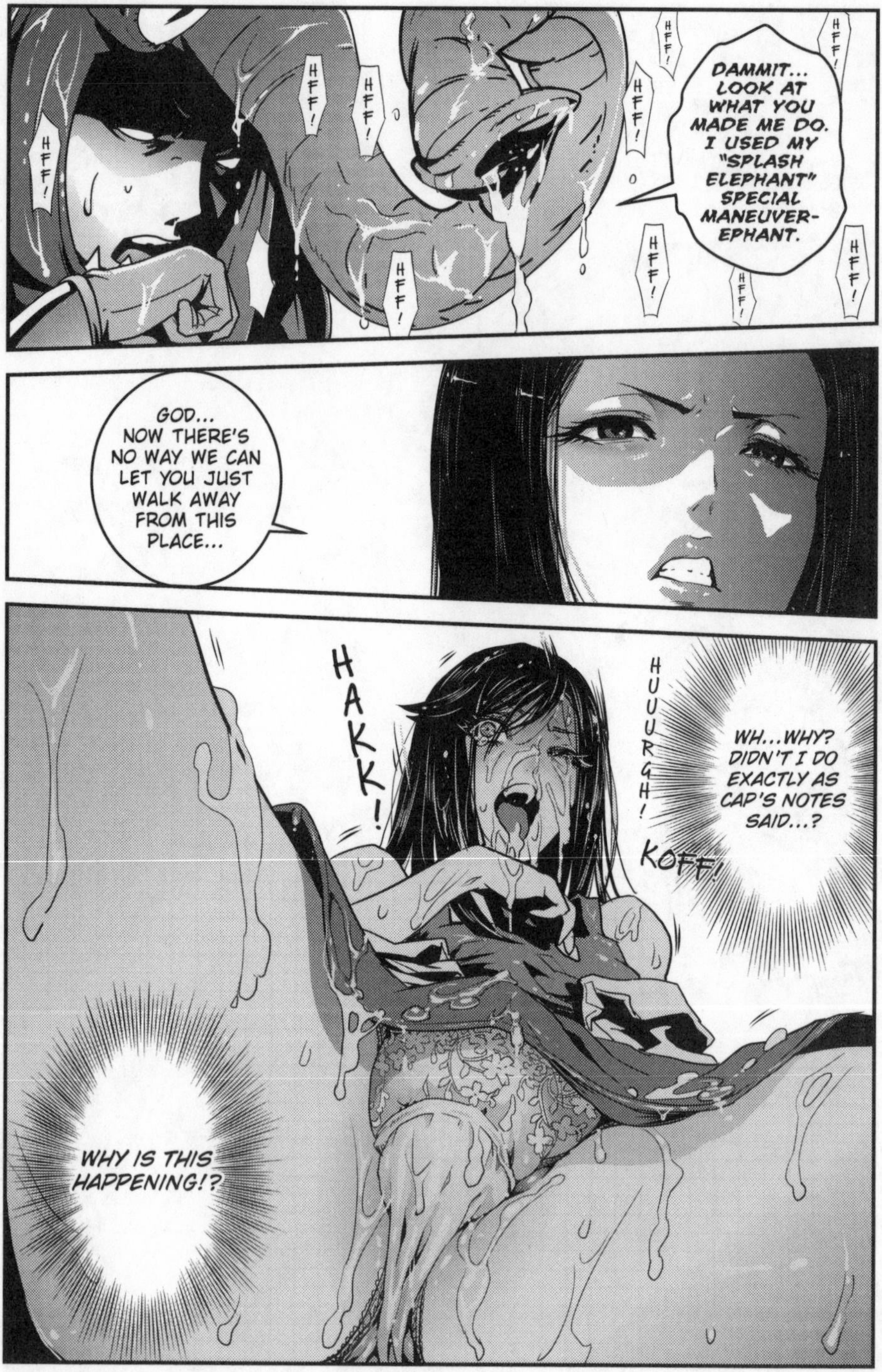
HFF!
HFF!
HFF!
DAMMIT... LOOK AT WHAT YOU MADE ME DO. I USED MY "SPLASH ELEPHANT" SPECIAL MANEUVER-EPHANT.
HFF!
HFF!
HFF!
HFF!
HFF!
HFF!
HFF!
HFF!
GOD... NOW THERE'S NO WAY WE CAN LET YOU JUST WALK AWAY FROM THIS PLACE...
WH...WHY? DIDN'T I DO EXACTLY AS CAP'S NOTES SAID...?
HUUURGH!
KOFF!
HAKK!
WHY IS THIS HAPPENING!?

Chapter 4: End

Chapter 5: After Interview

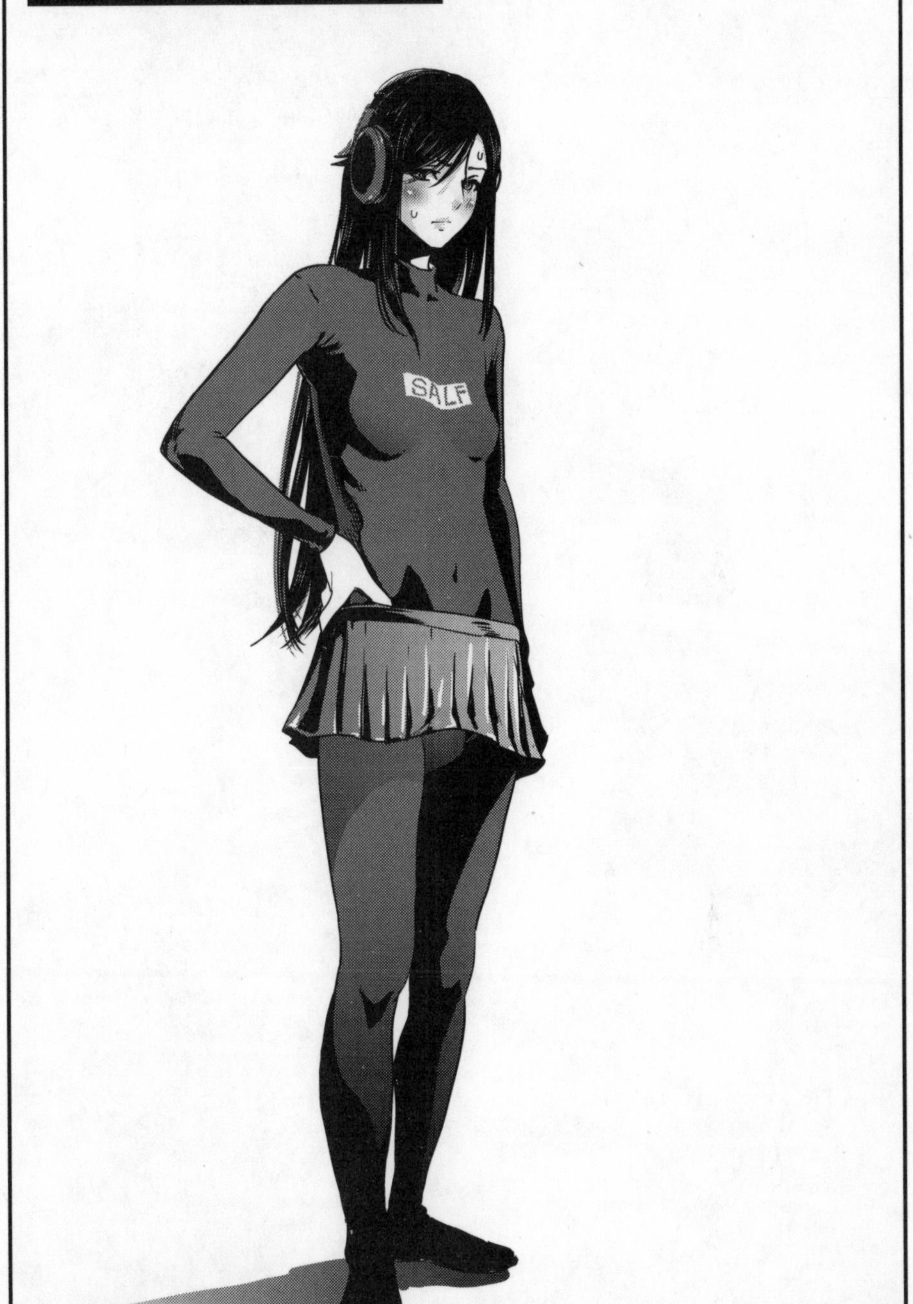

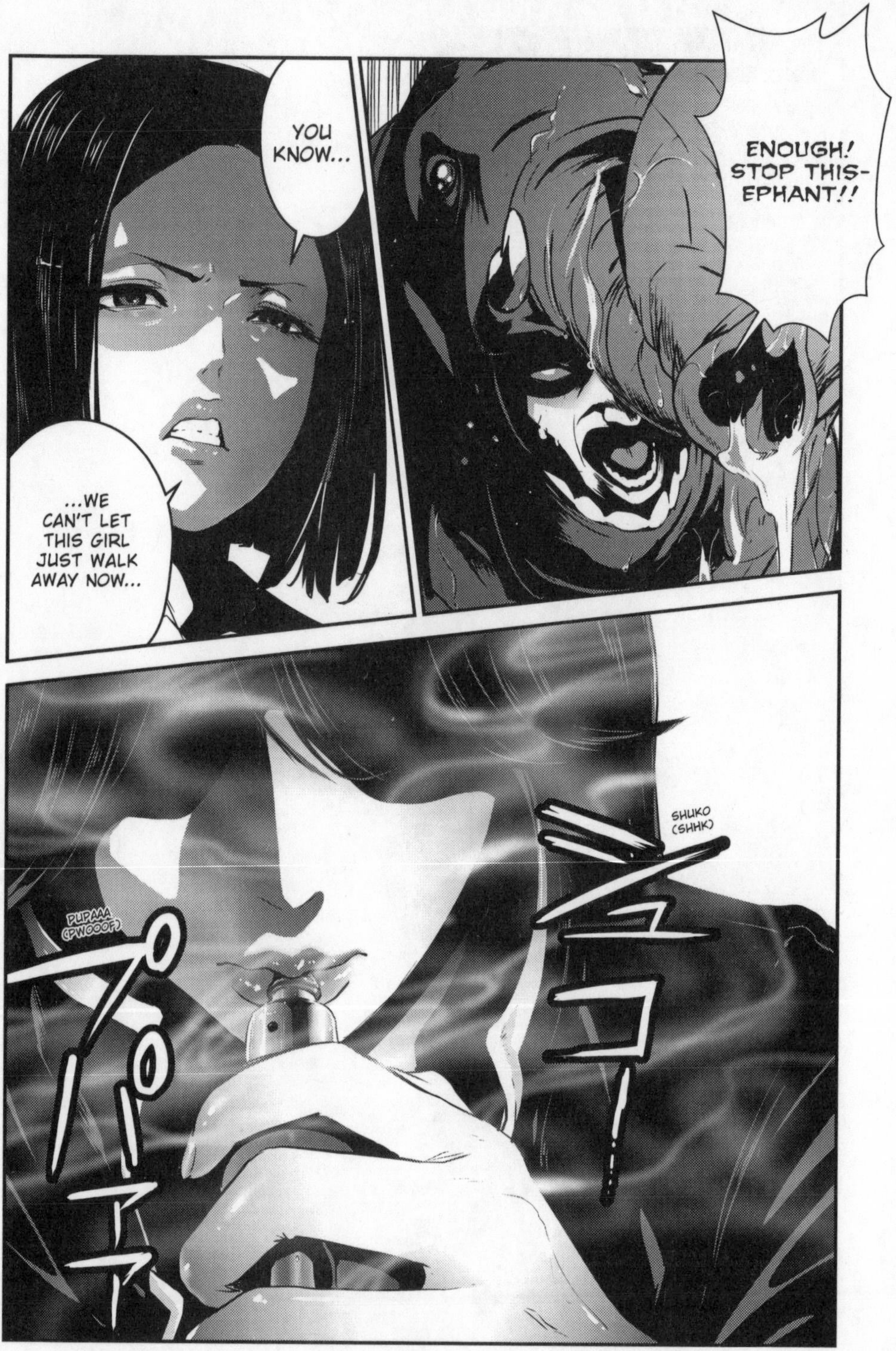
ENOUGH! STOP THIS-EPHANT!!
YOU KNOW...
...WE CAN'T LET THIS GIRL JUST WALK AWAY NOW...
SHUKO (SHHK)
PUPAAA (PWOOOF)

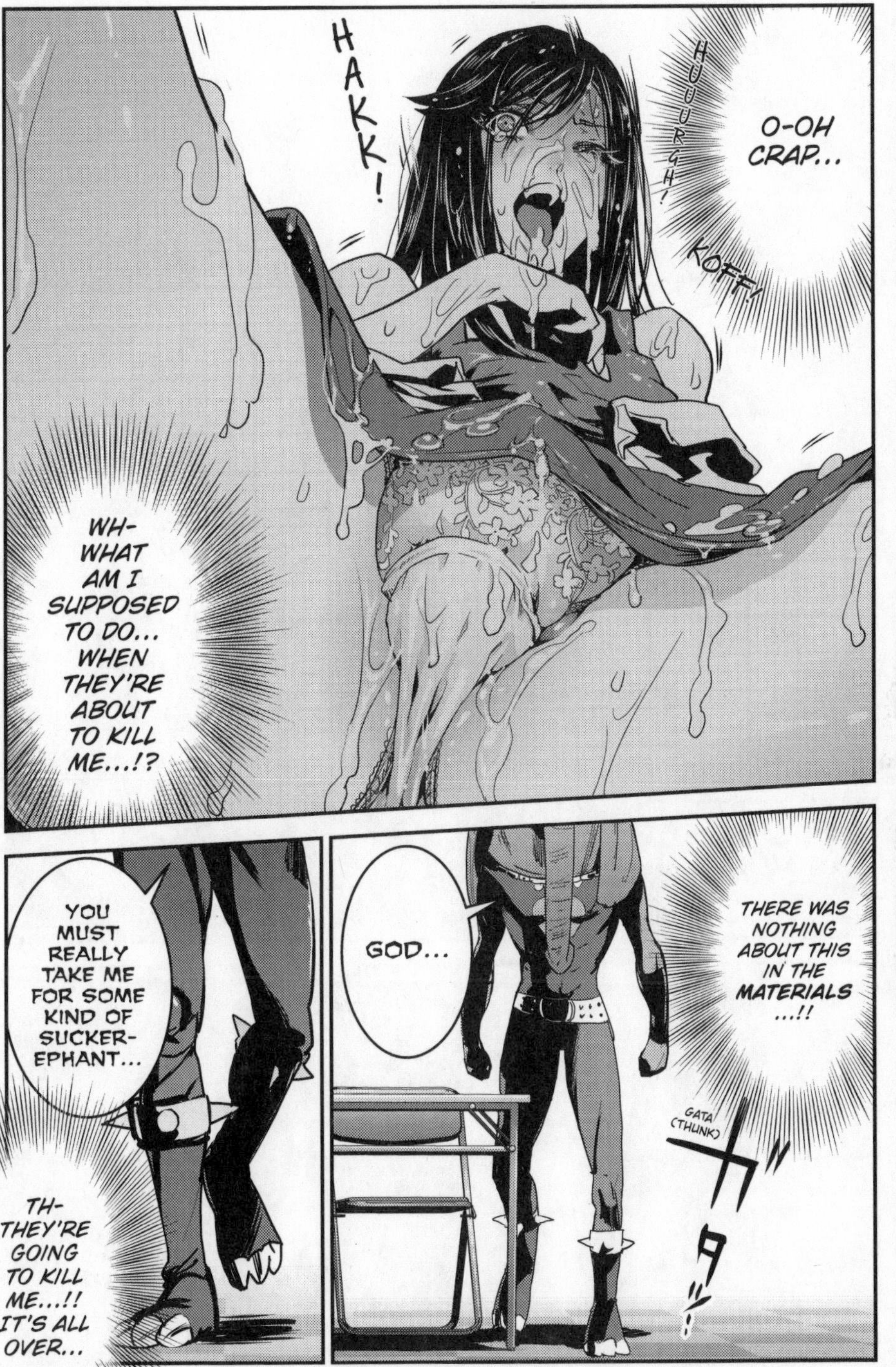
O-OH CRAP...
HUUUURGH!
HAKK!
KOFF!
WH-WHAT AM I SUPPOSED TO DO... WHEN THEY'RE ABOUT TO KILL ME...!?
THERE WAS NOTHING ABOUT THIS IN THE MATERIALS ...!!
GOD...
GATA (THUNK)
YOU MUST REALLY TAKE ME FOR SOME KIND OF SUCKER-EPHANT...
TH-THEY'RE GOING TO KILL ME...!! IT'S ALL OVER...

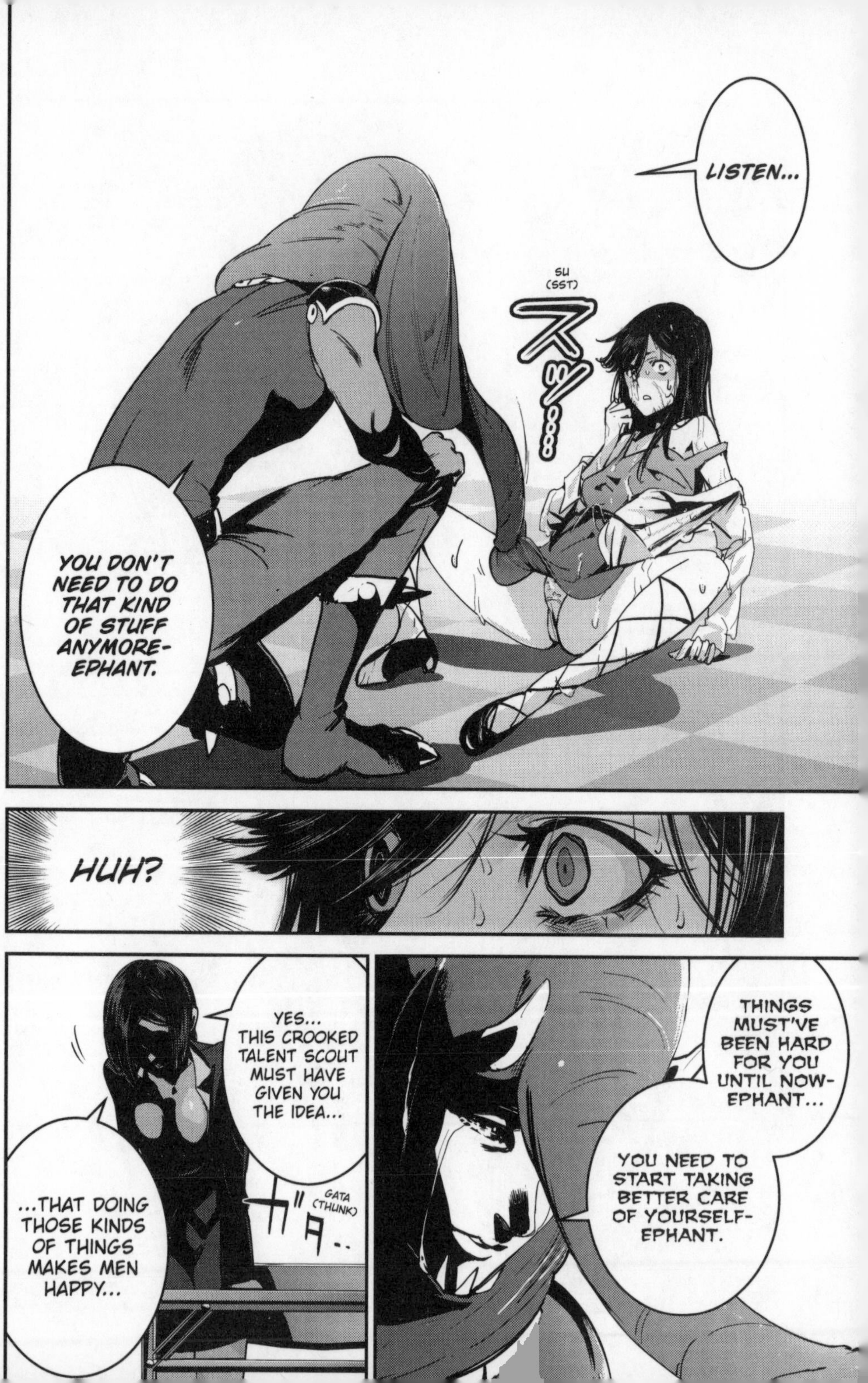
LISTEN...
SU (SST)
YOU DON'T NEED TO DO THAT KIND OF STUFF ANYMORE-EPHANT.
HUH?
THINGS MUST'VE BEEN HARD FOR YOU UNTIL NOW-EPHANT...
YOU NEED TO START TAKING BETTER CARE OF YOURSELF-EPHANT.
YES... THIS CROOKED TALENT SCOUT MUST HAVE GIVEN YOU THE IDEA...
GATA (THUNK)
...THAT DOING THOSE KINDS OF THINGS MAKES MEN HAPPY...

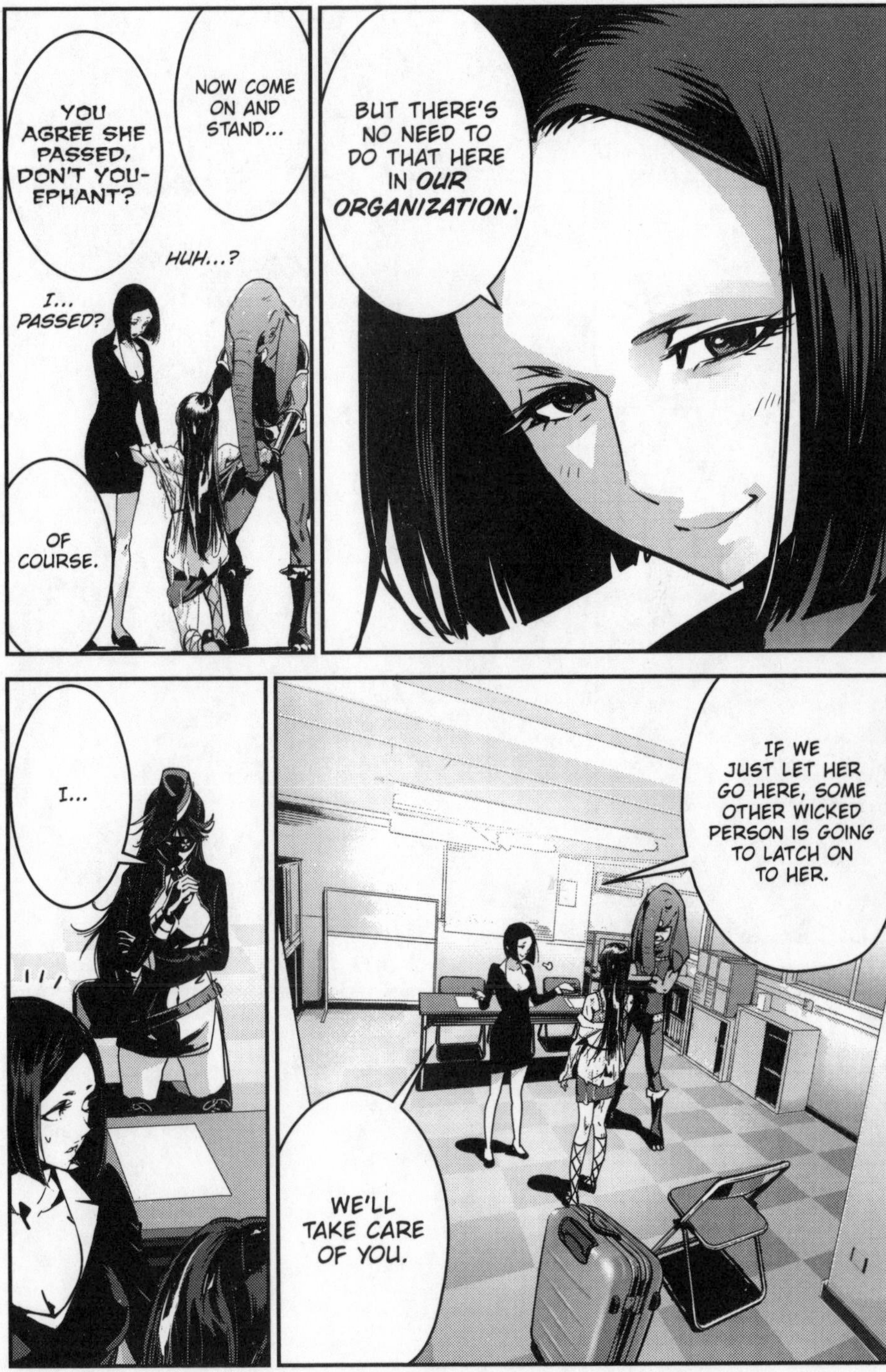
BUT THERE'S NO NEED TO DO THAT HERE IN OUR ORGANIZATION.
NOW COME ON AND STAND...
YOU AGREE SHE PASSED, DON'T YOU-EPHANT?
HUH...?
I... PASSED?
OF COURSE.
IF WE JUST LET HER GO HERE, SOME OTHER WICKED PERSON IS GOING TO LATCH ON TO HER.
WE'LL TAKE CARE OF YOU.
I...

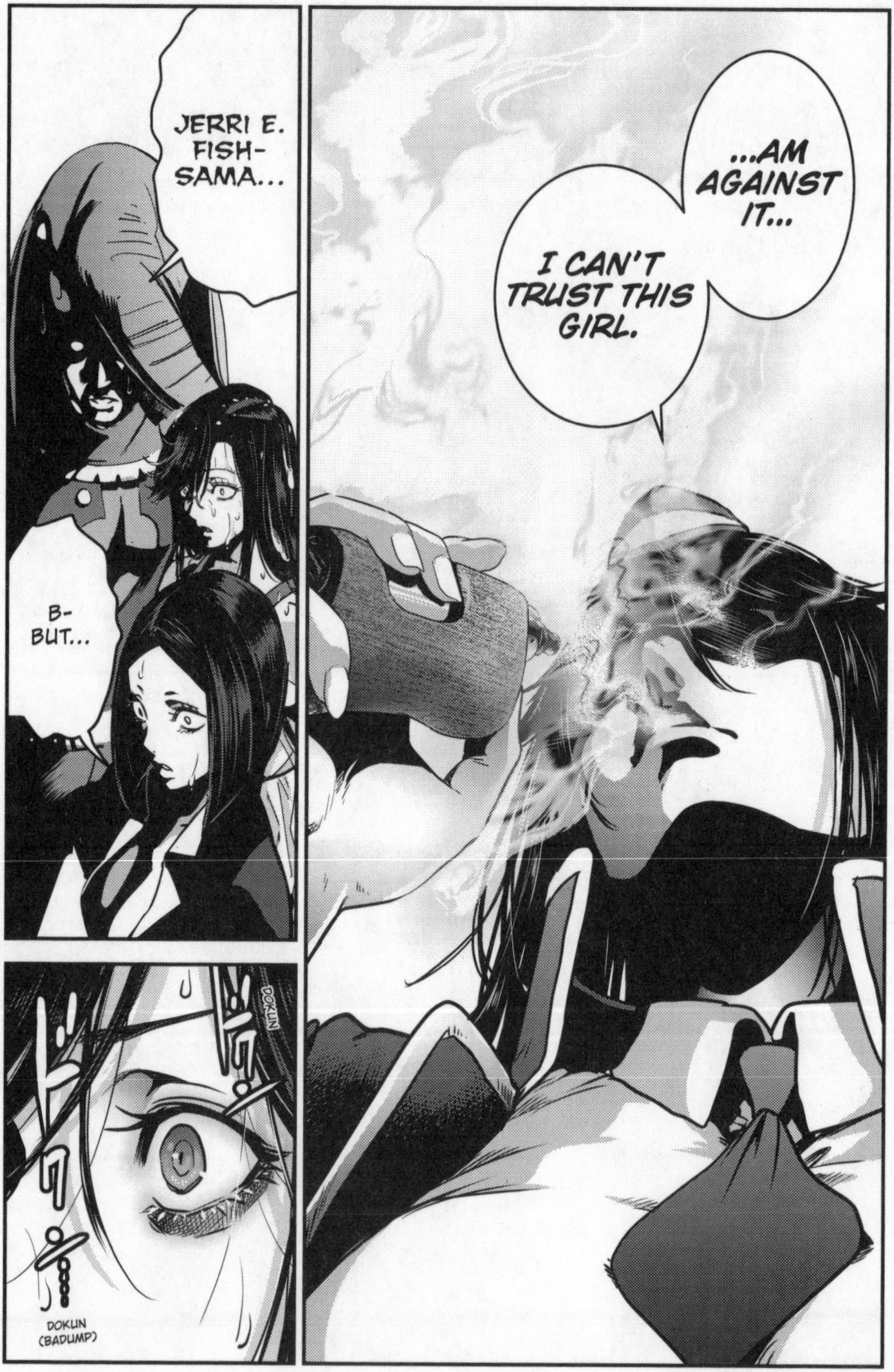
...AM AGAINST IT...
I CAN'T TRUST THIS GIRL.
JERRI E. FISH-SAMA...
B-BUT...
DOKUN
DOKUN (BADUMP)

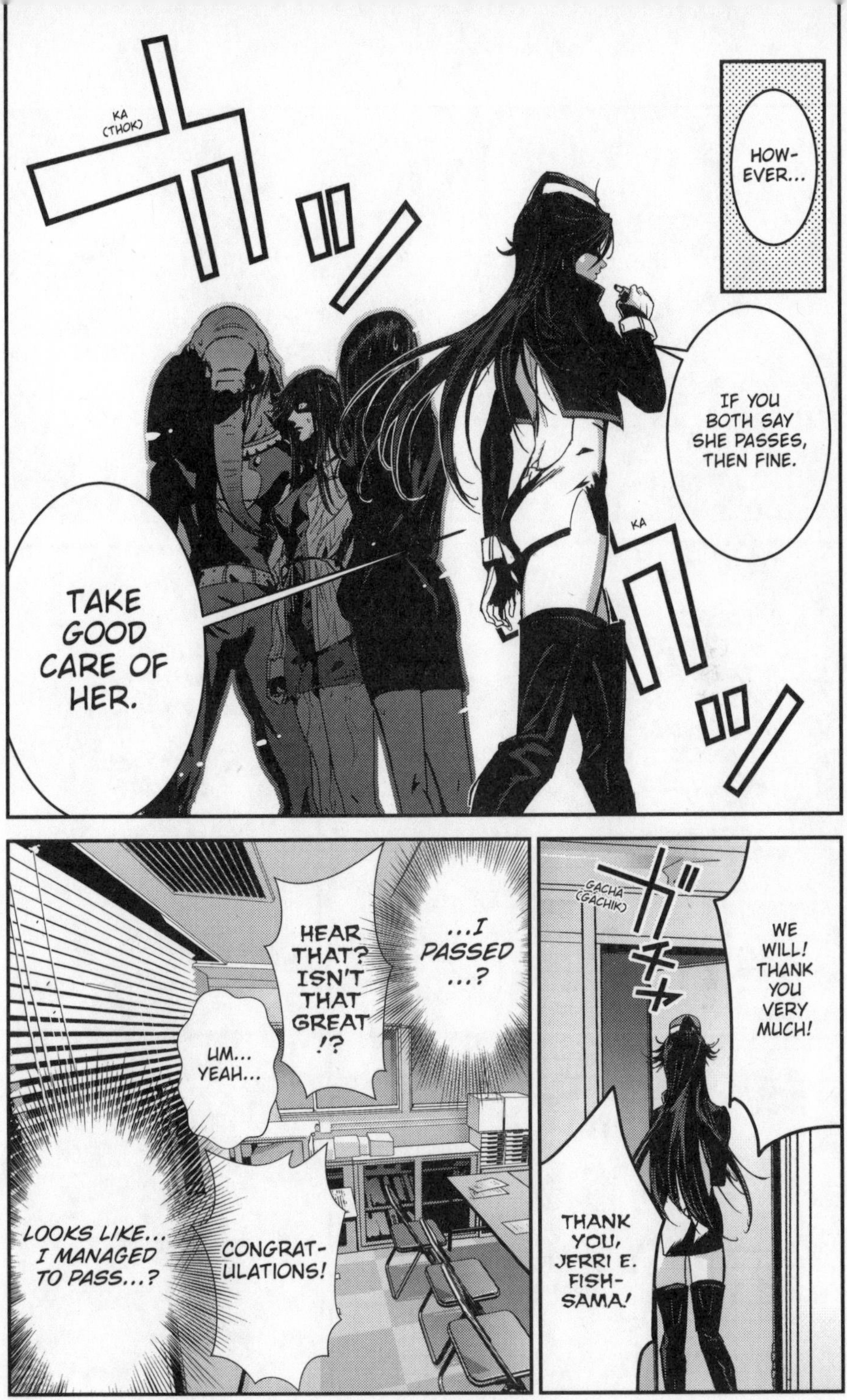
HOW-EVER...
IF YOU BOTH SAY SHE PASSES, THEN FINE.
KA
KA (THOK)
TAKE GOOD CARE OF HER.
GACHA (GACHIK)
WE WILL! THANK YOU VERY MUCH!
THANK YOU, JERRI E. FISH-SAMA!
...I PASSED...?
HEAR THAT? ISN'T THAT GREAT!?
UM... YEAH...
CONGRAT-ULATIONS!
LOOKS LIKE... I MANAGED TO PASS...?

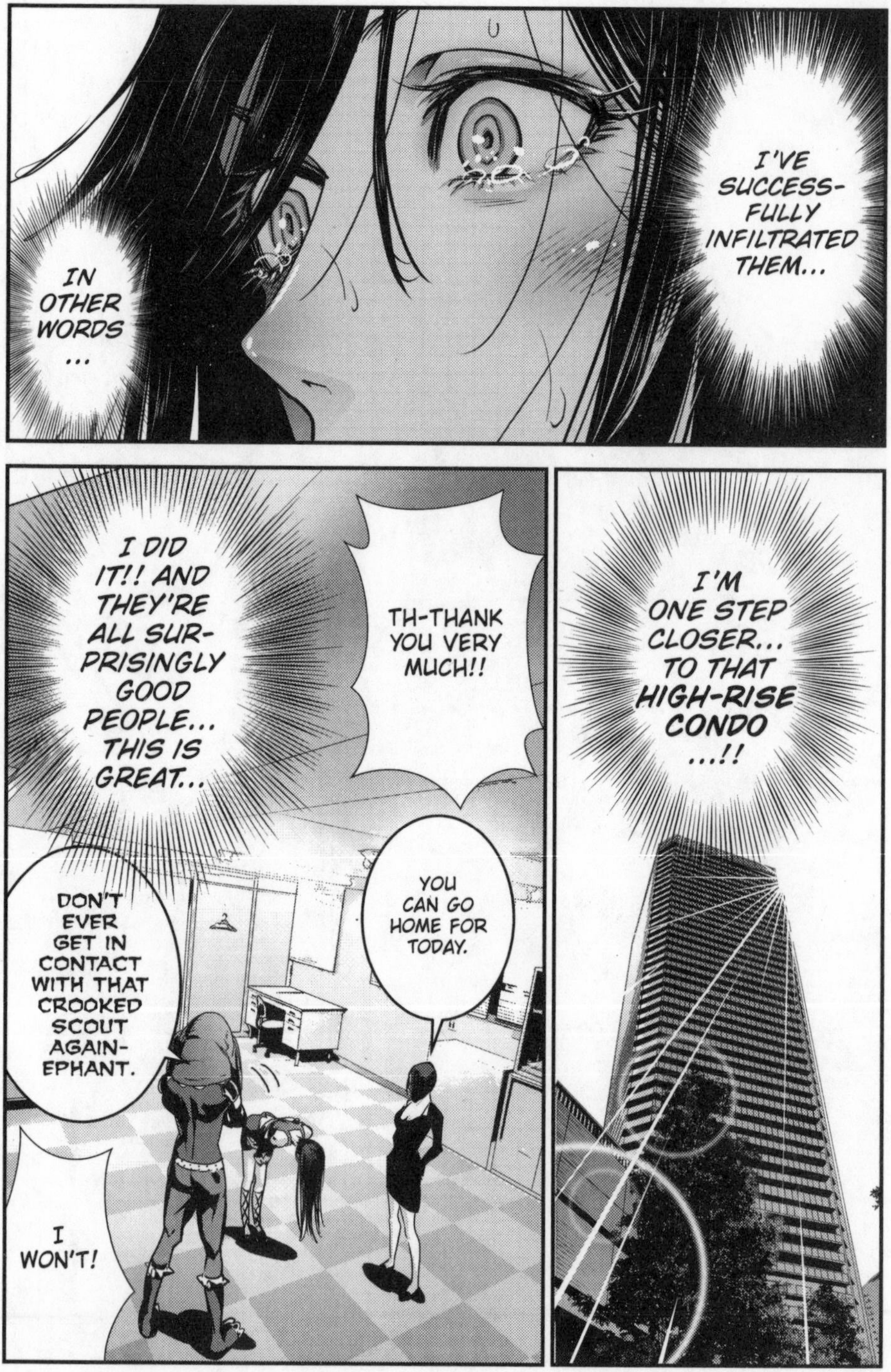
I'VE SUCCESS-FULLY INFILTRATED THEM...
IN OTHER WORDS...
I'M ONE STEP CLOSER... TO THAT HIGH-RISE CONDO...!!
TH-THANK YOU VERY MUCH!!
I DID IT!! AND THEY'RE ALL SUR-PRISINGLY GOOD PEOPLE... THIS IS GREAT...
YOU CAN GO HOME FOR TODAY.
DON'T EVER GET IN CONTACT WITH THAT CROOKED SCOUT AGAIN-EPHANT.
I WON'T!

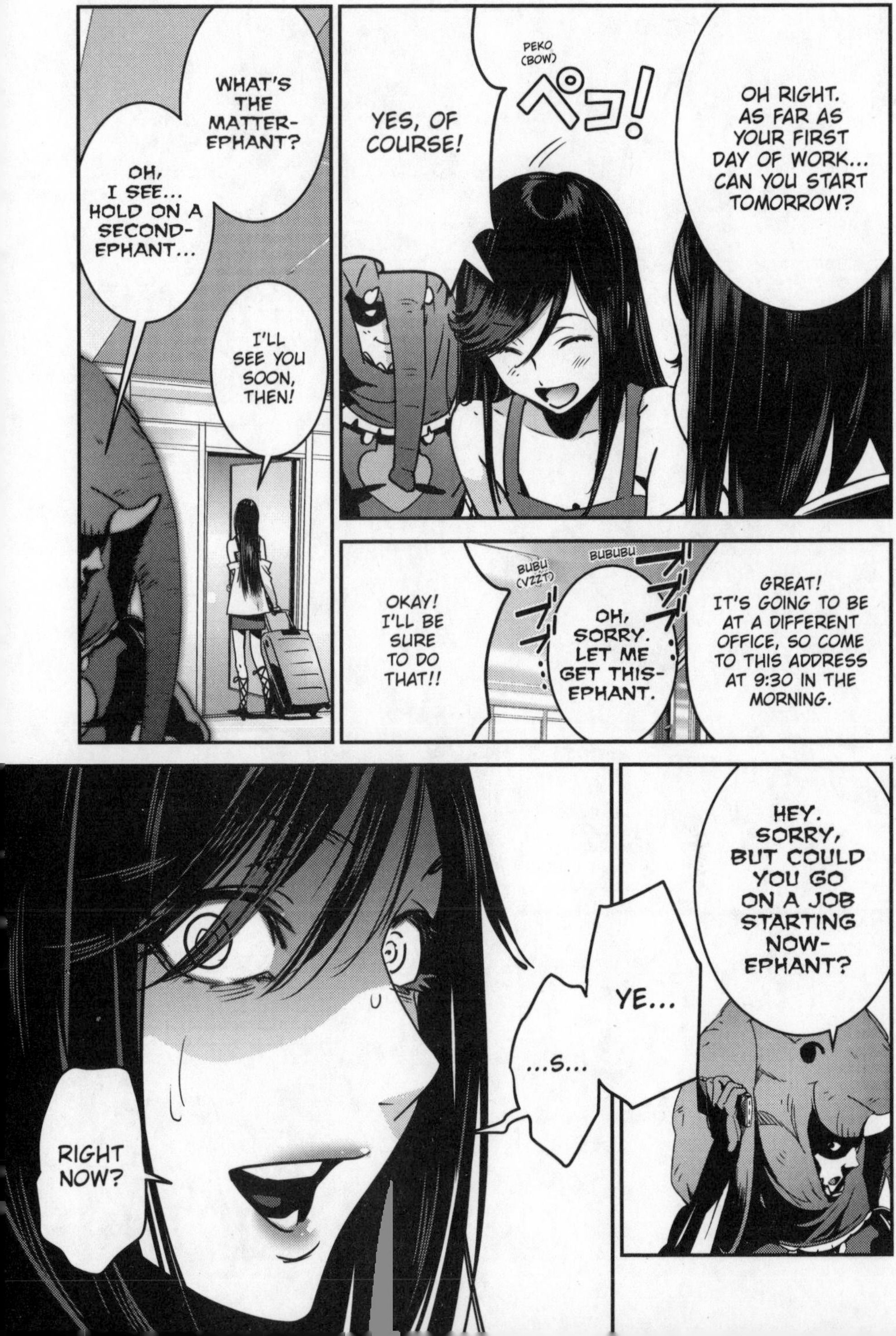
OH RIGHT. AS FAR AS YOUR FIRST DAY OF WORK... CAN YOU START TOMORROW?
PEKO (BOW)
YES, OF COURSE!
GREAT! IT'S GOING TO BE AT A DIFFERENT OFFICE, SO COME TO THIS ADDRESS AT 9:30 IN THE MORNING.
BUBUBU
OH, SORRY. LET ME GET THIS-EPHANT.
BUBU (VZZT)
OKAY! I'LL BE SURE TO DO THAT!!
WHAT'S THE MATTER-EPHANT?
OH, I SEE... HOLD ON A SECOND-EPHANT...
I'LL SEE YOU SOON, THEN!
HEY. SORRY, BUT COULD YOU GO ON A JOB STARTING NOW-EPHANT?
YE...
...S...
RIGHT NOW?

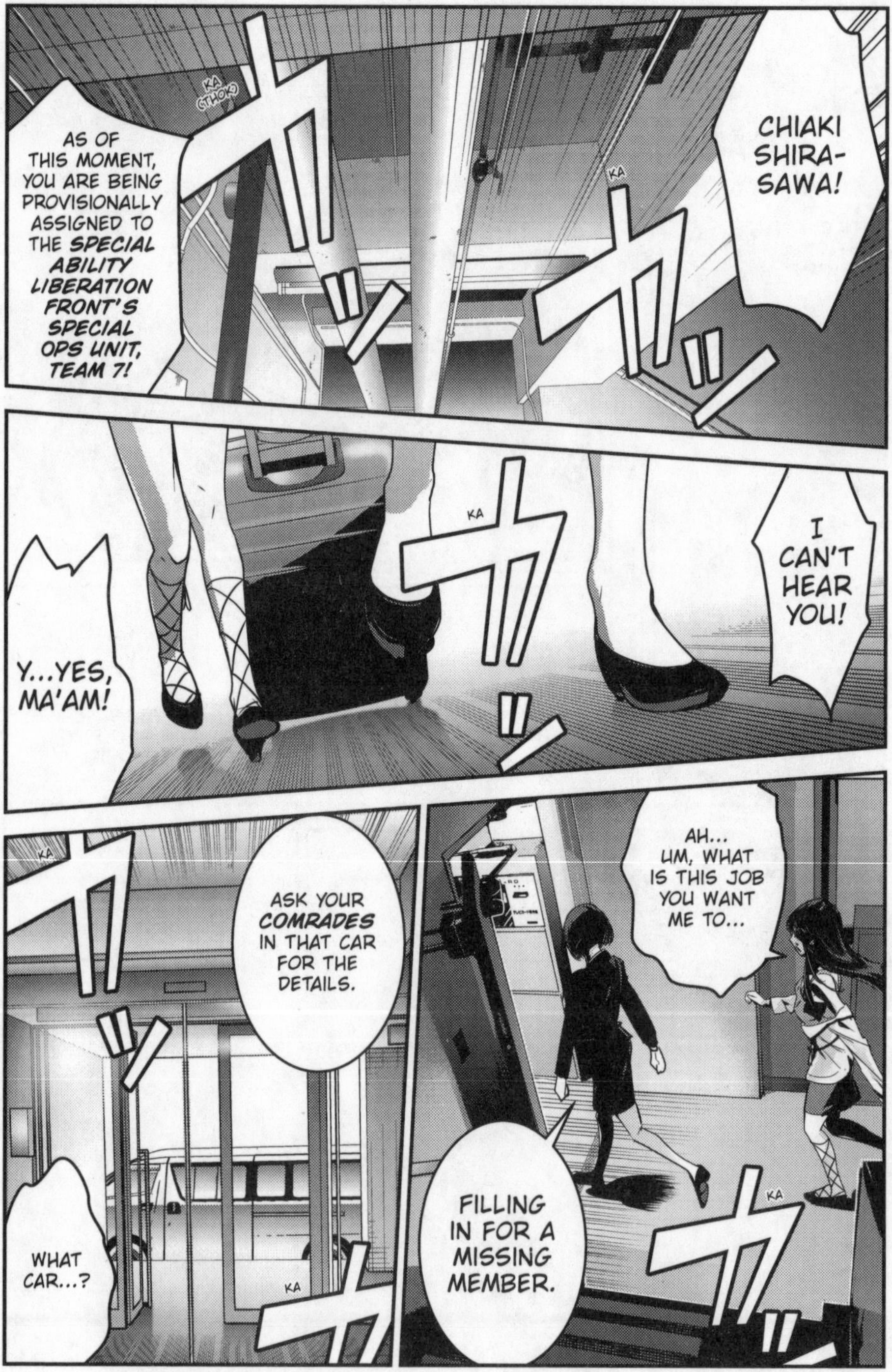
CHIAKI SHIRA-SAWA!
KA
KA (THOK)
AS OF THIS MOMENT, YOU ARE BEING PROVISIONALLY ASSIGNED TO THE ***SPECIAL ABILITY LIBERATION FRONT'S SPECIAL OPS UNIT, TEAM 7!***
I CAN'T HEAR YOU!
KA
Y...YES, MA'AM!
AH... UM, WHAT IS THIS JOB YOU WANT ME TO...
FILLING IN FOR A MISSING MEMBER.
KA
KA
ASK YOUR ***COMRADES*** IN THAT CAR FOR THE DETAILS.
WHAT CAR...?
KA

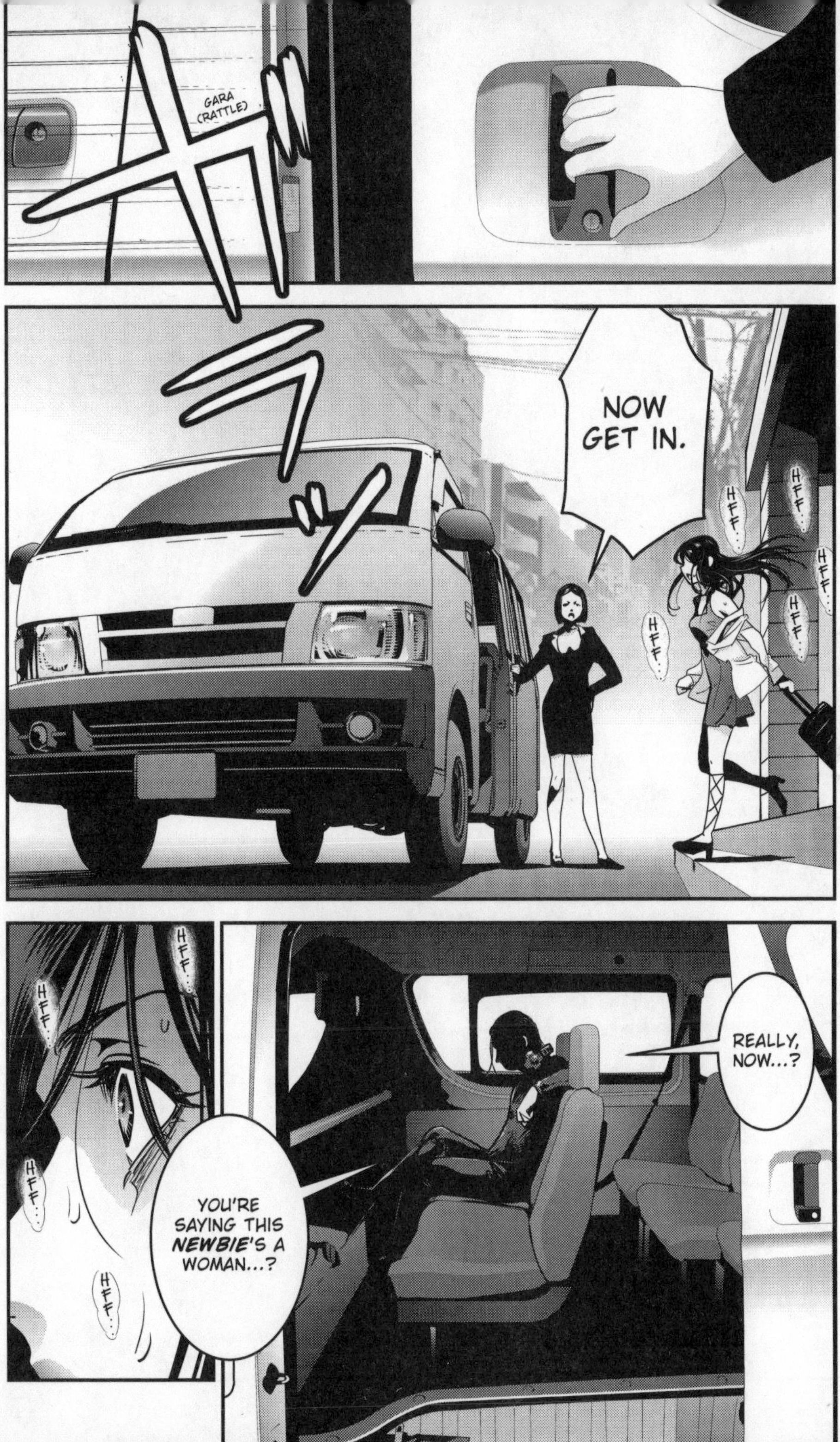
GARA (RATTLE)
NOW GET IN.
HFF...
HFF...
HFF...
HFF...
HFF...
REALLY, NOW...?
YOU'RE SAYING THIS *NEWBIE*'s A WOMAN...?
HFF...
HFF...
HFF...
HFF...

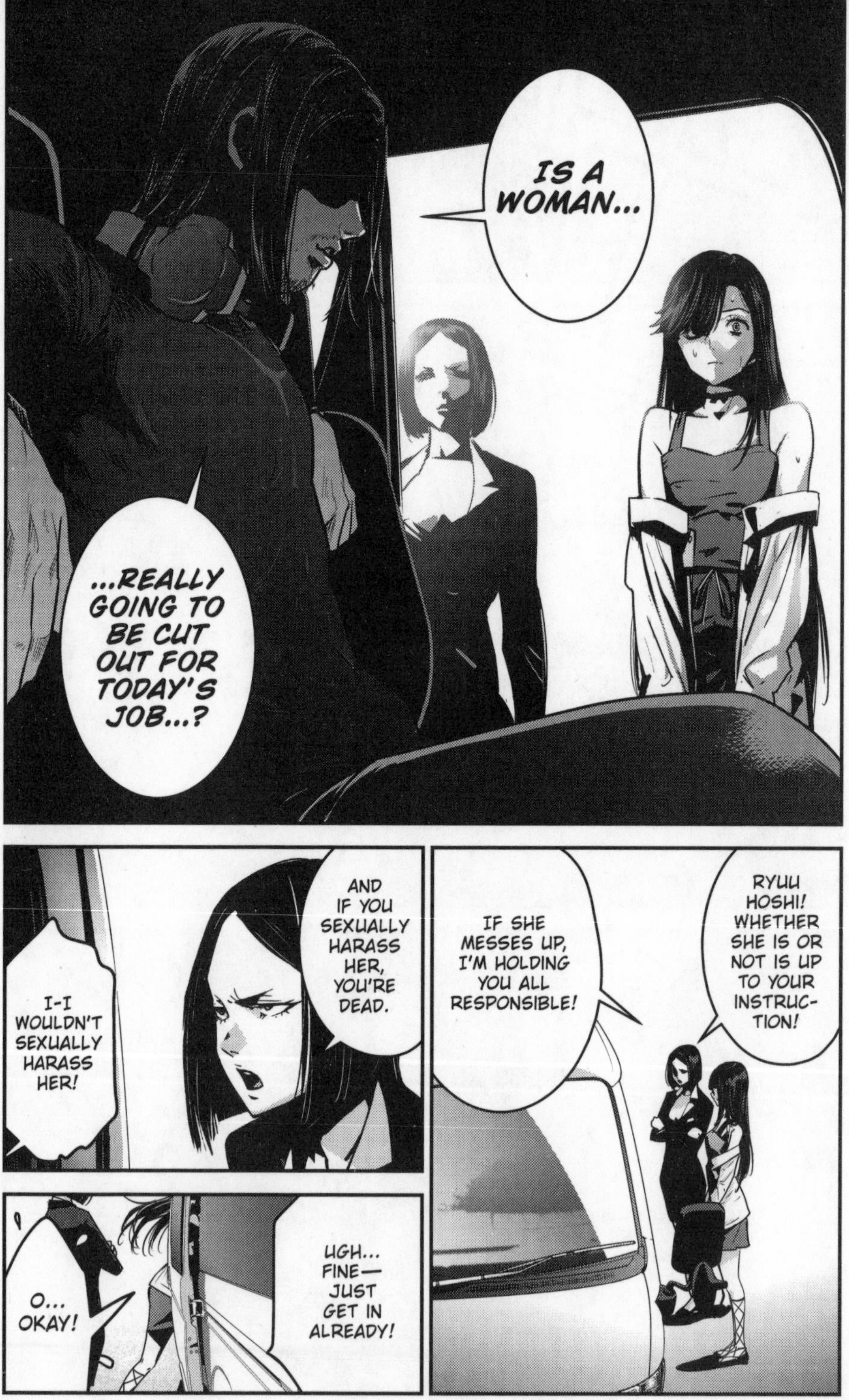
IS A WOMAN...
...REALLY GOING TO BE CUT OUT FOR TODAY'S JOB...?
RYUU HOSHI! WHETHER SHE IS OR NOT IS UP TO YOUR INSTRUCTION!
IF SHE MESSES UP, I'M HOLDING YOU ALL RESPONSIBLE!
AND IF YOU SEXUALLY HARASS HER, YOU'RE DEAD.
I-I WOULDN'T SEXUALLY HARASS HER!
UGH... FINE—JUST GET IN ALREADY!
O... OKAY!

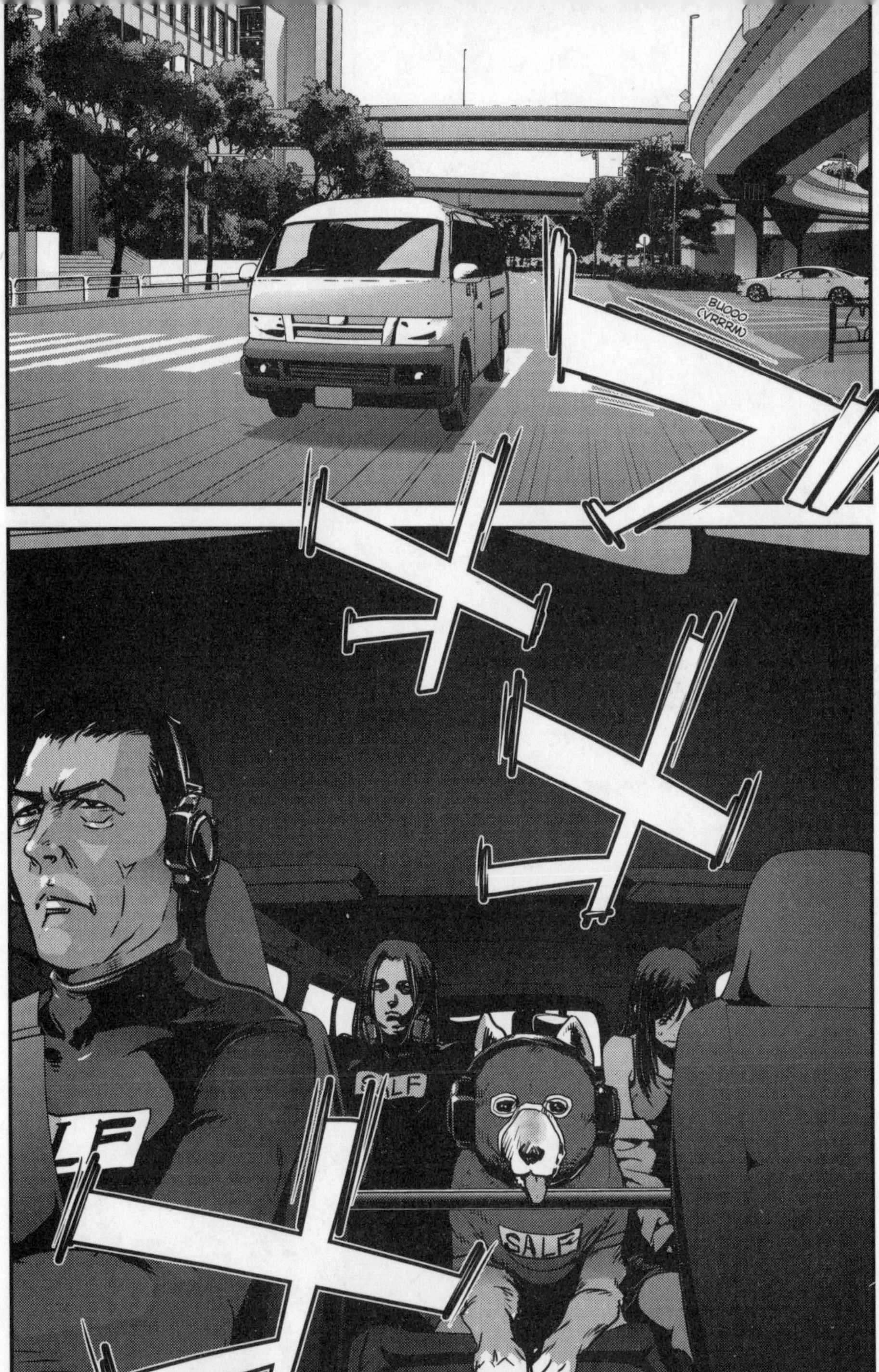
BUOOO
(VRRRM)
SALF
SALF

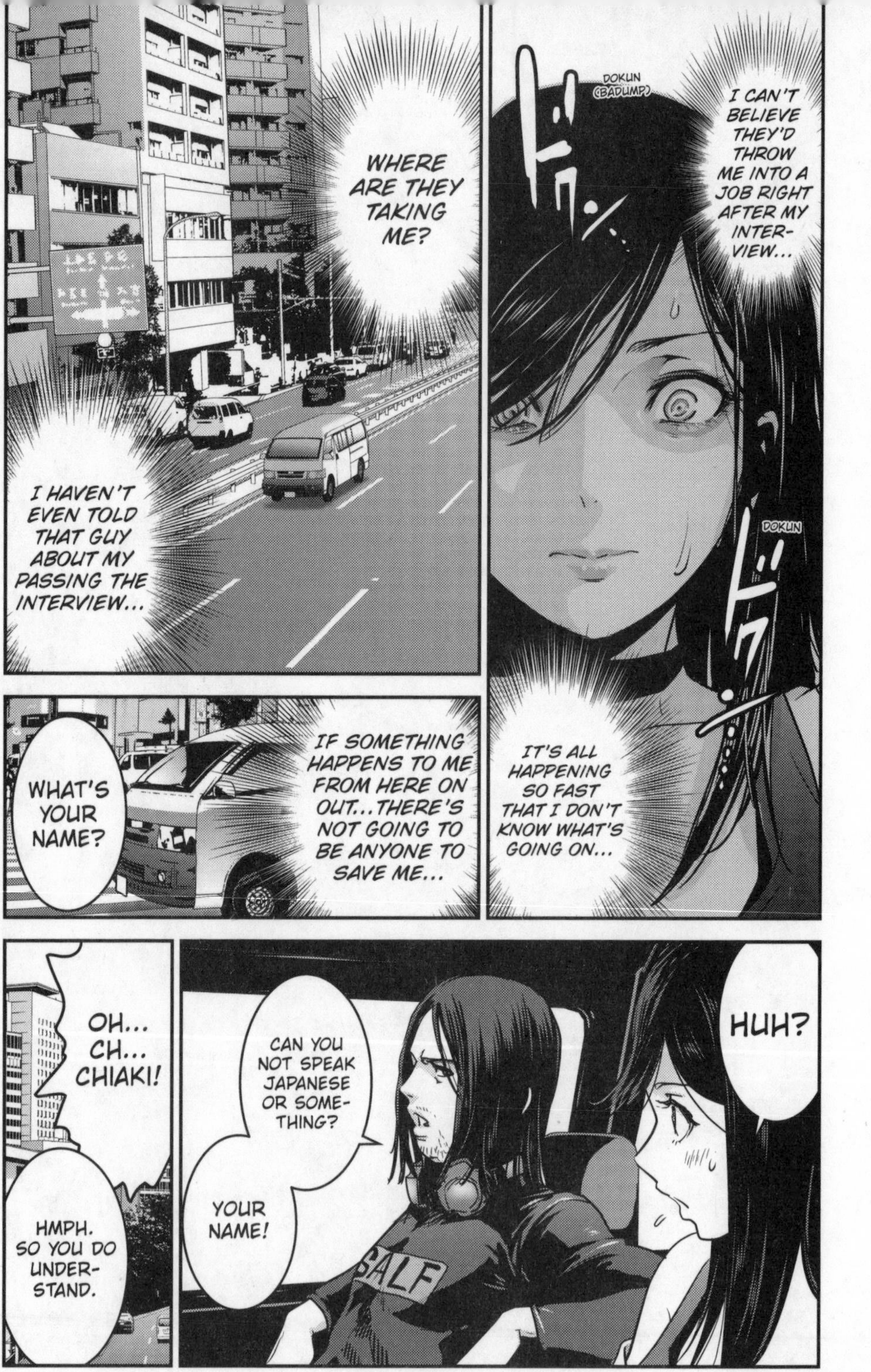
DOKUN (BADUMP)
I CAN'T BELIEVE THEY'D THROW ME INTO A JOB RIGHT AFTER MY INTER-VIEW...
DOKUN
IT'S ALL HAPPENING SO FAST THAT I DON'T KNOW WHAT'S GOING ON...
WHERE ARE THEY TAKING ME?
I HAVEN'T EVEN TOLD THAT GUY ABOUT MY PASSING THE INTERVIEW...
IF SOMETHING HAPPENS TO ME FROM HERE ON OUT...THERE'S NOT GOING TO BE ANYONE TO SAVE ME...
WHAT'S YOUR NAME?
HUH?
CAN YOU NOT SPEAK JAPANESE OR SOME-THING?
YOUR NAME!
SALF
OH... CH... CHIAKI!
HMPH. SO YOU DO UNDER-STAND.

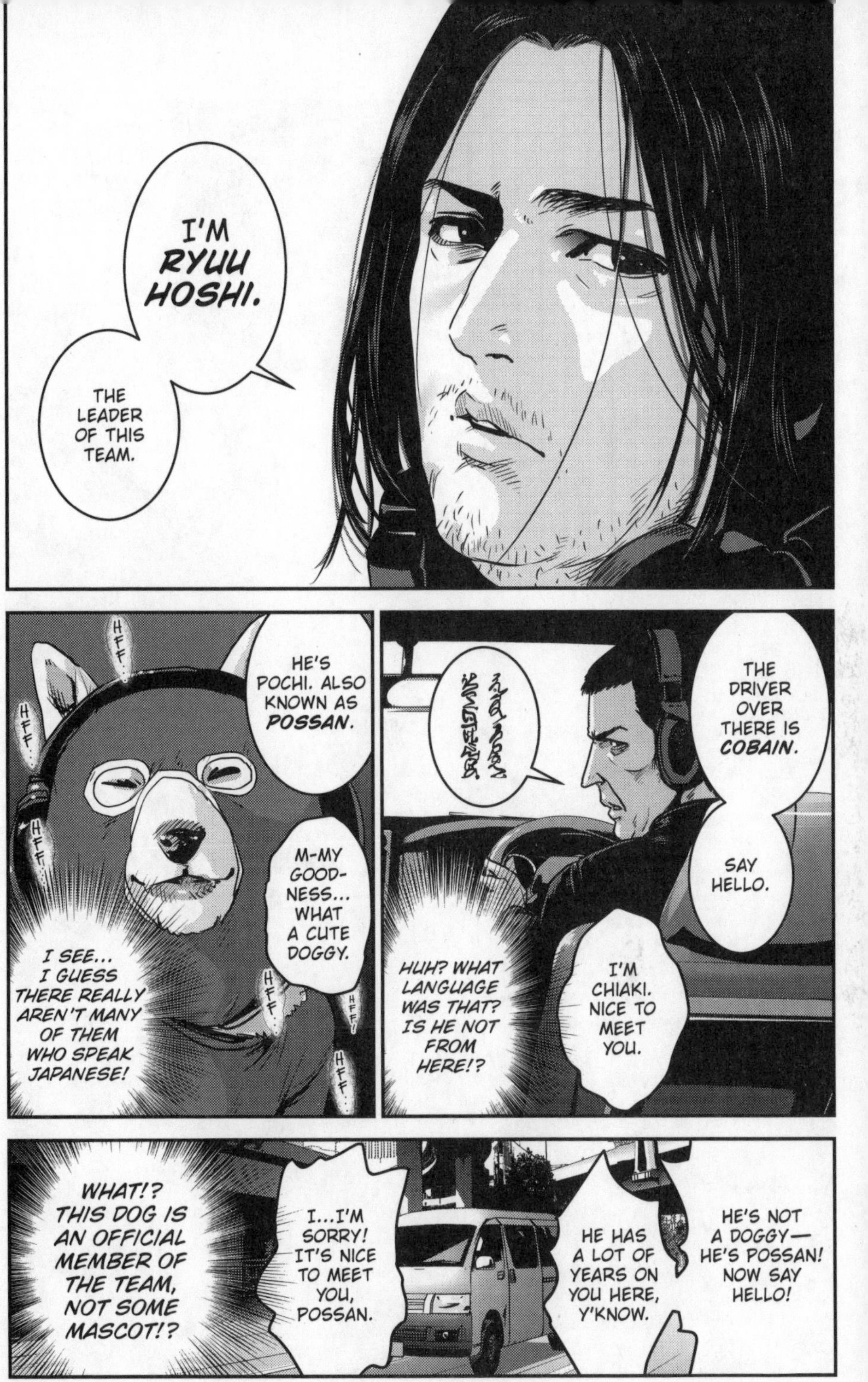
I'M RYUU HOSHI.
THE LEADER OF THIS TEAM.
THE DRIVER OVER THERE IS COBAIN.
SAY HELLO.
I'M CHIAKI. NICE TO MEET YOU.
HUH? WHAT LANGUAGE WAS THAT? IS HE NOT FROM HERE!?
HE'S POCHI. ALSO KNOWN AS POSSAN.
M-MY GOODNESS... WHAT A CUTE DOGGY.
HFF...
HFF...
HFF...
I SEE... I GUESS THERE REALLY AREN'T MANY OF THEM WHO SPEAK JAPANESE!
HFF...
HFF!
HFF...
HE'S NOT A DOGGY— HE'S POSSAN! NOW SAY HELLO!
HE HAS A LOT OF YEARS ON YOU HERE, Y'KNOW.
I...I'M SORRY! IT'S NICE TO MEET YOU, POSSAN.
WHAT!? THIS DOG IS AN OFFICIAL MEMBER OF THE TEAM, NOT SOME MASCOT!?

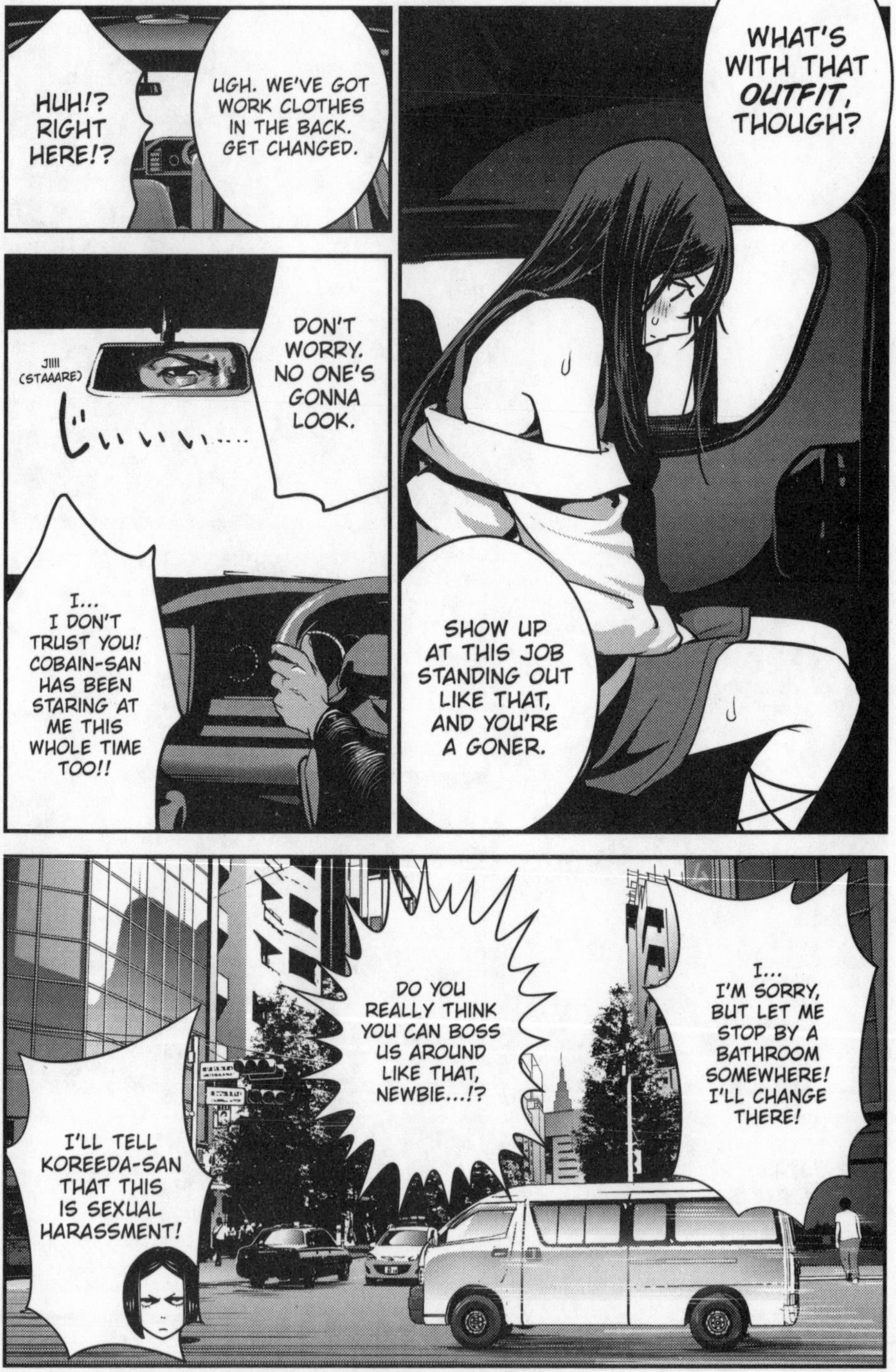
WHAT'S WITH THAT *OUTFIT*, THOUGH?
SHOW UP AT THIS JOB STANDING OUT LIKE THAT, AND YOU'RE A GONER.
UGH. WE'VE GOT WORK CLOTHES IN THE BACK. GET CHANGED.
HUH!? RIGHT HERE!?
DON'T WORRY. NO ONE'S GONNA LOOK.
じぃぃぃ....
JIIII (STAAARE)
I... I DON'T TRUST YOU! COBAIN-SAN HAS BEEN STARING AT ME THIS WHOLE TIME TOO!!
I... I'M SORRY, BUT LET ME STOP BY A BATHROOM SOMEWHERE! I'LL CHANGE THERE!
DO YOU REALLY THINK YOU CAN BOSS US AROUND LIKE THAT, NEWBIE...!?
I'LL TELL KOREEDA-SAN THAT THIS IS SEXUAL HARASSMENT!

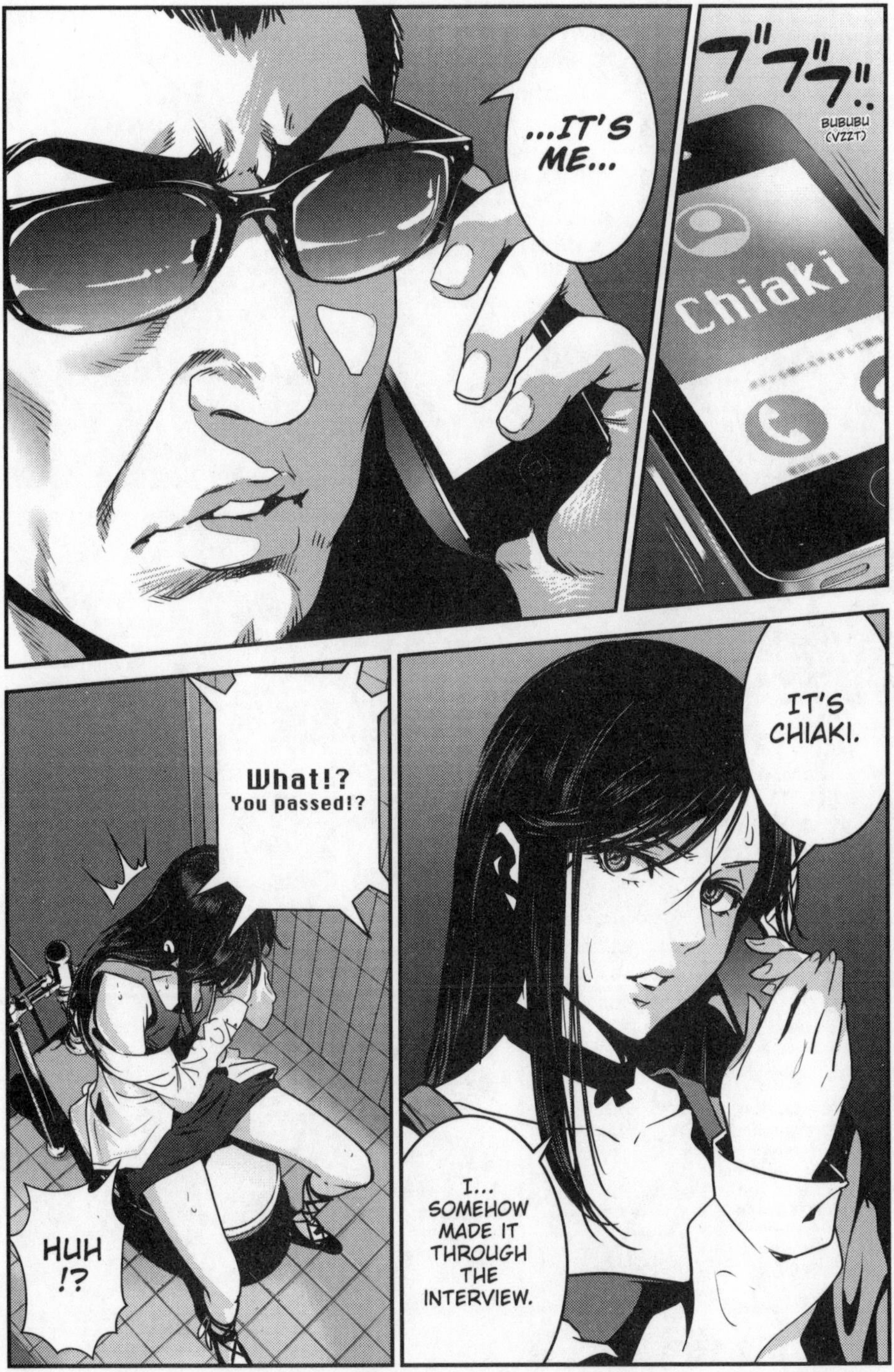

ブブブ..
BUBUBU (VZZT)
Chiaki
...IT'S ME...
IT'S CHIAKI.
I... SOMEHOW MADE IT THROUGH THE INTERVIEW.
What!? You passed!?
HUH !?

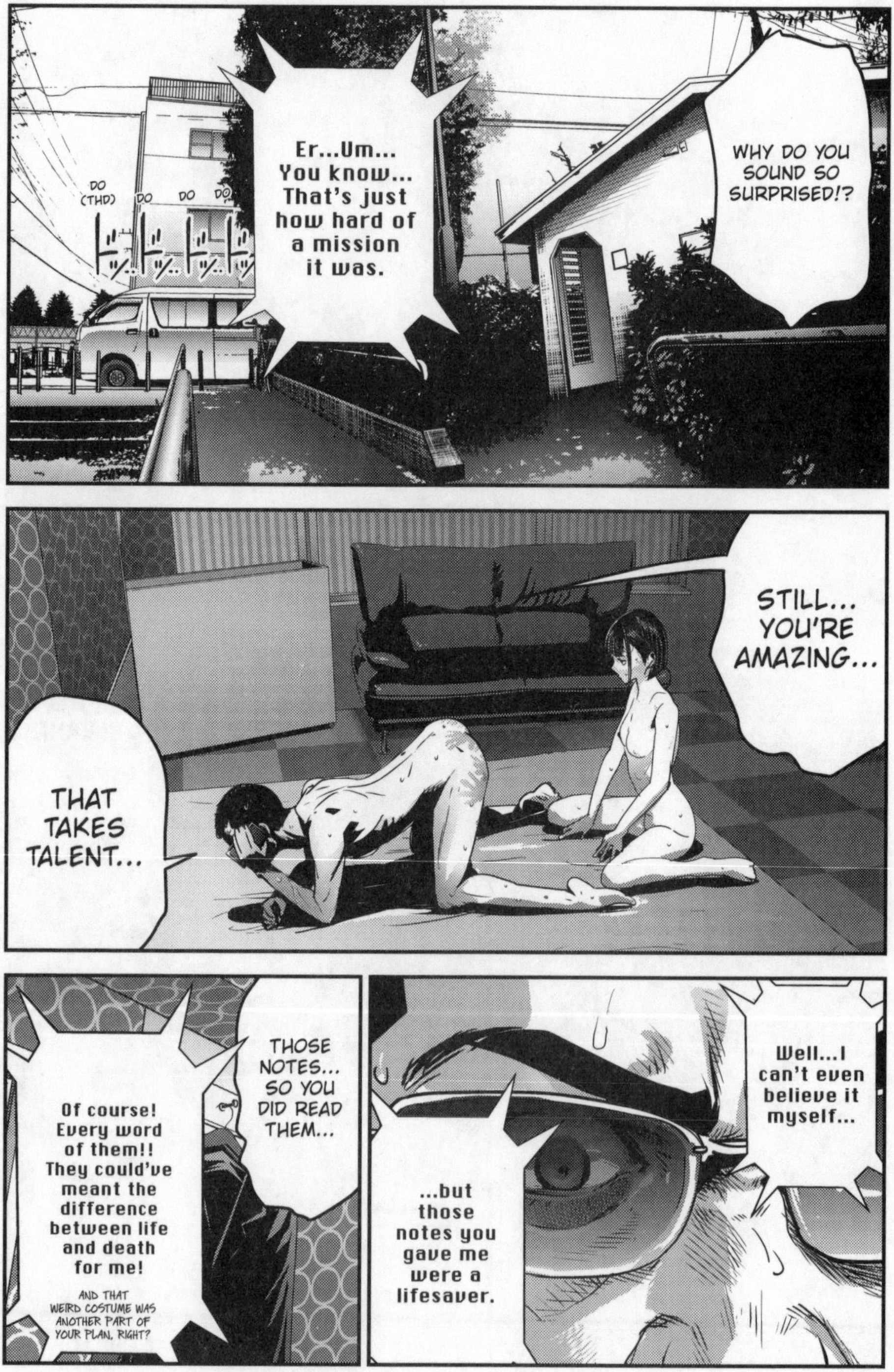
WHY DO YOU SOUND SO SURPRISED!?
Er...Um... You know... That's just how hard of a mission it was.
DO (THD) DO DO DO
STILL... YOU'RE AMAZING...
THAT TAKES TALENT...
Well...I can't even believe it myself...
...but those notes you gave me were a lifesaver.
THOSE NOTES... SO YOU DID READ THEM...
Of course! Every word of them!! They could've meant the difference between life and death for me!
AND THAT WEIRD COSTUME WAS ANOTHER PART OF YOUR PLAN, RIGHT?

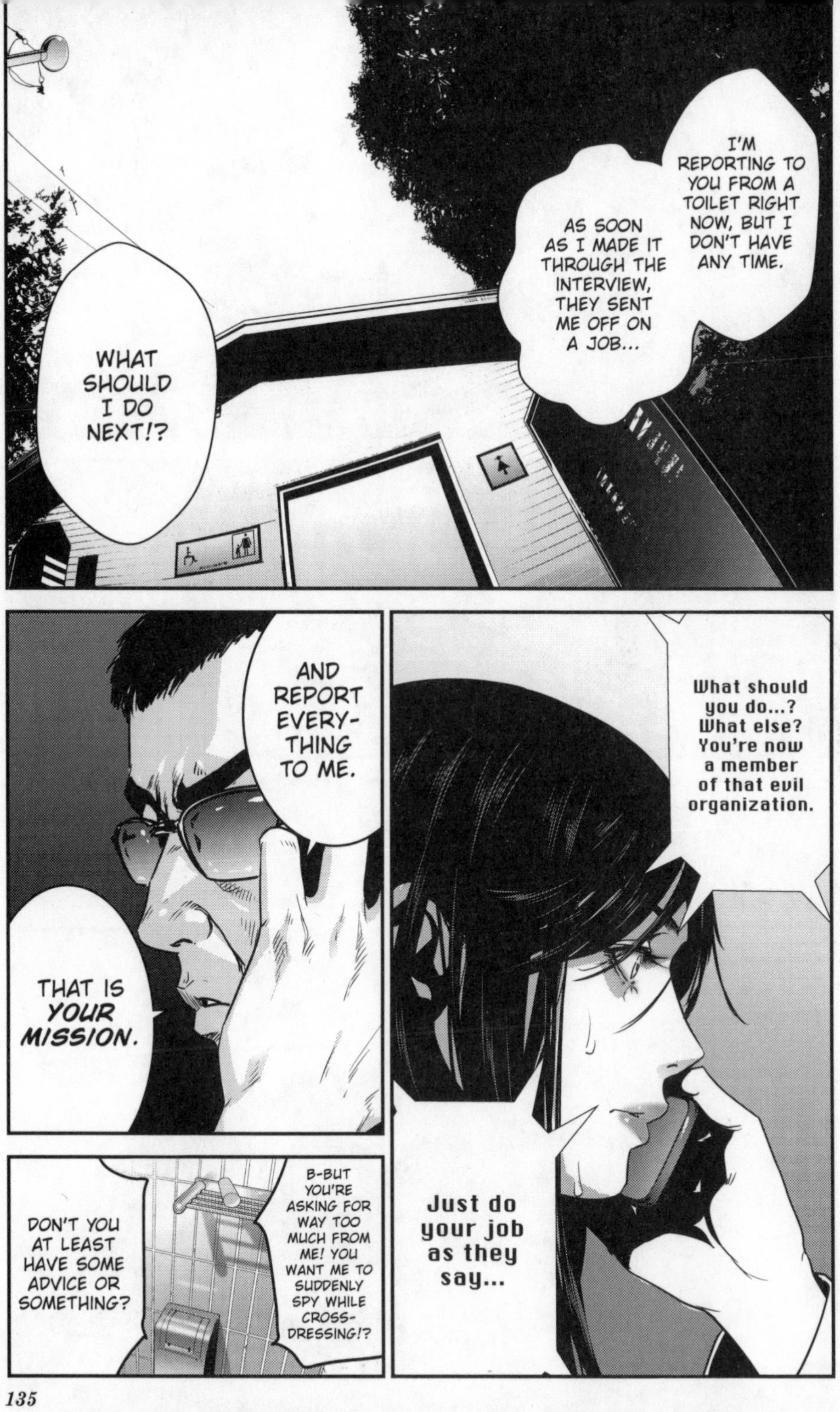
I'M REPORTING TO YOU FROM A TOILET RIGHT NOW, BUT I DON'T HAVE ANY TIME.
AS SOON AS I MADE IT THROUGH THE INTERVIEW, THEY SENT ME OFF ON A JOB...
WHAT SHOULD I DO NEXT!?
What should you do...? What else? You're now a member of that evil organization.
Just do your job as they say...
AND REPORT EVERY-THING TO ME.
THAT IS *YOUR MISSION*.
B-BUT YOU'RE ASKING FOR WAY TOO MUCH FROM ME! YOU WANT ME TO SUDDENLY SPY WHILE CROSS-DRESSING!?
DON'T YOU AT LEAST HAVE SOME ADVICE OR SOMETHING?

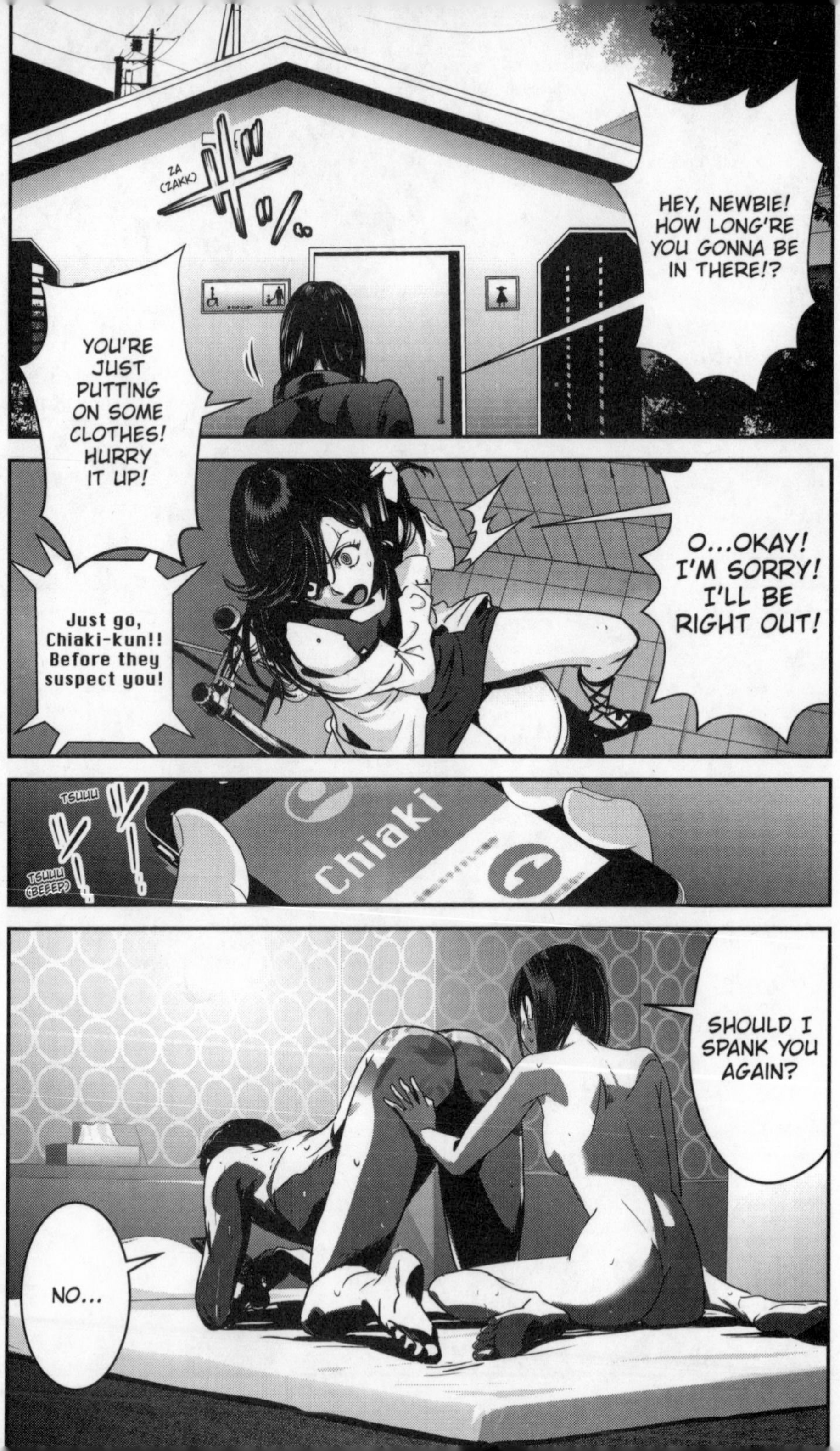
HEY, NEWBIE! HOW LONG'RE YOU GONNA BE IN THERE!?
ZA (ZAKK)
YOU'RE JUST PUTTING ON SOME CLOTHES! HURRY IT UP!
O...OKAY! I'M SORRY! I'LL BE RIGHT OUT!
Just go, Chiaki-kun!! Before they suspect you!
Chiaki
TSUUU
TSUUU (BEEEP)
SHOULD I SPANK YOU AGAIN?
NO...

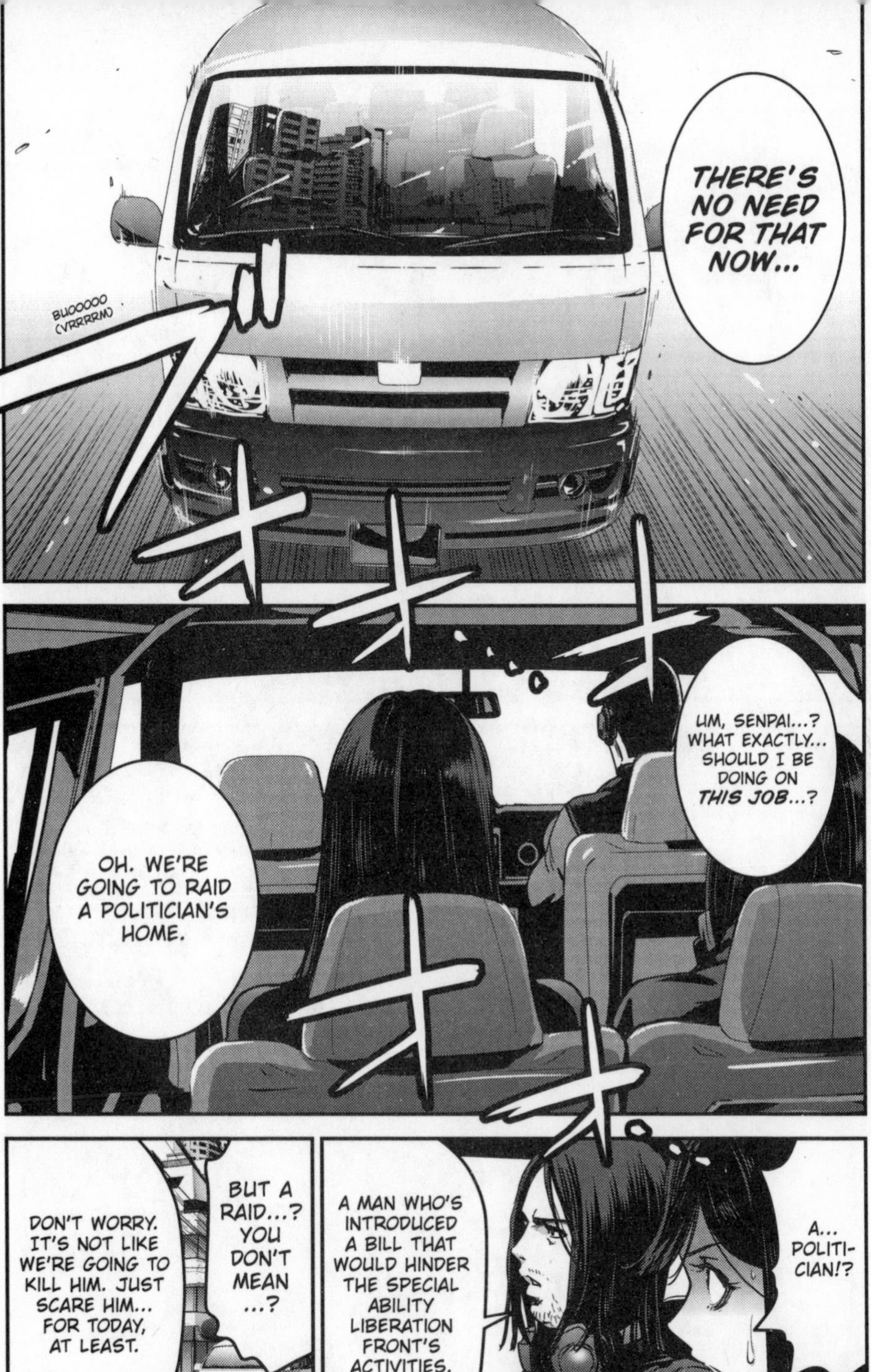
THERE'S NO NEED FOR THAT NOW...
BUOOOOO (VRRRRM)
UM, SENPAI...? WHAT EXACTLY... SHOULD I BE DOING ON THIS JOB...?
OH. WE'RE GOING TO RAID A POLITICIAN'S HOME.
A... POLITI-CIAN!?
A MAN WHO'S INTRODUCED A BILL THAT WOULD HINDER THE SPECIAL ABILITY LIBERATION FRONT'S ACTIVITIES.
BUT A RAID...? YOU DON'T MEAN ...?
DON'T WORRY. IT'S NOT LIKE WE'RE GOING TO KILL HIM. JUST SCARE HIM... FOR TODAY, AT LEAST.

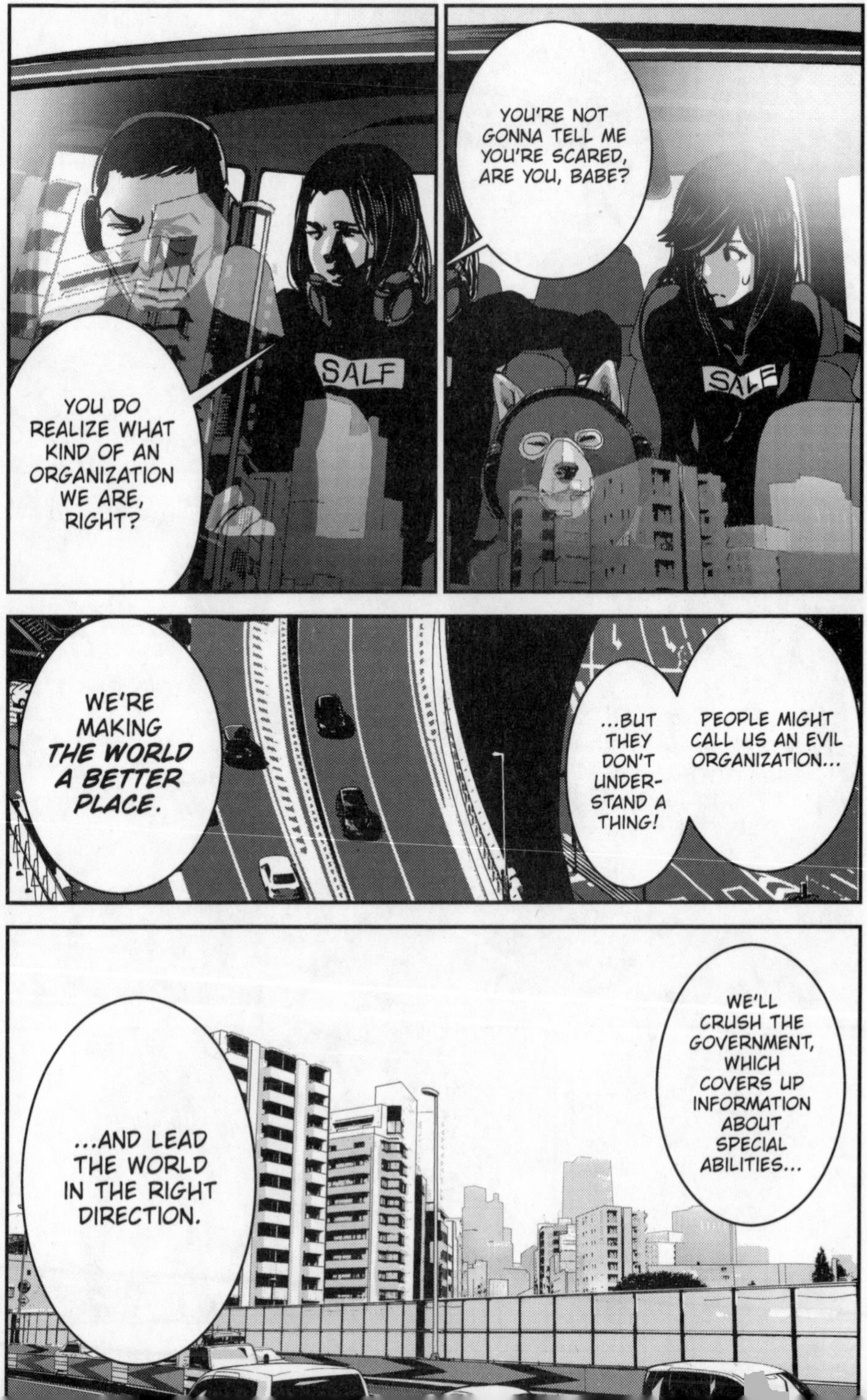
YOU'RE NOT GONNA TELL ME YOU'RE SCARED, ARE YOU, BABE?
SALF
SALF
YOU DO REALIZE WHAT KIND OF AN ORGANIZATION WE ARE, RIGHT?
PEOPLE MIGHT CALL US AN EVIL ORGANIZATION...
...BUT THEY DON'T UNDER-STAND A THING!
WE'RE MAKING *THE WORLD A BETTER PLACE*.
WE'LL CRUSH THE GOVERNMENT, WHICH COVERS UP INFORMATION ABOUT SPECIAL ABILITIES...
...AND LEAD THE WORLD IN THE RIGHT DIRECTION.

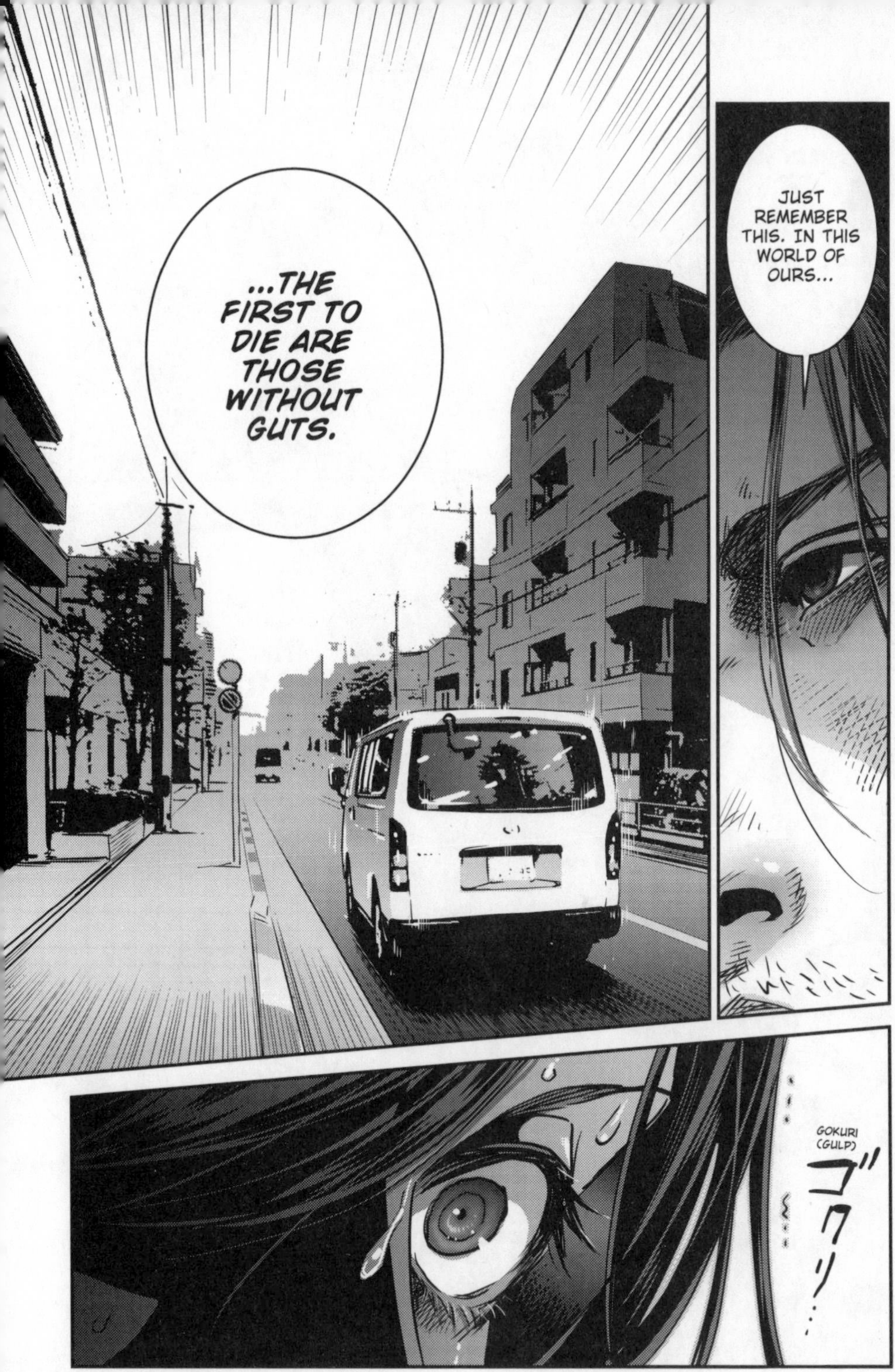
JUST REMEMBER THIS. IN THIS WORLD OF OURS...
...THE FIRST TO DIE ARE THOSE WITHOUT GUTS.
GOKURI (GULP)
ゴクリ…

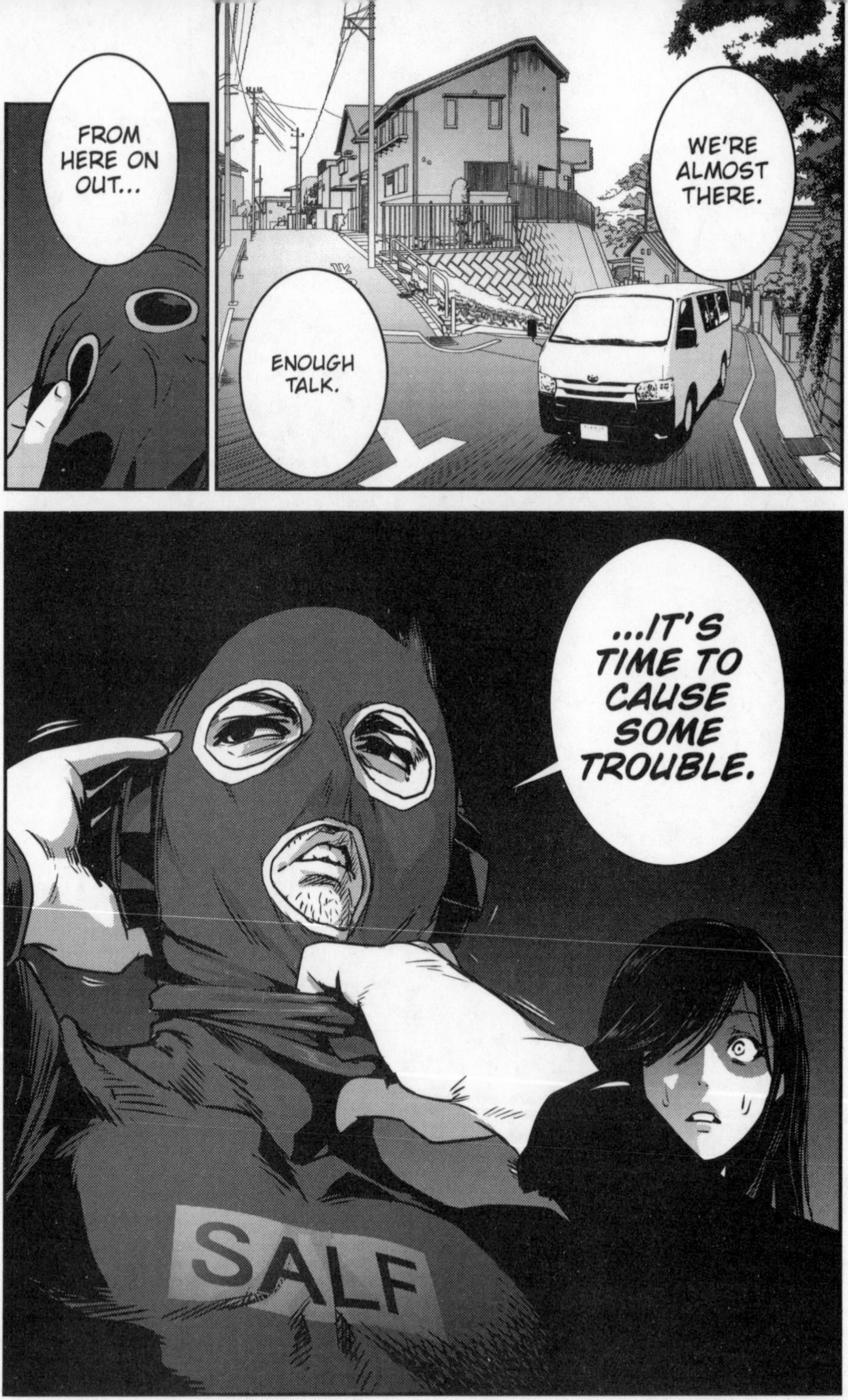
WE'RE ALMOST THERE.
ENOUGH TALK.
FROM HERE ON OUT...
...IT'S TIME TO CAUSE SOME TROUBLE.
SALF

Chapter 5: End

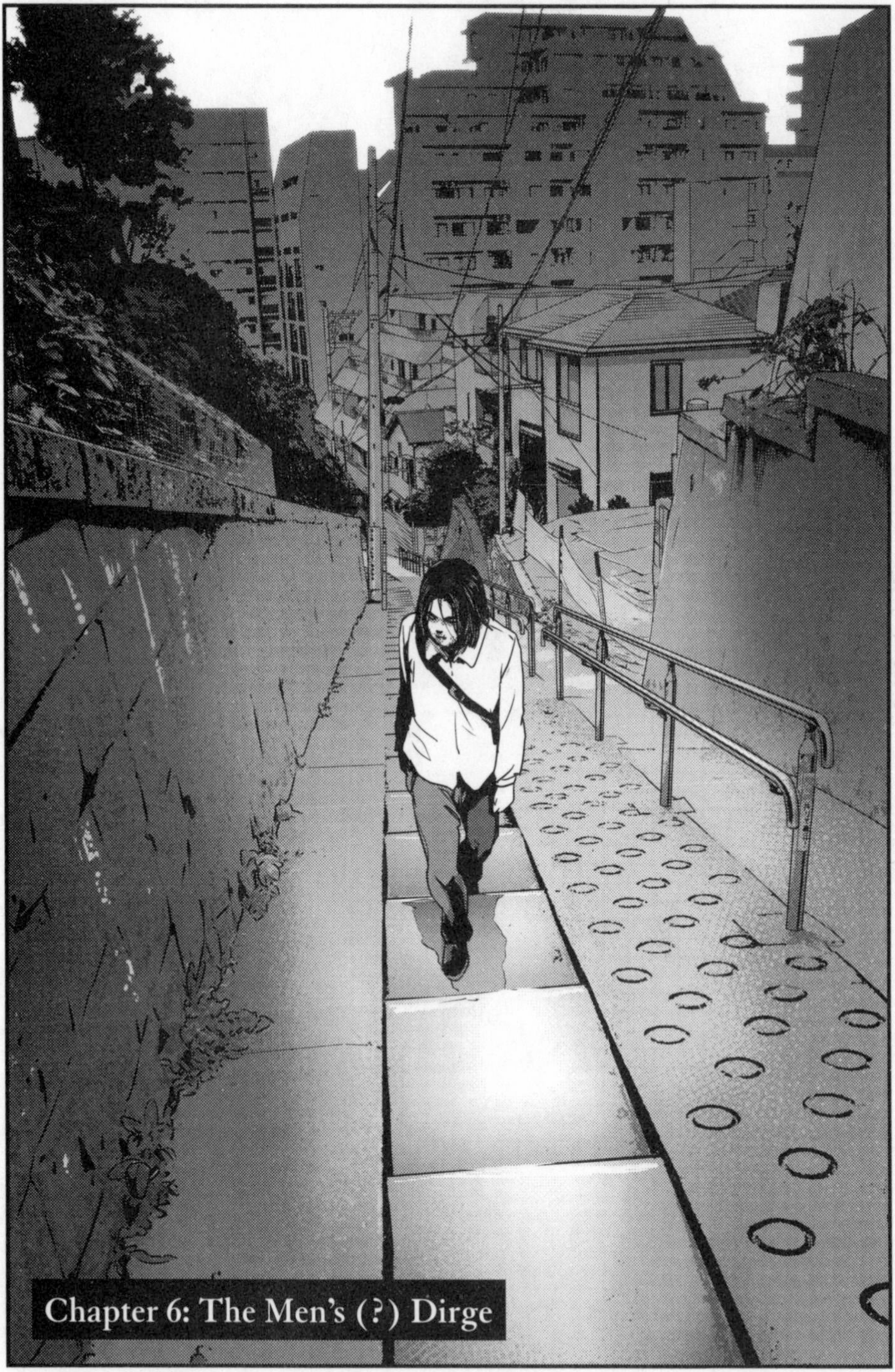
Chapter 6: The Men's (?) Dirge

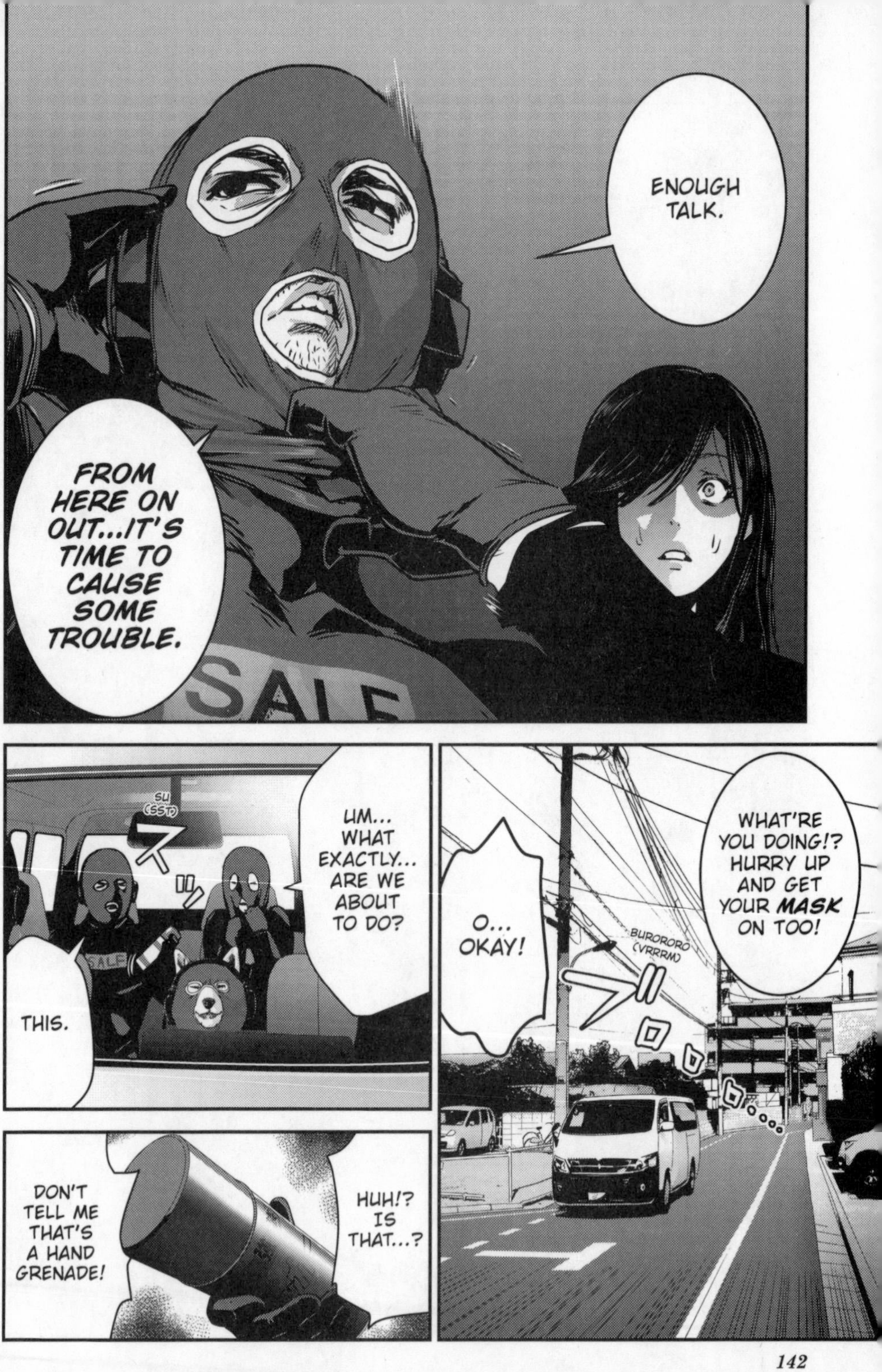
ENOUGH TALK.
FROM HERE ON OUT...IT'S TIME TO CAUSE SOME TROUBLE.
WHAT'RE YOU DOING!? HURRY UP AND GET YOUR MASK ON TOO!
O... OKAY!
BURORORO (VRRRM)
UM... WHAT EXACTLY... ARE WE ABOUT TO DO?
SU (SST)
THIS.
HUH!? IS THAT...?
DON'T TELL ME THAT'S A HAND GRENADE!

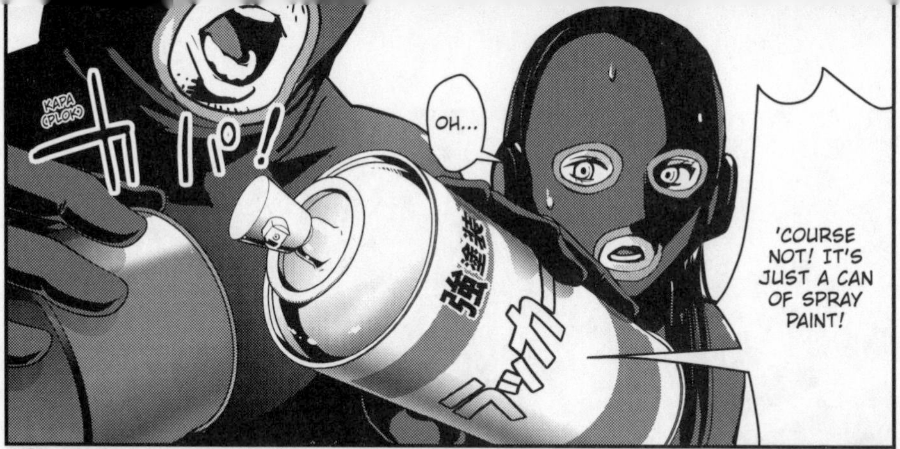
KAPA (PLOK)
OH...
'COURSE NOT! IT'S JUST A CAN OF SPRAY PAINT!
LABEL: STRONGCOAT INDUSTRIES, LACQUER

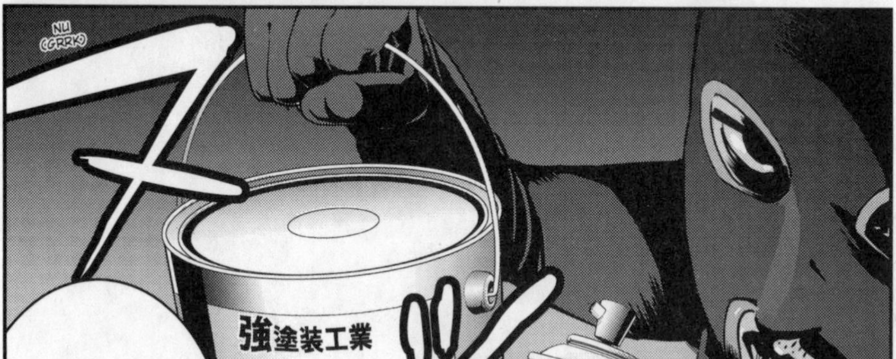
NU (GRRK)
強塗装工業
強 ペンキ
強塗装
WE'RE GONNA COVER THAT BASTARD'S HOME IN CURSES TODAY.
LABEL: STRONGCOAT INDUSTRIES, STRONG PAINT

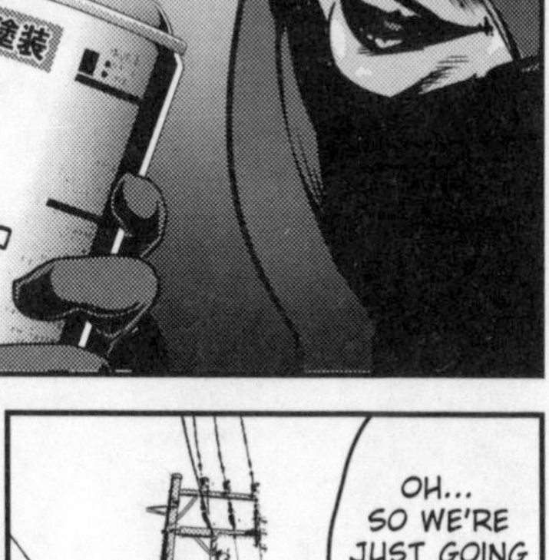
OH... SO WE'RE JUST GOING TO GRAFFITI HIS PLACE? PHEW...
HUH? WHAT'S THAT!? ARE YOU MAKING LIGHT OF THIS JOB!?

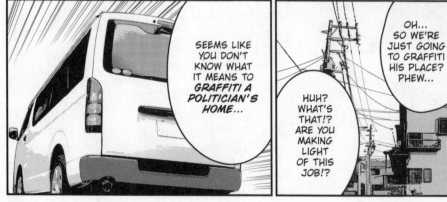

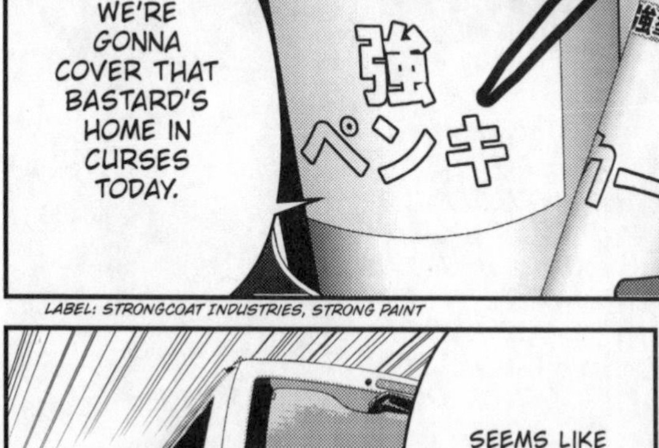
SEEMS LIKE YOU DON'T KNOW WHAT IT MEANS TO ***GRAFFITI A POLITICIAN'S HOME***...

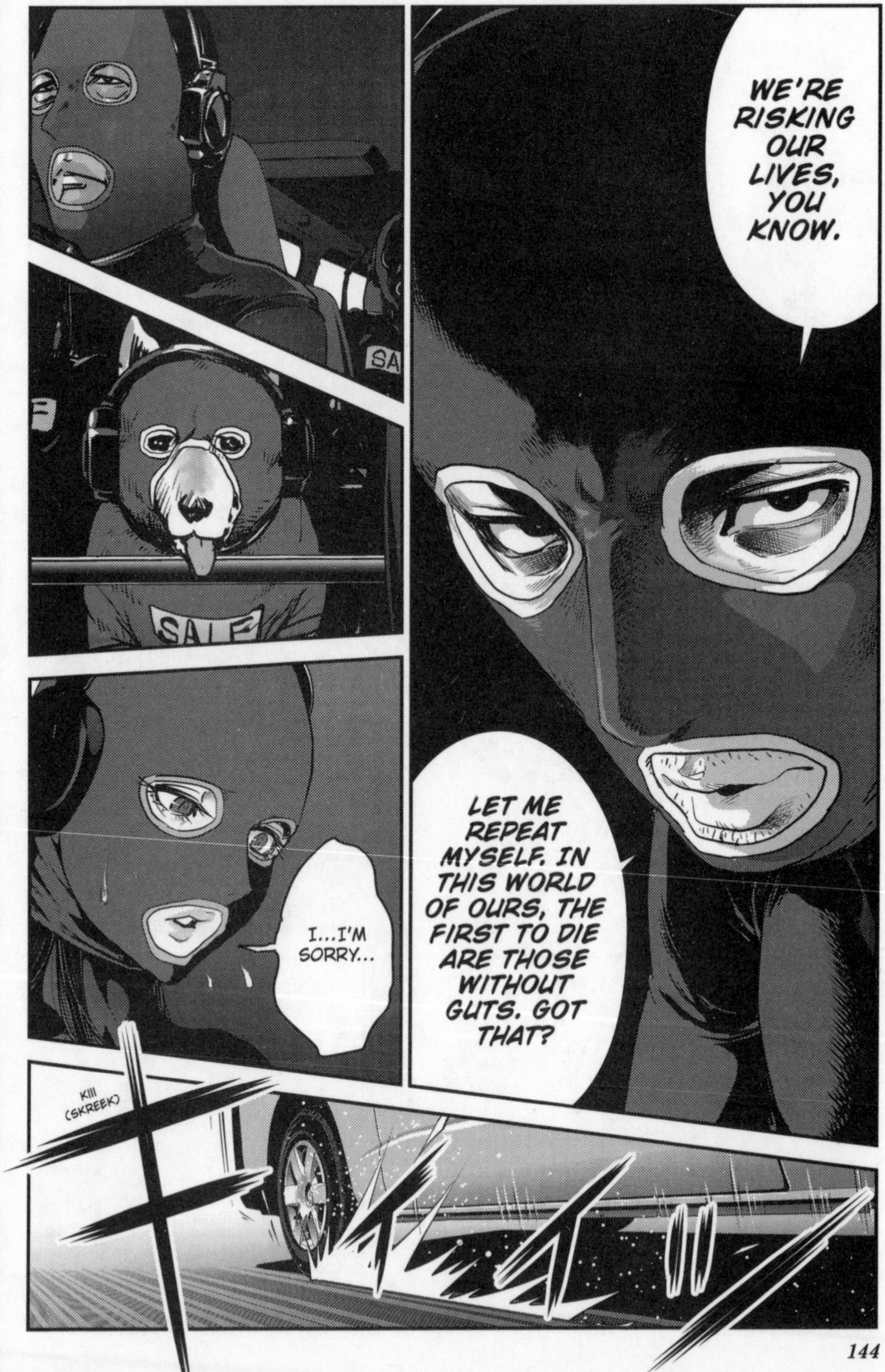
WE'RE RISKING OUR LIVES, YOU KNOW.
LET ME REPEAT MYSELF. IN THIS WORLD OF OURS, THE FIRST TO DIE ARE THOSE WITHOUT GUTS. GOT THAT?
I...I'M SORRY...
KIII (SKREEK)

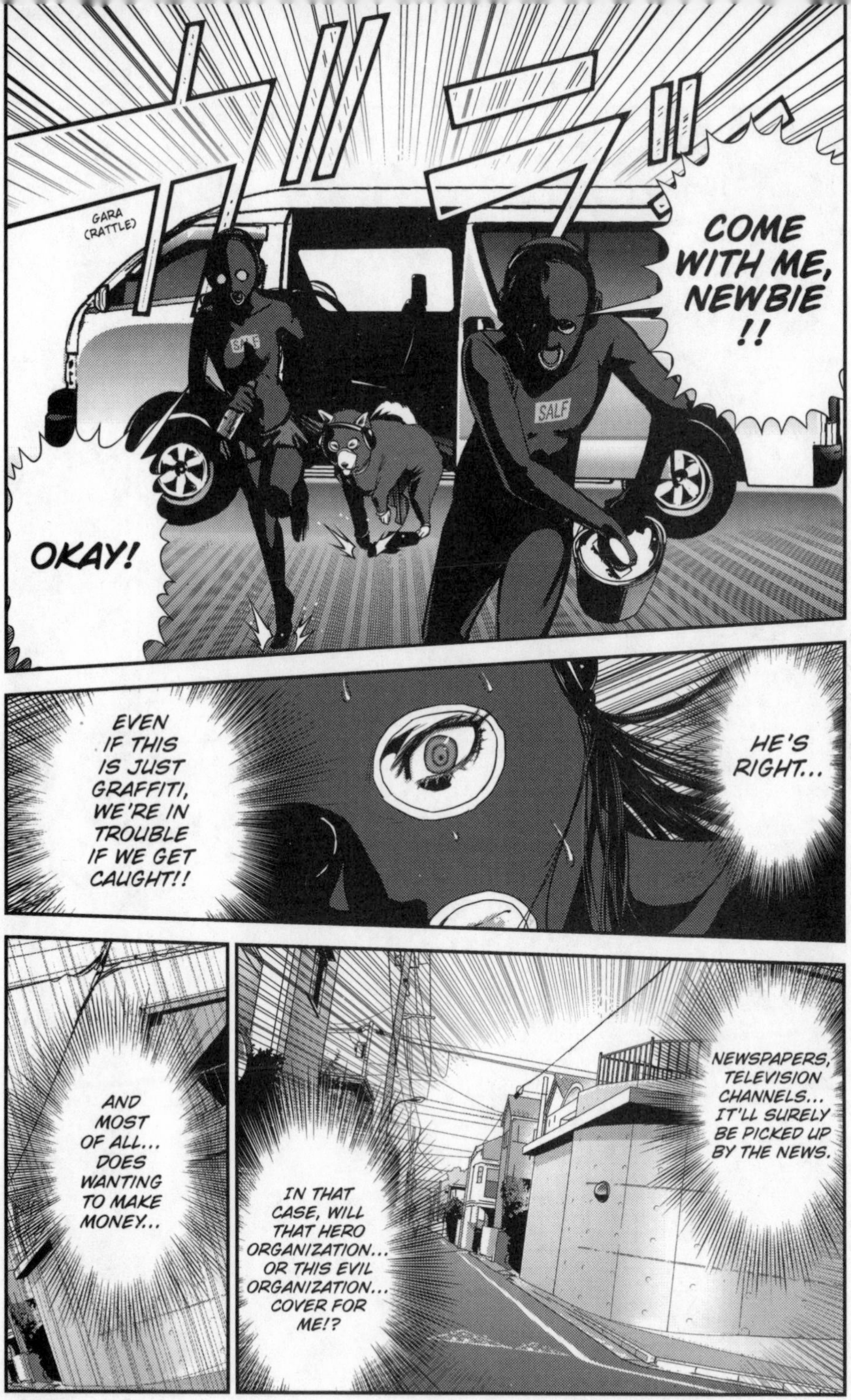
GARA (RATTLE)
COME WITH ME, NEWBIE!!
OKAY!
HE'S RIGHT...
EVEN IF THIS IS JUST GRAFFITI, WE'RE IN TROUBLE IF WE GET CAUGHT!!
NEWSPAPERS, TELEVISION CHANNELS... IT'LL SURELY BE PICKED UP BY THE NEWS.
IN THAT CASE, WILL THAT HERO ORGANIZATION... OR THIS EVIL ORGANIZATION... COVER FOR ME!?
AND MOST OF ALL... DOES WANTING TO MAKE MONEY...

...JUSTIFY MY BECOMING A CRIMINAL!?

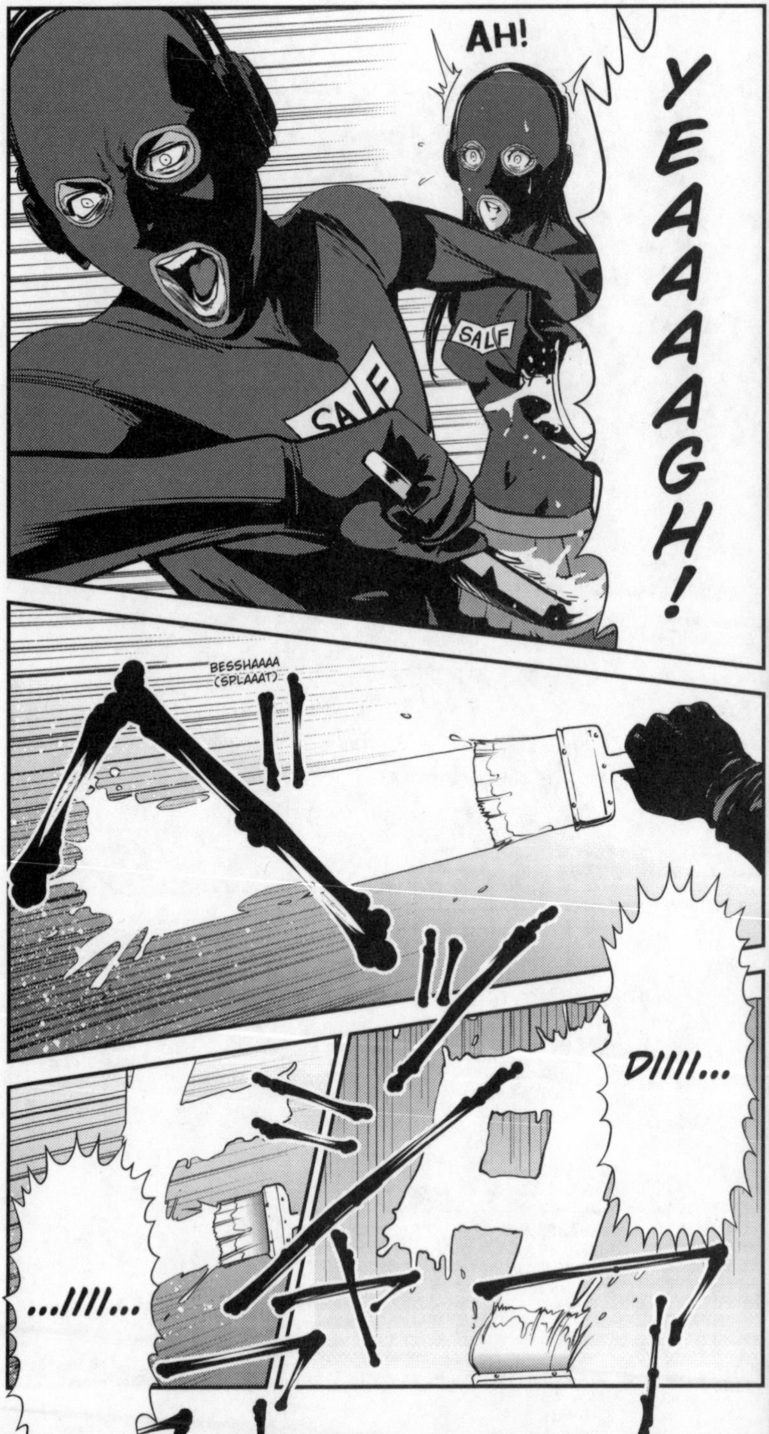
YEAAAAGH!
AH!
SALF
SALF
BESSHAAAA (SPLAAAT)
DIIII...
...IIII...

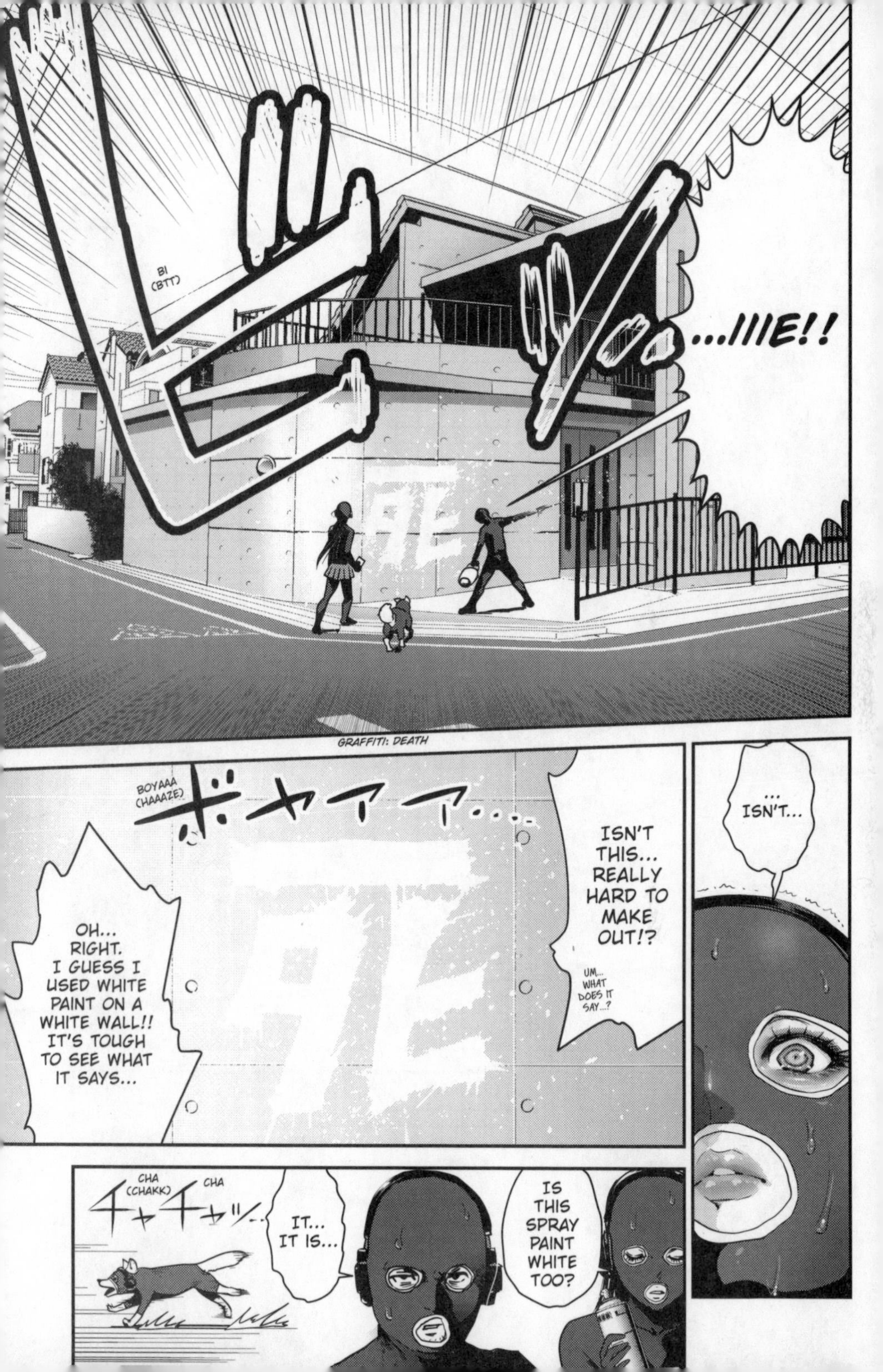
...IIIE!!
BI (BTT)
GRAFFITI: DEATH
... ISN'T...
BOYAAA (HAAAZE)
ISN'T THIS... REALLY HARD TO MAKE OUT!?
UM... WHAT DOES IT SAY...?
OH... RIGHT. I GUESS I USED WHITE PAINT ON A WHITE WALL!! IT'S TOUGH TO SEE WHAT IT SAYS...
IS THIS SPRAY PAINT WHITE TOO?
IT... IT IS...
CHA (CHAKK) CHA

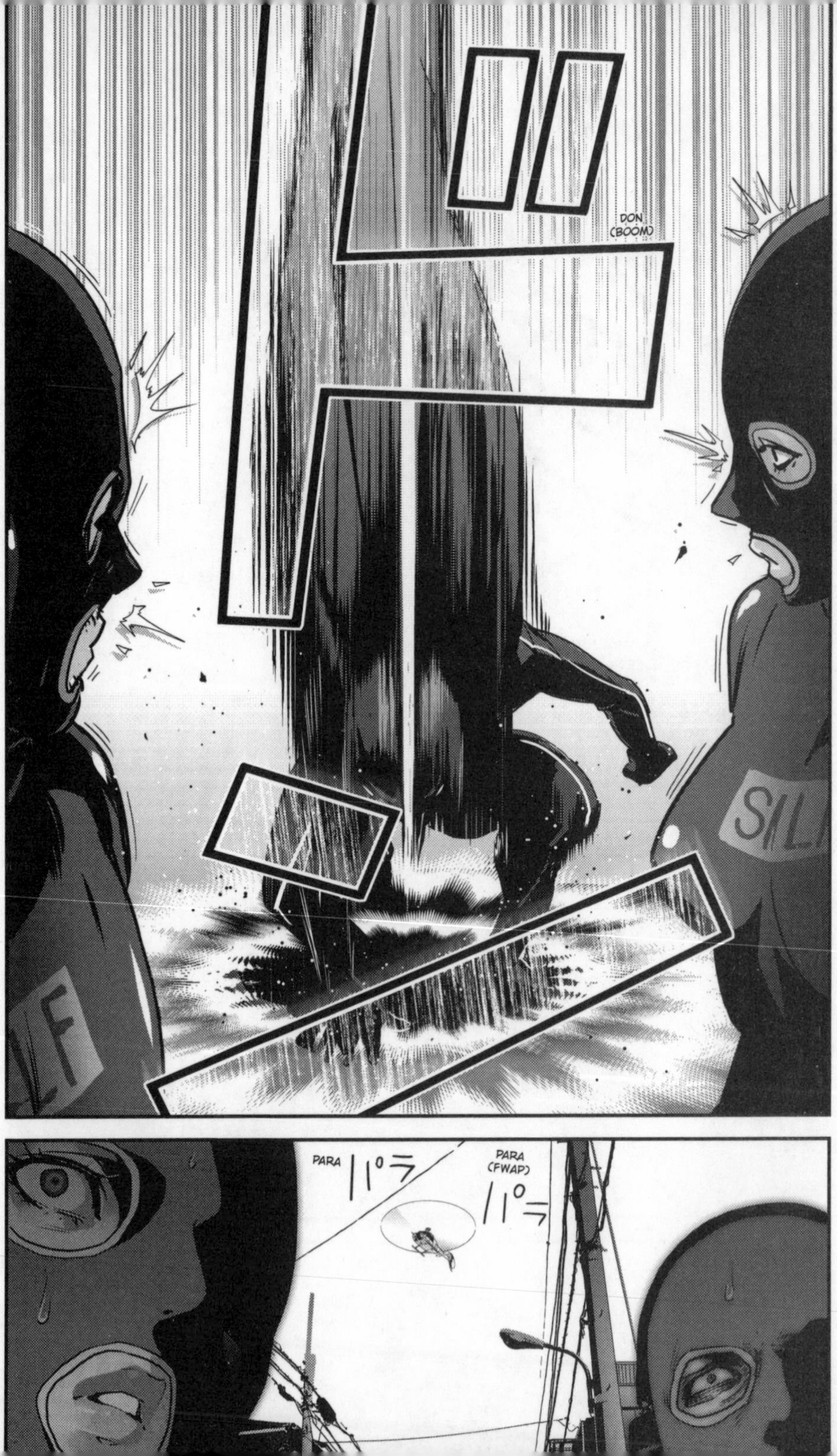
DON
(BOOM)
PARA
(FWAP)
パラ
PARA
パラ

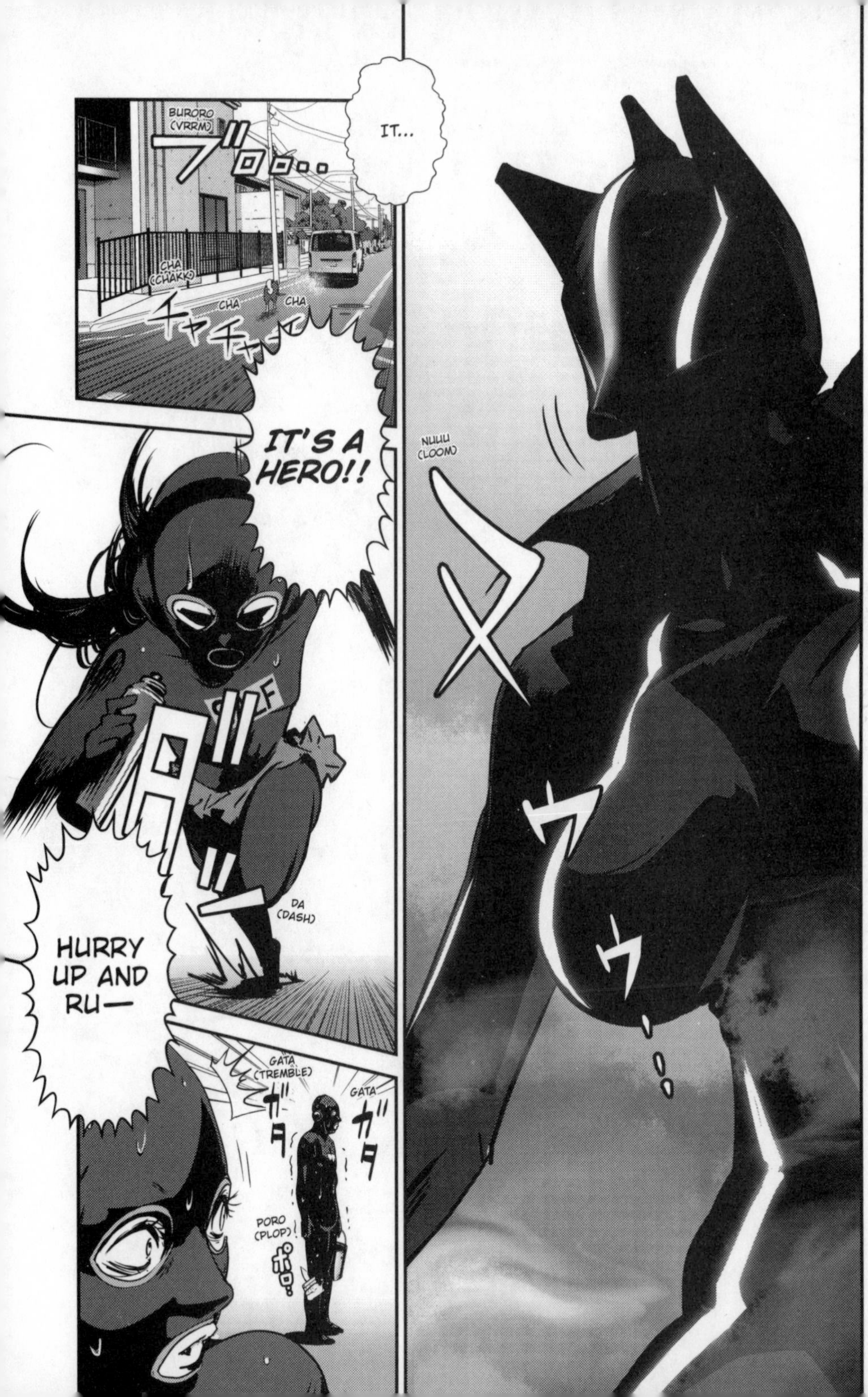
NUUU
(LOOM)
BURORO
(VRRM)
IT...
CHA
(CHAKK)
CHA
CHA
IT'S A HERO!!
DA
(DASH)
HURRY UP AND RU—
GATA
(TREMBLE)
GATA
PORO
(PLOP)

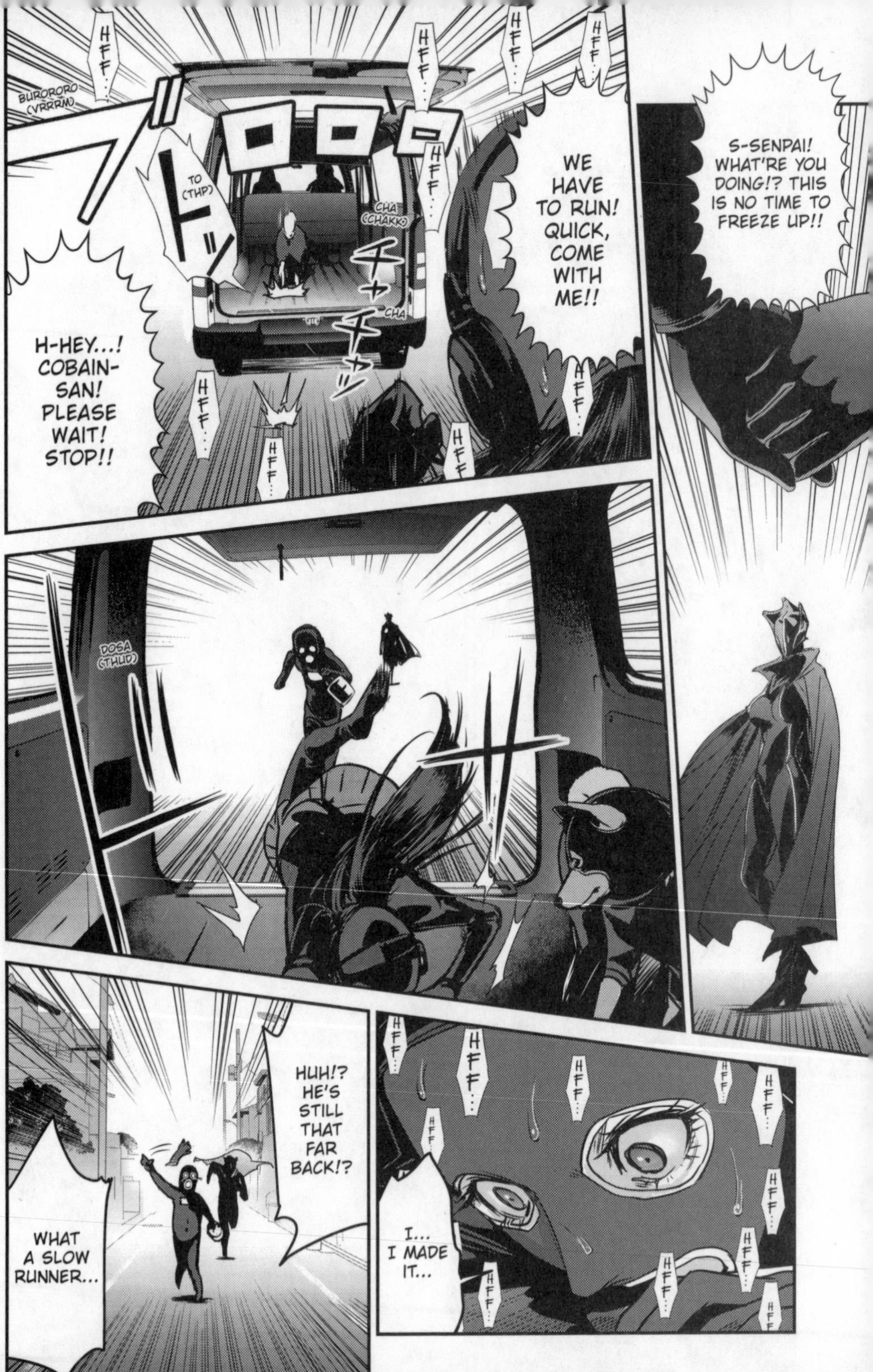
S-SENPAI! WHAT'RE YOU DOING!? THIS IS NO TIME TO FREEZE UP!!
HFF...
HFF...
HFF...
WE HAVE TO RUN! QUICK, COME WITH ME!!
HFF...
CHA (CHAKK)
CHA
BURORORO (VRRRM)
TO (THP)
HFF...
HFF...
HFF...
H-HEY...! COBAIN-SAN! PLEASE WAIT! STOP!!
DOSA (THUD)
HFF...
HFF...
HFF...
HFF...
HFF...
HFF...
HFF...
HFF...
HFF...
HFF...
I... I MADE IT...
HUH!? HE'S STILL THAT FAR BACK!?
WHAT A SLOW RUNNER...

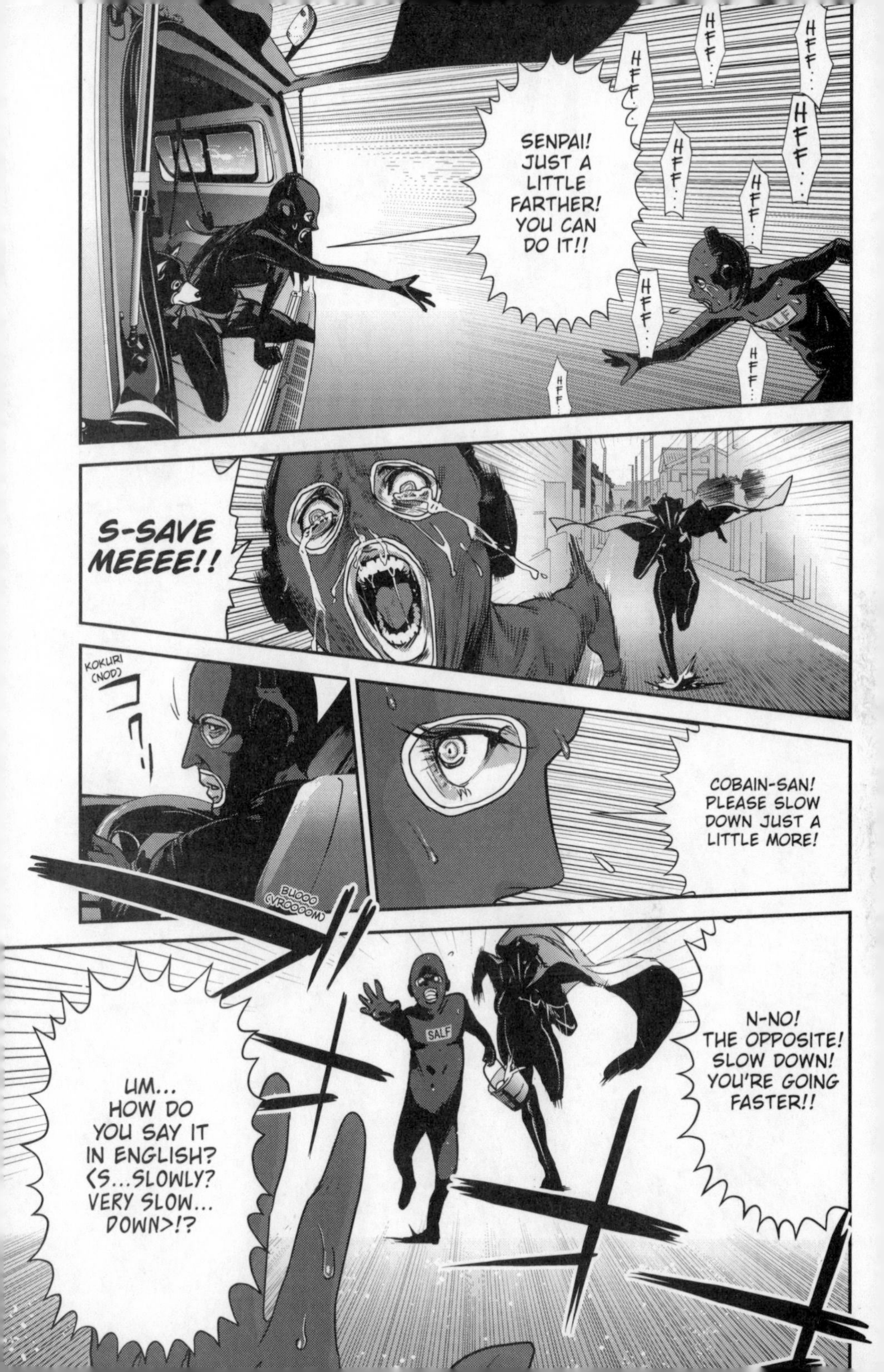
HFF...
HFF...
HFF...
HFF...
HFF...
HFF...
HFF...
HFF...
SENPAI! JUST A LITTLE FARTHER! YOU CAN DO IT!!
S-SAVE MEEEE!!
COBAIN-SAN! PLEASE SLOW DOWN JUST A LITTLE MORE!
BUOOO (VROOOOM)
KOKURI (NOD)
N-NO! THE OPPOSITE! SLOW DOWN! YOU'RE GOING FASTER!!
UM... HOW DO YOU SAY IT IN ENGLISH? <S...SLOWLY? VERY SLOW... DOWN>!?

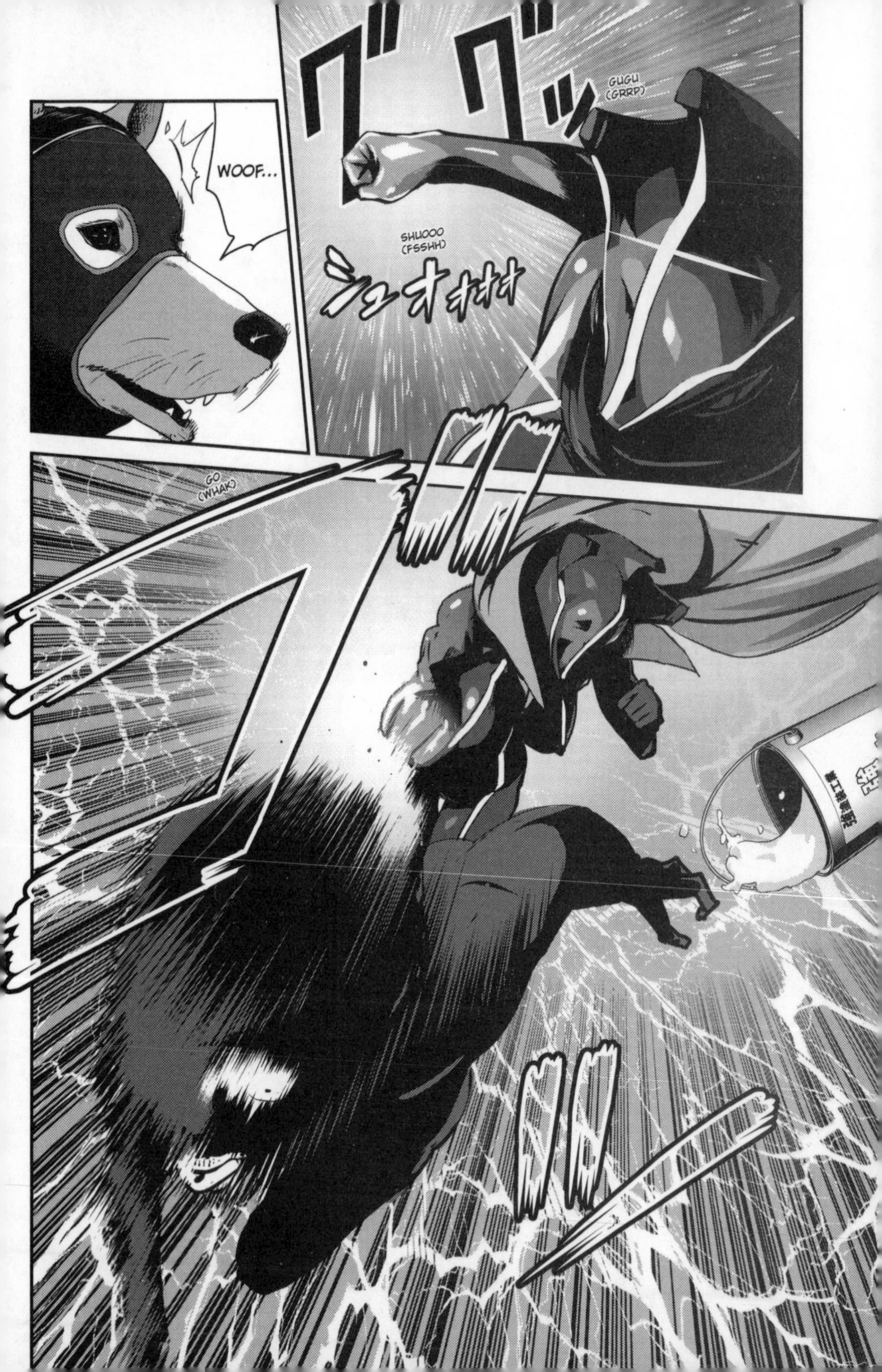
GUGU (GRRP)
SHUOOO (FSSHH)
WOOF...
GO (WHAK)

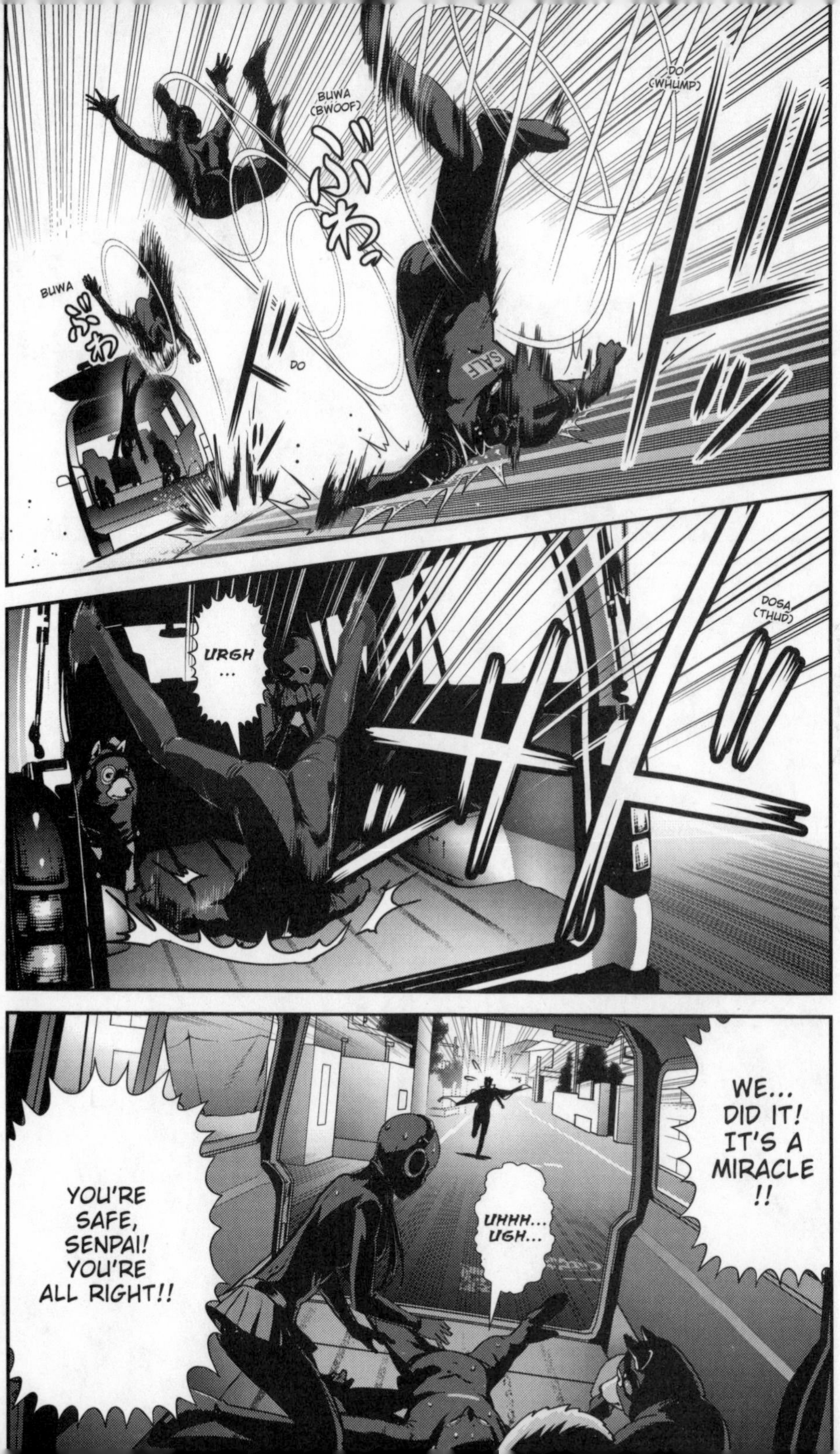
DO (WHUMP)
BUWA (BWOOF)
BUWA
DO
DOSA (THUD)
URGH ...
WE... DID IT! IT'S A MIRACLE !!
UHHH... UGH...
YOU'RE SAFE, SENPAI! YOU'RE ALL RIGHT!!

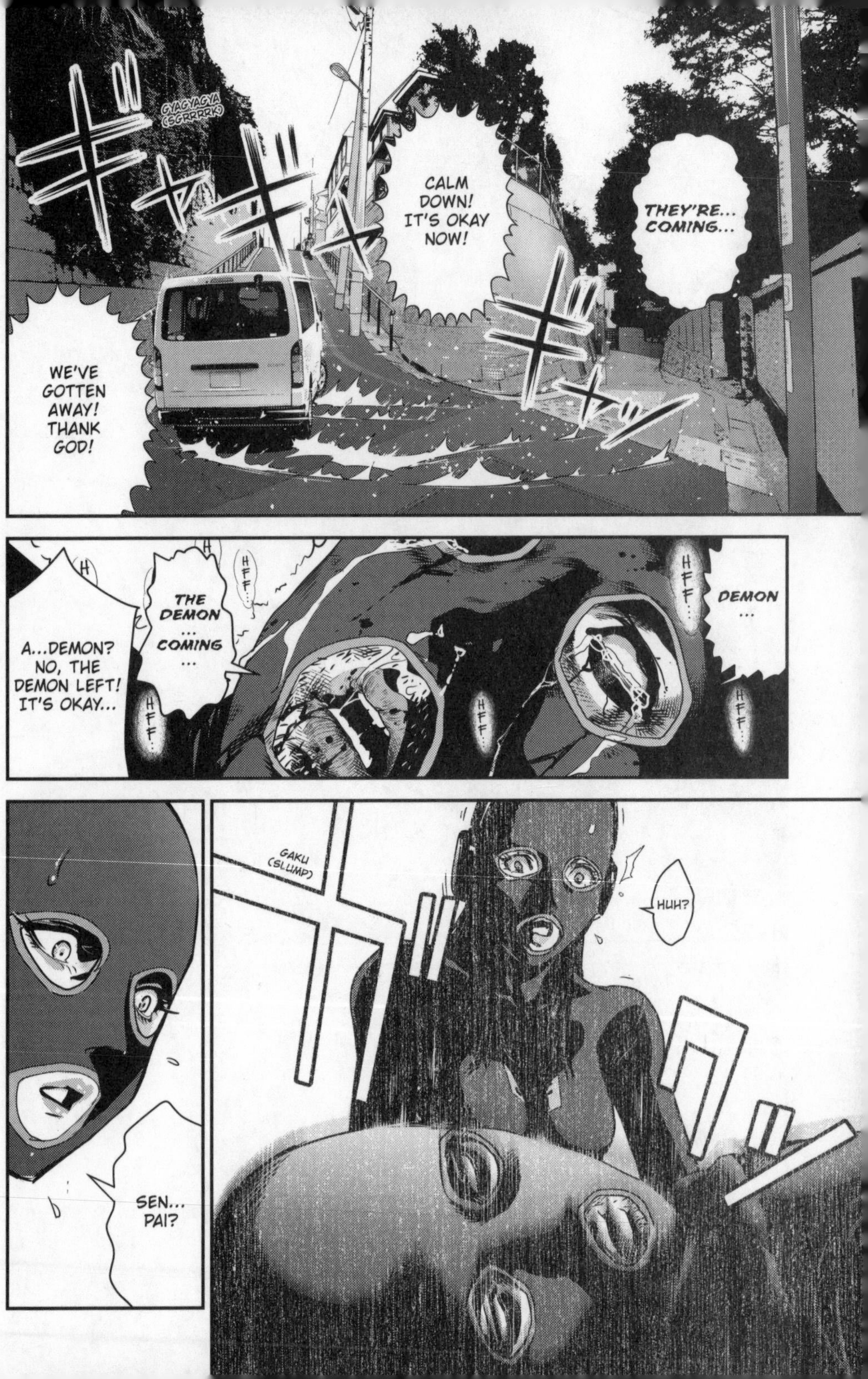
THEY'RE... COMING...
CALM DOWN! IT'S OKAY NOW!
GYAGYAGYA (SGRRRRK)
WE'VE GOTTEN AWAY! THANK GOD!
DEMON...
HFF...
HFF...
HFF...
THE DEMON... COMING...
HFF...
A...DEMON? NO, THE DEMON LEFT! IT'S OKAY...
HFF...
HUH?
GAKU (SLUMP)
SEN... PAI?

ペロ
PERO
ペロ
PERO (CLICK)
...
HE... WASN'T LYING...

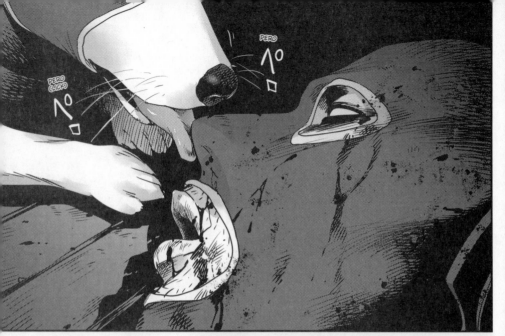

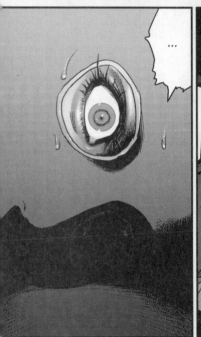

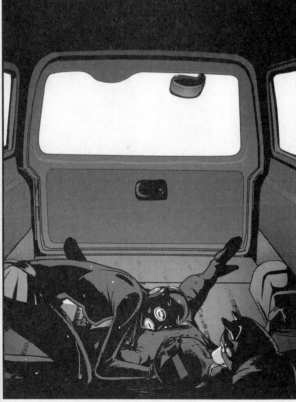

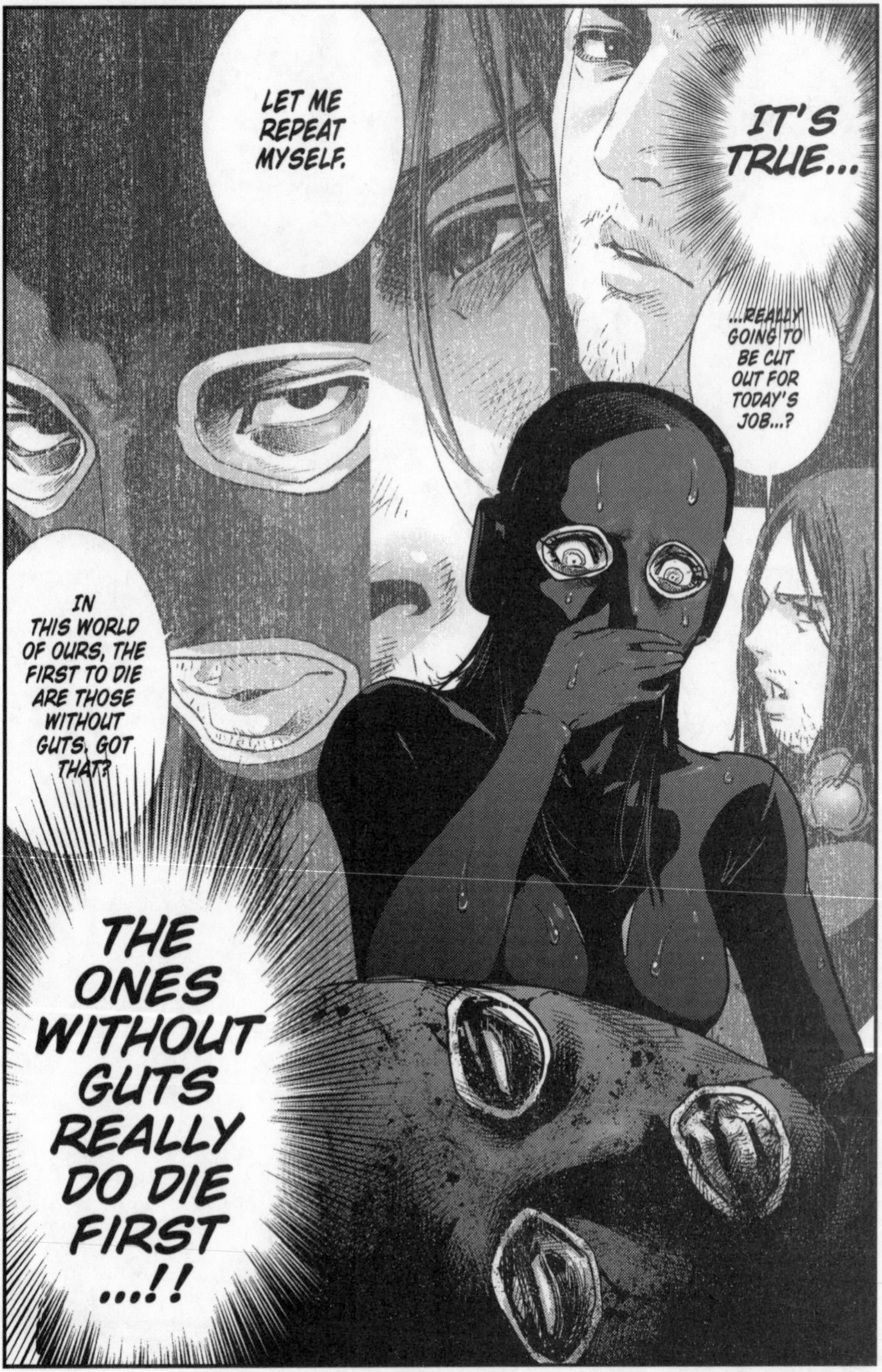
IT'S TRUE...
...REALLY GOING TO BE CUT OUT FOR TODAY'S JOB...?
LET ME REPEAT MYSELF.
IN THIS WORLD OF OURS, THE FIRST TO DIE ARE THOSE WITHOUT GUTS. GOT THAT?
THE ONES WITHOUT GUTS REALLY DO DIE FIRST ...!!

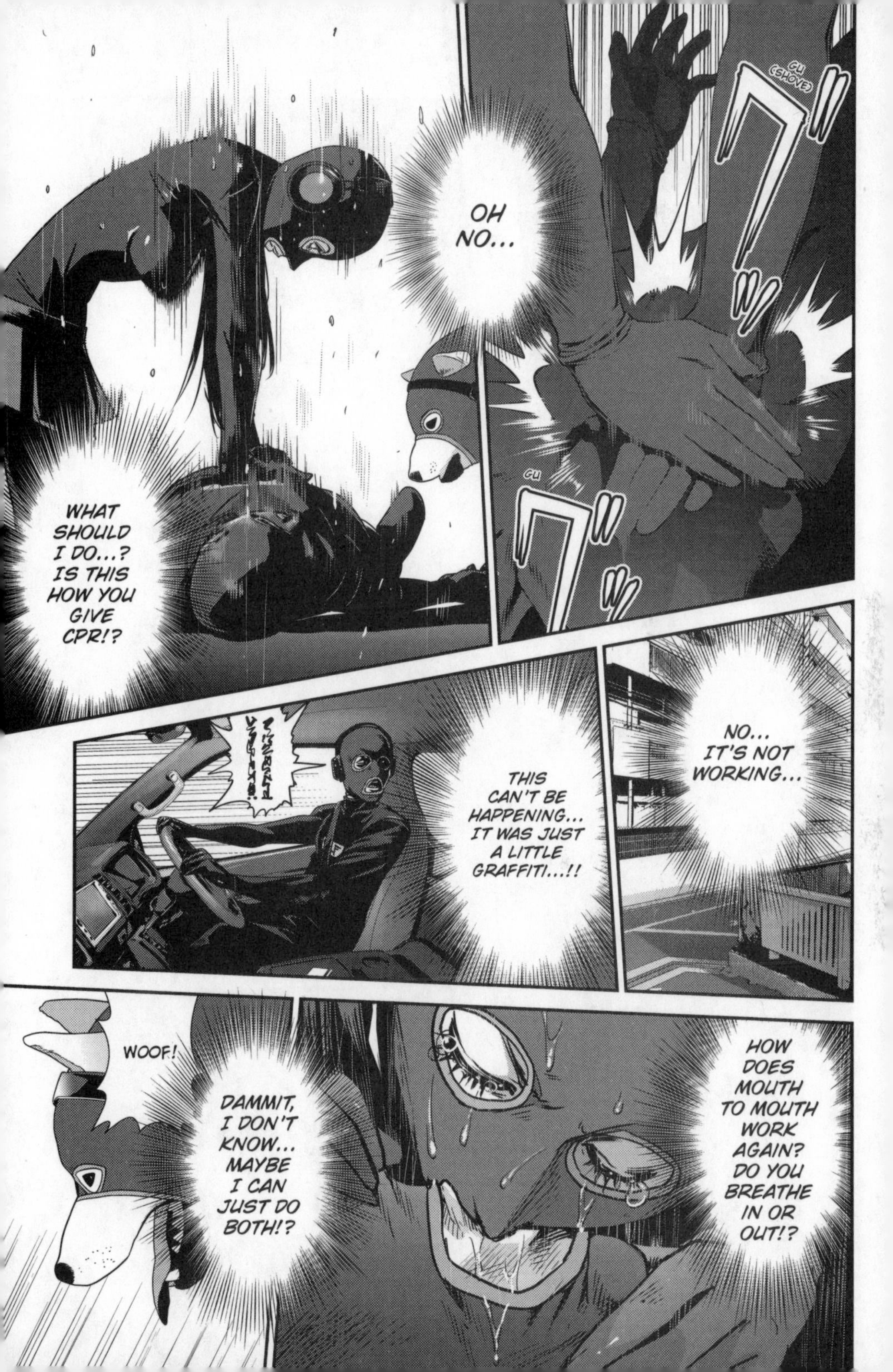
GU (SHOVE)
GU
OH NO...
WHAT SHOULD I DO...? IS THIS HOW YOU GIVE CPR!?
NO... IT'S NOT WORKING...
THIS CAN'T BE HAPPENING... IT WAS JUST A LITTLE GRAFFITI...!!
HOW DOES MOUTH TO MOUTH WORK AGAIN? DO YOU BREATHE IN OR OUT!?
DAMMIT, I DON'T KNOW... MAYBE I CAN JUST DO BOTH!?
WOOF!

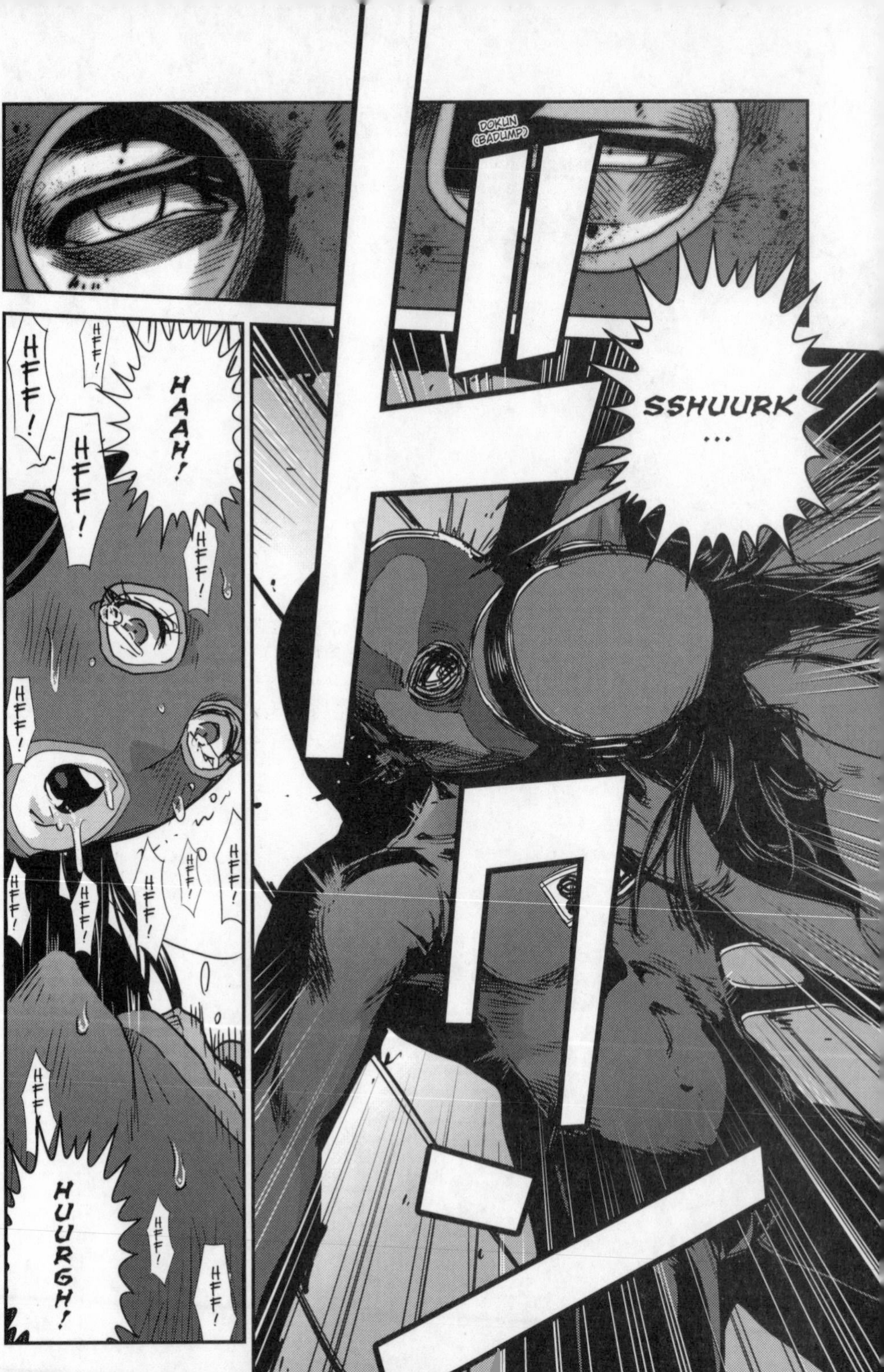

DOKUN (BADUMP)
SSHUURK ...
HAAH!
HFF!
HFF!
HFF!
HFF!
HFF!
HFF!
HFF!
HFF!
HFF!
HFF!
HFF
HFF!
HFF!
HUURGH!

GUI
(TUG)

...DON'T "HUH" ME...

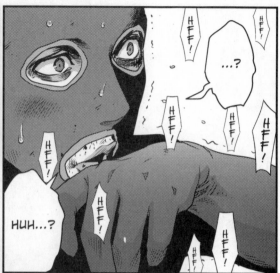

HFF!
HFF!
...?
HFF!
HFF!
HFF!
HUH...?
HFF!
HFF!
HFF!
HFF!

YOU GUTLESS COWARD...

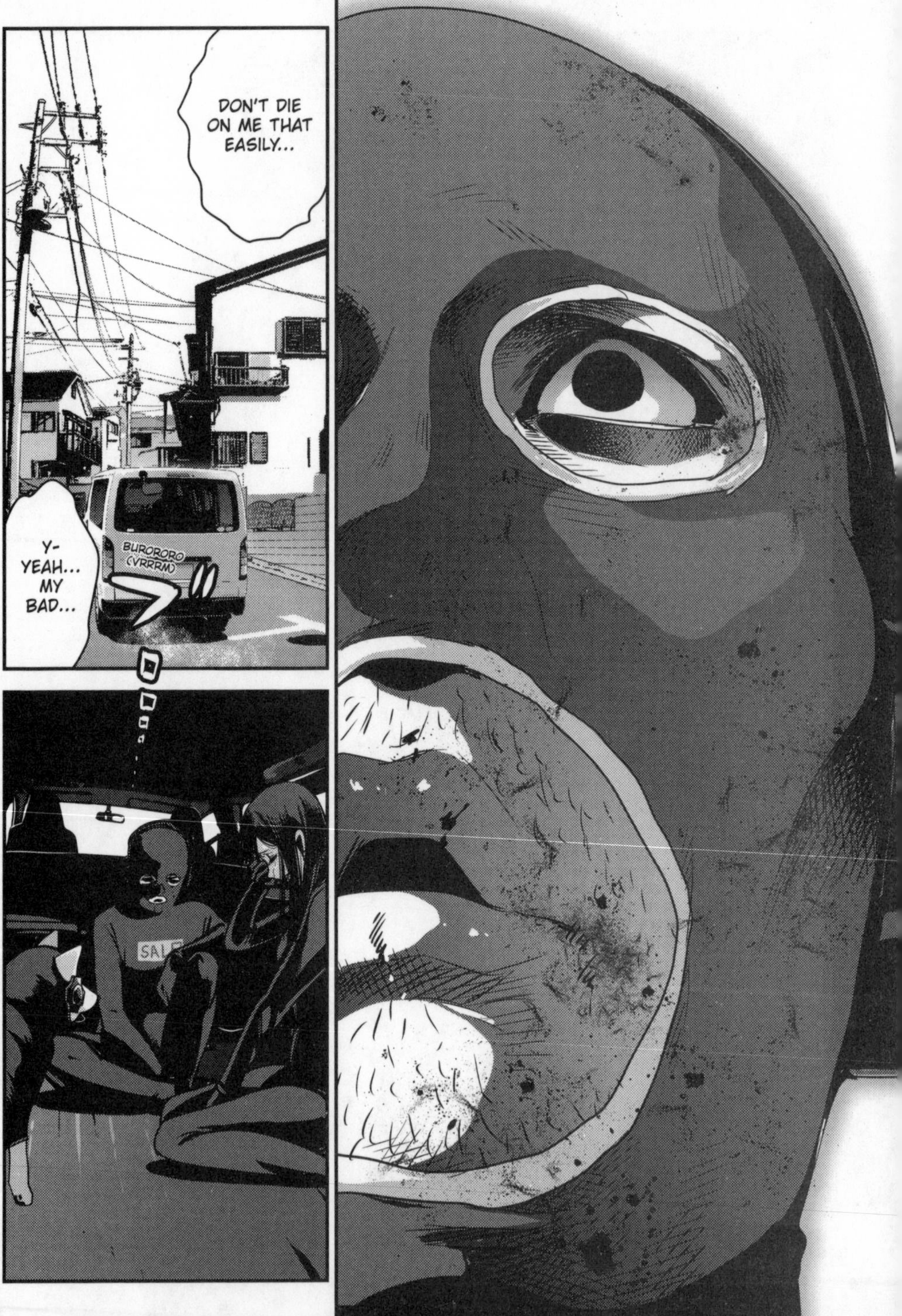
DON'T DIE ON ME THAT EASILY...
BURORORO (VRRRM)
Y-YEAH... MY BAD...

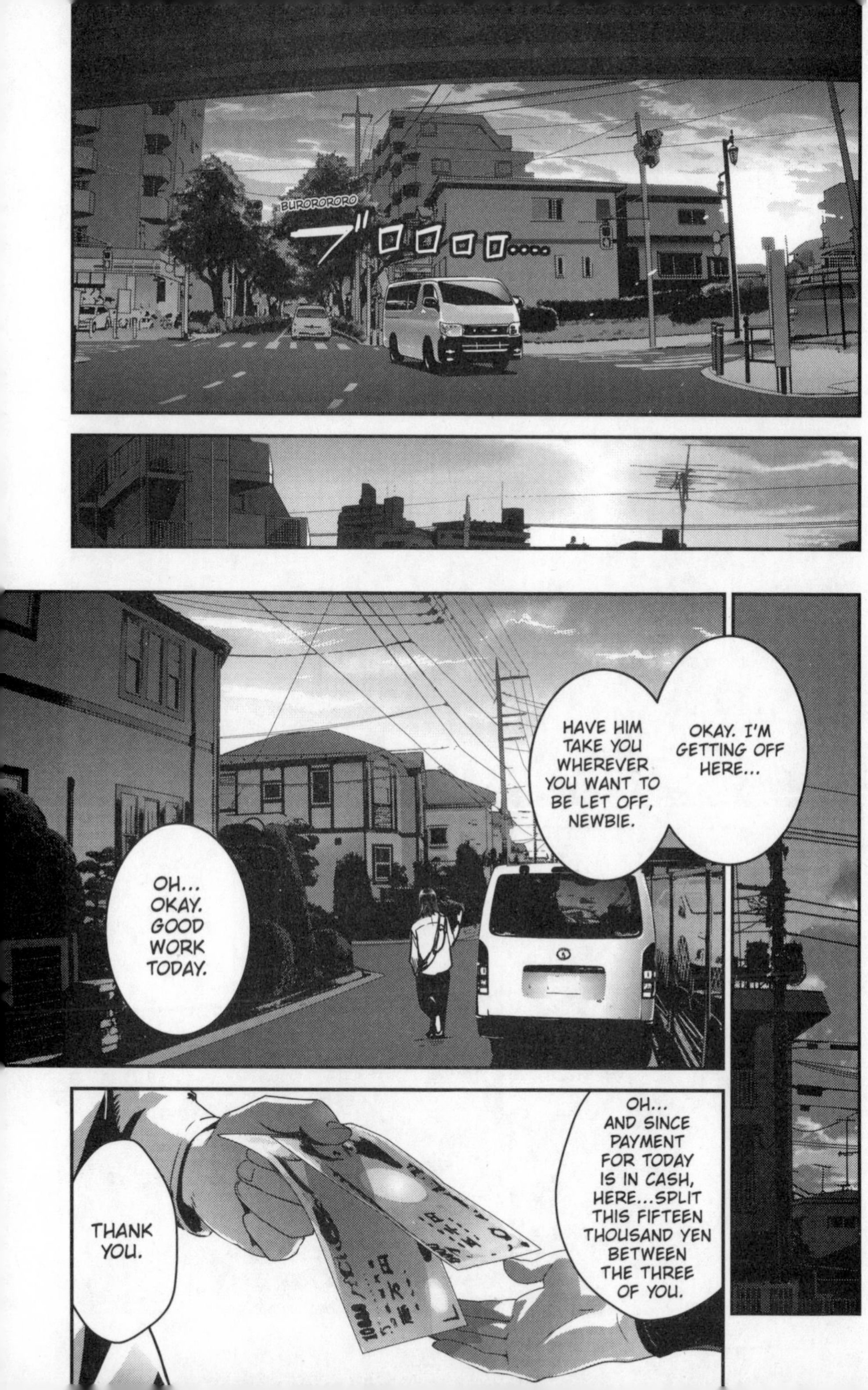
BURORORORO
ブロロロロ……
OKAY. I'M GETTING OFF HERE...
HAVE HIM TAKE YOU WHEREVER YOU WANT TO BE LET OFF, NEWBIE.
OH... OKAY. GOOD WORK TODAY.
OH... AND SINCE PAYMENT FOR TODAY IS IN CASH, HERE...SPLIT THIS FIFTEEN THOUSAND YEN BETWEEN THE THREE OF YOU.
THANK YOU.

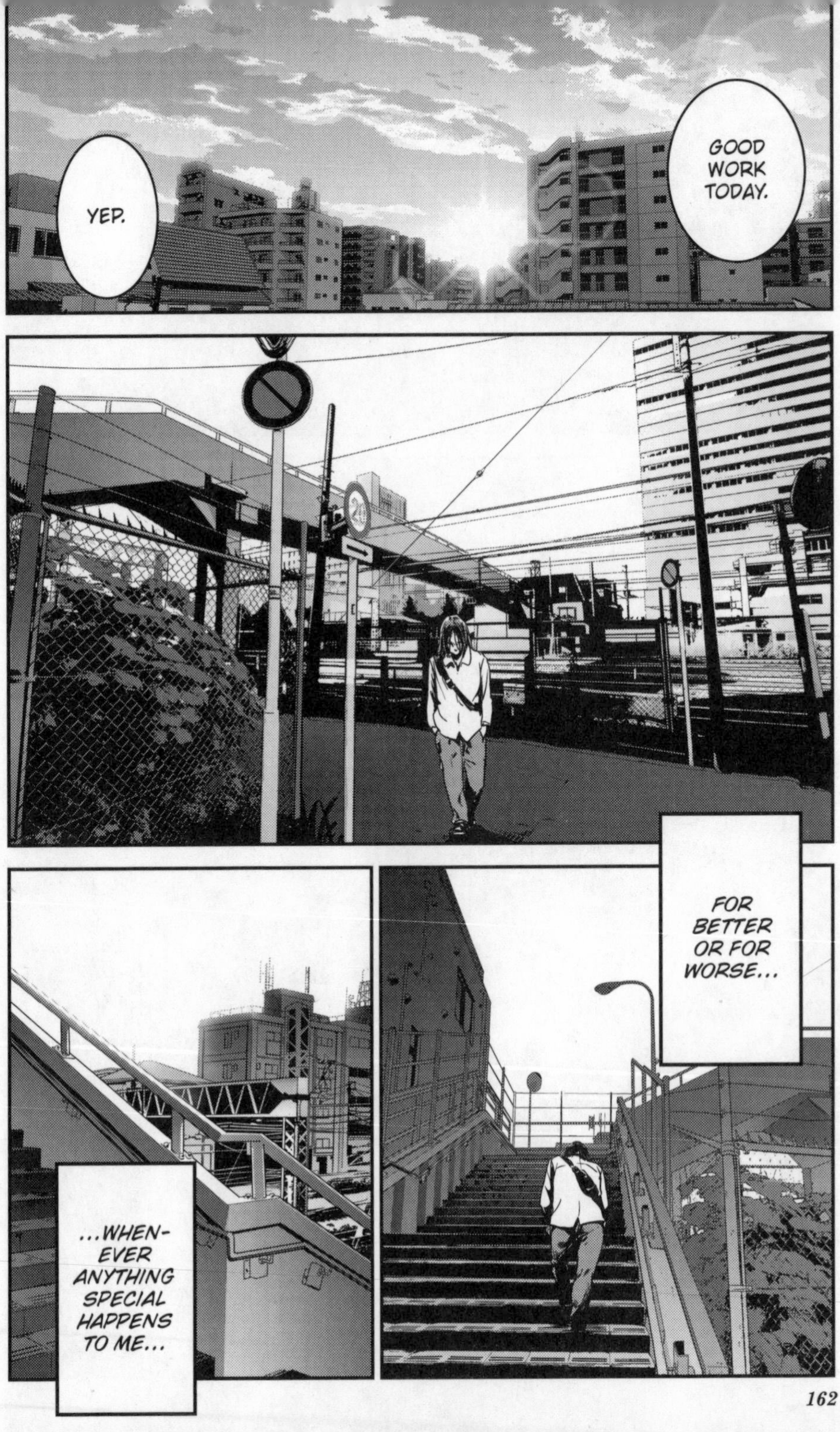
GOOD WORK TODAY.
YEP.
FOR BETTER OR FOR WORSE...
...WHEN-EVER ANYTHING SPECIAL HAPPENS TO ME...

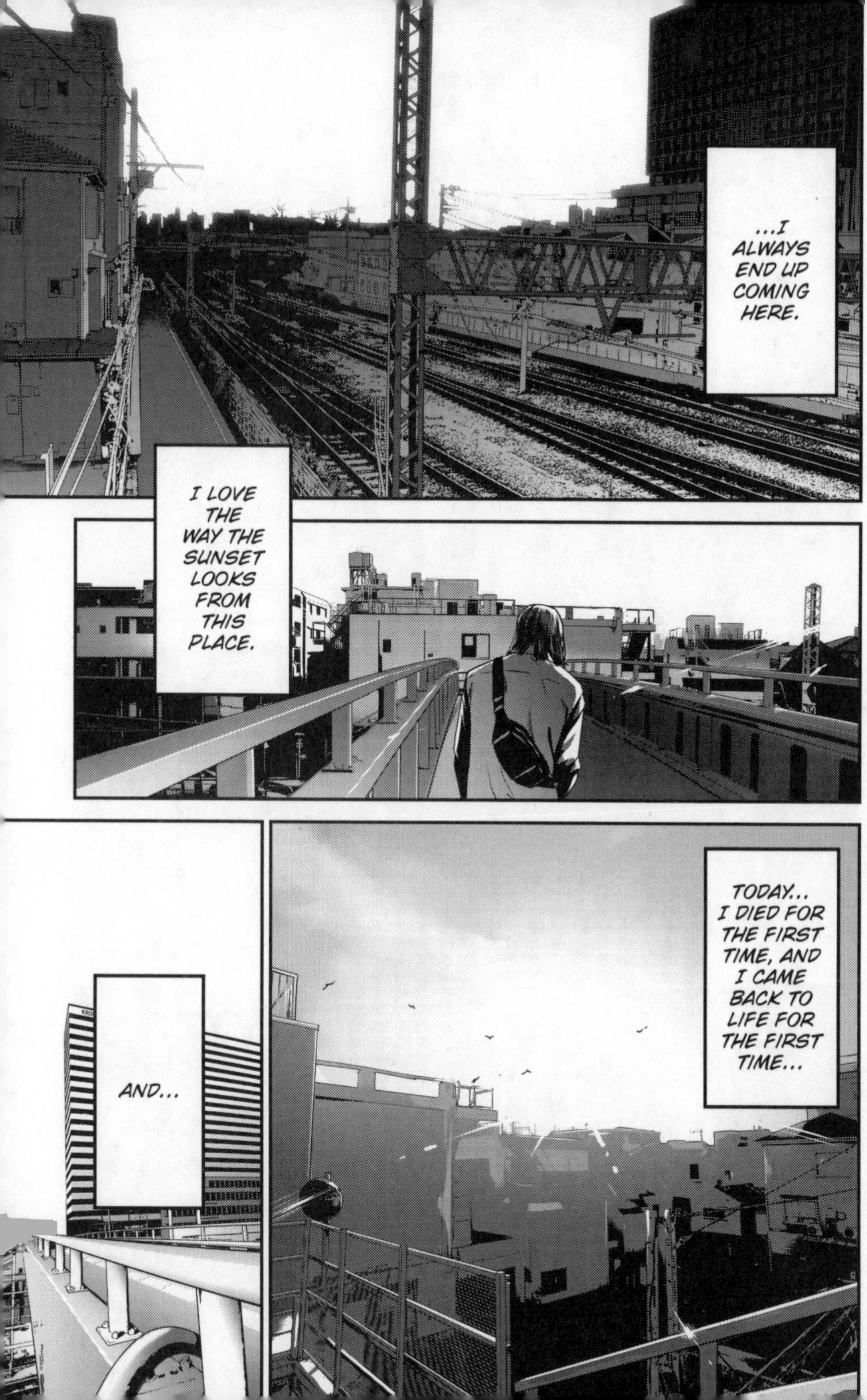
...I ALWAYS END UP COMING HERE.
I LOVE THE WAY THE SUNSET LOOKS FROM THIS PLACE.
TODAY... I DIED FOR THE FIRST TIME, AND I CAME BACK TO LIFE FOR THE FIRST TIME...
AND...

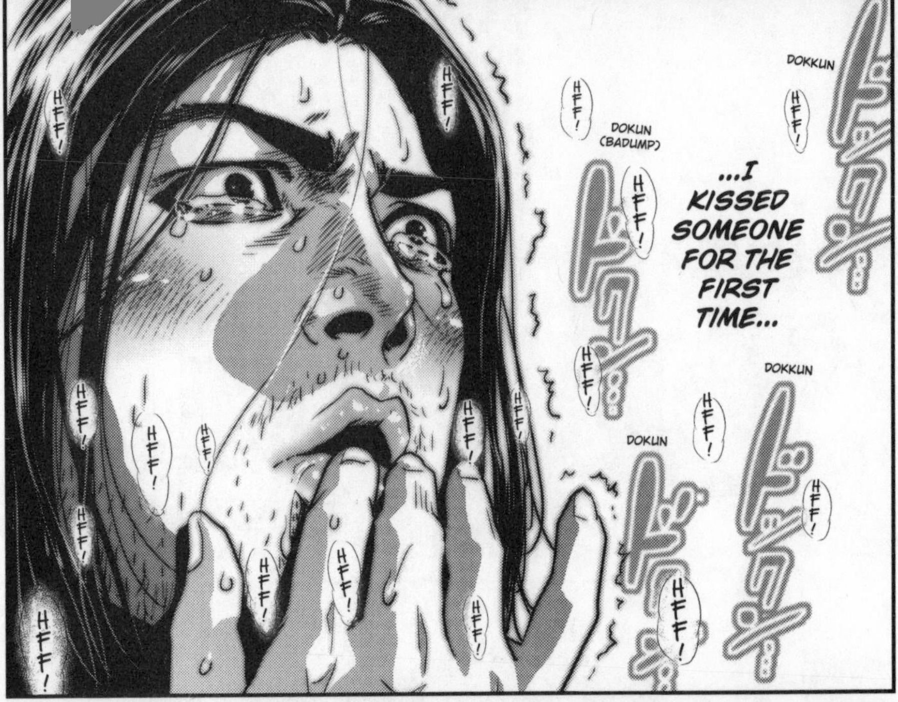
DOKKUN
HFF!
DOKUN (BADUMP)
HFF!
...I KISSED SOMEONE FOR THE FIRST TIME...
DOKKUN
DOKUN

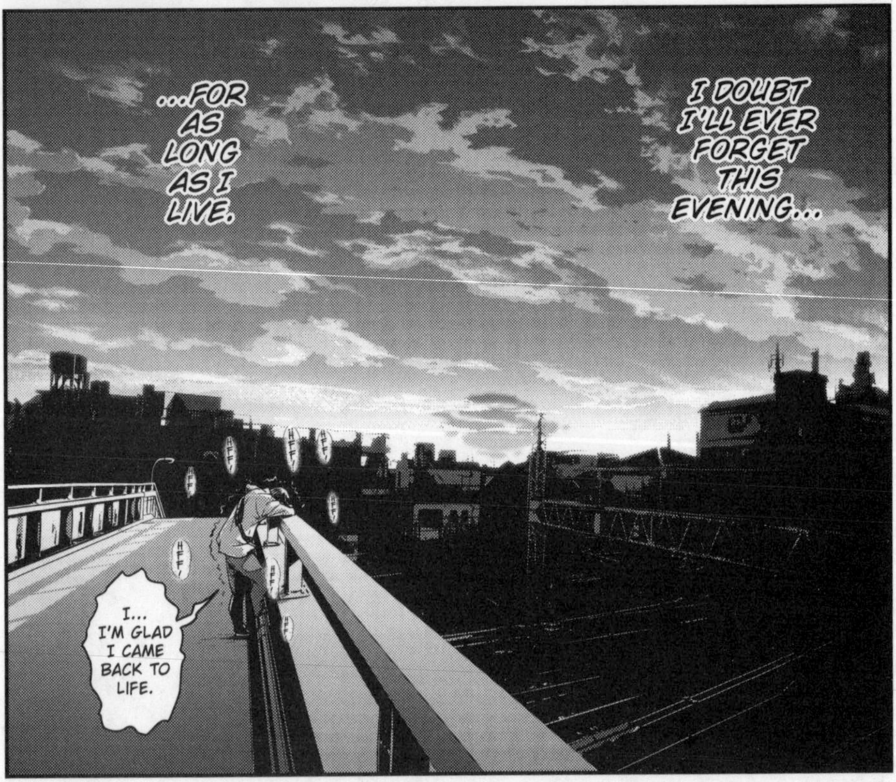
I DOUBT I'LL EVER FORGET THIS EVENING...
...FOR AS LONG AS I LIVE.
HFF!
I... I'M GLAD I CAME BACK TO LIFE.

SIGNS: CHICKEN SKEWERS, WE USE KISHU BINCHOTAN CHARCOAL, CHICKEN JASON / CHICKEN

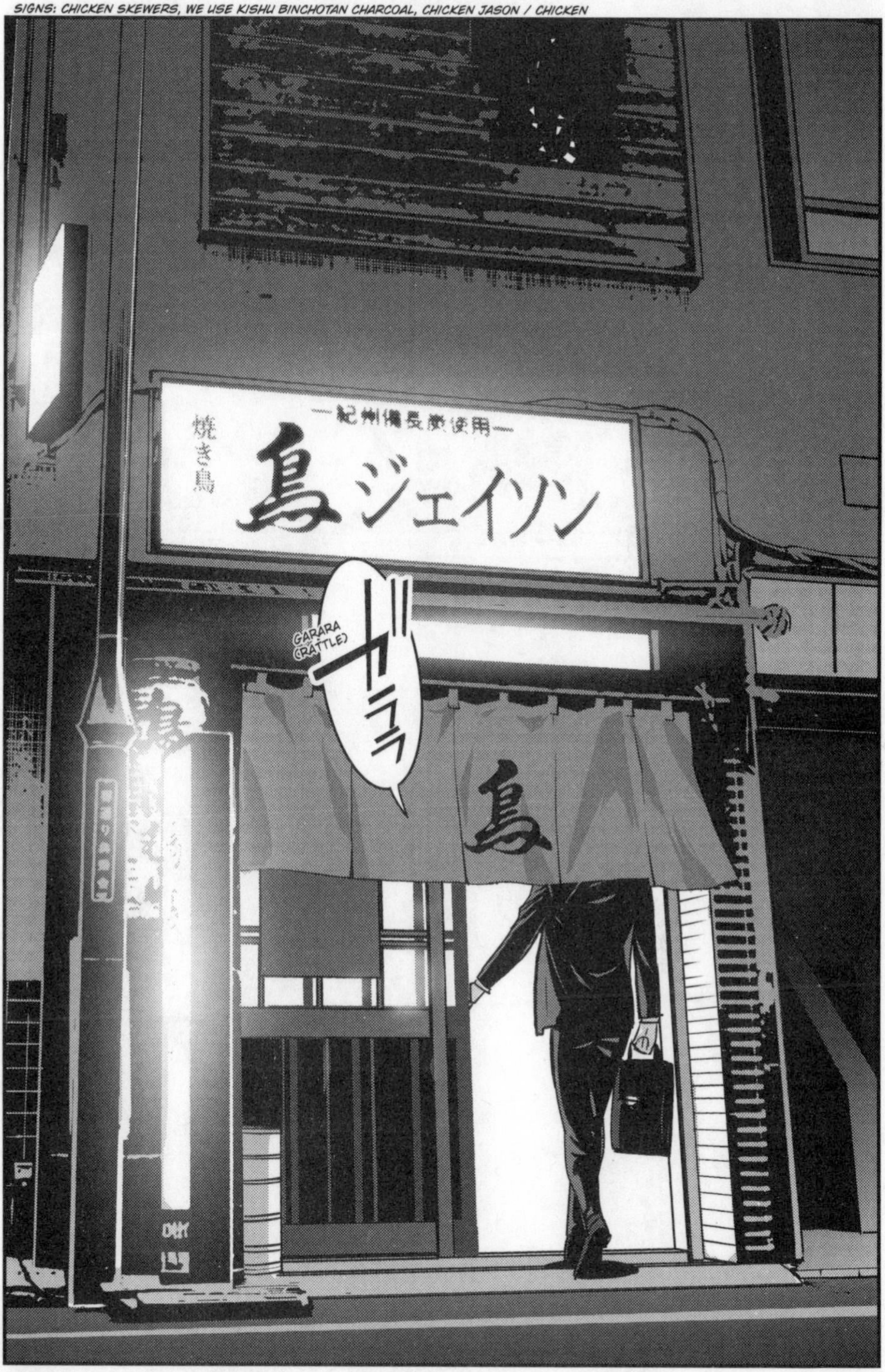
―紀州備長炭使用―
焼き鳥
鳥ジェイソン
ガララ
GARARA (RATTLE)
鳥

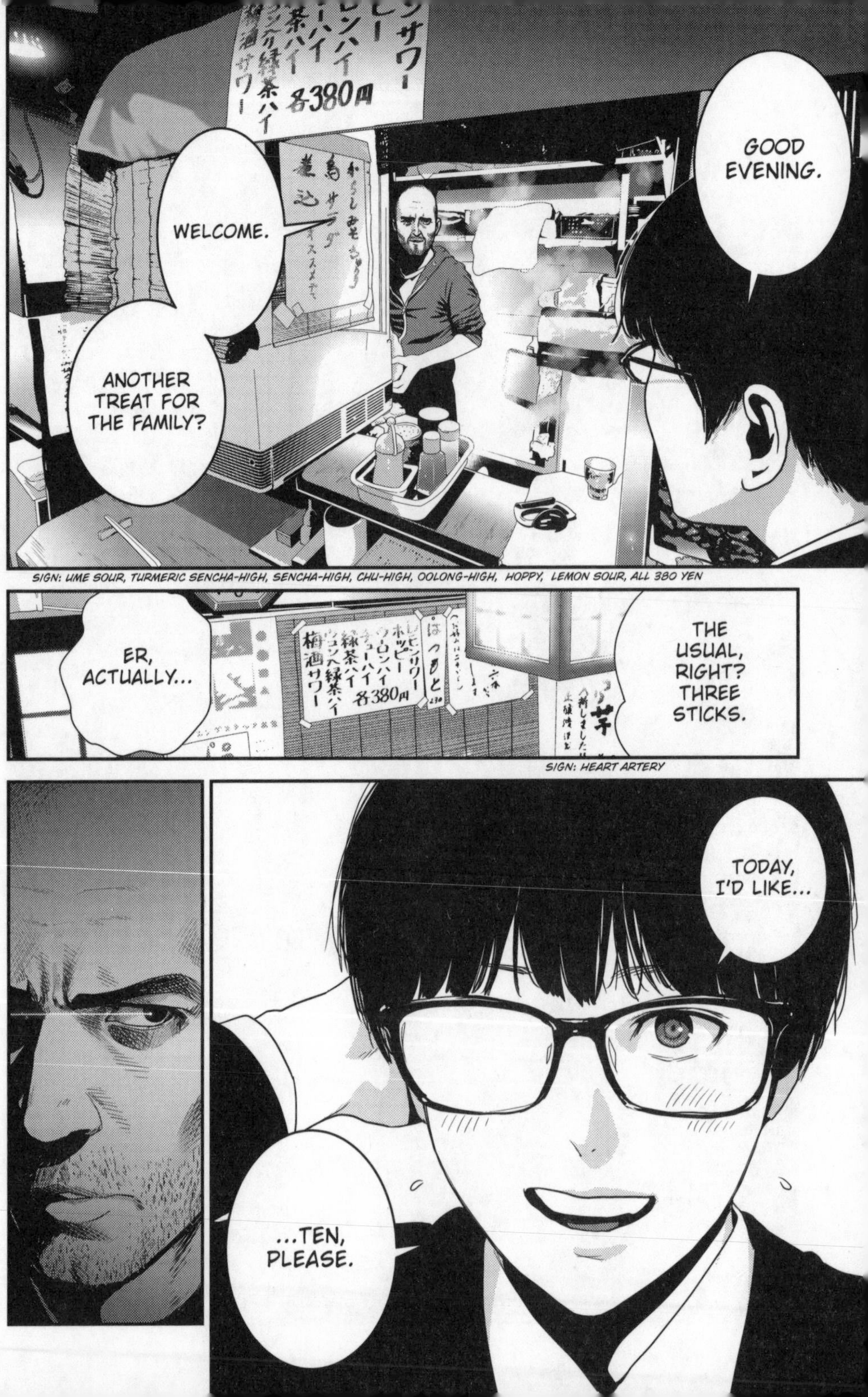
GOOD EVENING.
WELCOME.
ANOTHER TREAT FOR THE FAMILY?
SIGN: UME SOUR, TURMERIC SENCHA-HIGH, SENCHA-HIGH, CHU-HIGH, OOLONG-HIGH, HOPPY, LEMON SOUR, ALL 380 YEN
THE USUAL, RIGHT? THREE STICKS.
ER, ACTUALLY...
SIGN: HEART ARTERY
TODAY, I'D LIKE...
...TEN, PLEASE.

SIGNS: CHICKEN SKEWERS, WE USE KISHU BINCHOTAN, CHICKEN JASON

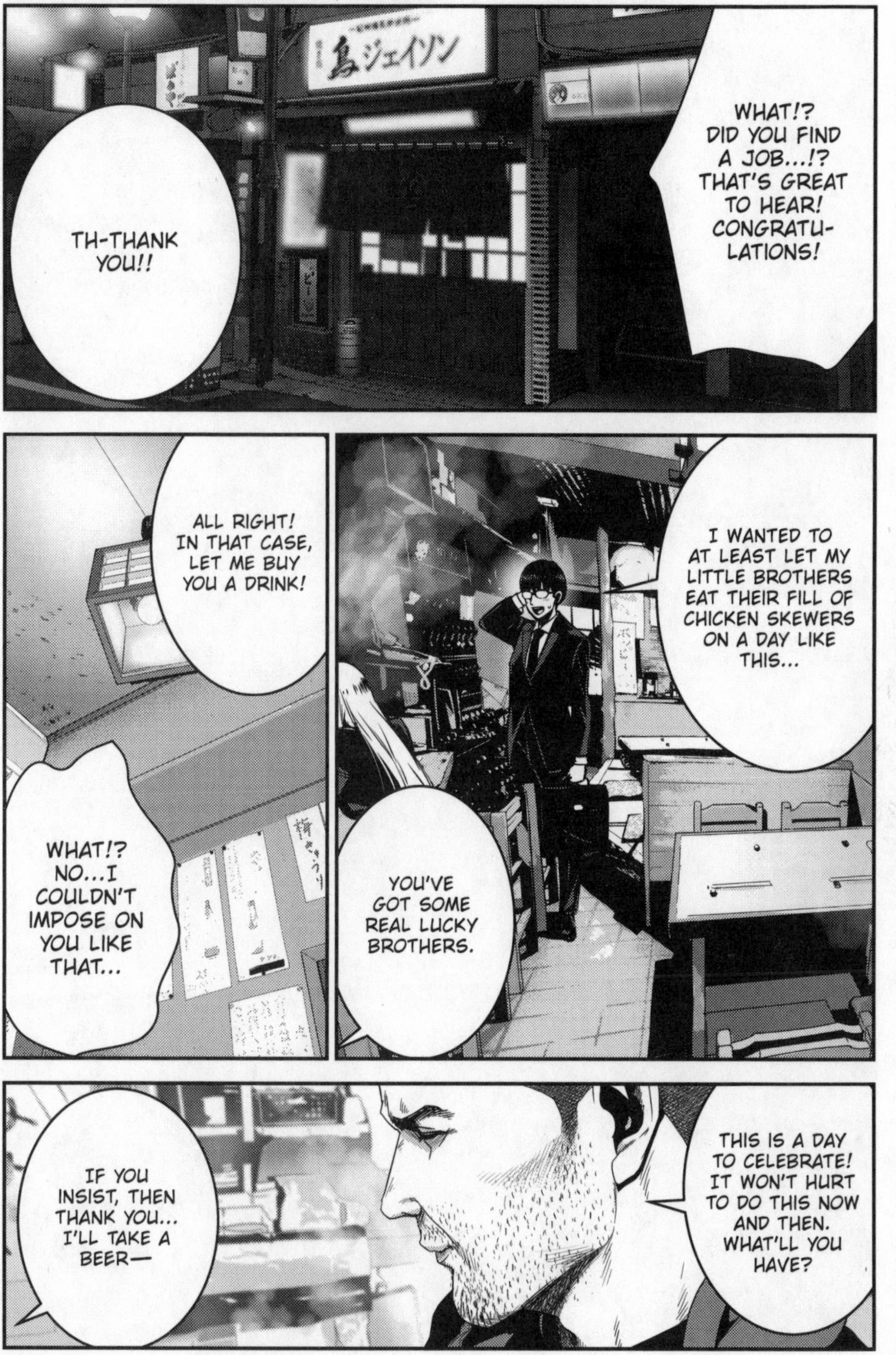
WHAT!? DID YOU FIND A JOB...!? THAT'S GREAT TO HEAR! CONGRATULATIONS!
TH-THANK YOU!!
I WANTED TO AT LEAST LET MY LITTLE BROTHERS EAT THEIR FILL OF CHICKEN SKEWERS ON A DAY LIKE THIS...
YOU'VE GOT SOME REAL LUCKY BROTHERS.
ALL RIGHT! IN THAT CASE, LET ME BUY YOU A DRINK!
WHAT!? NO...I COULDN'T IMPOSE ON YOU LIKE THAT...
THIS IS A DAY TO CELEBRATE! IT WON'T HURT TO DO THIS NOW AND THEN. WHAT'LL YOU HAVE?
IF YOU INSIST, THEN THANK YOU... I'LL TAKE A BEER—

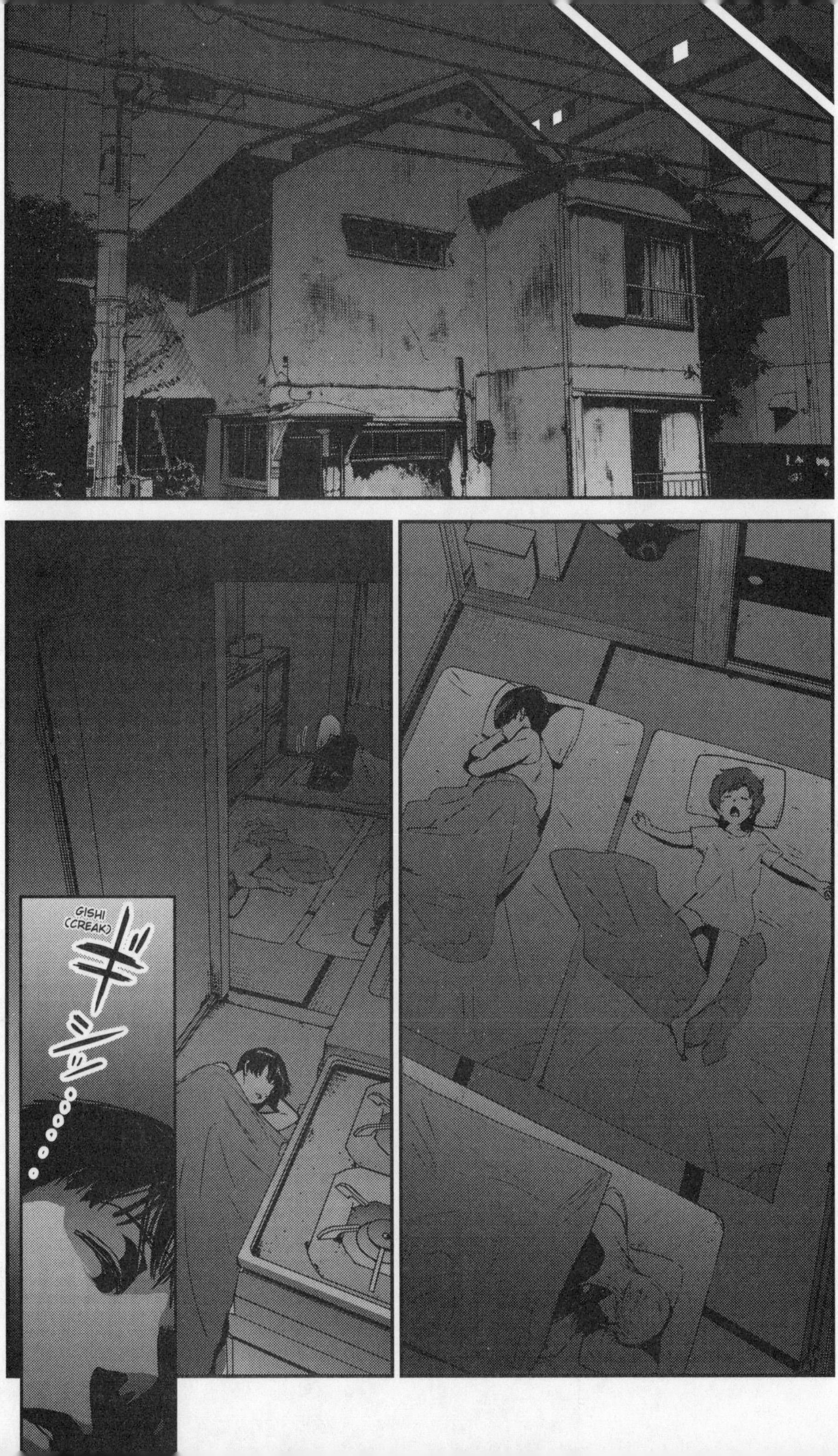
GISHI (CREAK)
ギシ
....

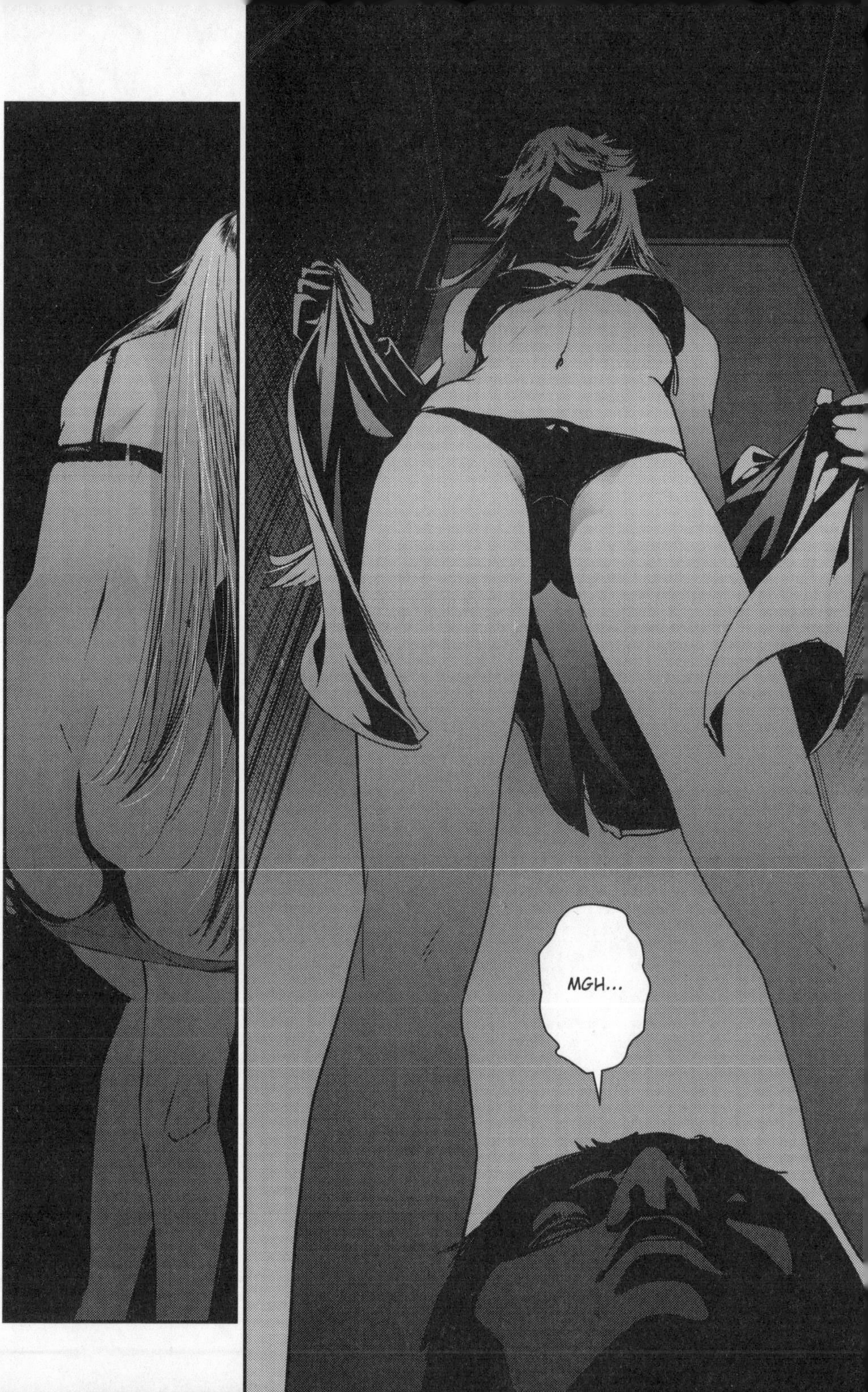
MGH...

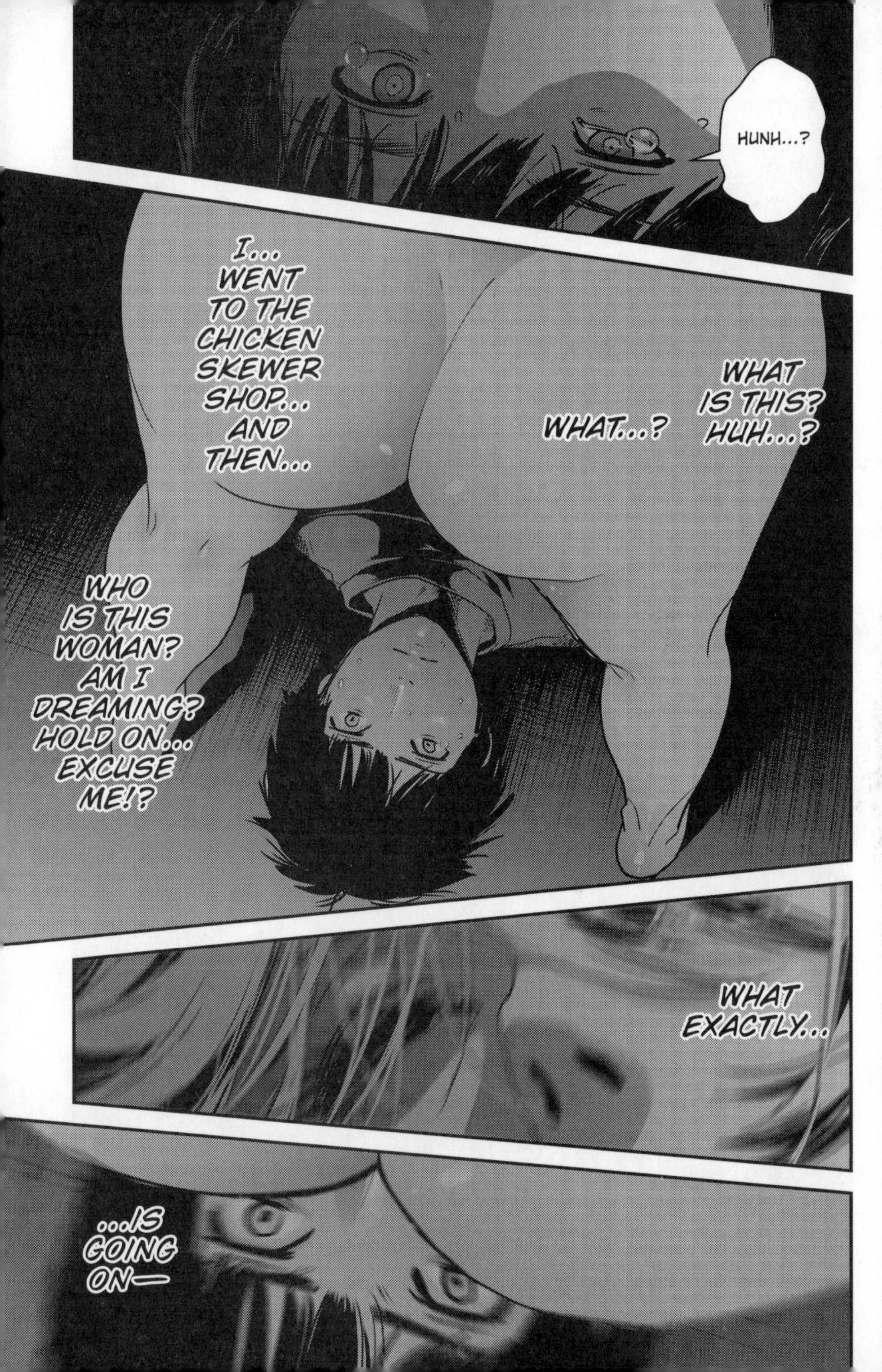
HUNH...?
WHAT IS THIS? HUH...?
WHAT...?
I... WENT TO THE CHICKEN SKEWER SHOP... AND THEN...
WHO IS THIS WOMAN? AM I DREAMING? HOLD ON... EXCUSE ME!?
WHAT EXACTLY...
...IS GOING ON—

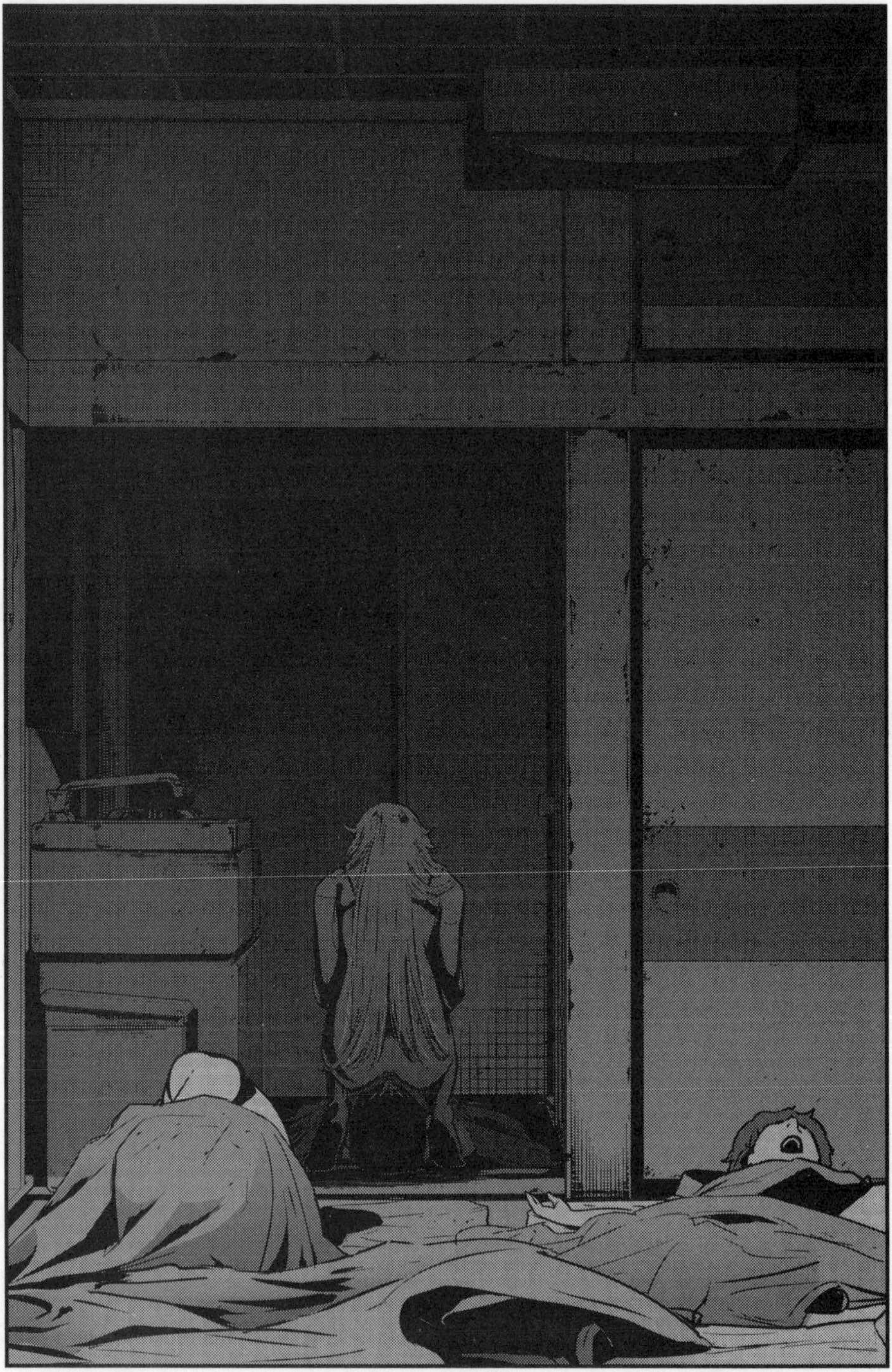

RaW Hero ① End

RaWHERO Translation Notes

Common Honorifics

no honorific: Indicates familiarity or closeness; if used without permission or reason, addressing someone in this manner would constitute an insult.

-san: The Japanese equivalent of Mr./Mrs./Miss. If a situation calls for politeness, this is the fail-safe honorific.

-kun: Used most often when referring to boys, this indicates affection or familiarity. Occasionally used by older men among their peers, but it may also be used by anyone referring to a person of lower standing.

-chan: An affectionate honorific indicating familiarity used mostly in reference to girls; also used in reference to cute persons or animals of either gender.

senpai: A suffix used to address upperclassmen or more experienced coworkers.

dono: Conveys an indication of respect for the addressee.

sama: Extremely formal and conveys an enormous amount of respect for the addressee.

(o)nii: Literally means "older brother" but can refer to older unrelated boys.

(o)nee: Literally means "older sister" but can refer to older unrelated girls.

GENERAL
100 yen is approximately $1 USD.

1 meter is approximately 3.2 feet.

The names of Chiaki and his brothers are based on the Japanese words for seasons: Chi**aki** ("fall"), Chi**haru** ("spring"), and Chi**natsu** ("summer").

PAGE 2
The chapter titles not only reference what happens in the story but are also references to movies and popular culture. However, the Japanese titles for non-Japanese films can sometimes be drastically different from the originals, so the Japanese versions are maintained in some cases.

"Dear Daddy" is the Japanese title for the 2009 film *World's Greatest Dad*.

"It's a Terrible Life" is a reference to the 1946 Christmas film *It's a Wonderful Life*.

"For My Brothers" is taken from the 2014 film *For My Brother*.

"Exam" is from the 2009 thriller by the same name.

"After Interview" is a reference to the 2017 action film *Aftermath*.

"The Men's (?) Dirge," without the question mark, is the Japanese name for the 1986 Hong Kong gangster film released in English as *A Better Tomorrow*.

PAGE 18
Chicken skewers, or *yakitori*, is a Japanese style of grilled chicken served on skewers. It's similar to chicken shish kebabs.

PAGE 22
Gropers (or train gropers/*chikan*) are an infamous problem on trains in Japan, especially during crowded rush hours. Designated women-only train cars are one attempt to prevent this crime.

PAGE 166
The different drinks listed are all alcoholic beverages and cocktails. **Ume sour** is a pickled plum whiskey sour. **Sencha** and **oolong** are types of tea. **"High"** is short for drinks mixed with highballs. **Chu-high** is *shochu* (a Japanese rice-based alcohol) plus highball.

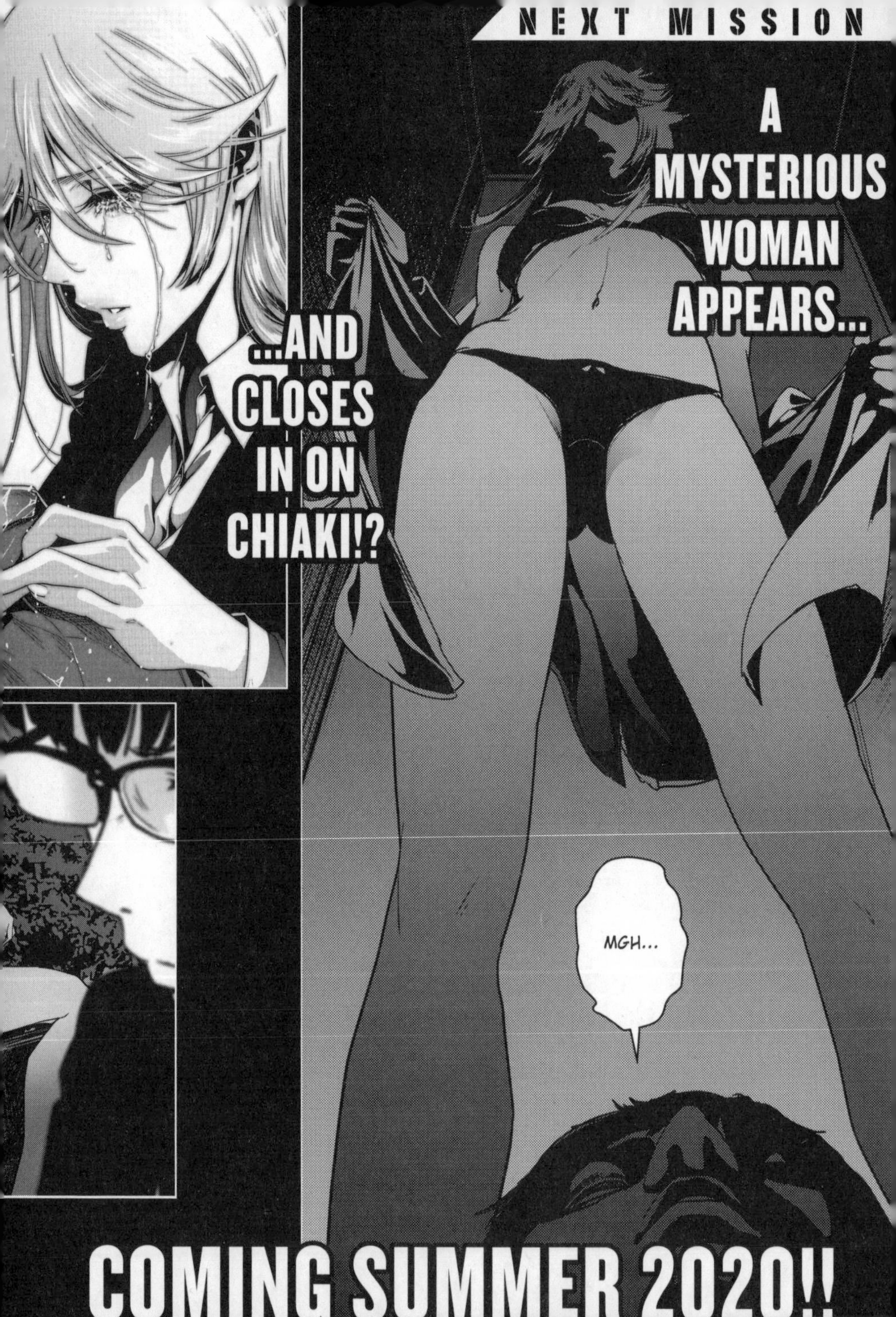
NEXT MISSION
A MYSTERIOUS WOMAN APPEARS...
...AND CLOSES IN ON CHIAKI!?
MGH...
COMING SUMMER 2020!!

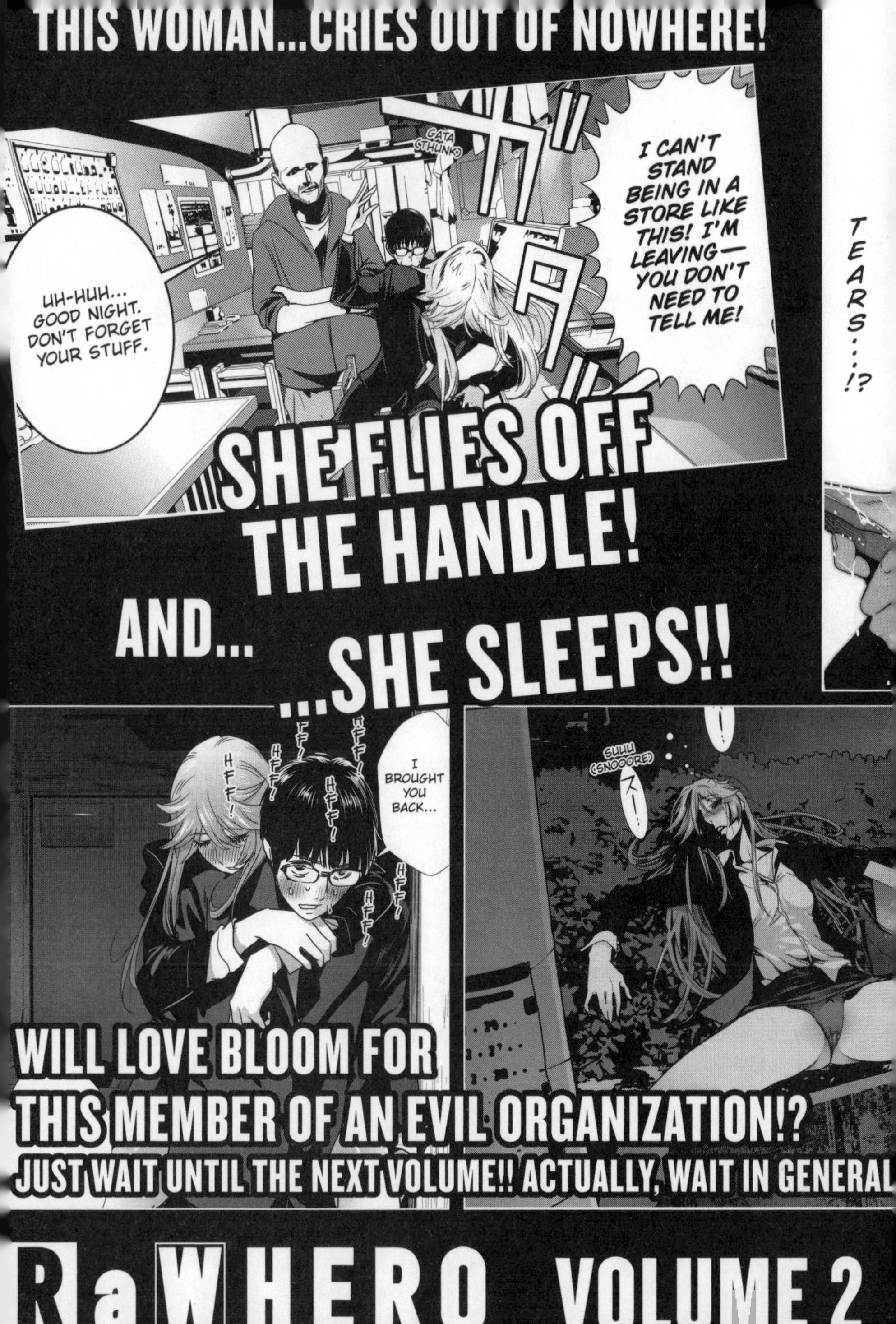
THIS WOMAN...CRIES OUT OF NOWHERE!
TEARS...!?
I CAN'T STAND BEING IN A STORE LIKE THIS! I'M LEAVING—YOU DON'T NEED TO TELL ME!
GATA (THUNK)
UH-HUH... GOOD NIGHT. DON'T FORGET YOUR STUFF.
SHE FLIES OFF THE HANDLE!
AND...
...SHE SLEEPS!!
SUUU (SNOOORE)
I BROUGHT YOU BACK...
HFF!
HFF!
HFF!
HFF!
HFF!
WILL LOVE BLOOM FOR THIS MEMBER OF AN EVIL ORGANIZATION!?
JUST WAIT UNTIL THE NEXT VOLUME!! ACTUALLY, WAIT IN GENERAL
RaWHERO VOLUME 2

RAW HERO ①

AKIRA HIRAMOTO

Translation: **Ko Ransom**

Lettering: **Phil Christie**

RAW HERO Vol. 1
©Akira Hiramoto 2019. All rights reserved.
First published in Japan in 2019 by Kodansha Ltd., Tokyo.
Publication rights for this English edition arranged through Kodansha Ltd., Tokyo.

English translation © 2020 by Yen Press, LLC

Yen Press
150 West 30th Street, 19th Floor
New York, NY 10001

Visit us at yenpress.com
facebook.com/yenpress
twitter.com/yenpress
yenpress.tumblr.com
instagram.com/yenpress

First Yen Press Edition: February 2020

Yen Press is an imprint of Yen Press, LLC.
The Yen Press name and logo are trademarks of Yen Press, LLC.

Library of Congress Control Number: 2019956807

ISBNs: 978-1-9753-9924-5 (paperback)
978-1-9753-0937-4 (ebook)

10 9 8 7 6 5 4 3 2

WOR

Printed in the United States of America